Andrew Warren, Managing ... ...td.

Welcome to this exciting new edition of our Guide to Recommended Country Houses, Small Hotels and Inns, Great Britain & Ireland.

I am pleased to announce that Johansens is now part of The Condé Nast Publications Ltd., publishers of Vogue, House & Garden, Condé Nast Traveller and other prestigious monthly magazines.

New ownership has resulted in some exciting changes that we hope you agree, make the Guide easier to use and our recommendations easier to locate in alphabetical order by country and then by county.

By opening both cover flaps you can now refer to the contents of the Guide and the amenity symbol definitions whilst the guide is laid open at the hotel of your choice.

We feel sure that you will enjoy visiting our recommendations for 2003; these can also be found, some offering special rates and featuring their chef's favourite recipes, on our website www.johansens.com

Please remember to mention Condé Nast Johansens when you make a reservation and again when you check in. You will be made to feel very welcome.

THE CONDÉ NAST JOHANSENS PROMISE

Condé Nast Johansens is the most comprehensive illustrated reference to annually inspected, independently owned hotels throughout Great Britain, Europe and North America.

It is our objective to maintain the trust of Guide users by recommending through annual inspection a careful choice of accommodation offering quality, excellence and value for money.

Our team of over 60 dedicated Regional Inspectors visited almost 3000 hotels, country houses, inns and resorts throughout 30 countries to select only the very best for recommendation in the 2003 editions of our Guides.

No hotel can appear in our guides unless they meet our exacting standards.

Scotland & Ireland

Turn to the page shown for the start of each county

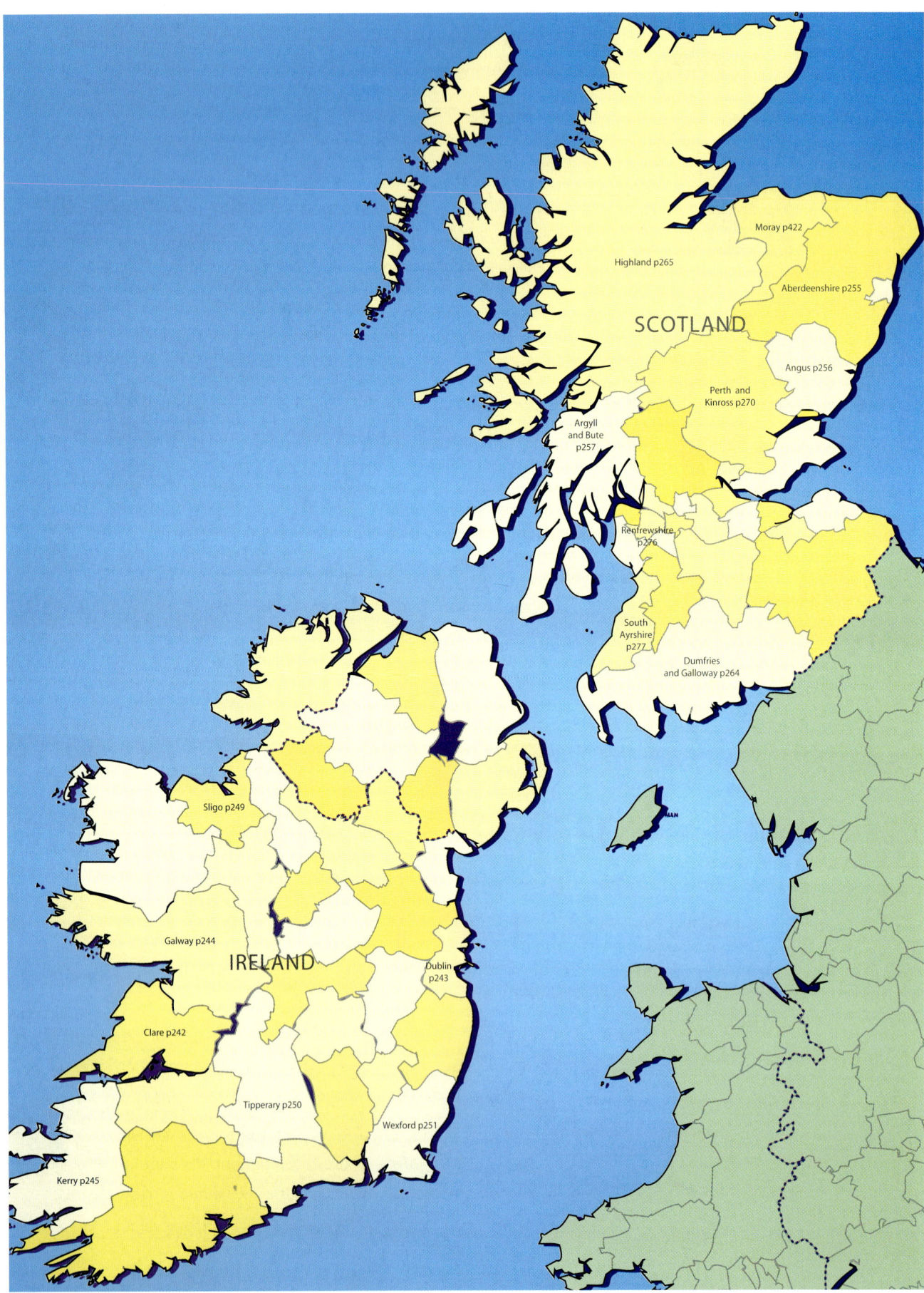

ENGLAND, WALES & CHANNEL ISLANDS
Turn to the page shown for the start of each county

Condé Nast Johansens Guides
Recommending only the finest hotels in the world

As well as this guide Condé Nast Johansens also publishes the following titles:

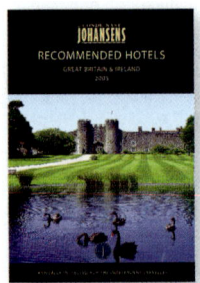

Recommended Hotels, Great Britain & Ireland

440 unique and luxurious hotels, town houses, castles and manor houses chosen for their superior standards and individual character

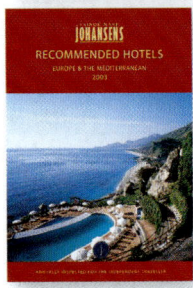

Recommended Hotels, Europe & the Mediterranean

320 continental gems featuring châteaux, resorts and charming countryside hotels

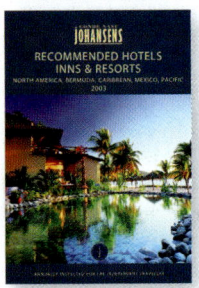

Recommended Hotels, Inns & Resorts, North America, Bermuda, Caribbean, Mexico, Pacific

200 hotels including many hidden properties from across the region

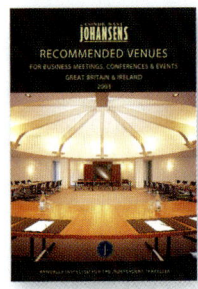

Recommended Venues for Business Meetings, Conferences and Events, Great Britain & Europe

230 venues that cater specifically for a business audience

Worldwide Listings Pocket Guide

Features all recommended hotels and serves as the perfect companion when travelling light

When you purchase two guides or more we will be pleased to offer you a reduction in the cost.

The complete set of Condé Nast Johansens guides may be purchased as 'The Chairman's Collection'.

To order guides please complete the order form on page 351 or call FREEPHONE 0800 269 397

CONDÉ NAST JOHANSENS

Condé Nast Johansens Ltd., 6-8 Old Bond Street, London W1S 4PH
Tel: +44 (0)20 7499 9080 Fax: +44 (0)20 7152 3565
Find Condé Nast Johansens on the Internet at: www.johansens.com
E-Mail: info@johansens.com

Publishing Director:	Stuart Johnson
P.A. to Publishing Director:	Fiona Galley
Hotel Inspectors:	Jean Branham
	Geraldine Bromley
	Robert Bromley
	Julie Dunkley
	Pat Gillson
	Martin Greaves
	Joan Henderson
	Marie Iversen
	Pauline Mason
	John O'Neill
	Mary O'Neill
	Fiona Patrick
	John Sloggie
	David Wilkinson
Production Director:	Daniel Barnett
Production Manager:	Kevin Bradbrook
Production Controller:	Laura Kerry
Senior Designer:	Michael Tompsett
Copywriters:	Norman Flack
	Debra Giles
	Rozanne Paragon
	Leonora Sandwell
Sales and Marketing Director:	Tim Sinclair
Promotions & Events Manager:	Adam Crabtree
Client Services Director:	Fiona Patrick
P.A. to Managing Director:	Siobhan Smith
Managing Director:	Andrew Warren

Whilst every care has been taken in the compilation of this Guide, the publishers cannot accept responsibility for any inaccuracies or for changes since going to press, or for consequential loss arising from such changes or other inaccuracies, or for any other loss direct or consequential arising in connection with information describing establishments in this publication.

Recommended establishments, if accepted for inclusion by our inspectors, pay an annual subscription to cover the costs of inspection, the distribution and production of copies placed in hotel bedrooms and other services.

No part of this publication may be copied or reproduced, stored in a retrieval system or transmitted, in any form or by any means, electronic, mechanical, photocopy, recording or otherwise, without the prior permission of the publishers.

The publishers request readers not to cut, tear or otherwise mark this Guide except Guest Reports, Brochure Requests and Order Coupons. No other cuttings may be taken without the written permission of the publishers.

Copyright © 2002 Condé Nast Johansens Ltd.

Condé Nast Johansens Ltd. is part of The Condé Nast Publications Ltd.

ISBN 1 903665 08 6

Printed in England by St Ives plc
Colour origination by Arkima Ltd

Distributed in the UK and Europe by Portfolio, Greenford (bookstores). In North America by Whitehurst & Clarke, New York (direct sales) and Hunter Publishing, New Jersey (bookstores). In Australia and New Zealand by Bookwise International, Wingfield, South Australia.

WWW.JOHANSENS.COM

Visit the Condé Nast Johansens website to:

- Print out detailed **road maps**
- See up-to-date accommodation **Special Offers**
- Access each **recommended hotel's own website**
- Find details of places to visit nearby - **historic houses, castles, gardens, museums and galleries**

Condé Nast Johansens Home Page

Search for hotels and business venues

Access local places to visit

Link to latest Special Offers

Users can log in as an Online Member to receive regular e-mail updates, complete guest survey reports and create their own Personal Portfolio of favourite recommended hotels

Example of Recommended Hotel's Web Entry

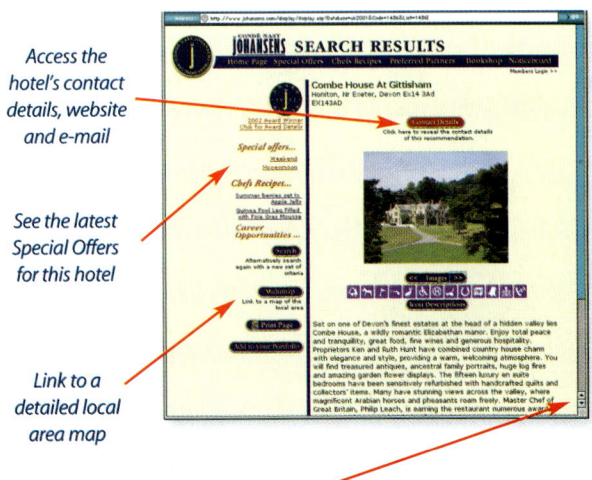

Access the hotel's contact details, website and e-mail

See the latest Special Offers for this hotel

Link to a detailed local area map

Scroll down to find details of places to visit nearby

Home cinema from two speakers

The *New* Bose 3·2·1 digital home entertainment system

The critics approved: "Even though I knew the midrange and high frequency sound were emanating from only two speakers at the front of the room, it sure didn't sound that way – I know I heard swords clanking where surround speakers should have been." – Sound & Vision (US)

Bass module not shown

For information about our products or the address of an authorised Bose dealer near you call 0800-317942 and quote ref. JG02.

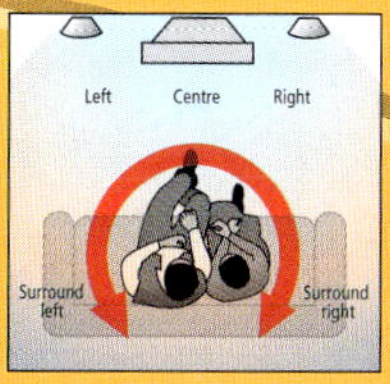

Hear it! Believe it! Ask for a demonstration.

Better sound through research®
www.bose.co.uk

2002 Awards For Excellence

The winners of the Condé Nast Johansens 2002 Awards for Excellence

The Condé Nast Johansens 2002 Awards for Excellence were presented at the Awards Dinner held at The Dorchester hotel, London on November 12th, 2001. Awards were made to those properties worldwide that represented the finest standards and best value for money in luxury independent travel. An important source of information for these awards was the feedback provided by guests who completed Johansens Guest Survey reports. Guest Survey forms can be found on page 352.

Most Excellent Country House Award

GLENAPP CASTLE – South Ayrshire, Scotland

"A Scottish home away from home, in which to unwind. A truly memorable stay"

Most Excellent Traditional Inn Award

THE CROWN HOTEL – Lincolnshire, England, p131

"The friendly staff, relaxing atmosphere and a fresh innovative approach to service"

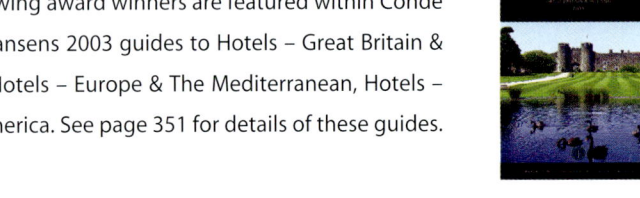

The following award winners are featured within Condé Nast Johansens 2003 guides to Hotels – Great Britain & Ireland, Hotels – Europe & The Mediterranean, Hotels – North America. See page 351 for details of these guides.

Most Excellent Country Hotel Award
Northcote Manor Country Hotel – Devon, England

Most Excellent City Hotel Award
Hotel On The Park – Gloucestershire, England

Most Excellent London Hotel Award
The Colonnade, The Little Venice Town House – London, England

Most Excellent Value for Money Award
The Gibbon Bridge Hotel – Lancashire, England

Most Excellent Service Award
Combe House Hotel – Devon, England

Most Excellent Restaurant Award
Maison Talbooth – Essex, England

Most Excellent Coastal Hotel Award
The Grand Hotel – Eastbourne, England

Europe: The Most Excellent City Hotel
Hotel Rector – Salamanca, Spain

Europe: The Most Excellent Country Hotel
Château de Vault de Lugny– Avallon, France

Europe: The Most Excellent Waterside Resort
Domaine de Rochevilaine – Billiers, France

North America: Most Outstanding Hotel
Wheatleigh – Massachusetts, USA

North America: Most Outstanding Inn
The Willows – California, USA

North America: Most Outstanding Resort
Turtle Island –Yasawa Islands, Fiji

Condé Nast Johansens Special Award for Excellence
Henderson Village – Georgia, USA

Knight Frank Award for Excellence and Innovation
Nicholas Dickenson & Nigel Chapman

Rise and Shine

While you're away, get each day off to a flying start.

Because the world doesn't stop when you do. Sudden market shifts and new global business developments can change everything. But if you know you're in touch, you can relax.

Which is why the FT provides you with essential tools and business information to help keep you ahead, wherever you are.

During your stay you can get constant access to the very latest business developments and market news from Europe's leading business resource, making sure you retain your competitive edge even whilst at leisure.

Ask for the FT at your hotel's reception.

ENGLAND

Recommendations in England appear on pages 12-231

For further information on England, please contact:

Cumbria Tourist Board
Ashleigh, Holly Road, Windermere, Cumbria LA23 2AQ
Tel: +44 (0)15394 44444
Web: www.gocumbria.co.uk

East of England Tourist Board
Toppesfield Hall , Hadleigh, Suffolk IP7 5DN
Tel: +44 (0)1473 822922
Web: www.eastofenglandtouristboard.com

Heart of England Tourist Board
Larkhill Road, Worcester, Worcestershire WR5 2EZ
Tel: +44 (0)1905 761100
Web: www.visitheartofengland.com

Northumbria Tourist Board
Aykley Heads, Durham DH1 5UX
Tel: +44 (0)191 375 3028
Web: www.visitnorthumbria.com

North West Tourist Board
Swan House, Swan Meadow Road, Wigan, Lancashire WN3 5BB
Tel: +44 (0)1942 821 222
Web: www.visitnorthwest.com

South East England Tourist Board
The Old Brew House, Warwick Park, Tunbridge Wells, Kent TN2 5TU
Tel: +44 (0)1892 540766
Web: www.seetb.org.uk

Southern Tourist Board
40 Chamberlayne Road, Eastleigh, Hampshire SO50 5JH
Tel: +44 (0) 23 8062 5400
Web: www.visitsouthernengland.com

South West Tourist Board
Woodwater Park, Exeter, Devon EX2 5WT
Tel: +44 (0)870 442 0830
Web: www.westcountrynow.com

Yorkshire Tourist Board
312 Tadcaster Road, York, Yorkshire YO24 1GS
Tel: +44 (0)1904 707961
Web: www.ytb.org.uk
Yorkshire and North & North East Lincolnshire.

English Heritage
Customer Services Department , PO Box 569, Swindon SN2 2YP
Tel: +44 (0) 870 333 1181
Web: www.english heritage.org.uk

Historic Houses Association
2 Chester Street, London SW1X 7BB
Tel: +44 (0)20 7259 5688
Web: www.hha.org.uk

The National Trust
36 Queen Anne's Gate, London SW1H 9AS
Tel: +44 (0)20 7222 9251
Web: www.nationaltrust.org.uk

Images from www.britainonview.com

or see **pages 306-309** for details of local attractions to visit during your stay.

APSLEY HOUSE

141 NEWBRIDGE HILL, BATH, SOMERSET BA1 3PT

1 mile from the centre of Bath, this elegant Georgian house was built in 1830 by the Duke of Wellington and is set in a delightful garden. The hosts, Nicholas and Claire Potts, greet guests with a warm welcome into their home. There are magnificently proportioned reception rooms which have been refurbished in great style and comfort with splendid views across Bath. A quite delicious breakfast is the only meal served, although drinks are available. Nicholas and Claire will recommend local restaurants and inns, which visitors will enjoy. The bedrooms are invitingly romantic with lovely drapery and delightful en suite bathrooms. Televisions almost seem to intrude in this timeless décor. There are many things to see and do in Bath, the centre of which is just a 20 minute stroll from Apsley House through Victoria Park. The magnificent architecture includes the Assembly Rooms, mentioned so often in Jane Austen's and Georgette Heyer's historical novels, the Royal Crescent and the Roman Baths with the new luxurious spa facility opening this year. Fascinating museums, the thriving theatre and excellent shopping all add to the enjoyment of this lovely city. The Cotswolds, Mendip Hills, Stourhead, Stonehenge, Avebery and Longleat are within driving distance. Private parking is available.

Directions: The Hotel lies 1 mile west of the centre of Bath, on the A431 which branches off the A4, the Upper Bristol Road.

Web: www.johansens.com/apsleyhouse
E-mail: info@apsley-house.co.uk
Tel: 01225 336966
Fax: 01225 425462

Price Guide:
single £65–£85
double £75–£140

Our inspector loved: *The spacious Georgian rooms and high ceilings.*

The County Hotel

18/19 PULTENEY ROAD, BATH, SOMERSET BA2 4EZ

The County Hotel, winner of the AA Guest Accommodation of the Year Award 2001, the Little Gem Award by the RAC and the English Tourism Councils Gold Award, stands in the centre of Bath. It is an attractive stone-built building with a frontage enhanced by arched sash windows and twin balconies ornamented with open stone balustrades. Completely refurbished in 1999, décor and sympathetic modernisation have resulted in the creation of elegant, relaxing accommodation. The 22 exquisite en suite bedrooms have every home comfort. Many have splendid views over the Cricket ground and Bath Abbey. Breakfast is served in an intimate dining room which opens onto a conservatory where morning coffee, afternoon tea and light lunches can be ordered. Dinner is not available but the hotel's owners will happily help select one of the many nearby restaurants for an evening out. Drinks can be enjoyed in the stylish bar or lounge. The hotel has a non-smoking policy apart from the bar area. Bath's attractions include the Roman Baths, Pump Room, Royal Crescent, the thriving theatres and fascinating museums. Ample parking available.

Our inspector loved: The attention to detail and cleanliness throughout.

Directions: From M4 Jct18 take A46 and A4 towards Bath. Just before the city centre turn left onto A36 ring road and follow signs for Exeter and Wells. The hotel is on the right after the Holburne Museum.

Web: www.johansens.com/countyhotelbath
E-mail: reservations@county-hotel.co.uk
Tel: 01225 425003
Fax: 01225 466493

Price Guide:
single £75
double £100–£170

BATH & NORTH EAST SOMERSET - BATH

OLDFIELDS
102 WELLS ROAD, BATH, SOMERSET BA2 3AL

Oldfields is a large, elegant and traditional Victorian bed & breakfast with panoramic views of Bath. It is superbly positioned, only 8 minutes walk from the city centre and is built from the honey-coloured stone for which Bath is famous. Although the house is equipped with every modern feature to ensure that visitors experience maximum comfort and convenience, it retains many of the elaborate cornices and artistry of its original character. The bedrooms are beautifully furnished with rich fabrics and antiques and offer a full range of amenities. A delicious choice of breakfast to include full English, fresh seasonal fruits and smoked salmon with scrambled eggs are served in the magnificent dining room overlooking the city of Bath. Newspapers are provided and for those with time to linger over breakfast, there is unlimited tea and coffee. There is also a drawing room, gardens and private car park, which make Oldfields the perfect choice for a visit to Bath. You are assured of a warm welcome from the resident hosts, Rod and Alex Kitcher. Hot-air ballooning, golf and horse riding can be arranged. Bath is nearby with its famous Roman baths and pump room as well as the Book Museum and No. 1 Royal Crescent and is the perfect centre to explore the Cotswolds, Glastonbury and Wells Cathedral, Stonehenge, Salisbury, Bristol and South Wales. Oldfields is a strictly non-smoking hotel.

Directions: From the M4, junction 18, follow signs for Bath city centre, then take the A367 (signpost for Radstock). Oldfields is situated on the corner of Upper Oldfield Park, the first turning on the right.

Web: www.johansens.com/oldfields
E-mail: info@oldfields.co.uk
Tel: 01225 317984
Fax: 01225 444471

Price Guide:
single £59–£69
double/twin £69–£100

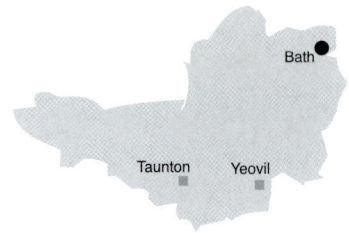

Our inspector loved: The value for money in a convenient location.

Tasburgh House Hotel

WARMINSTER ROAD, BATH BA2 6SH

The impressive, red brick Victorian façade can only hint at the warmth, style, comfort and excellent service provided in the 3 floors of its interior. A former gentleman's residence built in the 1890's this Hotel majestically rises high over 7 acres of beautifully tended terraced gardens and meadow park just ½ mile from Bath's city centre. Guests can enjoy spectacular views over and beyond the Avon and a stroll through landscaped gardens and grounds featuring over 1,000 trees down to the Kennet and Avon Canal. The towpath provides a picturesque walk into the city. Sympathetically extended and personally run by the owner, Tasburgh offers traditional English elegance and tasteful décor with all modern comforts. The Reception Hall, with original floor tiling and stained-glass windows, is particularly attractive. The Drawing Room has typical Victorian features such as high ceiling, marble fireplace and large bay window and there is a lovely, light conservatory with a spectacular chandelier and French doors leading onto a terrace. Bedrooms are elegantly decorated, en suite and appointed to a high standard. Some have a four poster or half-tester bed and original marble surround fireplace. Many have scenic views. Excellent gourmet breakfasts are provided in a sunny Dining Room and in winter the Drawing Room is warmed by a large open fire.

Our inspector loved: *The 'author' teddy bears in each of the bedrooms.*

Directions: Leave Bath by entering Warminster Road (A36) via Beckford Road with Sydney Gardens to the right. Tasburgh House is on the left after passing Trossachs Drive.

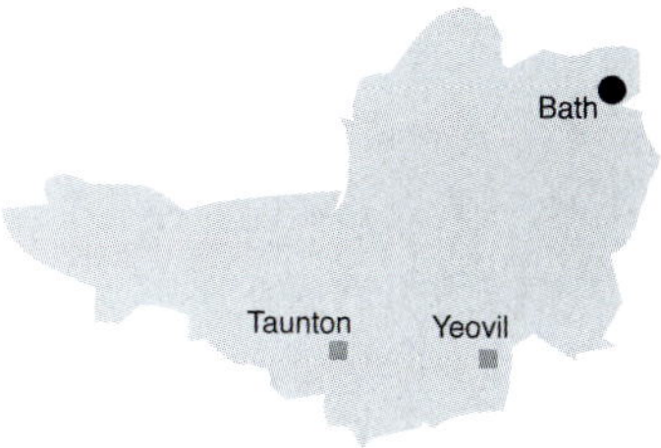

Web: www.johansens.com/tasburgh
E-mail: hotel@bathtasburgh.co.uk
Tel: 01225 425096

Price Guide:
single £67
double/twin £90–£120

Villa Magdala

HENRIETTA ROAD, BATH, SOMERSET BA2 6LX

Directions: From the M4, junction 18, take the A46 to Bath. Turn right into London Road, left at the lights, over Cleveland Bridge then take the second turning right into Henrietta Road.

Web: www.johansens.com/villamagdala
E-mail: jsvilla@villamagdala.co.uk
Tel: 01225 466329
Fax: 01225 483207

Price Guide:
single £65–£85
double £80–£120

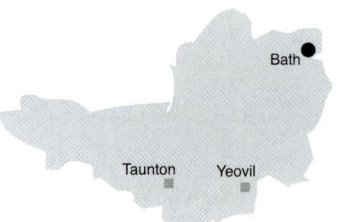

Built in 1868, the Villa Magdala is steeped in a most interesting history. The property takes its name from one of Sir Charles Napier's victories in Ethiopia as Sir Charles himself was a resident in the road at the time of construction. All the attractions of Bath are within easy reach, making the house an ideal choice for those wishing to discover the city. The 18 bedrooms are well-appointed and feature an array of modern conveniences from colour televisions and hairdryers to refreshment trays. All are en suite. The airy dining room provides a most convivial ambience in which to enjoy a traditional English breakfast whilst at dinnertime, the attentive owners Roy & Lois Thwaites are pleased to recommend some of the many nearby restaurants and brasseries. Pulteney Bridge, the Roman Baths and Pump Room are only a 5 minute walk away whilst keen shoppers will be pleased with the variety of individual and specialist shops in the centre of Bath. The National Trust village of Lacock is worth a visit and the area abounds with many stately homes and museums. There are delightful canalside walks along the Kennet and Avon Canal.

Our inspector loved: Its wonderful location in the centre of Bath.

BATH LODGE HOTEL

NORTON ST PHILIP, BATH, SOMERSET BA2 7NH

The Bath Lodge Hotel, originally called Castle Lodge, was built between 1806 and 1813 as one of six lodges added to a former gentleman's residence known as Farleigh House. This splendid building, with its towers, battlements, portcullis and heraldic shields, is redolent of Arthurian romance and offers guests a delightful setting in which to escape the stresses and strains of modern life. The rooms, which are superbly decorated and furnished, are beautifully located and have many castellated features within them. three rooms overlook the magnificent natural gardens with their cascading stream and the adjacent deer forest. The main entrance hall, lounge and conservatory all contain oak beamed ceilings, natural masonry and large log burning fireplaces. All the rooms are furnished in keeping with this unique building. An excellent breakfast is served at the Hotel. The Hotel has a no-smoking policy. Bath Lodge is an ideal location for enjoying the attractions of the World Heritage City of Bath. Stonehenge, Longleat, Wells and Bristol are also within easy reach.

Our inspector loved: *The interesting turret bedrooms.*

Directions: From Bath take the A36 Warminster road. Bath Lodge is on your left after approximately 7 miles.

Web: www.johansens.com/bathlodge
E-mail: info@bathlodge.com
Tel: 01225 723040
Fax: 01225 723737

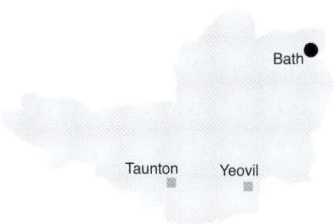

Price Guide:
single from £40
double £75–£120

BATH & NORTH EAST SOMERSET - STANTON WICK (NR BATH)

THE CARPENTERS ARMS

STANTON WICK, NR PENSFORD, SOMERSET BS39 4BX

Directions: Exit M4 at junction 19 and join M32 to Bristol. Pick up A37 to Chelwood Bridge then take right turn onto A368 towards Stanton Wick.

Web: www.johansens.com/carpentersarms
E-mail: carpenters@dial.pipex.com
Tel: 01761 490202
Fax: 01761 490763

Price Guide:
single from £62
double from £84.50

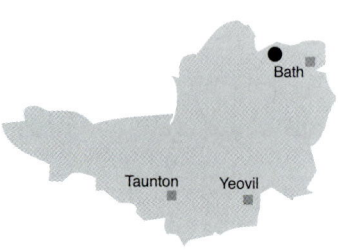

On arriving at this charming and picturesque country inn, converted from a group of miners' cottages, guests could be forgiven for thinking themselves in the depths of the English countryside. Tucked away in this peaceful rural hamlet however, The Carpenters' Arms is actually only a short drive from Bath and Bristol. A real gem of a country inn, the attentive staff see to it that total comfort is guaranteed and matched by fine wine and cuisine. The dining room is beautifully presented with crisp white table linen and sparkling glass to offset the imaginative and frequently changing menu that offers many seafood specialities. The more informal Coopers Parlour offers something more than pub food and is a great place to relax for a light lunch or hearty supper, before retiring to the comfortable lounge for coffee. With flower-decked patios and crackling log fires, The Carpenters Arms is a great retreat for a summer or winter break; the delightful en suite bedrooms are decorated individually in cottage style to a superb standard. This is an area with plenty of interest – Cheddar Gorge, Longleat, Bath and Wells are all within easy distance, or relax fly fishing on the Chew Valley Lakes. Weekend breaks available from £185.

Our inspector loved: The overall atmosphere and charm.

The Leatherne Bottel Riverside Inn & Restaurant

THE BRIDLEWAY, GORING-ON-THAMES, BERKSHIRE RG8 0HS

Uniquely situated on the banks of the Thames, surrounded by water meadows and rolling hills, The Leatherne Bottel offers peace and tranquillity with no distractions except for ducks and swans and the odd rowing eight. Chef, Julia Storey, who has been at The Leatherne Bottel for 5 years, lovingly and passionately prepares meals from the finest of fresh ingredients, whilst dining guests can dip their toes in the river! Annie Bonnet, who runs the Inn and restaurant, grows her own herbs and salad leaves to create unusual salads which may include mustard, orach, miburna, lemon basil and pineapple sage. There is also an abundance of fish, shellfish and caviar in the summer and game in the winter. Much thought and time has been taken to choose the wine list which includes hidden treasures in wooden boxes and wonderful armagnacs and cognacs together with possibly the finest and largest selections of cigars in the south. A lighter lunch menu is available from Monday to Friday and a set dinner menu costs £19.50 for 3 courses. A full à la carte menu is on offer every day and the restaurant is open for Sunday lunch but closes Sunday evenings.

Our inspector loved: The riverside terrace on a sunny day.

Directions: Signed off the B4009 Goring–Wallingford road. From the M4, junction12: 15 minutes. From the M40, junction 6: 15 minutes. Oxford is 30 minutes drive and London is 60 minutes.

Web: www.johansens.com/leathernebottel
E-mail: leathernebottel@aol.com
Tel: 01491 872667
Fax: 01491 875308

Price Guide: (dinner for 2 including wine) £90–£120

BERKSHIRE - MAIDENHEAD (COOKHAM DEAN)

THE INN ON THE GREEN

THE OLD CRICKET COMMON, COOKHAM DEAN, BERKSHIRE SL6 9NZ

With commanding views over the village green and beyond, The Inn on the Green is situated in the heart of the picturesque village, Cookham Dean. A heartfelt welcome is warmly offered in this family-run hotel, which has recently been completely refurbished to an extremely high standard, with bright colour schemes, imaginative décor and comfortable furniture. A cosy bar is the perfect place to relax and the adjoining dining room opens onto a spacious terrace in the summer, an ideal spot for early evening dining. The idyllic gardens that surround the Hotel are a haven for birds and have been lovingly cared for. Individually decorated bedrooms are beautifully appointed and benefit from all modern conveniences such as D.V.D. and surround sound, some with a marvellous four poster bed. Guests can explore the local woods, which provide many excellent walks and the Thames, which is only 2 kilometres away, winds through the beautiful Thames Valley; an enchanting day out. Local attractions include Windsor Castle, the second home of the Royal family, Legoland and the pretty riverside town of Marlow, which has numerous unique shops and restaurants. The Hotel is also within easy reach of Oxford, Eton, Henley and Heathrow.

Directions: From the M4 take junction 8/9 towards Marlow. Follow the signs to Cookham Dean and turn right by the war memorial on the Old Cricket Common.

Web: www.johansens.com/innonthegreen
E-mail: reception@theinnonthegreen.com
Tel: 01628 482638
Fax: 01628 487474

Price Guide:
single from £100
double from £110

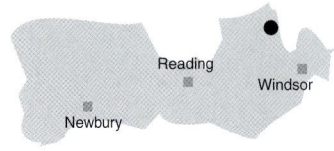

Our inspector loved: This tucked away hostelry.

MELBOURN BURY

MELBOURN, CAMBRIDGESHIRE, NR ROYSTON SG8 6DE

Set in extensive grounds with a lake and wildfowl, Melbourn Bury is an elegant manor house. It has had only two ownerships since the 1500s. The first owners were the monks of Ely and then in 1850, the property was purchased by the ancestors of Sylvia Hopkinson. Gracious reception rooms are furnished with antiques and fine paintings, while the en suite bedrooms are comfortable and have charming views of the gardens. Fresh flowers and log fires are extra touches which guests will appreciate. Adjoining the library is a 19th century billiard room with a full-size table. Delicious home cooking encompasses traditional English recipes and continental dishes prepared in cordon bleu style. Dinner is by prior arrangement. Lunches and dinners for up to 22 persons seated; more can be accommodated buffet-style – small conferences, receptions and exhibitions. Closed at Christmas and Easter. Places of interest nearby include Cambridge, Duxford Air Museum, Audley End, Ely, Wimpole Hall and Hatfield House.

Our inspector loved: The sight of the snowdrops sweeping over the lawn to the lake and folly.

Directions: Off A10, 10 miles south of Cambridge, 3rd turning on left to Melbourn; 2 miles north of Royston, 1st turning on right to Melbourn. Entrance is 300 yards on left after the turning. Look for the white gate posts and lodge cottage.

Web: www.johansens.com/melbournbury
E-mail: melbournbury@biztobiz.co.uk
Tel: 01763 261151
Fax: 01763 262375

Price Guide:
single £65
double £100

CAMBRIDGESHIRE - WISBECH (OUTWELL)

CROWN LODGE HOTEL

DOWNHAM ROAD, OUTWELL, WISBECH, CAMBRIDGESHIRE PE14 8SE

Directions: Crown Lodge is situated in the village of Outwell, on the A1122 between Wisbech and Downham Market town.

Web: www.johansens.com/crownlodge
E-mail: crownlodgehotel@hotmail.com
Tel: 01945 773391
Fax: 01945 772668

Price Guide:
single £55
double £70

Situated on the banks of Well Creek with its abundance of wild ducks and swans, the Crown Lodge is a cosy family-run hotel. With magnificent views of the surrounding Fenland, it is the ideal base for exploring one of Britain's most naturally beautiful regions. Upon entering, the visitor is immediately struck by the welcoming ambience created by the many soothing watercolours and prints that adorn the walls of the restaurant, bar and public rooms. The excellently designed rooms are all bright and airy, and offer every home comfort, including television, telephone modem point, double glazing and central heating. The restaurant, a deserved recipient of an AA Rosette, creates delicious fare from the freshest of local produce, accompanied by a fine selection of wines. After dinner relaxation is assured, as guests can avail of the snooker room and squash courts. For the business traveller, there are first-class conference facilities, as well as top-of-the-range word processing services. A short drive away is the cathedral city of Ely, Sandringham, the Queen's country residence and the historic seat of learning in nearby Cambridge. Those who prefer the "sport of kings" can visit the Newmarket horse-racing track. Weekend break rates available.

Our inspector loved: *The cosy comfort and cheerful pictures.*

22

Frogg Manor Hotel & Restaurant

FULLERS MOOR, NANTWICH ROAD, BROXTON, CHESTER CH3 9JH

A human sized frog with a polka dot tie points towards Frogg Manor, a beautiful Grade II listed Georgian manor house which, from its elevated position high in the Broxton Hills, affords a most spectacular view across Cheshire to the Welsh Mountains. Surrounded by 9 acres of woods and carefully tended gardens this original, eccentric and bourgeois Hotel is bursting with character and is home to several hundred frogs made from brass, wood and everything else you can think of. Plush surroundings, lavish décor and magnificent antique furniture set the scene; the Hotel has been excellently refurbished recently to maintain a high standard of comfort. The romantic conservatory restaurant serves delicious English style cuisine that is freshly prepared by proprietor, John Sykes and complemented by an extensive list of fine wines. After dinner the comfortable and cosy lounge is the perfect place to enjoy a fine scotch, coffee and chocolates. Luxurious bedrooms are individually and creatively decorated with attention to detail and quality such as fine Egyptian cottons and the best mattresses. Guests can explore the unspoilt local landscapes with rolling hills, sandstone cliffs, idyllic villages and ancient churches. Chester, the only completely walled city left in Britain, is nearby and features charming timbered houses and ancient Roman remains.

Directions: From Chester take the A41 towards Whitchurch, then the A534 towards Nantwich. The Hotel is on the right.

Web: www.johansens.com/froggmanor
E-mail: info@froggmanorhotel.co.uk
Tel: 01829 782629
Fax: 01829 782459

Price Guide:
single £65–£130
double/twin £92–£170

Our inspector loved: The eccentric charm of this Georgian country hotel.

CHESHIRE - CHESTER (BROXTON)

BROXTON HALL COUNTRY HOUSE HOTEL

WHITCHURCH ROAD, BROXTON, CHESTER, CHESHIRE CH3 9JS

Directions: Broxton Hall is on the A41 Whitchurch – Chester road, eight miles between Whitchurch and Chester.

Web: www.johansens.com/broxtonhall
E-mail: reservation@broxtonhall.co.uk
Tel: 01829 782321
Fax: 01829 782330

Price Guide:
single £70–£85
double/twin £75–£130

Built in 1671 by a local landowner, Broxton Hall is a black and white half-timbered building set in five acres of grounds and extensive gardens amid the rolling Cheshire countryside. The mediaeval city of Chester is eight miles away. The hotel provides every modern comfort while retaining the ambience of a bygone age. The reception area reflects the character of the entire hotel, with its magnificent Jacobean fireplace, plush furnishings, oak panelled walls and carved mahogany staircase. On cool evenings log fires are lit. The small but well-appointed bedrooms are furnished with antiques and have en suite bathrooms as well as every modern comfort. Overlooking the gardens, the restaurant receives constant praise and AA and RAC Rosettes. French and English cuisine is served, using local game in season and freshly caught fish. There is an extensive wine list. Breakfast may be taken in the sunny conservatory overlooking the lawned gardens. The hotel is an ideal venue for business meetings and conferences. Broxton Hall is the perfect base from which to visit the North Wales coast and Snowdonia. There are a number of excellent golf courses nearby and racecourses at Chester and Bangor-on-Dee.

Our inspector loved: The cosy antique filled rooms.

BROOK MEADOW HOTEL
HEATH LANE, CHILDER THORNTON, CHESHIRE CH66 7NS

Set in 4 acres of landscaped gardens amidst beautiful rural surroundings, this graceful Hotel offers privacy and tranquillity with impeccable service and first class facilities. Elegant reception rooms feature stunning open fireplaces, magnificent attention to detail, antiques and comfortable sofas to create a gracious and warm ambience. The bedrooms and suites are equally luxurious with wonderful spa baths and fine décor. Peaceful gardens have sweeping lawns, colourful flowers and a gentle flowing stream. Black swans gracefully cruise around the island on a lovely romantic lake, where there is a delightful wedding pavilion, the perfect place to say your vows (the Hotel has a license to carry out wedding ceremonies there). Newly-weds will love the romantic Bridal Suite, which has a fabulous four poster bed. Delicious cuisine makes use of Cheshire's finest local produce and is complemented by a choice of superior wines, vintage champagnes, malts, cognacs and ports. The conservatory and terrace, which overlook the gardens, fountains and cascade, are ideal for a more informal dining atmosphere. A fully-equipped gym, squash courts and steam room is available just 7 miles away and numerous championship golf courses are nearby. Guests can explore the picturesque villages of Cheshire or the countryside and coast of Wirral and North Wales.

Our inspector loved: The wedding pavilion surrounded by a small lake.

Directions: From the M6 take the M56 to North Wales/Runcorn. From the M53 to Liverpool, exit junction 5 for the A41 to Chester. Fork right at Total Garage onto the A550 Welsh Road then follow signs to Brook Meadow.

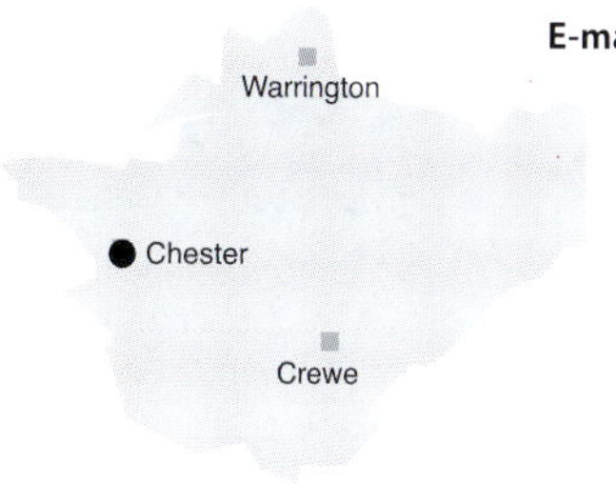

Web: www.johansens.com/brookmeadow
E-mail: brookmeadowhotel@btconnect.com
Tel: 0151 339 9350
Fax: 0151 347 4221

Price Guide:
single £70–£110
double/twin £90–£130
suite £150

CHESHIRE - CHESTER (TARPORLEY)

WILLINGTON HALL HOTEL

WILLINGTON, NR TARPORLEY, CHESHIRE CW6 0NB

Directions: Take the A51 from Tarporley to Chester and turn right at the Bull's Head public house at Clotton. Willington Hall Hotel is one mile ahead on the left.

Web: www.johansens.com/willingtonhall
E-mail: enquiries@willingtonhall.co.uk
Tel: 01829 752321
Fax: 01829 752596

Price Guide:
single £70–£85
double £110–£120

Built by Cheshire landowner Charles Tomkinson, Willington Hall was converted into a hotel by one of his descendants and in 1999 was bought by Stuart and Diana Begbie. Set in 17 acres of woods and parkland, the hotel affords wonderful views across the Cheshire countryside towards the Welsh mountains. There are both formally landscaped and 'wild' gardens, which create a beautiful backdrop for the handsome architectural proportions of the house. The hotel is a comfortable and friendly retreat for those seeking peace and seclusion. Under the personal supervision of Diana and Stuart, Willington Hall has acquired a good reputation with local people for its extensive bar meals and à la carte restaurant, along with friendly and attentive service. The menus offer traditional English cooking, with a French influence. Willington Hall is an ideal location for visiting the Roman city of Chester, Tatton Park, Beeston Castle and Oulton Park racetrack. North Wales is easily accessible. The hotel is closed on Christmas Day.

Our inspector loved: The recently refurbished bedrooms.

Trelawne Hotel – The Hutches Restaurant

MAWNAN SMITH, NR FALMOUTH, CORNWALL TR11 5HS

A very friendly welcome awaits guests, who will be enchanted by the beautiful location of Trelawne Hotel, on the coast between the Rivers Fal and Helford. Large picture windows in the public rooms, including the totally refurbished spacious lounge/bar, ensure that guests take full advantage of the panoramic vistas of the ever-changing coastline. The bedrooms are charming, many with views of the sea. The soft colours of the décor, the discreet lighting and attention to detail provide a restful atmosphere, in harmony with the Wedgwood, fresh flowers and sparkling crystal in The Hutches Restaurant, which has been awarded 2 AA Rosettes. The menu changes daily and offers a variety of inspired dishes, including local seafood, game and fresh vegetables. Ideally located for coastal walks along Rosemullion Head and the picturesque Helford Estuary. There are also a wealth of famous gardens within the area. 'Slip Away Anyday' spring, autumn and winter breaks. Closed January. The Royal Duchy of Cornwall is an area of outstanding beauty, with many National Trust and English Heritage properties to visit and a range of leisure pursuits to enjoy.

Our inspector loved: The beautiful location and first class cuisine.

Directions: From Truro follow A39 towards Falmouth, turn right at Hillhead roundabout, take exit signposted Maenporth. Carry on for 3 miles and Trelawne is at the top overlooking Falmouth bay.

Web: www.johansens.com/trelawne
Tel: 01326 250226
Fax: 01326 250909

Price Guide:
single £74–£82
double £106–£140

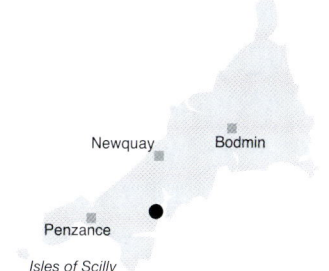

CORNWALL - FOWEY

THE OLD QUAY HOUSE HOTEL
28 FORE STREET, FOWEY, CORNWALL PL23 1AQ

The Old Quay House is a 19th century former temperance house located in the heart of the picturesque port of Fowey. With its own private quay residents may dine facing one of the most beautiful marine panoramas on Cornwall's south coast. Following a five month refurbishment programme beginning in November 2002, the owners, Roy and Jane Carson, aim to present a hotel noted for its relaxed atmosphere, high quality rooms, excellent service and cuisine. Chef, Henry Wood, will continue to serve contemporary, light, healthy cuisine using the highest quality local produce. Fowey is steeped in maritime history, the home to buccaneers and authors, laying claim to notable residents such as Daphne du Maurier and Arthur Quillar Couch. There are numerous nearby walks offering spectacular views of the estuary and coastline and the seaboard location provides arguably the best sailing in the UK.

Directions: From the A390 towards St. Austell turn left onto the B3269 to Fowey. Just before entering Fowey go across a mini-roundabout then continue until the bottom of the hill. Turn left into Lostwithiel Street, go past the church into Fore Street. The Hotel is a couple of hundred yards on the right hand side.

Web: www.johansens.com/oldquayhouse
E-mail: info@theoldquayhouse.com
Tel: 01726 833302
Fax: 01726 833668

Price Guide:
single £100
double/twin from £120

Our inspector loved: *From walking in from Fore Street, to be greeted by the magical estuary location.*

Cormorant On The River, Hotel & Riverside Restaurant

GOLANT BY FOWEY, CORNWALL PL23 1LL

Only 5 miles from the Eden Project, the Cormorant stands high above the beautiful Fowey Estuary with magnificent views over the shimmering waters and the Cornish countryside. The subject of an upgrading programme, this is a warm, friendly and inviting Hotel with 11 entirely individual bedrooms. All have en suite, with colour television, radio, direct dial telephone and extensive views over the estuary and creeks. Guests can relax in an extremely comfortable lounge which has full-length picture windows and a log fire in winter. The bar is small and welcoming. Guests can also enjoy lounging on the terrace near the Hotel's heated swimming pool which has superb river views. This corner of Cornwall is a living larder of wholesome produce all made use of of by the enthusiastic chef and served in a pretty candlelit restaurant; a choice of good and imaginative menus is on offer. Guests can enjoy miles of walking along the coastline, fishing villages, Lanhydrock House and gardens and many National Trust properties. Fishing, riding and golf can be arranged locally.

Our inspector loved: *The wonderful elevated location overlooking the ever changing estuary.*

Directions: From Exeter, take the A30 towards Bodmin and then the B3269 towards Fowey. After 6 miles turn left at a staggered junction to Golant. Bear right as you approach the estuary and continue along the water's edge. The Hotel is on the right.

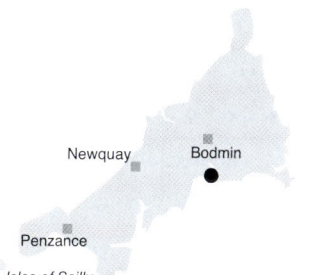

Web: www.johansens.com/cormorant
E-mail: relax@cormoranthotels.co.uk
Tel: 01726 833426

Price Guide:
single £65–£100
double £110–£170

CORNWALL - ISLES OF SCILLY (BRYHER)

HELL BAY

BRYHER, ISLES OF SCILLY, CORNWALL TR23 0PR

Directions: The Isles of Scilly are reached by Helicopter or boat from Penzance or fixed wing aircraft from Bristol, Exeter, Newquay and Lands End. The hotel can make all necessary travel arrangements and will co-ordinate all transfers to Bryher on arrival.

Web: www.johansens.com/hellbay
E-mail: contactus@hellbay.co.uk
Tel: 01720 422947
Fax: 01720 423004

Price Guide: (including dinner
suites £160–£300

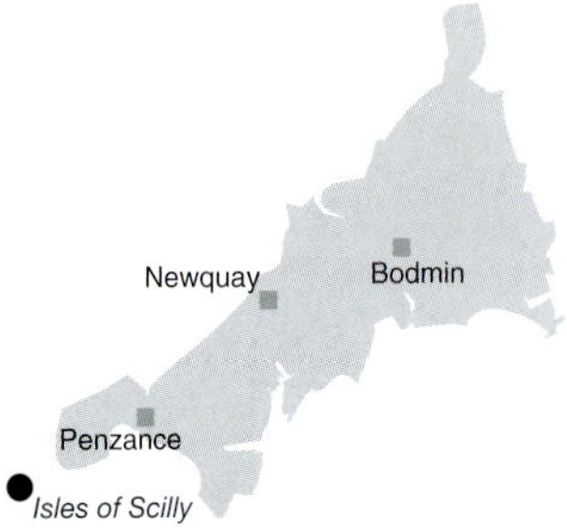

Bryher is the smallest community of the Isles of Scilly, 28 miles west of Land's End and Hell Bay its only hotel. It stands in a spectacular and dramatic setting in extensive lawned grounds on the rugged West Coast overlooking the unbroken Atlantic Ocean. Described as a 'spectacularly located getaway from it all destination that is a paradise for adults and children alike' .. and it is. Outdoor heated swimming pool, gym, sauna, spa bath, children's playground, games room and par 3 golf course ensure there is never a dull moment. Daily boat trips available so that you can discover the islands, the world famous tropical Abbey Garden is on the neighbouring island of Tresco. White sanded beaches abound with an array of water sports available. Dining is an integral part of staying at Hell Bay and the food will not disappoint, as you would expect seafood is a speciality. Stylish and design led re-development, due winter 2002/3, set to enhance an already very distinctive property. Open April to November.

Our inspector loved: The away-from-it-all feel. Fresh pollution free air and beautiful magical views.

CORNWALL - LOOE

TREHAVEN MANOR HOTEL
STATION ROAD, LOOE, CORNWALL PL13 1HN

The Trehaven Manor Hotel, built of beautiful traditional Cornish stone, was originally a vicarage and stands serenely high above the picturesque seaside town of Looe. Approached along a sweeping driveway, this enchanting 19th-century house is a haven of tranquillity and commands wonderful views over the idyllic estuary and beyond to the Looe bridge. The spacious bedrooms are tastefully presented in a relaxed environment with comfortable furniture, bright colour co-ordinated fabrics and all modern conveniences. Home-made scones and delicious Cornish clotted cream are served in the elegant lounge on arrival. A tasty breakfast is prepared using fresh local ingredients and served in the sunny restaurant with bay fronted windows. Dinner bed and breakfast breaks are available from September through to May. Many fine other restaurants may be recommended in the area with pre-booking arrangements organised by the hotel during the summer. Looe which is within a three minute walk away is an ideal base to explore charming Cornwall and its stunning sandy beaches. National Trust houses and gardens are in abundance or guests can visit the monkey sanctuary, Eden Project and Lost Gardens of Helegan. Tennis, bowling and boat trips for fishing or pleasure are available.

Our inspector loved: *The magnificent location and the warm welcoming feel throughout.*

Directions: A38 over Tamar Bridge. Carry on until Trerulfoot roundabout and take exit for Looe.

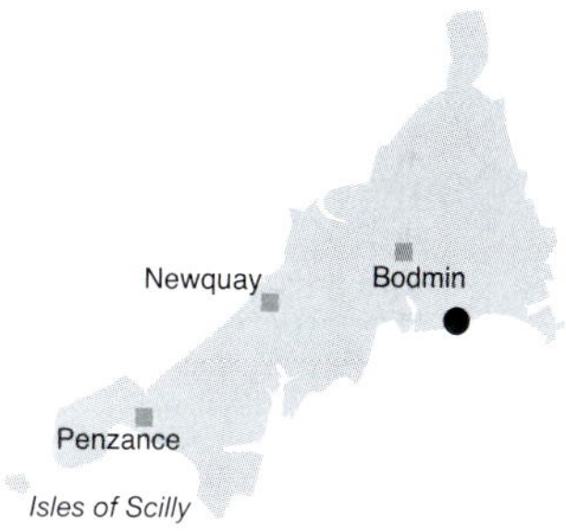

Web: www.johansens.com/trehavenlooe
E-mail: enquiries@trehavenhotel.co.uk
Tel: 01503 262028
Fax: 01503 265613

Price Guide:
single £50
double/twin £80–£130

CORNWALL - MEVAGISSEY

Trevalsa Court Hotel

SCHOOL HILL, MEVAGISSEY, ST AUSTELL, CORNWALL PL26 6TH

Directions: On approaching Mevagissey on the B3273 from St Austell go through Pentewan, climb the hill and turn left at the crossroads at the top. Trevalsa Court Hotel is ½ mile on the left.

Web: www.johansens.com/trevalsa
E-mail: trevalsacourthotel@yahoo.co.uk
Tel: 01726 842468
Fax: 01726 844482

Price Guide:
single £50–£60
double/twin £90–£120
suite £150

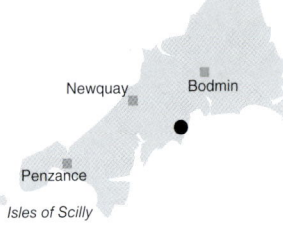

Built overlooking the sea in the 1930's the Trevalsa was discovered by owners Klaus Wagner and Matthias Mainka in 1999, who lovingly set to work to restore the casual but elegant atmosphere of a country house. Blending traditional and modern styles, its oak panelled hall and dining room, beautiful lounge and mullioned windows recall the ambience of a bygone age, whilst the newly refurbished en suite bedrooms are simply and classically furnished. All principal bedrooms have splendid sea views and on the ground floor are 3 rooms particularly suitable for elderly or less able guests. The Hotel's grounds are above the sheltered Polstreath Beach and access to its sloping sands and coves for swimming and fishing is directly available from the garden. A footpath also leads to the harbour and typically Cornish streets of Mevagissey and St Austell, with its 18 hole golf course and modern sports centre, is just 5 miles away. Trevalsa Court can be reached by car without passing through Mevagissy's narrow roads and its location makes it an excellent base for touring all parts of Cornwall. The award winning Lost Gardens of Heligan and the Eden Project, fast becoming a top visitor destination for the 21st century, are nearby.

Our inspector loved: *The wonderful warm welcome and feeling of relaxation.*

HIGHER FAUGAN COUNTRY HOUSE HOTEL

CHYWOONE HILL, NEWLYN, CORNWALL TR18 5NS

A tree-overhung drive meandering into lawned gardens provides an attractive welcome to this gracious hotel situated on the outskirts of Newlyn overlooking Mount's Bay and St Michael's Mount. Built in 1904 as the family home of artist Stanhope Forbes, R.A., founder of the Newlyn School of Art, Higher Faugan lies in 10 acres of magnificent grounds and offers seclusion, tranquillity and old world charm. An exquisite staircase leads to 11 well-appointed en suite bedrooms, all with views of the gardens and some looking onwards to the sea. The beautiful lawns, flower borders and woodlands incorporating an Italian sunken garden were featured in many of the paintings of Stanhope and Elizabeth Forbes. Excellent cuisine is provided in the elegant dining room which incorporates the original Edwardian conservatory with doors leading onto the garden. The extensive five-course table d'hôte menu varies daily and features locally caught fish and organic vegetables. The area is rich in National Trust properties, sandy beaches and picturesque fishing villages. St Michael's Mount with its famous castle-like mansion, the Merry Maidens, a group of Bronze Age stone and the Eden project are within easy reach. Painting and activity breaks.

Our inspector loved: This delightful, peacefully located country house - yet only minutes from Penzance sea front and town.

Directions: From M5 Jct30 follow A30 past Penzance to pick up signs for Newlyn. Entrance is on the right hand side of Chywoone Hill (B3315).

Web: www.johansens.com/higherfaugan
E-mail: reception@higherfaugan-hotel.co.uk
Tel: 01736 362076
Fax: 01736 351648

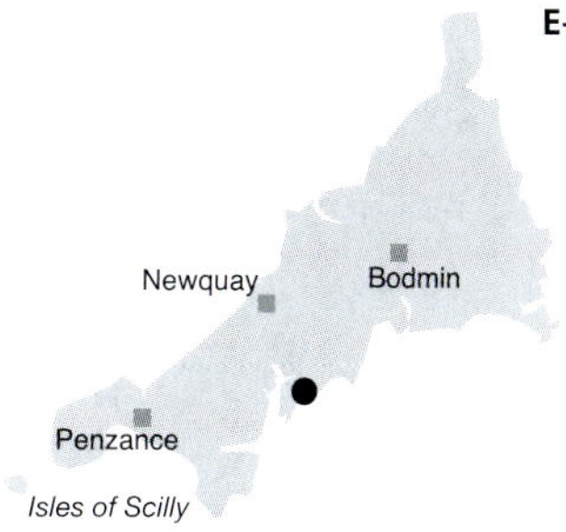

Price Guide:
single £60–£80
double/twin £90–£120

JUBILEE INN

PELYNT, NR LOOE, CORNWALL PL13 2JZ

Directions: From Plymouth, cross Tamar Bridge and follow the main road to Looe. Leave Looe on the Polperro road and turn right for Pelynt.

Web: www.johansens.com/jubileeinn
E-mail: rickard@jubileeinn.com
Tel: 01503 220312
Fax: 01503 220920

Price Guide:
single £35–£44
double £60–£70

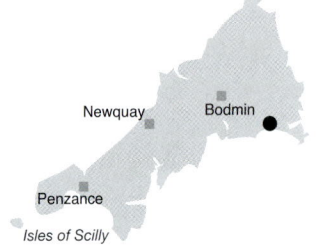

The Jubilee has been an inn since the 16th century, changing its name from The Axe in 1887 to mark the 50th anniversary of Queen Victoria's accession. The low beamed ceilings, open hearths and old prints create an air of tradition and charm throughout. The unique spiral staircase designed by artist, Stuart Armfield leads to the various size bedrooms which are tastefully furnished in a cottage style; three are for families and one is a bridal suite. With a residents' lounge, three bars, a beer garden plus a large garden with a children's play area there are plenty of places to relax. and enjoy an Al Fresco meal and drink. An impressive à la carte menu and friendly, professional service are offered in the dining room. The inn's speciality is fish and shellfish, which come straight off the boats in nearby Looe. An extensive bar menu and traditional Sunday lunches are also on offer. The inn now has a non smoking family room. The Duchy of Cornwall nurseries, National Trust Properties, Monkey Sanctuary are a selection of the many interesting places to visit. Bodmin Moor, numerous picturesque villages and beautiful coastline are all to be explored. The Eden Project is only ½ hour away. Special breaks arranged.

Our inspector loved: *The charm and character are enchanting.*

CORNWALL - ST. AUSTELL (TREGREHAN)

BOSCUNDLE MANOR
TREGREHAN, ST. AUSTELL, CORNWALL PL25 3RL

Just one mile from the sea, Boscundle Manor is a small, mid 18th century country house hotel within 8 acres of beautiful wooded grounds that comprises of a golf practice area with two greens and several teeing positions, old tin mine remains and indoor and outdoor swimming pools. All the bedrooms are en suite and feature a fridge, T.V., tea and coffee making facilities, direct dial telephone and hairdryer. Most rooms also have a C.D. player and nearly all the double or twin rooms have spa baths. As well as the bedrooms in the Manor, the separate Garden Room makes an ideal bridal suite and The Cottage provides ideal accommodation for families. An elegant dining room offers cuisine created with local fresh fish and produce, as well as an excellent cheeseboard and selection of wines from around the world; special diets can be catered for. Other facilities include badminton and a croquet lawn. Boscundle Manor is the closest hotel to the world famous Eden Project which is just a 3 minute drive or 20 minute walk away. It is also ideally placed for sightseeing around Cornwall with its numerous gardens, fishing villages and coastal walks.

Our inspector loved: The beautiful grounds and tasteful, comfortable presentation.

Directions: 2 miles east of St. Austell and ¼ mile east of the A391/A390 junction, turn left towards Tregrehan and follow brown tourist signs.

Web: www.johansens.com/boscundle
E-mail: stay@boscundlemanor.co.uk
Tel: 01726 813557
Fax: 01726 814997

Price Guide:
single £80–£90
double/twin £140–£160
suite £170–£190

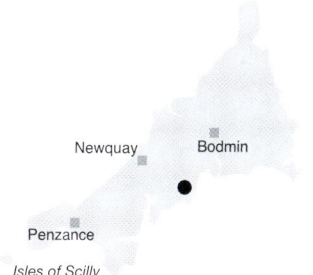

THE COUNTRYMAN AT TRINK HOTEL

OLD COACH ROAD, ST IVES, CORNWALL TR26 3JQ

Directions: A30, A3074 to St Ives, then B3311 for about two miles.

Web: www.johansens.com/countrymanattrink
E-mail: enquiries@the-countryman-hotel-stives.co.uk
Tel: 01736 797571
Fax: 01736 797571

Price Guide:
single £38
double £65–£70

Five minutes drive from the quaint town of St Ives is the Countryman Hotel at Trink. St Ives has become a mecca for artists and one of the latest attractions is the new Tate Gallery with its collection of modern paintings and contemporary exhibits. Cornwall has a wealth of interesting things to see not least its dramatic coastline ideal for lovers of nature and walkers. The Countryman dates from the 17th century. Today the small hotel has been renovated to meet the needs of the modern visitor, all rooms have en suite shower and toilet, colour television and tea making facilities. The atmosphere of the hotel is friendly and inviting, the emphasis being on cheerful service and good value for money. This is a totally no smoking hotel. In the restaurant, Howard Massey, the chef-patron, likes cooking to order from his varied and interesting menu containing Cornish fish supported by a sensibly priced wine-list. St Ives has always had a tradition for generous hospitality. A former mayor, the legendary John Knill, bequeathed £10 for an annual banquet. Prices may have altered a little but the high quality of the local cooking has not changed. Places of interest nearby include the Tate Gallery, Barbara Hepworth's house, Lands End and St Michael's Mount. Golf and riding available.

Our inspector loved: *The simplicity, which is the charm.*

THE PORT WILLIAM

TREBARWITH STRAND, NR TINTAGEL, CORNWALL PL34 0HB

The Port William is a delightful old inn, romantically situated 50 yards from the sea overlooking the beach and cliffs at Trebarwith Strand. The small but charming bedrooms have recently been refurbished and offer every modern amenity, including baths with showers, colour TVs, hair dryers and hospitality trays. Each bedroom is positioned so that guests can enjoy spectacular views during the day and dramatic sunsets over the sea in the evening. Well behaved children and dogs are welcome! All the bedrooms are non-smoking. Restaurant: The Inn enjoys an excellent local reputation for the quality of its food. An extensive breakfast menu and lunches and dinners are prepared using only the freshest produce, with home-cooked dishes and a range of superb fish courses and seafood among the specialities. A good selection of vegetarian food is always available. Service is friendly and informal. Proprietory brands and local Cornish ales are available. The unique and stunning display of seahorses and other marine species are guaranteed to relax the most stressed of travellers. In this area, noted for its outstanding beauty, there is no shortage of leisure activities. Apart from magnificent walks, there are plenty of opportunities for surfing, sea-fishing and golf. Nearby: Tintagel Castle, King Arthur's Great Halls and a host of National Trust properties. Winter breaks available.

Our inspector loved: The stunning spectacular location.

Directions: Follow B3263 from Camelford to Tintagel, then south to Trebarwith via Treknow.

Web: www.johansens.com/portwilliam
E-mail: william@eurobell.co.uk
Tel: 01840 770230
Fax: 01840 770936

Price Guide:
single £56–£65
double £75–£90

Tredethy House

HELLAND BRIDGE, BODMIN, CORNWALL PL30 4QS

Directions: From the A30 exit Bodmin, take the exit marked Helland from the roundabout and after 1½ miles turn left again signposted Helland.

Prior to going to press Tredethy House was sold as a private house. In a central location, just west of Bodmin Moor, Tredethy House is the ideal base for exploring Cornwall. Set in 9 acres of grounds and with beautiful views over the countryside, this elegant manor house dates back to Tudor times, with later Victorian additions providing spacious accommodation in beautifully proportioned rooms. The 15 bedrooms are all individual in their design and style; 11 in the main house and 4 courtyard suites yet are united by their elegant décor and excellent facilities. Families will love the spacious courtyard suites with their additional sitting rooms and dogs are welcome too with blankets and throws provided. Local Cornish produce features prominently in the exciting dinner menu with unusual dishes such as: fried parmesan crumbed Cornish brie with a lemon and lime gremolata or pan fried medallions of prime Cornish beef wrapped in bacon with seared aubergine and smoked cheese on a rich pan gravy. Children are also extremely well catered for with a 2 course high tea prepared nightly. Pencarrow House and the local vineyard are well worth a visit and there are plenty of walks along Bodmin Moor or the Camel Trail.

Trehellas House Hotel & Restaurant

WASHAWAY, BODMIN, CORNWALL PL30 3AD

This early 18th century Grade II listed Cornish courthouse, steeped in history, is surrounded by 2 acres of grounds. Inside, its traditional features act as a backdrop for many stunning Oriental artefacts. The beamed, atmospheric restaurant with its beautifully preserved Delabole slate floor and elegant décor serves dishes from Thailand, India and Asia together with English and European dishes. An extensive wine list includes wines from the local Camel Valley vineyard. Following a recent refurbishment the 10 bedrooms are all en suite and comfortably furnished with patchwork quilts and iron bedsteads. The chandelier-lit Courtroom Suite still retains the magistrates dais and moulded cornice and has its own woodburner which can be lit upon request. Outside, guests may wish to stroll in the pleasant gardens or enjoy the heated swimming pool and for the more energetic there are many walks along the Camel trail. The village of Rock is a popular base for sailing and fishing and at nearby Daymer Bay is the little church where poet John Betjeman is buried. The Eden Project is just 12 miles away. Tickets are available from the hotel.

Our inspector loved: *The relaxing atmosphere and interesting, varied cuisine.*

Directions: Washaway is located on the A389 half-way between the towns of Bodmin and Wadebridge. Approaching from Bodmin, Trehellas House is situated to the right, set back from the main road and accessed by a slip road.

Web: www.johansens.com/trehellas
E-mail: trehellashouse@aol.com
Tel: 01208 72700
Fax: 01208 73336

Price Guide:
single £40–£85
double from £82.50
suite from £130

GREY FRIAR LODGE

CLAPPERSGATE, AMBLESIDE, CUMBRIA LA22 9NE

Directions: From Ambleside take A593 towards Coniston for approx. 1½ miles.

Web: www.johansens.com/greyfriar
E-mail: greyfriar@veen.freeserve.co.uk
Tel: 015394 33158
Fax: 015394 33158

Price Guide:
single £38–£90
double/twin £54–£98

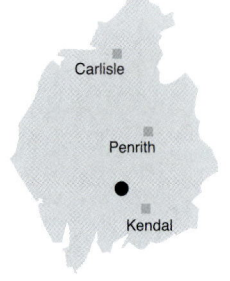

This traditional Cumbrian country house hotel has breathtaking views over unspoilt countryside and the Brathay river to the dramatic mountains beyond. Standing amidst a flower-filled garden one mile from Lake Windermere and just a few minutes from Ambleside town centre, Grey Friar Lodge was built in 1869 as a vicarage, known as the Bishops House. Tastefully converted into an attractive hotel, it has a tranquil atmosphere created by joint owner and chef Pamela Veen's attention to detail, décor and furnishings. The charming, hospitable lodge has earned many awards in the past, such as AA Small Hotel of the Year 1997 and RAC Small Hotel of the North 1994. The lounges offer total comfort and countryside views, which can also be enjoyed from the verandah and terrace. Each of the cosy en suite bedrooms is individually furnished with antique pictures, patchwork quilts and every facility from colour television to tea and coffee tray; most have antique or four-poster beds. Pamela's set menus will satisfy the most discerning diner and are complemented by a wine list reflecting husband David's desire for quality, interest and value. Nearby attractions include the Lake District, Stockghyll Force waterfall, Kirkstone Pass, Wordsworth Museum and the National Trust property of Townend.

Our inspector loved: *The lovely views across the Brathay river.*

NANNY BROW COUNTRY HOUSE HOTEL & RESTAURANT

CLAPPERSGATE, AMBLESIDE, CUMBRIA LA22 9NF

Away from the tourists visiting Ambleside at the northern end of Lake Windermere, a Victorian architect built Nanny Brow for himself on this magnificent site on Loughrigg Fell, overlooking the dramatic Langdale Pikes and the gently meandering River Brathay. Set in five acres of landscaped gardens and woodland, the house is now an elegant hotel which retains its country house charm and has been awarded many accolades such as AA Romantic Hotel and two AA Red Rosettes. Guests appreciate the welcoming atmosphere of the panelled Entrance Hall and find the Lounge with its comfortable furniture and log fires very restful. The pretty bedrooms each, individually styled, have been thoughtfully equipped with many extras. The romantic Garden Suites have balconies or seating areas outside their sitting rooms. Guests mingle in the inviting Bar, before dining by candlelight in the Restaurant. The ever-changing five course menu features the chef's inspired rendition of traditional English dishes, complemented by many fine wines. Fishing, putting and spa facilities, with membership of a private leisure club are available and all the attractions of nearby Lake Windermere are within easy reach. Special breaks available.

Our inspector loved: *This attractive hotel, built by a Victorian member of the Arts and Crafts movement.*

Directions: From Ambleside A593 Coniston Road for 1m. Nanny Brow is on the right.

Web: www.johansens.com/nannybrow
E-mail: reservations@nannybrow.co.uk
Tel: 015394 32036
Fax: 015394 32450

Price Guide:
single £95–£150
double £170–£260
suite £300

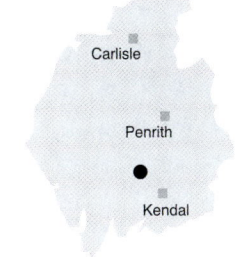

UNDERWOOD

THE HILL, MILLOM, CUMBRIA LA18 5EZ

Andrew and Wendy Miller personally run this delightful non-smoking country house which was once a Victorian vicarage. Beautifully restored, it stands within eight acres of landscaped gardens, meadows and paddocks, between the picturesque Whicham Valley and Duddon Estuary. The tranquil and elegant surroundings include two relaxing lounges, as well as an indoor heated swimming pool with steam room and a tennis court. Each of the 5 fully equipped bedrooms are en suite and individually furnished. Hosts Andrew and Wendy pride themselves on offering guests the utmost in comfort and hospitality, and every evening prepare and serve a four-course dinner which combines the best in local ingredients, along with a carefully selected wine list. A hearty breakfast provides the perfect start for those wishing to explore the surrounding area. Lakes Coniston, Windermere and Wastwater are within easy reach, and there is plenty of opportunity to enjoy the attractions of Cumbria by car or on foot. The less adventurous can unwind with a relaxing swim, a stroll around the grounds or a game of croquet.

Our inspector loved: *Wendy's hospitality and Andrew's cuisine using mainly local and home grown produce.*

Directions: Leave M6 at Jct36. Follow A590 towards Barrow-in-Furness, at Greenodd turn right onto A5902 towards Millom until reaching A5093. Turn left here, go through 'The Green' and 'The Hill'. After ½ mile Underwood House is on the right.

Web: www.johansens.com/underwood
E-mail: enquiries@underwoodhouse.co.uk
Tel: 01229 771116
Fax: 01229 719900

Price Guide:
single £35–£65
double/twin £70–£100

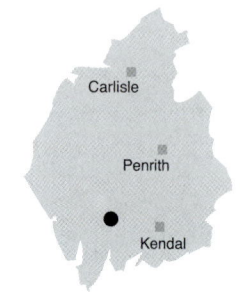

CROSBY LODGE COUNTRY HOUSE HOTEL

HIGH CROSBY, CROSBY-ON-EDEN, CARLISLE, CUMBRIA CA6 4QZ

Crosby Lodge is a romantic country mansion that has been converted into a quiet efficient hotel without spoiling any of its original charm. Grade II listed, it stands amid pastoral countryside close to the Scottish Lowlands and the Lake District. Spacious interiors are elegantly furnished and appointed to provide the maximum of comfort. The personal attention of Michael and Patricia Sedgwick ensures that a high standard of service is maintained. All of the bedrooms are beautifully equipped, most with antique beds and half-testers. Two bedrooms are situated in the converted courtyard stables overlooking the walled garden and in these rooms guests are welcome to bring their pet dogs. In The Lodge restaurant, extensive menus offer a wide and varied choice of dishes. Traditional English recipes are prepared by James Sedgwick, along with continental cuisine complemented by an extensive international wine list. Tables are set with cut glass and gleaming silver cutlery and in keeping with the gracious surroundings. Crosby Lodge, with its spacious grounds, is a superb setting for weddings, parties, business and social events. Closed 24 December to 20 January. Special breaks available.

Our inspector loved: The beautiful antique furniture and fresh flower arrangements.

Directions: From M6 junction 44 take A689 Brampton road for three miles; turn right through Low Crosby. Crosby Lodge is on the right at High Crosby.

Web: www.johansens.com/crosbylodge
E-mail: info@crosbylodge.co.uk
Tel: 01228 573618
Fax: 01228 573428

Price Guide:
single £89–£95
double £115–£160

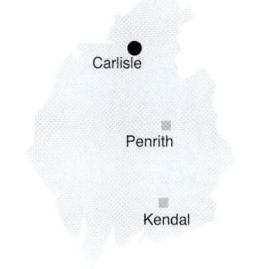

43

The Tarn End House Hotel

TALKIN TARN, BRAMPTON, CUMBRIA CA8 1LS

Directions: From M6 junction 43 take A69 to Brampton. From the centre of Brampton take B6413 towards Castle Carrock and Talkin Tarn. Go over the railway and past Brampton Golf Club and turn left to Talkin village – the hotel is on the left.

Web: www.johansens.com/tarnendhouse
Tel: 016977 2340
Fax: 016977 2089

Price Guide:
single £40–£58
double £55–£85

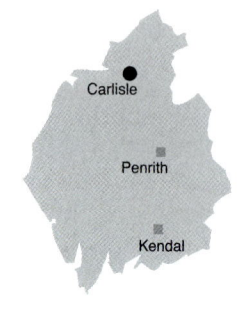

The Tarn End House Hotel has idyllic surroundings at any time of year. This former estate farm house is over 100 years old and is set in its own grounds, with lawns running down to the shores of Talkin Tarn. A very warm welcome and traditional hospitality are guaranteed. The nicely furnished bedrooms have every modern facility and offer exceptional views. This is an ideal spot in which to escape from the world and there is a good choice of leisure activities. Long walks can be taken over the surrounding fells, or the more active can take advantage of rowing, wind-surfing or sailing on the Tarn. There are good golf courses nearby and river fishing and rough shooting can be arranged. The inn enjoys a very good reputation for its cuisine. Guests can savour a meal chosen from two menus – à la carte or table d'hôte. Bar snacks are also available at lunchtime. Hadrian's Wall, Lanercost Priory and the City of Carlisle with its historic castle are all nearby. The River Gelt is an ideal place to visit for bird-watchers and the Scottish borders are within easy reach.

Our inspector loved: *The stunning location as the only house overlooking Talkin Tarn.*

WHITE MOSS HOUSE

RYDAL WATER, GRASMERE, CUMBRIA LA22 9SE

Set in a fragrant garden of roses and lavender, White Moss House was once owned by Wordsworth, who often rested in the porch here between his wanderings. Built in 1730, it overlooks beautiful Rydal Water in the heart of the Lake District. Many famous and interesting walks through fells and lakeland start from the front door. Guests have free use of the local leisure club and swimming pool and free fishing on local rivers and lakes. It has been described by a German gourmet magazine as 'probably the smallest, most splendid hotel in the world'. Proprietors Peter and Susan Dixon have created an intimate family atmosphere with a marvellous degree of comfort and attention to detail. The five bedrooms in the main house and the two in the Brockstone Cottage Suite are individually furnished, and most have lake views. Chef Peter Dixon has won international acclaim for his culinary skills including 2 AA Rosettes and a Red Star. The restaurant is deservedly famous for food prepared with imagination and style – 'the best English food in Britain', said The Times – and offers an extensive wine list of over 300 bins. Special breaks available. Closed December and January. Places to visit nearby include Dove Cottage and Rydal Mount (Wordsworth's houses) are both one mile away

Our inspector loved: *Peter's imaginative and delicious dinner, complimented by a comprehensive and inexpensive wine list.*

Directions: White Moss House is off the A591 between Rydal Water and Grasmere, on the right as you drive north to Grasmere.

Web: www.johansens.com/whitemoss
E-mail: dixon@whitemoss.com
Tel: 015394 35295
Fax: 015394 35516

Price Guide: (including 5-course dinner)
single £80–£95
double £130–£190

THE QUEEN'S HEAD HOTEL

MAIN STREET, HAWKSHEAD, CUMBRIA LA22 0NS

Directions: Leave M6 at Jct36. Take A590 to Newby Bridge then 2nd right and follow road for eight miles into Hawkshead. Drive through village car park, turn right up the main street; the hotel is on the right.

Web: www.johansens.com/queenshead
E-mail: enquiries@queensheadhotel.co.uk
Tel: 015394 36271
Fax: 015394 36722

Price Guide:
single £40–£50
double/twin £63–£92

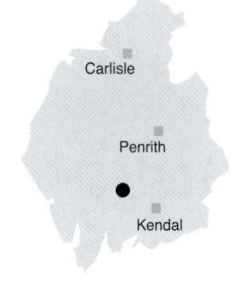

Situated on the edge of Estwaite Water overlooked by Grizedale Forest, Hawkshead is a charming village in the centre of the Lake District with narrow cobbled streets and half-timbered cottages. The 16th-century Queen's Head Hotel is located in the centre of the village and boasts many period features such as low oak beamed ceilings, panelled walls and large open fireplaces. A warm ambience is created in the cosy lounge bar, which serves hand pumped ales and displays the famous Girt Clog, measuring a full twenty inches in length, which was worn by John Waterson. Extremely comfortable non-smoking bedrooms, some with four-poster beds, have en suite bathrooms and lovely décor. Two family rooms are available. Mouth-watering English cuisine including venison, pheasant and mallard as well as delicious seafood specialities is accompanied by an extensive international wine list. 3 award-winning self-catering cottages with all modern conveniences are situated at the rear of the hotel and are ideal for longer stays. Guests can visit the Beatrix Potter Museum, Village Heritage Centre and Parish Church or explore the lush fells and Tarn Hows, the jewel of the Lakes.

Our inspector loved: *The welcoming friendly atmosphere of this pretty Lakeland village centre inn.*

SAWREY HOUSE COUNTRY HOTEL & RESTAURANT

NEAR SAWREY, HAWKSHEAD, AMBLESIDE, CUMBRIA LA22 0LF

Marooned in 3 acres of sculpted gardens designed for lazy indolence, Sawrey House is a non-smoking hotel which is a quintessential English rural hideaway. Built in the 1830's with slate from the local quarry, it is one of the prettiest buildings in the pristine conservation hamlet of Near Sawrey. Next door is 'Hilltop' once the home of Beatrix Potter and visitors to Near Sawrey cannot fail to be captivated by the village's quaint tranquillity which so inspired her writings. Owners, Shirley and Colin Whiteside, are justifiably proud of their chef's dinners which have received 2 AA Rossettes and their comfortable dining room, which has spectacular views over Esthwaite water and the lush forests beyond. Guests can take afternoon tea in the spacious lounge or relax in the bar for pre dinner drinks. The whole area is surrounded by National Trust land and is idyllic for walking. The Hotel is centrally situated, with the Windermere ferry only minutes from the House and Hawkshead, Ambleside and Coniston are only a few minutes drive away. For the more energetic, Sawrey House will organise horse riding, fishing, sailing and even hot-air ballooning. Langdale and the Grizedale Forest are amongst the many natural attractions in the near vicinity. Special breaks available.

Our inspector loved: Stunning views across the garden towards Esthwaite water.

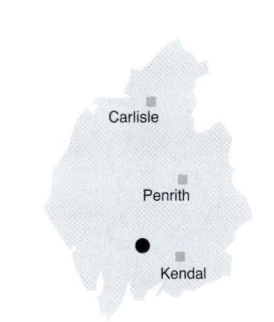

Directions: Take junction 36 off the M6 and follow the A591 in the direction of Windermere and continue to Ambleside. Take sign B5286, then the B5285 to Near Sawrey. Sawrey House is on the right.

Web: www.johansens.com/sawreyhouse
E-mail: enquiries@sawrey-house.com
Tel: 015394 36387
Fax: 015394 36010

Price Guide:
single £50–£65
double £100–£140

THE LEATHES HEAD

BORROWDALE, KESWICK, CUMBRIA CA12 5UY

Directions: From M6 Jct40 take A66 to Keswick, then B5289 to Borrowdale. The hotel is on the left 3½ miles from Keswick. From the south, approach Keswick on A591.

Web: www.johansens.com/leatheshead
E-mail: enq@leatheshead.co.uk
Tel: 017687 77247
Fax: 017687 77363

Price Guide: (including dinner)
single £60–£86
double/twin £100–£160.

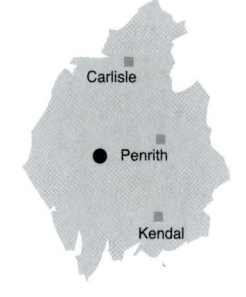

The Leathes Head is an Edwardian country house set in a lovely location within the Borrowdale Valley. Log fires burn in the sitting room in winter and a delightful conservatory overlooks the Fells, affording guests the full benefit of the Hotel's elevated position. Recently refurbished by owners Roy and Janice Smith it combines the charm and elegance of a bygone age with up-to-date standards of comfort. All bedrooms are en suite with a wide range of facilities, and two superior double aspect rooms boast magnificent views stretching across to Catbells and Maiden Moor. Downstairs there are rooms suitable for the less mobile, and in nearby Portinscale a selection of self-catering apartments are available. Food is excellent, and award-winning chef David Jackson has built a well deserved reputation for his daily changing menus and dishes which, where possible, include locally sourced ingredients. This high standard is also reflected in the extensive wine list. Guests can choose from a varied collection of books and board games, enjoy a leisurely walk or cycle ride, or simply relax with a drink in the bar. Special breaks available.

Our inspector loved: *While eating breakfast watching the Woodpeckers and Red Squirrels eating the bird nuts.*

DALE HEAD HALL LAKESIDE HOTEL

THIRLMERE, KESWICK, CUMBRIA CA12 4TN

On the edge of Thirlmere, Cumbria's most central lake, with only the sound of the birds breaking the silence stands Dale Head Hall. It is a truly scenic gem. At the foot of Helvellyn, almost completely surrounded by lush woodlands, this glorious 16th century house reigns alone on the shores of the lake and must surely command one of the most tranquil settings in the Lake District. Hosts Alan and Shirley Lowe and family, having restored the 16th century authenticity of the house, now offer exceptional accommodation and service. The hotel was deservedly runner-up for the Johansens 1995 Most Excellent Country House Hotel. Bar and lounge are both delightful, sharing views over lake and mountains. The oak panelled dining room is the ideal place to enjoy the hotel's superb cuisine (Good Food Guide; 2 AA Red Rosettes). The bedrooms are extremely welcoming, warm and spacious and have all the things that you will expect to find, plus those little extras that make your stay so very special. Dale Head is one of those wonderful secrets which you would like to keep for yourself. English Tourism Council Gold Award. Special offers available.

Our inspector loved: *That this is the only building on Lake Thirlmere. Peace and quiet virtually ensured.*

Directions: On the A591, halfway between Keswick and Grasmere. The hotel is situated along a private driveway overlooking Lake Thirlmere.

Web: www.johansens.com/daleheadhall
E-mail: onthelakeside@daleheadhall.info
Tel: 017687 72478
Fax: 017687 71070

Price Guide: (including 5-course dinner)
single £90–£120
double £130–£195

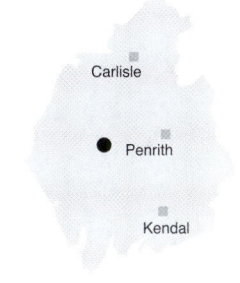

CUMBRIA - KESWICK (NEWLANDS)

SWINSIDE LODGE HOTEL

GRANGE ROAD, NEWLANDS, KESWICK, CUMBRIA CA12 5UE

Directions: M6 junction 40 take the A66 bypassing Keswick – over main roundabout – take second left. Go through Portinscale towards Grange; hotel is two miles further on the right.

Web: www.johansens.com/swinsidelodge
E-mail: info@swinsidelodge-hotel.co.uk
Tel: 017687 72948
Fax: 017687 72948

Price Guide: (including 4 course dinner)
single £88–£98
double £140–£188

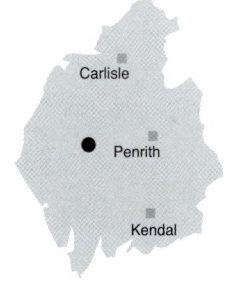

Swinside Lodge, situated at the foot of Catbells, is a Victorian lakeland house, surrounded by hills, valleys and woodland, and close to the shores of Derwentwater. Kevin & Susan Kniveton's house has seven attractive en suite bedrooms, each offering a high degree of comfort and equipped with colour TV, radio, hairdryer, tea making facilities plus a wealth of extras. Begin your day with a hearty Cumbrian breakfast and later return to the comfort of the charming sitting rooms before enjoying your four-course dinner, skilfully cooked by Andrew Carter, in the intimate candle-lit dining room. Menus change daily and a typical meal could include wild mushroom souffle on a dressed salad with red pepper vinaigrette, a delicious soup with home-baked rolls followed by pan-fried breast and stuffed leg of guinea fowl with a red wine and shallot sauce with freshly cooked vegetables. A choice of puddings or a variety of British farmhouse cheeses is followed by coffee and home-made petit fours. Vegetarian and specialist diets can be provided. An AA Red Star hotel with 2 Rosettes for food, RAC Blue Ribbon Award and ETB Gold Award, Swinside Lodge is a non-smoking house and is licensed. Places of interest nearby include Keswick Pencil Museum, Castlerigg Stone Circle, Wordsworth's birthplace, excellent walks from the house.

Our inspector loved: *The delicious dinner served in this peaceful house at the foothills of Catbells.*

Hipping Hall

COWAN BRIDGE, KIRKBY LONSDALE, CUMBRIA LA6 2JJ

Hipping Hall dates back from the 15th Century and is set in three acres of walled gardens on the Cumbria/North Yorkshire borders, so an ideal centre from which to tour both the Lake District and Yorkshire Dales. Having just four double rooms and two cottage suites, this is an especially suitable venue for small groups wanting a place to themselves – families or friends celebrating an anniversary, golfing parties, corporate entertaining etc – and these house parties (available throughout the year) are a feature of Hipping Hall's success. Guests will enjoy the comfort and informality of staying with Jean and Richard Skelton. The well-equipped bedrooms are largely furnished with antiques and all have attractive bathrooms. Guests help themselves to drinks from an honesty bar in the conservatory before feasting on the delights of the à la carte menu. A typical dinner may start with asparagus roasted in sea salt with mustard hollandaise, followed by a noisette trio of beef, veal and lamb with petite vegetable bundles and hot pot potatoes, and rounded off with toblerone fondue with fresh fruit & marshmallows. Places of interest nearby include The Lake District, The Yorkshire Dales, The Settle to carlisle Railway, Brontë country and Sizergh castle.

Our inspector loved: *The magnificent main sitting room.*

Directions: Hipping Hall lies on the A65, two miles east of Kirkby Lonsdale towards Settle & Skipton, eight miles from M6 junction 36.

Web: www.johansens.com/hippinghall
E-mail: hippinghal@aol.com
Tel: 015242 71187
Fax: 015242 72452

Price Guide:
single £75
double £96–£120

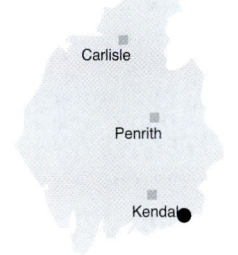

Temple Sowerby House Hotel

TEMPLE SOWERBY, PENRITH, CUMBRIA CA10 1RZ

Directions: On A66, 7 miles from exit 40 off M6, between Penrith and Appleby.

Web: www.johansens.com/templesowerby
E-mail: stay@temple-sowerby.com
Tel: 017683 61578
Fax: 017683 61958

Price Guide:
single £70–£75
double £99–£125

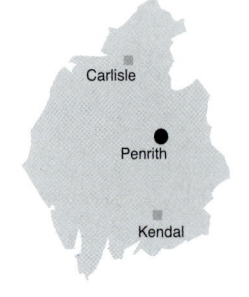

Formerly the principal residence of the village, this delightful country house hotel is overlooked by Cross Fell, the highest peak in the Pennines. Set in a one-acre walled garden, Temple Sowerby House offers its guests a peaceful and relaxing stay. Paul and Julie Evans provide a warm and hospitable welcome upon which the hotel prides itself. Awarded an AA Rosette, the hotel has two dining rooms – the candlelit Restaurant and the Garden Room, a lovely setting for private entertaining. The seasonally inspired à la carte menu might include a starter of terrine of pigeon, duck & chicken layered with pistachio nuts, followed by turbot with a parsley & parmesan crust with saffron rice and lime beurre blanc, rounded off with chocolate & raspberry tart. The individually furnished bedrooms, many just recently upgraded, all have private bathrooms. Four of the rooms, including two on the ground floor, are situated in the Coach House, just a few steps from the main house. During the winter months, apéritifs are taken by the fireside, while in summer, guests can take drinks on the Terrace and enjoy views across the croquet lawn and garden. Private fishing takes place on the River Eden, two miles away. Special themed breaks available including wine, antiques and activities.

Our inspector loved: The secluded walled garden.

FAYRER GARDEN HOUSE HOTEL

LYTH VALLEY ROAD, BOWNESS-ON-WINDERMERE, CUMBRIA LA23 3JP

Awarded The Cumbrian Tourist Board Hotel of the Year 2002, this lovely Victorian House overlooks Lake Windermere in spacious gardens and grounds. Owned and run by Iain and Jackie Garside this very comfortable hotel, where guests can enjoy the spectacular views over the water, offers a real welcome and marvellous value for money. The delightful lounges and bar and the superb air-conditioned restaurant all enjoy Lake views. There is an excellent table d'hôte menu in the award-winning restaurant changing daily using local produce where possible, fish, game and poultry and also a small à la carte choice. The wine list is excellent and very reasonably priced. Many of the attractive bedrooms face the Lake, some having four-poster beds and whirlpool baths en suite. There are also ground floor rooms suitable for the elderly or infirm. The nearby Parklands Leisure Complex has an indoor pool, sauna, steam room, badminton, snooker and squash complimentary to hotel residents. Special breaks available. The Windermere Steamboat Museum, boating from Bowness Pier and golf at Windermere Golf Club and The Beatrix Potter Attraction are all close by.

Our inspector loved: *The air-conditioned dining room with stunning views of Lake Windermere.*

Directions: Junction 36 off the M6, A590 past Kendal. Take B5284 at the next roundabout, turn left at the end and the hotel is 350 yards on the right.

Web: www.johansens.com/fayrergarden
E-mail: lakescene@fayrergarden.com
Tel: 015394 88195
Fax: 015394 45986

Price Guide: (including dinner)
single £69–£99
double £99–£199

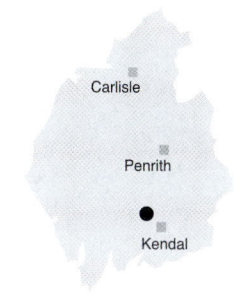

LINTHWAITE HOUSE HOTEL

CROOK ROAD, BOWNESS-ON-WINDERMERE, CUMBRIA LA23 3JA

Directions: From the M6 junction 36 follow Kendal by-pass (A590) for 8 miles. Take B5284 Crook Road for 6 miles. 1 mile beyond Windermere Golf Club, Linthwaite House is signposted on left.

Web: www.johansens.com/linthwaitehouse
E-mail: admin@linthwaite.com
Tel: 015394 88600
Fax: 015394 88601

Price Guide:
single £90–£120
double/twin £90–£220
suite £240–£270

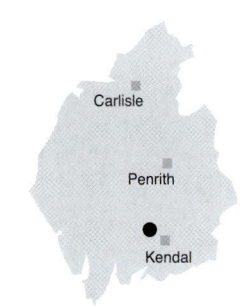

Situated in 14 acres of gardens and woods in the heart of the Lake District, Linthwaite House overlooks Lake Windermere and Belle Isle, with Claife Heights and Coniston Old Man beyond. Here, guests will find themselves amid spectacular scenery, yet only a short drive from the motorway network. The hotel combines stylish originality with the best of traditional English hospitality. Superbly decorated en suite bedrooms, most of which have lake or garden views. The comfortable lounge is the perfect place to unwind and there is a fire on winter evenings. In the restaurant, excellent cuisine features the best of fresh, local produce, accompanied by a fine selection of wines. Within the hotel grounds, there is a 9-hole putting green and a par 3 practice hole. Fly fishermen can fish for brown trout in the hotel tarn. Guests have complimentary use of a private swimming pool and leisure club nearby, while fell walks begin at the hotel's front door. The area around Linthwaite abounds with places of interest: this is Beatrix Potter and Wordsworth country, and there is much to interest the visitor.

Our inspector loved: Walking through the landscaped gardens up to the town.

BROADOAKS COUNTRY HOUSE
BRIDGE LANE, TROUTBECK, WINDERMERE, CUMBRIA LA23 1LA

Tucked away in Troutbeck, one of the prettiest areas of the Lake District, Broadoaks is a wonderful retreat from which to explore this beautiful part of England. Views from the first floor are truly breathtaking, reaching over Lake Windermere and the Troutbeck Valley into the ten acres of private grounds that belong to the hotel. Designed to be relaxing and luxurious, yet mindful of the graceful building's Victorian past, all bedrooms are furnished with four poster or antique brass bedsteads, and are fully equipped with the latest Jacuzzi, spa whirlpool and sunken bath. Rich oak panelling runs from the entrance hall into the cosy music room with Bechstein piano and open fire, where guests can enjoy pre-dinner drinks or after dinner coffee. Rich red damask compliments the Victorian dining-room and is a splendid setting for the award-winning restaurant, that has a wide reputation and a choice of a la carte and house menus. All guests have use of a local private leisure club, and complimentary mountain bike hire or can relax in the grounds trying their hand at pitch and put. Golf, fishing and clay-pigeon shooting can also be arranged.

Our inspector loved: *The beautiful views over Troutbeck Valley.*

Directions: M6 junction 36, A590/591 to Windermere. Go over small roundabout towards Ambleside, then right into Bridge Lane. Broadoaks is ½ mile on right.

Web: www.johansens.com/broadoaks
E-mail: trev@broakoaksf9.co.uk
Tel: 01539 445566
Fax: 01539 488766

Price Guide:
single £65–£160
double £110–£210

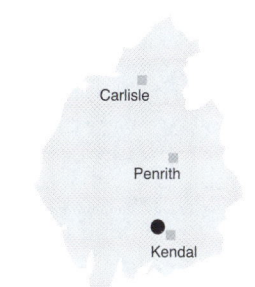

THE PEACOCK INN

ROWSLEY, NR. MATLOCK, DERBYSHIRE DE4 2EB

Directions: M1/exit 28, head for A6. Rowsley is midway between Matlock and Bakewell.

E-mail: jpeacock.gm@jarvis.co.uk
Web: www.johansens.com/peacockrowsley
Tel: 01629 733518
Fax: 01629 732671

Price Guide:
single £125
double/twin £125

Once the Dower House to Haddon Hall, this superb 17th century country house is now a marvellous hotel with gardens leading down to the River Derwent. When first a hotel in 1820 it attracted bathers who plunged into the nearby River Wye! Fishermen are spoilt here. There are 12 rods on the River Wye and two on the Derwent. Tickets are available and the Head Keeper offers advice and tuition. Fish caught will be cooked by the hotel or put in the freezer. Walkers and fishermen get a delicious picnic in a thermally insulated knapsack. The hotel is beautifully furnished with antiques. The bedrooms are extremely comfortable and thoughtfully equipped. Resident and non-resident diners can enjoy an apéritif in the delightful bar or lounge before dining in one of the three rooms, two of which feature furniture by "Mousey" Thompson. Both lunch and dinner are served in traditional style and smoking during food service is discouraged. A special diet can be catered for with prior notice. Special rates may be available on weekdays at certain times of the year. There are excellent facilities for small meetings in a delightfully furnished room. Places of interest nearby: Haddon Hall, Chatsworth, Crich Tram Museum.

Our inspector loved: *This historic building.*

DANNAH FARM COUNTRY HOUSE
BOWMAN'S LANE, SHOTTLE, NR BELPER, DERBYSHIRE DE56 2DR

Set amidst undulating countryside high above the Ecclesbourne Valley on the edge of the Peak District, Dannah Farm is an exceptional 18th-century Georgian farmhouse conversion on the Chatsworth Estate. In addition to obtaining 5 AA Diamonds, the hotel has won National Awards for Excellence and Tourism in the region and offers a unique service within a tranquil and relaxed environment. Bedrooms overlooking rolling pastures and large pretty gardens are beautifully furnished with antiques and old pine; some have four-poster beds, private sitting rooms, Japanese-style tubs and whirlpool baths. The award-winning restaurant has a fine reputation for serving imaginative meals in elegant surroundings. Aromas of freshly baked bread, home-made soups and piquant sauces escaping from the kitchen whet the appetite and for breakfast there are free-range eggs and organic sausages. Dinner is by prior arrangement. The countryside is criss-crossed with footpaths in all directions, whilst places of interest nearby include Chatsworth, Haddon Hall, Dovedale and water sports at Carsington.

Our inspector loved: *The Japanese bath tub, such fun.*

Directions: From Derby take A6 Matlock road. At Duffield turn left onto B5023 towards Wirksworth. At traffic lights at Cowers Lane turn right onto A517 towards Belper, then first left to Shottle. Bowman's Lane is 100 yds past crossroads in the village.

Web: www.johansens.com/dannah
E-mail: reservations@dannah.demon.co.uk
Tel: 01773 550273/550630
Fax: 01773 550590

Price Guide:
single £54
double/twin £79.50
suite £99–£120

BIGGIN HALL

BIGGIN-BY-HARTINGTON, BUXTON, DERBYSHIRE SK17 0DH

In the heart of the Derbyshire countryside Biggin Hall is a charming 17th century building, amidst 8 acres of its own grounds. The house itself is a haven of English country house tranquillity, and many guests have commented on the therapeutic effects of the Biggin air. The Hotel is ideally placed for the airports at Manchester, East Midlands and Sheffield which makes it a perfect destination for both weekend retreats and business meetings; the Peak district making a welcome break from city hustle and bustle. The house itself has recently undergone a comprehensive restoration project, with all the stone mullioned leaded windows being returned to their original grandeur and the conversion of the Courtyard, Bothy and Lodge to guest accommodation. All guests rooms have been carefully furnished with period pieces and the master suite has spectacular oak beams and a four poster bed. The Hotel prides itself on its daily menu of locally produced meat and vegetables, that carefully considers all dietary requests and places its emphasis on free-range wholefoods and natural flavours. This is prime country for walkers, although Derbyshire has a plethora of places to visit; Chatsworth House and Haddon Hall being the most well-known, whilst the market towns of Buxton, Bakewell and Ashbourne are delightful.

Directions: At the end of Biggin village, off A515, 9m from Ashbourne and 10m from Buxton.

Web: www.johansens.com/bigginhall
E-mail: enquiries@bigginhall.co.uk
Tel: 01298 84451
Fax: 01298 84681

Price Guide:
single £50–£80
double £60–£104

Our inspector loved: James Moffett's style, life floats by.

Boar's Head Hotel
LICHFIELD ROAD, SUDBURY, DERBYSHIRE DE6 5GX

This 17th-century house was lost from the famous Vernon estate through a game of cards! It is now a well known local hostelry, having been run by the Crooks family for many years. Guests will be welcomed by the architectural beauty of this very old building. There is a bar, with natural brick walls, horse brasses and hunting horns. The residents' lounge looks onto a pretty patio where drinks are served in summer months. Much thought has been given to furnishing the delightful bedrooms which have every possible facility, including teletext and Sky television. Visitors enjoy a choice of real ales and excellent home-cooked dishes with the chef's specials listed on a blackboard. There are two restaurants, the elegant Royal Boar with an imaginative à la carte menu and the less formal Hunter's Table Carvery and Bistro offering fresh fish, pasta dishes and splendid roasts, both at lunchtime and in the evening. The Royal Boar is closed on Sunday evenings, but is famous for its Sunday lunch. A fascinating wine list covers vineyards worldwide, with 70 entries including 6 house wines and a selection of 10 half-bottles. Alton Towers and Uttoxeter Racecourse are attractions nearby. Other guests will enjoy Chatsworth House, Sudbury Hall, Tutbury Castle and the Bass Museum of brewing. Special weekend breaks available.

Our inspector loved: *The traditional menus in the restaurant including some timeless favourites from the last few decades.*

Directions: The hotel is on A515, just south of A50 from Stoke on Trent to Derby.

Web: www.johansens.com/boarsheadburton
Tel: 01283 820344
Fax: 01283 820075

Price Guide:
single from £42.50
double from £52.50

DERBYSHIRE - CHESTERFIELD

NEW

BUCKINGHAM'S HOTEL & RESTAURANT WITH ONE TABLE

85 NEWBOLD ROAD, CHESTERFIELD, DERBYSHIRE S41 7PU

Directions: Exit M1 at junction 29 and take A617 to Chesterfield town centre. Then take road towards Sheffield. At mini roundabout turn left into Newbold Road.

Web: www.johansens.com/buckinghams
E-mail: info@buckinghams-table.com
Tel: 01246 201041
Fax: 01246 550059

Price Guide:
single £50-£70
double/twin £65-£80

With its deep green exterior highlighted by sparkling white windows and entrance door and an access walkway colourfully flanked by flowers and ornamental trees, Buckingham's is one of the most attractive city hotels you are likely to visit. It oozes ambience and charm, complemented by a degree and quality of service to be expected by an establishment owned and run by a Master Chef. Nick Buckingham and his wife, Tina, who took up the Hotel challenge in the summer of 2000 and quickly earned a reputation for warm and friendly hospitality with attention to detail and superlative food. Situated in a residential area of Chesterfield, just a 5 minute walk from the town centre, Buckingham's was originally a pair of Victorian semi-detached houses. Sympathetic conversion has resulted in a relaxing venue with all modern facilities. Each spacious, en suite bedroom is delightfully decorated and furnished and has a high standard of home comforts, including toy rubber ducks in the bathroom. Guests can enjoy a chat over drinks in a well-stocked bar before enjoying excellent cuisine in an intimate dining room. Alternatively guests can arrange to have dinner in the Hotel's Restaurant with one table. A pick-up facility is available from the railway station, by request.

Our inspector loved: The dining concept and the impressive selection of over 50 beers.

LITTLEOVER LODGE HOTEL
222 RYKNELD ROAD, LITTLEOVER, DERBY, DERBYSHIRE DE23 7AN

A warm and friendly welcome by the Crooks family awaits guests at this busy country hotel, or 'restaurant with rooms'. Formerly a farmhouse, Littleover Lodge has been extended to provide modern and well-presented accommodation. In addition to the 13 recently refurbished, spacious bedrooms, which are equipped with every modern facility, there are three superb suites, all with upstairs balcony bedrooms and cosy day areas, offering the ultimate in relaxation and comfort. The Lodge Carvery is open lunchtimes and evenings and serves an extensive daily changing menu, whilst your choice from the exquisite à la carte menu in the restaurant might include King scallops wrapped in pancetta, followed by pan-fried wild boar steak placed onto seasonal vegetables served with Armagnac, mushrooms and cream sauce, and rounded off by iced mango parfait with fruit coulis. Situated amid beautiful rural countryside, Littleover Lodge stands only minutes from Derby city centre with its Cathedral and Assembly Rooms, famed for snooker events. It is the perfect base from which to explore the numerous attractions nearby including Calke Abbey, Derbyshire Cricket Ground, Chatsworth House and Alton Towers. Sporting enthusiasts can visit Uttoxeter Race Course, which is also within easy reach. Special weekend breaks available.

Our inspector loved: The split-level suites with spacious living areas.

Directions: Leave M1 at junction 24, take A50 towards Stoke, then take A38 towards Derby, first slip road signed for Littleover.

Web: www.johansens.com/littleover
Tel: 01332 510161
Fax: 01332 514010

Price Guide:
single £45
double/twin £65
suites £75

THE CHEQUERS INN

FROGGATT EDGE, HOPE VALLEY, DERBYSHIRE S32 3ZJ

Directions: The Inn is situated on the A625, which links Bakewell and Sheffield, 6 miles from Bakewell on Froggatt Edge.

Web: www.johansens.com/chequerscalver
E-mail: info@chequers-froggatt.com
Tel: 01433 630231
Fax: 01433 631072

Price Guide:
single £45–£55
double/twin £45–£75

As new owners, since February 2002, Jonathan and Joanne Tindall have worked hard to instil their pleasant personalities into this popular Country Inn. Its tradition for hospitality dates back to the 16th century when it was built on the old pack horse road. A Grade II listed building, the Inn was originally 4 houses and has been extensively refurbished yet retains many of its charming period features including a horse mounting block and the old stables. Each of the 5 bedrooms has its own personality and is cosy with comfortable, characteristic furnishings alongside private bathroom and individually controlled heating. The Chequers prides itself on its cuisine and chef, Michael Smith, creates a wide variety of European and British dishes comprising the freshest ingredients, including local game in season. On cooler evenings guests can relax in the warmth of crackling open fires in the bar or enjoy breathtaking views of the setting sun from the elevated secret woodland garden. The surrounding Peak District area is ideal walking country and the Inn is perfectly situated for exploring along the Derwent River or Peak trails. Nearby is the historic castle and caverns of Castleton, Haddon Hall, Chatsworth House and the lively market town of Bakewell, famous for its puddings.

Our inspector loved: *The well-balanced menu following a delightful walk in the surrounding area.*

The Wind In The Willows

DERBYSHIRE LEVEL, GLOSSOP, DERBYSHIRE SK13 7PT

Situated 12 miles from the centre of Manchester, with good road and rail links, The Wind in the Willows is a delightful, family-owned early Victorian Country House, which has retained its original charm including oak-panelled rooms, traditional furnishings and open log fires. The hotel is situated within five acres of land with unspoilt views of the Peak District National Park, and surrounded by the heather-clad hills of the Pennines. The setting provides an escape from the pressures of modern day life into the atmosphere and elegant surroundings of a bygone era. Past winner of the AA Courtesy and Care and the AA Romantic Hotel Awards, the hotel has gained an excellent reputation for first-class home cooking served in the charming period dining room. The traditionally styled en suite bedrooms are decorated with predominantly antique furniture and numerous personal touches. A small conference suite accommodates prestigious corporate meetings in peaceful, uninterrupted surroundings. Adjoining the grounds is a splendid 9-hole golf course, where guests can play within the beautiful scenery of the local countryside. Many activities can be arranged locally, including sailing, horse riding, hang gliding, fly fishing and pot holing. Places of interest nearby include Chatsworth, Haddon Hall, Castleton, Bakewell and Holmfirth.

Our inspector loved: *The tranquillity of this hotel which is only 12 miles from Manchester.*

Directions: One mile east of Glossop on A57, 400 yards down the road opposite the Royal Oak.

Web: www.johansens.com/windinthewillows
E-mail: info@windinthewillows.co.uk
Tel: 01457 868001
Fax: 01457 853354

Price Guide:
single £85–£100
double £105–£140

THE MAYNARD ARMS

MAIN ROAD, GRINDLEFORD, DERBYSHIRE S32 2HE

Directions: Leaving Sheffield take the A625. Continue on this road until it becomes the A6187. Turn left onto the B6521, The Maynard Arms is on the left just as you enter Grindleford.

Web: www.johansens.com/maynardarms
E-mail: info@maynardarms.co.uk
Tel: 01433 630321
Fax: 01433 630445

Price Guide: (incl. continental breakfast)
single £69
double £79

The owners of this Victorian inn have transformed its ambience and image into a very stylish small hostelry at this superb location overlooking the beautiful Derbyshire Peak National Park. The en suite bedrooms, which include two suites, are charming, comfortable and well equipped. Guests booking Friday and Saturday nights may stay in their room free on the Sunday night (except before Bank Holidays). The excellent restaurant offers a primarily traditional English fare featuring local game when in season, together with a carefully selected wine list. An extensive range of bar food is served at lunchtime and in the evenings in the Longshaw Bar – the busy hub of the inn. The second, quieter, bar is ideal for a drink before dinner and has a big log fire in winter months. There is a peaceful lounge with a view of the pretty gardens and the Dales. Chatsworth, Haddon Hall and Castleton are spectacular reminders of the heritage of the region. The market town of Bakewell is fascinating. Walkers have an endless choice of directions to take. Fishing is on the Derwent. Golf, pony-trekking and even gliding can be arranged locally. Regional theatres abound.

Our inspector loved: It's traditional values.

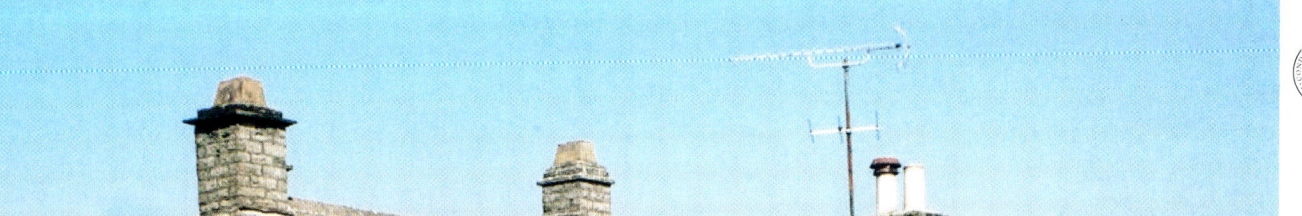

THE PLOUGH INN

LEADMILL BRIDGE, HATHERSAGE, DERBYSHIRE S30 1BA

Situated by the meandering River Derwent, in 9 acres of grounds, lies the beautifully restored 16th-century Plough Inn. The proprietors Bob and Cynthia Emery always ensure a warm and friendly welcome whether in winter by the roaring log fires or during summer in the garden, surrounded by an abundance of flower baskets and beds. 3 double bedrooms in the main building are accessed by an external staircase, and the 2 newly converted luxury suites offer en suite bathrooms, sitting area, video player and hi-fi. They have been restored using local materials, leaving exposed beams and stonework. Meals are served daily, either in the cosy bar or in the intimate restaurant. The extensive menu offers something to please every taste. Bob, a former butcher, and head chef John, who trained in some of London's most prestigious restaurants, always strive to use the finest quality produce to create dishes ranging from good old home-baked pies to fine International cuisine complemented by an extensive wine list and friendly informal service. Castleton, with its world-famous Blue John mines, is only 10 minutes along the picturesque Hope Valley. Bakewell, Haddon Hall and 18th-century Chatsworth House are only a little further afield. The Plough Inn is in proximity of Sheffield, Manchester and East Midland airports.

Directions: From M1 exit 29 take A617 west, then via A619 and A623 shortly after north onto B6001 towards Hathersage.

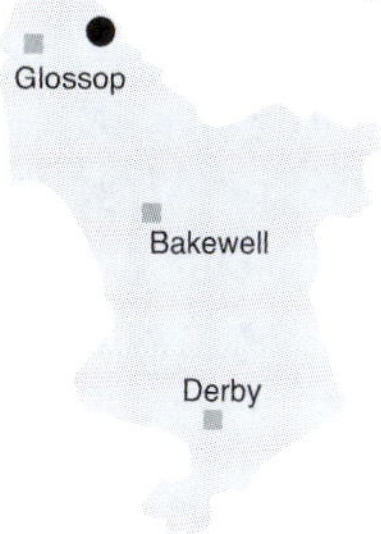

Web: www.johansens.com/ploughinnhathersage
E-mail: theploughinn@leadmillbridge.fsnet.co.uk
Tel: 01433 650319
Fax: 01433 651049

Price Guide:
single from £49.50
double from £69.50
suite from £99.50

Our inspector loved: *The cheerfulness & welcome of this delightful inn*

Santo's Higham Farm

MAIN ROAD, HIGHAM, DERBYSHIRE DE55 6EH

Directions: Exit M1 at junction 28 and take A38 to Alfreton. Then join A61 towards Chesterfield. Higham is reached after approximately 4 miles.

Web: www.johansens.com/santoshighamfarm
E-mail: reception@santoshighamfarm.demon.co.uk
Tel: 01773 833812/3/4
Fax: 01773 520525

Price Guide:
single £65–£90
double £75–£100
suite: £110

This delightful and rambling former 15th century farmhouse stands in the heart of the beautiful Derbyshire countryside overlooking the Amber Valley. The hotel has been tastefully refurbished and extended over the past four years to an excellent standard and offers visitors every modern amenity to make a stay comfortable and memorable. Old character and atmosphere are immediately evident and many of its original and unique features are still on view. The bedrooms are superbly furnished and equipped, and each has a stylish and luxurious en suite bathroom. Two offer Jacuzzi air baths, two have four-poster beds and three boast waterbeds. A new Italian wing comprises eight bedrooms and there is an internationally themed wing of seven bedrooms. The hotel has a reputation for fine dining with excellent à la carte and table d'hôte cuisine being attentively served in Guiseppe's restaurant, whilst less formal Italian and Continental meals are offered in the Sports Bar. Guests can go for interesting walks in the surrounding area and there is lake fishing, golf, riding and a leisure centre with indoor and outdoor swimming pools nearby. Conference facilities for up to 34 delegates.

Our inspector loved: The bathroom.

YEOLDON HOUSE HOTEL

DURRANT LANE, NORTHAM, NR BIDEFORD EX39 2RL

On arriving at Yeoldon House Hotel, guests are assured of two things: a generous and warm welcome, and a totally relaxing atmosphere. Set beside the river Torridge and with lawns sloping down towards the water's edge, the sense of serenity is instant, and enhanced by the heartfelt greetings of the proprietors. The ambience is one of home-from-home comfort – relaxed and casual, but with a little added luxury. Each bedroom has its own style whether it be a cosy single, a grand four-poster or a split level suite; some have balconies from which to admire the spectacular Devon scenery. Soyer's restaurant is a source of great pride for Yeoldon House – named after the Victorian chef Alexis Soyer, it has an air of casual elegance and offers an interesting table d'hôte menu of locally-sourced meat, fish and vegetables, catering for all palates. Breakfast too is served here, and it is a perfect setting from which to watch the sun rise over the river. This part of Devon boasts magnificent and unspoilt scenery, and the coastal path is a must for walkers. Guests can visit the picturesque village of Clovelly, Exmoor, Rosemoor Gardens, Lorna Doone country, Lundy Island and the North Devon beaches. 3 nights mini breaks available.

Our inspector loved: The warm and sincere welcome and offer of most relaxing break.

Directions: Leave M5 at Jct27 and join A361 towards Barnstaple, then A39 towards Bideford. At Torridge Bridge roundabout follow signs for Northam.

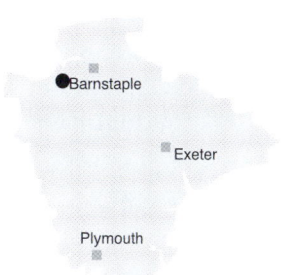

Web: www.johansens.com/Yeoldon
E-mail: yeoldonhousehotel@aol.com
Tel: 01237 474400
Fax: 01237 476618

Price Guide:
single £60–£65
double/twin £90–£105.

THE EDGEMOOR

HAYTOR ROAD, BOVEY TRACEY, SOUTH DEVON TQ13 9LE

Built in 1870, The Edgemoor Country House Hotel, owned and managed by Rod and Pat Day, stands in a peaceful location in two acres of grounds literally on the eastern boundary of the Dartmoor National Park. There are 12 charming bedrooms, two of which are on the ground floor. All have en suite bathrooms and some have four-poster beds. The public rooms look over the hotel grounds and provide comfortable and sophisticated surroundings in which guests enjoy their stay. In the restaurant, chef Edward Elliott prepares modern English cuisine incorporating locally produced West Country specialities. The wine list offers an interesting and varied selection. The Edgemoor, which has received the Westcountry Cooking "Best Hotel in Devon 2001" award, provides an excellent touring base for the area. Castle Drogo, Becky Falls and Haytor are worth a visit. With the hotel's close proximity to Dartmoor, walkers and nature lovers are well catered for. Shooting, fishing and riding can be arranged locally.

Our inspector loved: *The warm friendly welcome and the delightful location on the Dartmoor boundary.*

Directions: On leaving the M5, join the A38 in the direction of Plymouth. At Drumbridges roundabout, take A382 towards Bovey Tracey. At the second roundabout turn left and after approximately ½ mile, fork left at the sign for Haytor.

Web: www.johansens.com/edgemoor
E-mail: edgemoor@btinternet.com
Tel: 01626 832466
Fax: 01626 834760

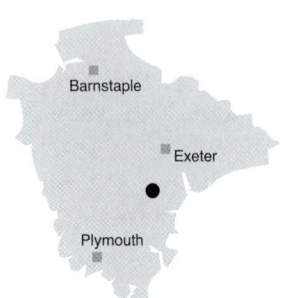

Price Guide:
single £55–£70
double/twin £85–£120

THE NEW INN

COLEFORD, CREDITON, DEVON EX17 5BZ

Those wishing to escape the hectic pace of everyday life will be delighted with this lovely 13th century thatched inn, located in a truly secluded valley beside a bubbling brook featuring newly designed gardens which are a delight. The New Inn, a Grade II listed building of cob, has been tastefully renovated and refurbished over the years. Today it retains the character and ambience of a past era. A warm welcome is extended to guests from owners Irene and Paul Butt and their talkative parrot, Captain! The resident ghost, Sebastian, is also reputed to be friendly... The AA 4 Diamond rated accommodation is excellent, with spacious and individually-appointed bedrooms offering every comfort. In the winter months, the lounge is the place to sit and enjoy the cosy warmth of a log fire. Three full-time chefs create memorable dishes, using the best and freshest local ingredients. The menu includes delicious starters, such as sherried kidney tart, cream of Devon crab soup or grilled goats cheese with walnuts and walnut oil salad, and a good selection of speciality dishes, grills, snacks and sweets. An extensive choice of drinks, including traditional ales, is served in the bars. The wine list has been awarded many accolades for its selection. The cathedral city of Exeter, Dartmoor and Exmoor are all close by.

Our inspector loved: *The truly secluded location in a valley beside Babbling Brook - Really delightful.*

Directions: Take the A377 Exeter-Barnstable Road. Coleford is signed two miles from Crediton.

Web: www.johansens.com/newinncoleford
E-mail: new-inn@reallyreal-group.com
Tel: 01363 84242
Fax: 01363 85044

Price Guide:
single £55–£65
double £70–£80

DEVON - COMBE MARTIN

Coulsworthy House

COMBE MARTIN, DEVON EX34 0PD

The main part of this beautiful house was built in 1760 but some of the original farmhouse dates back to 1650. It stands in 6 ½ acres of gardens and woodlands, has its own ancient natural spring and adjoins the western boundary of the Exmoor National Park. Inside, there is an enchanting lounge with flagstoned floor, wooden beams, natural stone walls and an enormous inglenook complete with bread ovens. Bedrooms are spacious, peaceful and tasteful, offering every comfort. The atmosphere at Coulsworthy House is relaxed and the family of hosts extend a truly warm welcome. Local fresh produce is available in abundance and home-cooked meals can be provided by arrangement but the owners will gladly recommend local places to eat. As well as enjoying the stunning Exmoor countryside and sandy beaches at Woolacombe, Croyde and Saunton guests can take advantage of many fine gardens and stately homes throughout the surrounding area. Nearby there is fishing, a shooting school and horse riding together with excellent golf courses at Ilfracombe and Saunton.

Directions: Take the A399 from Blackmoor Gate towards Combe Martin and turn at a signpost for Trentishoe and Hunters Inn.

E-mail: .coulsworthy@tiscali.co.uk
Web: www.johansens.com/coulsworthy
Tel: 01271 882813

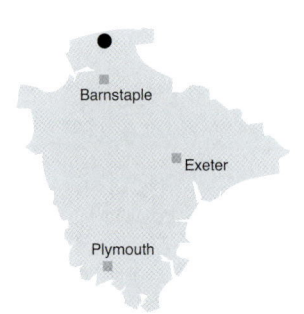

Price Guide:
single £80
double/twin from £100

Our inspector loved: The most beautiful location and the wonderfully warm sincere welcome and friendliness.

The Lord Haldon Country Hotel

DUNCHIDEOCK, NR EXETER, DEVON EX6 7YF

The impressive Lord Haldon Country Hotel, set amidst rolling hills and close to the cathedral city of Exeter, is a Relais du Silence hotel offering stunning views of the garden and the Devon countryside. It is a marvellous base from which to explore the many historic places of interest in the area. All bedrooms are individually and tastefully decorated in a country house style with colour co-ordinated fabrics; most enjoy picturesque views and there are family rooms available or four-poster suites. Fresh flowers adorn the rooms, which provide all the facilities expected in a quality hotel. An atmosphere of warmth and friendliness exudes from every corner, and the Preece family will ensure that you receive a high standard of service. Guests can enjoy a superb candle-lit dinner in the 2 AA Rosetted Courtyard Restaurant, which overlooks the courtyard and offers imaginative dishes using only the freshest ingredients. Special diets can be catered for and picnics can be provided on request. Just over a mile away is Haldon Forest, which has an unique Birds of Prey viewing point, and the rugged moorland of Dartmoor and the South Devon Coast are only a short drive away. Guests can also enjoy country pursuits such as clay pigeon shooting and fishing.

Our inspector loved: *The peaceful location yet so very accessible from M5 and Exeter airport.*

Directions: Exit Junction 31 off the M5 onto A30 and leave this dual carriageway at the first available exit signed Marsh Barton and Exeter.

Web: www.johansens.com/lordhaldon
E-mail: enquiries@lordhaldon.co.uk
Tel: 01392 832483
Fax: 01392 833765

Price Guide:
single £55–£65
double/twin £75–£120

DEVON - EXETER (HONITON)

COMBE HOUSE HOTEL & RESTAURANT
GITTISHAM, HONITON, NR EXETER, DEVON EX14 3AD

Directions: From M5 take exit 28 to Honiton and Sidmouth, or exit 29 to Honiton. Follow signs to Fenny Bridges and Gittisham. A303/A30 exit Honiton to Sidmouth.

Web: www.johansens.com/combehousegittisham
E-mail: stay@thishotel.com
Tel: 01404 540400
Fax: 01404 46004

Price Guide:
single £99–£125
double/twin £138–£190
suites £265

Combe House is a wildly romantic Grade 1 Elizabethan manor hidden in 3,500 acres of Devon's finest estates where magnificent Arabian horses and pheasants roam freely. Total peace and tranquillity together with generous hospitality can be enjoyed here in this warm and welcoming atmosphere created by the comfy sofas, flamboyant flowers and roaring log-fires. 15 intimate bedrooms and suites, many with panoramic views, are decorated with style and individuality. The candlit restaurant serves innovative, contemporary British cuisine prepared by Master Chef of Great Britain, Philip Leach, perfectly complemented by a well-chosen wine list, including a specialist Chablis collection. The recently restored Georgian Kitchen is the ideal setting for a highly individual private lunch or dinner, dining by lamps and candlelight. Down Combe's mile-long drive is Gittisham, once described by H.R.H. Prince Charles as, 'the ideal English Village,' with its thatched cottages, Norman church and village green. The World Heritage Jurassic coast, from Lyme Regis to Sidmouth, Honiton antique shops, numerous historic houses and gardens, the cathedral of Exeter and the wide open spaces of Dartmoor can all be explored.

Our inspector loved: *From when she drove through the gates along the driveway catching the first glimpse of the house - that was it.*

HOME FARM HOTEL
WILMINGTON, NR HONITON, DEVON EX14 9JR

Home Farm is an attractive thatched farmhouse, set in four acres of beautiful grounds. A small hotel since 1950, which the owners have tastefully restored to create a charming and relaxing ambience. The staff are friendly and children are made welcome. The public rooms have big bowls of flowers in summer and enchanting log fires in the winter. Value for money is an important criterion. The Residents' Lounge is comfortable and there is a cosy, well-stocked bar serving light meals. The restaurant, oak-beamed and with an inglenook fireplace, offers a marvellous à la carte choice as well as a good 'homemade' table d'hôte menu using local produce. The wine list is extensive. Bedrooms are in the main building or across a cobbled courtyard. All have private bathroom, telephone, colour television, hairdryer, radio alarm and tea/coffee making facilities. Wilmington is in the heart of 25 National Trust properties, 6 miles from the coast and there are six golf courses within 15 miles. Riding, water sports and fishing can be arranged. Honiton is known for its lace, as is Axminster for its carpets. A two bedroom lodge with stunning views is also available.

Our inspector loved: The charming character.

Directions: Take the A303 to Honiton, join the A35 signposted to Axminster. Wilmington is three miles further on and Home Farm is set back off the main road on the right.

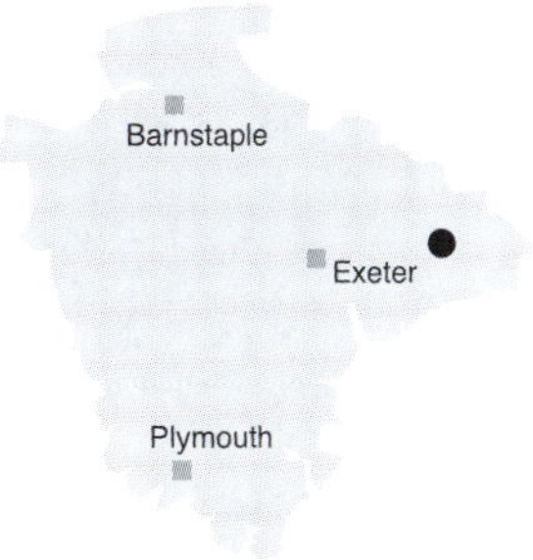

Web: www.johansens.com/homefarm
E-mail: homefarmhotel@breathemail.net
Tel: 01404 831278
Fax: 01404 831411

Price Guide:
single £39.50–£55
double £65–£100

ILSINGTON COUNTRY HOUSE HOTEL

ILSINGTON VILLAGE, NEAR NEWTON ABBOT, DEVON TQ13 9RR

Directions: From M5 join A38 at Exeter following Plymouth signs. After approximately 12 miles exit for Moretonhampstead and Newton Abbot. At roundabout follow signs for Ilsington.

Web: www.johansens.com/ilsington
E-mail: hotel@ilsington.co.uk
Tel: 01364 661452
Fax: 01364 661307

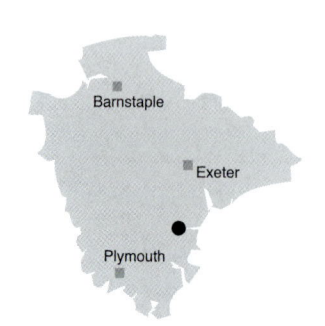

Price Guide:
single from £71
double/twin from £110

The Ilsington Country House Hotel stands in ten acres of beautiful private grounds within the Dartmoor National Park. Run by friendly proprietors, Tim and Maura Hassell, the delightful furnishings and ambience offer a most comfortable environment in which to relax. Stylish bedrooms all boast outstanding views across the rolling pastoral countryside and every comfort and convenience to make guests feel at home. The distinctive candle-lit dining room is perfect for savouring the superb cuisine, awarded an AA Rosette, created by talented chefs from fresh local produce. The library is ideal for an intimate dining party or celebration whilst the conservatory or lounge is the place for morning coffee or a Devon cream tea. There is a fully equipped purpose built gymnasium, heated indoor pool, sauna, steam room and spa. Some of England's most idyllic and unspoilt scenery surrounds Ilsington, with the picturesque villages of Lustleigh and Widecombe-in-the-Moor close by. Footpaths lead from the hotel on to Dartmoor. Riding, fishing and many other country pursuits can be arranged. Special breaks available.

Our inspector loved: *The beautiful location within the Dartmoor National Park.*

THE RISING SUN

HARBOURSIDE, LYNMOUTH, DEVON EX35 6EG

Recommended in every way, this award-winning 14th century thatched smugglers' inn is perfectly positioned on the picturesque harbour overlooking the East Lyn River. The building is steeped in history: Lorna Doone was partly written here and the inn's adjacent cottage – now luxuriously equipped for guests' use and pictured below – was reputedly the honeymoon retreat for the poet Shelley. The best of the inn's medieval character has been preserved: oak panelling, open fires and crooked ceilings, all enhanced by tasteful furnishings and modern comforts. The bedrooms lack nothing and, like the terraced gardens, have splendid views. Parking in Lynmouth can be difficult at the height of the season. The food served in the oak-panelled restaurant is of excellent quality. Classic modern cuisine is provided and also featured are local specialities such as fresh lobster. Good value bar meals are also available. Sea angling is available from the harbour and Exmoor National Park, The North Devon coastline and Doone Valley are all nearby.

Our inspector loved: *The idyllic location and total charm.*

Directions: Leave M5 at Jct23 (signed Minehead), follow A39 to Lynmouth. Or take A361, exit 27 (Tiverton) to South Molton, then B3226 towards Ilfracombe and then A39 at Blackmoor Gate to Lynmouth.

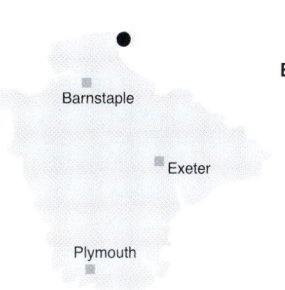

Web: www.johansens.com/risingsun
E-mail: risingsunlynmouth@easynet.co.uk
Tel: 01598 753223
Fax: 01598 753480

Price Guide:
single £66
double £110–£156

DEVON - LYNTON

Hewitt's - Villa Spaldi

NORTH WALK, LYNTON, DEVON EX35 6HJ

Directions: Leave the M5 at junction 23, signposted Minehead, follow the A39 to Lynton.

Web: www.johansens.com/hewitts
E-mail: hewitts.hotel@talk21.com
Tel: 01598 752293
Fax: 01598 752489

Price Guide:
single £85
double/twin from £140

This elegant, private 19th century country house offers total peace and seclusion within 27 acres of gardens and woodlands. Once the home of the eminent Victorian, Sir Thomas Hewitt, it stands regally on high cliffs overlooking Lynmouth Bay and beyond, Wales. Approached by a meandering, residential driveway, the house sits just minutes from the centre of Lynton and is perfectly placed for walks along the Exmoor coastal path. The character of the house has been superbly retained with wonderful antiques, a sweeping oak staircase and beautiful stained glass windows by Burnes-Jones. Two self catering apartments are available all year round, and the warm, friendly 'house party' ambience of Hewitt's means it lends itself perfectly to intimate gatherings. Dinner is available by prior arrangement and mouthwatering international dishes are created under the guidance of Italian chef and owner, Tito Spaldi. Local suppliers of venison, game, meats and cheeses are used to full advantage and the many fine wines on the accompanying list are truly first class. Guests can enjoy breakfast or a romantic dinner in the oak panelled dining room, or in the summer, on the cliff terrace overlooking the bay.

Our inspector loved: *The magnificent location and superb food. The Venison is mouthwatering.*

KITLEY HOUSE HOTEL & RESTAURANT

THE KITLEY ESTATE, YEALMPTON, PLYMOUTH, DEVON PL8 2NW

This imposing Grade I listed country house hotel, built of silver grey Devonshire "marble", is situated in 300 acres of richly timbered parkland at the head of one of Yealm estuary's wooded creeks, only ten minutes from the city of Plymouth. It is one of the earliest Tudor revival houses in England and has been splendidly restored to its former glory. Approached by a mile long drive through a magnificent private estate, Kitley is an oasis of quiet luxury, providing the highest standards in comfort, cuisine and personal service. A sweeping staircase leads to 18 spacious bedrooms and suites. Each has panoramic views over the estate and is richly appointed with furnishings designed to reflect the traditional elegance of the house whilst incorporating all modern facilities. The lounge area, with its huge open fireplace, and bar are stylish and relaxing. The restaurant is sumptuously decorated in burgundy and gold and provides the perfect atmosphere in which to enjoy the finest of cuisine – whatever the occasion. Guests can enjoy fishing in the private lake and golf, shooting and riding are nearby. Murder mystery dinners and mid week breaks available.

Our inspector loved: The standards, comfort and peace yet only 10 minutes from the city of Plymouth.

Directions: A38 towards Plymouth (A3121). Then turn right onto the A379. The hotel entrance is on the left after Yealmpton village.

Web: www.johansens.com/kitleyhouse
E-mail: sales@kitleyhousehotel.com
Tel: 01752 881555
Fax: 01752 881667

Price Guide:
single £95–£115
double/twin £110–£130
suite from £120

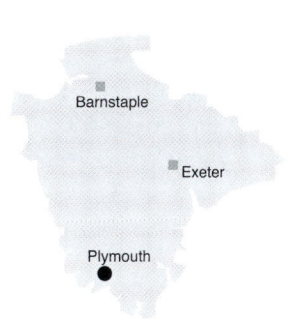

PRESTON HOUSE & LITTLE'S RESTAURANT

SAUNTON, BRAUNTON, NORTH DEVON EX33 1LG

Directions: From the M5, exit at junction 27 and take the A361 towards Barnstaple. Continue on to Braunton and then turn left at the traffic lights towards Croyde. The Hotel is on the left after approximately 2 miles.

Web: www.johansens.com/prestonhouse
E-mail: prestonhouse-saunton@zoom.co.uk
Tel: 01271 890472
Fax: 01271 890555

Price Guide:
single £65–£105
double £105–£165

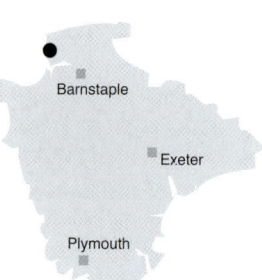

Magnificently placed on a clifftop, with breathtaking views extending as far as the eye can see over Saunton Bay and beyond, Preston House is a small private hotel offering personal service and an extremely inviting warm atmosphere. Quietly relaxing and informal, this completely smoke-free Hotel has been beautifully restored to a high standard with all the finishing touches, including tasteful eye-catching fabrics, stunning artworks and aesthetically pleasing design. Terraced lawns sweep towards the wide sandy beach and sea, a magnet for surfers worldwide. Cosy rooms are comfortable and individually appointed with calm colours and motifs, some with large balconies overlooking the sea and Lundy Island. Breakfast may be enjoyed in the conservatory and exceptional award winning British cuisine is lovingly prepared in Little's, a truly elegant restaurant with North Devon's most dramatic scenery as an awe-inspiring backdrop. There is an extensive bar and cellar to suit all tastes. A variety of activities are available whatever the weather: on the beach there is surfing, windsurfing, sand yachting and kite surfing whilst the theatre is perfect for a rainy day. For keen golfers there are 3 superb golf courses nearby and other outdoor activities include mountain biking, walking, shooting and horse riding.

Our inspector loved: The magnificent location - so tastefully and comfortably presented.

KINGSTON HOUSE
STAVERTON, TOTNES, DEVON TQ9 6AR

The Kingston Estate nestles amongst the rolling hills and valleys of the South Hams region of Devon, bounded by Dartmoor and the sea, with the focal point, Kingston House, commanding sweeping views of the moor. The Mansion, together with its superb cottages, have been restored by the Corfield family to their former glory and now offer some of the highest standard of accommodation to be found in the South West, boasting 3 period suites, reached by way of the finest example of a marquetry staircase in England. Dinner guests dine by candlelight in the elegant dining room at tables set with sparkling crystal, shining silver and starched linen. In winter, log fires crackle in the hearths, whilst in the summer pre-dinner drinks may be taken on the terrace overlooking the 18th century gardens. For every visitor, hospitality and comfort are assured in this magnificent historic setting. Places of interest nearby include Dartington Hall, Dartmouth, Totnes, Dartmoor and Devon's famous coastline. Sailing enthusiasts will be pleased to learn of the recent addition to the Kingston portfolio, "Winterwood," a 57 feet long yacht available for Crewed Charter by the day, or longer. The extremely comfortable and powerful yacht can accommodate up to 12 people by day, or two couples overnight.

Our inspector loved: The superb standards of accommodation and wonderful warm welcome.

Directions: Take A38 from Exeter or Plymouth, at Buckfastleigh take A384 Totnes Road for 2 miles. Turn left to Staverton. At Sea Trout Inn, take left fork to Kingston and follow signs.

Web: www.johansens.com/kingstonhouse
E-mail: info@kingston-estate.co.uk
Tel: 01803 762 235
Fax: 01803 762 444

Price Guide:
single £85–£95
double £130
suite £140–£150

DEVON - TAVISTOCK

BROWNS HOTEL, WINE BAR & BRASSERIE
80 WEST STREET, TAVISTOCK, DEVON PL19 8AQ

Directions: Tavistock is on the A386, a short distance from the M5 either via the A30 or the A38.

Web: www.johansens.com/brownstavistock
E-mail: enquiries@brownsdevon.co.uk
Tel: 01822 618686
Fax: 01822 618646

Price Guide:
single from £65
double/twin from £90

Browns is situated in the ancient market stannary town of Tavistock and originally an old coaching inn, has been lovingly restored whilst retaining many period features such as stunning slate flag stones and massive beams. Guests are pampered with attentive service and crackling log fires whilst rich fabrics and cosy furniture create a pleasant atmosphere that is relaxed and intimate. The 20 beautifully decorated bedrooms are spacious and comfortable with chic décor and superb facilities for the discerning traveller. Delightful modern British cuisine is offered in the Brasserie style restaurant, where an emphasis is placed on fresh fish and local produce and the Hotel's own well provides plenty of still and sparkling water of the purest quality. For leisure there is a gymnasium, for outdoor enthusiasts sailing, pony trekking, fishing, golf, bird watching and spectacular coastal walks can be enjoyed. In Tavistock, there are the remains of an abbey, old fashioned shops, thriving market and a canal to visit, it is the ideal base for exploring the beautiful secluded coves and sandy beaches of Devon and Cornwall. The local Church houses a window designed by William Morris dating back to the 14th century, which is breathtaking. Dartmoor is within easy reach with its tors and wild ponies.

Our inspector loved: *This Town House offering first class cuisine and superb accommadation.*

THE SEA TROUT INN

STAVERTON, NR. TOTNES, DEVON TQ9 6PA

Situated in a country valley setting The Sea Trout Inn dates from the 15th century and was named by a previous landlord who caught such a fish in the nearby River Dart. Several specimens of the prize fish now adorn the Inn in showcases. The 2 bars retain much of their period charm, with uneven floors, exposed oak beams, brass fittings and log fires. The bedrooms are decorated in an attractive cottage style, while the public rooms are cosy and inviting. Angling permits for trout, sea trout and salmon are available and the Inn offers special fishing breaks with tuition. Considered "Most people's ideal Devon inn," by Devon Today, 2001 and "The perfect Devon inn," by West Country Now, 2002, The Sea Trout Inn boasts 2 RAC Ribbons and 2 Red Rosettes for excellence. The Inn's restaurant is highly popular locally and has been acclaimed in many guides. Chef Joshua Martin creates finely balanced menus based on the best seasonal produce from local suppliers. Both table d'hôte (£16.50 for 2 courses or £19.75 for 3 courses) and à la carte menus are available. Dartmoor is excellent for walking, fishing and pony-trekking. Local attractions include the Devon coast, the Dart Valley Railway, Buckfast Abbey and Dartington Hall.

Our inspector loved: *This charming hidden retreat.*

Directions: Turn off the A38 on to the A384 at Buckfastleigh (Dartbridge) and follow the signs to Staverton.

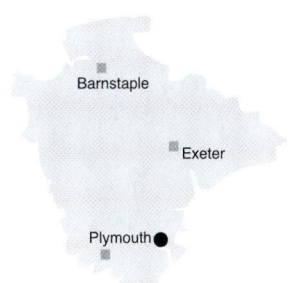

Web: www.johansens.com/seatroutinn
E-mail: enquiries@seatroutinn.com
Tel: 01803 762274
Fax: 01803 762506

Price Guide:
single £40–£50
double £55–£75

DEVON - VIRGINSTOW (NR OKEHAMPTON)

Percy's Country Hotel & Restaurant

COOMBESHEAD ESTATE, VIRGINSTOW, DEVON EX21 5EA

Directions: From Okehampton take A3079 to Metherell Cross. After 8.3 miles turn left. The hotel is 6.5 miles on the left.

Web: www.johansens.com/Percys
E-mail: info@percys.co.uk
Tel: 01409 211236
Fax: 01409 211275

Price Guide:
single £90–£125
double £140–£195

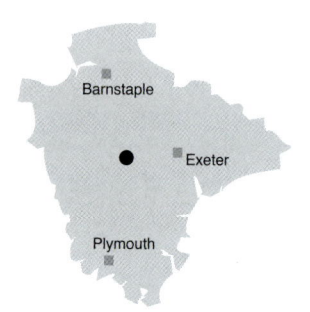

The Hotel's motto, "Relax...Taste...Enjoy..." is evident in this charming Devon hideaway. Set amongst 130 acres of unspoilt countryside, Percy's is ideal for those wishing to relax and unwind in a smoke and child-free environment and boasts breathtaking views over both Dartmoor and Bodmin Moor. Combining modern architectural intelligence with traditional country house comfort, guests are tempted from their own personal jacuzzi by the short, seasonal menu served in the highly accoladed restaurant. Here, Tina Bricknell-Webb, the only chef in Devon to have been awarded 4 Dining Awards by the RAC, creates contemporary country cuisine using only the finest local organic produce. Her unique style recently gained an unprecendented 9/10 from Giles Coren of The Saturday Times, who described Percy's as "a very rare place indeed." Wellington boots are at hand to explore the Estate's beauty spots and with the company of the resident labradors Bonnie, Tommy and Bonzo, guests can observe and enjoy the diverse and stunning wildlife in its natural habitat. Percy's is ideally situated to explore the Eden Project, RHS Gardens at Rosemoor and the region's many National Trust properties. Only minutes way, Roadford Reservoir offers excellent watersports and fishing with many interesting walks and superb tearooms overlooking the lake.

Our inspector loved: *The peaceful, 'away from it all' location.*

THE MANOR HOTEL
WEST BEXINGTON, DORCHESTER, DORSET DT2 9DF

The Manor Hotel, winner of the 1997 Johansens Most Excellent Inn Award and also mentioned in the Domesday Book, is in a wonderful setting, overlooking the beautiful Dorset countryside and spectacular Lyme Bay. The friendly atmosphere is apparent immediately on entering the inn, while the oak-panelling, stone walls and original fireplaces remind guests they are in the midst of history. The restaurant is brilliant, with two or three course menus that include wonderful choices - smoked duck breast and mango salad, lobster and scallop ragout, roast salmon and prawns with a lime and avocado salsa or roast pork with sage crust and apple sauce. Vegetarian dishes also feature and there is a children's menu. The wine list is exciting. Buffet meals, also including seafood, are served in the cosy cellar bar. There is an attractive conservatory for relaxing while children have their own play area outside. There are twelve charming en suite bedrooms and those at the top of the house have splendid views over the sea. This is Thomas Hardy country and there are famous gardens and historic houses to visit. Chesil Beach and Abbotsbury Swannery are nearby and water sports and country pursuits can be enjoyed.

Our inspector loved: *Its heritage coast location with views and walking the Dorset coastal path.*

Directions: West Bexington is on the B3157, 5 miles east of Bridport, 11 miles from Dorchester and Weymouth.

Web: www.johansens.com/manorbridport
E-mail: themanorhotel@bt.connect.com
Tel: 01308 897616
Fax: 01308 897035

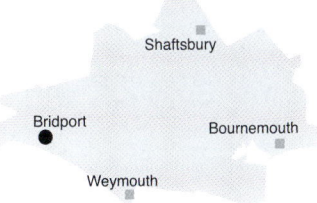

Price Guide:
single from £65
double £105–£140

Yalbury Cottage Hotel

LOWER BOCKHAMPTON, DORCHESTER, DORSET DT2 8PZ

Directions: Lower Bockhampton is a mile south of A35 between Puddletown and Dorchester.

Web: www.johansens.com/yalburycottage
E-mail: yalburycottage@aol.com
Tel: 01305 262382
Fax: 01305 266412

Price Guide:
single from £58
double from £90

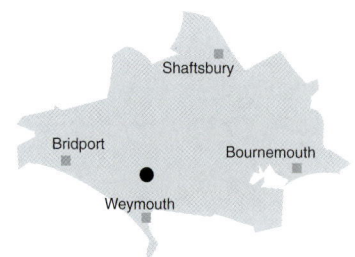

Yalbury Cottage Hotel is a lovely thatched house dating back about 300 years. It offers guests a warm welcome and friendly, personal service in a pleasing Dorset hamlet close to Thomas Hardy's home. The eight non-smoking en suite bedrooms are furnished in a simple country style, in keeping with the building. The comfortable lounge, complete with large Inglenook fireplace and low beamed ceiling, is the perfect place to relax, or enjoy a drink before dinner. Owner Kimberley Dent-Davis and her team of chefs pride themselves on the high standard of cuisine served in the attractive dining room. A good variety of imaginative dishes is available, for example, seared scallops on a warm potato and caper terrine with saffron and tomato dressing; roast loin of lamb with a white bean casserole, fresh broad beans and thyme jus; raspberry shortcake crème brûlée. Yalbury Cottage has been awarded 2 AA Rosettes for outstanding cuisine and a programme of gourmet dining events are memorable evenings. Places of interest nearby include Athelhampton House, Abbotsbury Swannery, Corfe Castle and Sherborne Castle. Yalbury Cottage, only 8 miles from the magnificent Heritage Coast, is an excellent basis from which to explore Dorset.

Our inspector loved: Simple room provision, with concentration on the inner man.

Acorn Inn

EVERSHOT, DORSET DT2 0JW

This beautiful 16th century inn lies in a wonderful part of West Dorset that found fame in one of Thomas Hardy's novels. Embedded in the literary mind as the 'Sow and Acorn' from the classic 'Tess of the d'Urbervilles', the owners take great pride in their hospitable approach and believe that offering a first class service and providing excellent value for money are paramount. There is an excellent selection of accommodation and the nine bedrooms are individually appointed with interesting antique furnishings. There is everything from a double bedroom with en suite shower or bathroom, to a king sized four poster bed with Jacuzzi bath. The non-smoking or smoking dining rooms offer an unashamedly British menu using fresh local fish, meat and game. Dishes such as hot shellfish (local West Bay crab, mussels and prawns) or fillet of local venison with red wine and thyme sauce with are complemented by a fine selection of wines. The village of Evershot is a very restful place with fabulous countryside and the Heritage coastline a few miles away, guests will find this inn the perfect location for a quiet weekend away in the countryside or a special midweek break. Places of interest nearby include Forde Abbey, Montacute House and the picturesque seaside town of Lyme Regis.

Our inspector loved: *Its village inn atmosphere and charming bedrooms.*

Directions: Evershot is 1 mile south of A37 midway between Yeovil and Dorchester.

Web: www.johansens.com/acorninnevershot
E-mail: stay@acorn-inn.co.uk
Tel: 01935 83228
Fax: 01935 83707

Price Guide:
single from £60
double £80–£120

THE EASTBURY HOTEL

LONG STREET, SHERBORNE, DORSET DT9 3BY

The Eastbury Hotel is a traditional town house which was built in 1740 during the reign of George II. During its recent refurbishment great care was taken to preserve its 18th-century character. In fine weather guests can enjoy the seclusion of the hotel's private walled garden, which encompasses an acre of shrubs and formal plants and a noteworthy listed walnut tree. Bedrooms are individually named after well-known English garden flowers and each is equipped with a full range of modern comforts and conveniences. The Eastbury is ideal for parents visiting sons or daughters who board at the Sherborne schools. Traditional English cooking is a feature of the Eastbury restaurant and the dishes are complemented by an extensive list of the world's fine wines. The numerous places of interest nearby include Sherborne with its magnificent 15th-century Perpendicular Abbey Church and two castles, in one of which Sir Walter Raleigh founded the national smoking habit. At Compton is a silk farm and a collection of butterflies. Beyond Yeovil is Montacute House (NT) and at Yeovilton is the Fleet Air Arm Museum.

Directions: Long Street is in the town centre, south of and parallel to the A30. Parking is at the rear of the hotel.

Web: www.johansens.com/eastbury
E-mail: eastbury.sherborne@virgin.net
Tel: 01935 813131
Fax: 01935 817296

Price Guide:
single £55.50–£78.50
double/twin £91–£121

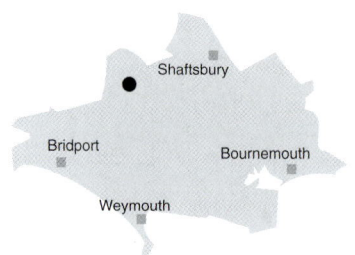

Our inspector loved: The ancient yew trees in the Hotel's walled garden.

KEMPS COUNTRY HOTEL & RESTAURANT

EAST STOKE, WAREHAM, DORSET BH20 6AL

This small and welcoming country hotel, surrounded by unspoilt Dorset countryside, overlooks the Frome Valley and offers lovely views of the Purbeck Hills. The house was originally a Victorian Rectory and its tasteful extension was undertaken with great care to preserve Victorian atmosphere. There are five bedrooms in the main house and another six with ground floor access facing the gardens and the Purbecks. Some have whirlpool baths and one features a traditional four-poster bed. Another four en suite bedrooms are located in the Old Coach House conversion. The bar features the ornate wallpaper and heavy hangings of the Victorian period. The comfortable dining room extends into the conservatory, from which guests can enjoy picturesque views of the hills. Kemps restaurant, which has been awarded an AA Rosette, enjoys an excellent local reputation for first-rate cuisine. The table d'hôte menu changes daily and there is also an à la carte menu and fresh fish board. Food is prepared to order, everything possible is home-made. Bargain breaks are available all year. Places of interest nearby include Lulworth Castle, Corfe Castle, Athelhampton House and Gardens, Monkey World and The Tank Museum.

Our inspector loved: *The light, bright Conservatory Restaurant.*

Directions: Situated in its own grounds on the A352 between Wareham and Wool.

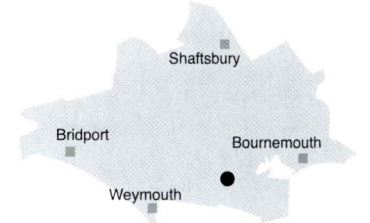

Web: www.johansens.com/kemps
E-mail: kemps.hotel@lineone.net
Tel: 01929 462563
Fax: 01929 405287

Price Guide:
single £55–£80
double/twin £88–£140

GROVE HOUSE

HAMSTERLEY FOREST, NR BISHOP AUCKLAND, CO DURHAM DL13 3NL

Grove House nestles at the heart of a beautiful garden in the middle of glorious Hamsterley Forest. Two small rivers run, on each side of the property, through 5,000 acres of old oaks and moors. It is an idyllic situation. Peaceful, quiet and historical, the house was built in 1830 as an aristocrat's shooting box and it exudes grandeur. There are fine furnishings and fabrics, stylish décor and open fires. The bedrooms, two doubles with en suite bathroom, a twin with en suite shower and toilet – have full facilities and are extremely comfortable. This is a non smoking house. Helene prepares five-course evening meals from the best fresh ingredients. Often on the set menu are venison and pheasant direct from the forest. Grove House is unlicensed so guests are invited to take their own wine. Those requiring total seclusion can stay at the adjoining, fully fitted, three-bedroomed Grove Cottage which has a large patio and a hillside rock garden. Places to visit nearby include Bowes Museum, Raby Castle, High Force Waterfall, Kilhope Wheel, Beamish open Air Museum and Durham Cathedral.

Our inspector loved: The location in the middle of Hamsterley Forest.

Directions: From A1(M) turn off onto A68 and just over 2 miles after Toft Hill turn left, through Hamsterley Village until the sign for "The Grove". Follow road to right, then left and after ½ a mile turn right to Hamsterley Forest and Grove House. Grove House is 3 miles further on.

Web: www.johansens.com/grovehouse
E-mail: grovehouse@dial.pipex.com
Tel: 01388 488203
Fax: 01388 488174

Price Guide: (including 5-course dinner)
single £47–£65
double £97–£110

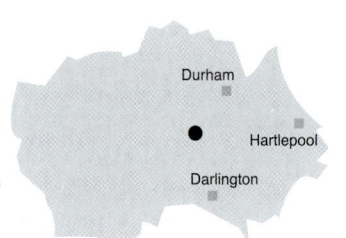

HORSLEY HALL

EASTGATE, NR STANHOPE, BISHOP AUCKLAND, CO. DURHAM DL13 2LJ

Horsley Hall is an elegant, three-story manor house nestling in the heart of Weardale, a designated area of outstanding natural beauty. Situated on the road south of the River Wear between Stanhope and Eastgate the hotel enjoys magnificent views across the Dale and easy access to local attractions. The Hall dates back to the 17th century and was once the home of the Hildyard family, whose existence in the Dale can be traced back nearly 500 years. The owners offer a warm, friendly North East welcome, attentive personal service and are justly proud of their hotel's reputation for homely comfort and good food. Liz is the chef and produces delicious cuisine and a varied choice of menus using the freshest of local produce. There are fine furnishings and fabrics, stylish décor and open fires throughout the Hall. The en suite bedrooms are extremely comfortable and have all the facilities to make a stay relaxing and enjoyable. They are all non smoking. The Hall is licensed for weddings and the Baronial Hall accommodates up to 80 guests for these, other private functions or business meetings.

Our inspector loved: *Dining in the Baronial Hall with spectacular views of Weardale.*

Directions: From the A68 take the A689 west to Stanhope. Then take the B6278 towards Brotherlee and Hasswicks. Horsley Hall (signposted) is on the right after approximately two miles.

Web: www.johansens.com/horsleyhall
E-mail: hotel@horsleyhall.co.uk
Tel: 01388 517239
Fax: 01388 517608

Price Guide:
single £47–£55
double £70–£85
family £109

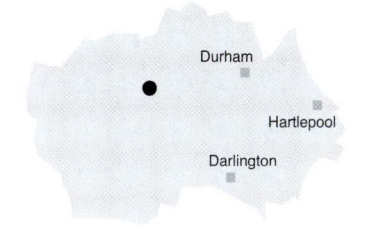

THE PUMP HOUSE APARTMENT
132 CHURCH STREET, GREAT BURSTEAD, ESSEX CM11 2TR

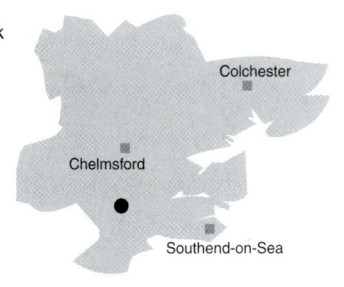

Situated in picturesque rural South East England, the Pump House Apartment is an immaculate two-storey apartment in the village of Great Burstead. Spacious and fully-equipped, it is an extremely comfortable home from home. Part of a modern house, Pump House is set in its own secluded gardens, with an oriental pond and paddocks. Visitors can avail of an outdoor swimming pool heated to 80 degrees from May to September, and a new, full-sized hot tub/spa set in a glazed Canadian Redwood Gazebo, located in suntrap walled courtyard with a decorative fountain. The house is very flexible and the air-conditioned Apartment can be let as a one, two or three-bedroom residence. Two beautifully appointed lounges are available in addition to an elegant dining room and well designed kitchen with views over the pretty gardens. The village of Great Burstead is steeped in history, and its 14th-century church has links with one of the Pilgrim Fathers and early settlers of the USA. London is 30 mins by train; Cambridge, Canterbury, Colchester and the Constable Country are within a 1-hour drive. Country walks are a pleasure, and golf, tennis and badminton are among the many sports available nearby.

Our inspector loved: The big hot tub in its gazebo in the sun trap walled garden.

Directions: Leave M25 at Jct29 and join A127. Travel in direction of Southend, then turn onto A176 (Noak Hill Road) towards Billericay. Church Street is on the right, the Pump House on the left before the church.

Web: www.johansens.com/pumphouse
E-mail: john.bayliss@willmottdixon.co.uk
Tel: 01277 656579
Fax: 01277 631160

Price Guide:
£425–£950 per week

THE CRICKETERS
CLAVERING, NR SAFFRON WALDEN, ESSEX CB11 4QT

As owners of The Cricketers since 1976, Trevor and Sally Oliver have done their utmost to maintain its traditional 16th century English country inn ambience. The beamed bar and restaurant, fresh flowers, gleaming brass and copper together with the cricket memorabilia all create a relaxed and friendly welcome. Excellent seasonal menus and an impressive wine list attract visitors from near and far and are widely recommended. Head Chef, Raymond Sexton, and his staff create fine cuisine using the freshest ingredients, be it a light snack or 3 course meal. All desserts are home-made; roast lunches and dinners are served throughout the week and Tuesday is Fish Day when fresh fish including lobster and crab is prepared straight from the market. The team is always happy to discuss any special requests. Bedrooms at The Cricketers are situated in the adjacent Pavilion and have good country style furnishings and individual décor. Each has a well-sized en suite bathroom, colour television and direct dial telephone. Located within easy reach of the M11 and Stansted Airport the Hotel is an excellent choice for both business and leisure guests. Nearby is the beautiful Jacobean mansion, Audley End, Newmarket for the races, and the university city of Cambridge.

Our inspector loved: The freshly shone brasses and fresh flowers.

Directions: Leave the M11 at junction 8, heading west, then turn right onto the B1383, signed Newport and left at the B1038 to Clavering.

Web: www.johansens.com/cricketers
E-mail: cricketers@lineone.net
Tel: 01799 550442
Fax: 01799 550882

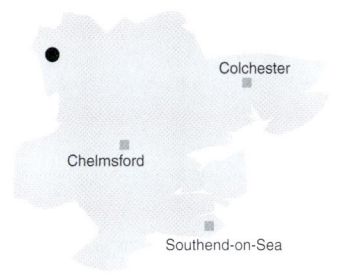

Price Guide:
single £70
double £100

THE CROWN HOUSE

GREAT CHESTERFORD, SAFFRON WALDEN, ESSEX CB10 1NY

Directions: Situated on B1383 leaving M11 at either Jct 9 or 10.

Web: www.johansens.com/crownhouse
Tel: 01799 530515 / 530257
Fax: 01799 530683

Price Guide: (per person)
single £55–£69.50
double/twin £39.75–£60

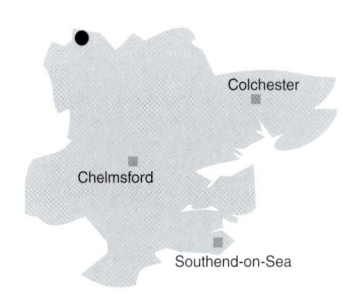

This Georgian hotel and restaurant, a restored coaching inn, or 'restaurant with rooms', is set within beautiful gardens in the pretty village of Great Chesterford. The building is truly historic; the front is built on a 4th-century Roman wall and several priest holes have been preserved. Oak-panelled walls and flagstone floors enhance the warm and friendly atmosphere, and there is one of only two oriel windows in the area. Glowing fires add to the warmth in winter, whilst comfortable leather chairs in the lounge/bar create a welcoming ambience. The luxurious, individually designed bedrooms are all en suite and provide all modern comforts. The restaurant, run by award-winning chef patron Keir Meikle, who trained at the Savoy, serves exquisite, innovative dishes, like the 'Crown Special', braised Scottish salmon with cucumber & ginger relish, herb polenta & cumin straw potatoes. Guests can enjoy the extensive menu, which is complemented by a carefully chosen wine list, in the intimate dining room or the vine-clad conservatory. The historic market town of Saffron Walden with its antiques shops, museum and castle is worth a visit, as are nearby Cambridge, Newmarket racecourse, Audley End and Duxford Air Museum. Stansted airport is within easy reach.

Our inspector loved: The double bath & big bathroom of The Crown Room

Bibury Court

BIBURY COURT, BIBURY, GLOUCESTERSHIRE GL7 5NT

Past visitors to Bibury Court are reputed to have included Charles II and during the reign of George III, the Prince Regent. This gracious mansion dates from Tudor times, but the main part was built in 1633 by Sir Thomas Sackville, an illegitimate son of the 1st Earl of Dorset. After generations of illustrious owners, it became a hotel in 1968. The great house is set on the outskirts of Bibury, which William Morris called "the most beautiful village in England". As a hotel, it is run on country house lines with one of the main objectives being the provision of good food and wine in informal and pleasurable surroundings. Log fires during the cooler months add to the comfort of guests. There are some lovely panelled rooms in the house, many containing antique furniture. Many of the bedrooms have four posters, all have private bathrooms and for those who like greater privacy there is the Sackville suite. Trout fishing is available in the Coln, which forms the southern boundary of the hotel's six acres of grounds, and there are golf courses at Burford and Cirencester. Water sports and riding are available nearby. Bibury Court is ideally placed for touring the Cotswolds, while Stratford, Oxford, Cheltenham and Bath are all within easy reach.

Our inspector loved: *Walking alongside the river Coln as it runs by this lovely little country house hotel.*

Directions: Bibury is on the B4425, seven miles from Burford and seven miles from Cirencester.

Web: www.johansens.com/biburycourt
E-mail: reservations@biburycourt.co.uk
Tel: 01285 740337
Fax: 01285 740660

Price Guide:
single from £115
double from £130
suite £200

THE GREEN DRAGON INN

COCKLEFORD, NR COWLEY, CHELTENHAM, GLOUCESTER GL53 9NW

Directions: 10 minutes from M5; 10 minutes from Cheltenham; 10 minutes from Gloucester; 15 minutes from Cirencester.

Web: www.johansens.com/greendragon
E-mail: green-dragon@buccaneer.co.uk
Tel: 01242 870271
Fax: 01242 870171

Price Guide:
single £49
double/twin £60
family room £80

Set in the heart of the picturesque Cotswold countryside in a tiny hamlet, the Green Dragon Inn is a secluded haven of tranquillity. Open log fireplaces, beamed ceilings and stone flagged floors add to the authentic atmosphere of historical charm and cosiness. Comfortable cottage style furniture has been beautifully hand crafted and the en-suite bedrooms are individually furnished in pleasing colours with all modern conveniences. The informal and friendly bars are perfect for unwinding and serve both traditional and unique modern pub food with real ales and fine wines. The Green Dragon restaurant serves delectable international dishes and homemade soups and al fresco dining is available on the delightful patio. A freshly prepared dessert selection includes irresistible cakes and ice creams in mouth-watering flavours using the finest organic ingredients and full cream Jersey milk. The surrounding towns of Cheltenham, Cirencester, Bibury and Bourton-on-the-water are a short drive away. Cheltenham racecourse is nearby for horse racing enthusiasts, or guests may simply enjoy the beautiful Cotswold countryside surrounding the hotel. There is a lovely function room that overlooks Cowley Lakes available for parties, weddings and business events.

Our inspector loved: *The cosy atmosphere of this little inn tucked away in a little hamlet.*

CHARLTON KINGS HOTEL
CHARLTON KINGS, CHELTENHAM, GLOUCESTERSHIRE GL52 6UU

Surrounded by the Cotswold Hills, on the outskirts of Cheltenham but just a few minutes by car to the heart of town, stands Charlton Kings Hotel. If you seek instant peace and solitude, follow the footpath running alongside the Hotel into the beautiful Cotswold countryside. The famous 'Cotswold Way' escarpment walk passes just ½ mile away. Quality, comfort and friendliness are the hallmarks of this lovely Hotel. All of the bedrooms have been beautifully refurbished and most boast views of the Coltswold Hills and countryside. Standard rooms offer a high degree of comfort while deluxe rooms are much larger with many upgraded facilities ideal for a longer stay or that special occasion. The restaurant offers a variety of dishes to satisfy the most discerning of diners and requests from vegetarians or vegans can be readily accommodated. The enthusiastic and experienced staff have a great knowledge of the surrounding area which enables them to recommend and help plan guests' visits to places of interest, local events and entertainment. Cheltenham Spa is famous for its architecture, festivals and racing, there is also plenty on offer in the way of theatres, restaurants as well as a distinguished selection of shops. To the north, east and south lie numerous charming Cotswold villages and to the west the Forest of Dean, Wye Valley, Malvern Hills and much more.

Our inspector loved: The friendliness of the staff.

Directions: The Hotel is the first property on the left coming into Cheltenham from Oxford on the A40 (the 'Welcome to Cheltenham' Boundary Sign is located in the front garden!).

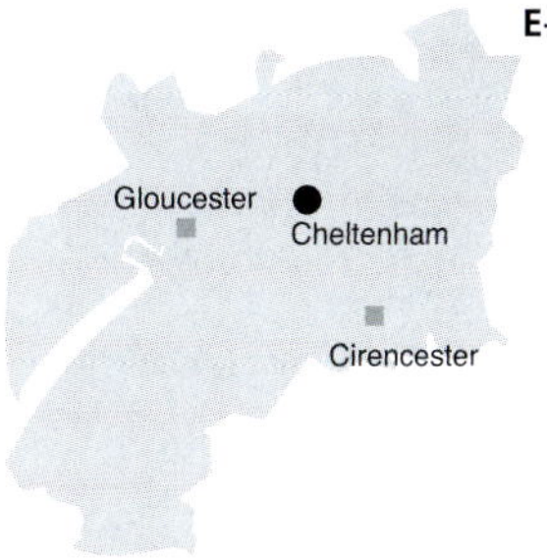

E-mail: enquiries@charltonkingshotel.co.uk
Web: www.johansens.com/charltonkings
Tel: 01242 231061
Fax: 01242 241900

Price Guide:
single £58.50–85
double £76–£120

THE WHITE HART INN

HIGH STREET, WINCHCOMBE, NR. CHELTENHAM, GLOUCESTERSHIRE GL54 5LJ

With its white and timber façade, 16th century charm and situation in the heart of an ancient town that was once the capital of Mercia, The White Hart is a typical old English coaching inn but with a difference! With a touch of Swedish modernity, introduced by owner Nicole Burr, a friendly, efficient Scandinavian staff provide a relaxed and informal ambience where the emphasis is on good service. Since purchasing The White Hart in the Autumn of 2000, the Burr family has financed an extensive refurbishment and modernization programme to cater for the most discerning visitor while at the same time retaining the Inn's authentic atmosphere of historical appeal. The beamed bar is cosily old fashioned while the brasserie-style restaurant is decorated in a Gustavian manner to reflect the family's Scandinavian influence. Cuisine is modern English with a Scandinavian contribution. Delectable smorgasbord buffet lunches and Scandinavian dinner menus are offered on Wednesdays and Fridays. Each 8 en suite bedroom is furnished to a high standard, individually designed and decorated. The Carl Larsson Room, for instance, is influenced and styled by the home of this famous Swedish artist while the Gustavian Room has a Swedish chandelier and traditional wallpapers and fabrics. Sudeley Castle and award winning gardens are nearby.

Directions: From Cheltenham take the B4632 for approximately 5 miles.

Web: www.johansens.com/whitehartcheltenham
E-mail: enquiries@the-white-hart-inn.com
Tel: 01242 602359
Fax: 01242 602703

Price Guide:
single £50–£60
double/twin £60–£125

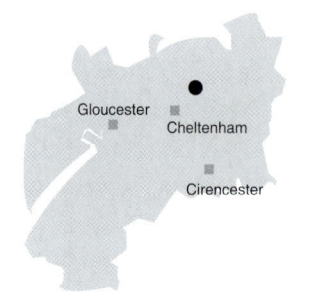

Our inspector loved: The little taste of Sweden in a Cotswold village inn.

THE MALT HOUSE

BROAD CAMPDEN, GLOUCESTERSHIRE GL55 6UU

The idyllic surroundings of The Malt House, a beautiful 17th century Cotswold home in the quiet village of Broad Campden, enhance the congenial atmosphere. Rooms, including residents' sitting rooms, combine comfortable furnishings with antiques and displays of fresh flowers. Most bedrooms overlook the wide lawns which lead to a small stream and orchard beyond. All of the recently refurbished rooms are individually decorated and have an en suite bathroom. The Windrush Suite has an 18th century four-poster bed and a family suite is also available. Dinner is served five days a week. The chef uses many ingredients from the kitchen gardens to prepare a table d'hôte menu, accompanied by a choice selection of wines. The English breakfasts are equally good. The Malt House has earned many awards for its standard of accommodation and meals including, most deservedly, 2 Rosettes for its food and Premier Select 5Q from the AA. Places of interest nearby include Hidcote Manor Gardens (N.T), Chipping Campden Church, The Cotswolds, Cheltenham, Stratford-upon-Avon, Oxford and Bath.

Our inspector loved: *This lovely little hotel with its very private garden and cottage style rooms.*

Directions: The Malt House is in the centre of the village of Broad Campden which is just one mile from Chipping Campden.

Web: www.johansens.com/malthouse
E-mail: nick@the-malt-house.freeserve.co.uk
Tel: 01386 840295
Fax: 01386 841334

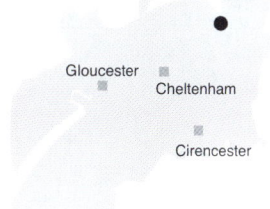

Price Guide:
single £59.50–£89.50
double £85–£118
suite £105–£128

THE WILD DUCK INN

DRAKES ISLAND, EWEN, CIRENCESTER, GLOUCESTERSHIRE GL7 6BY

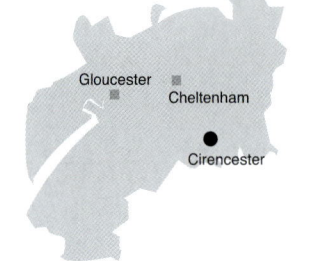

Here is a typical, lovely little picture postcard hotel; warm, welcoming and rich in history. Built of mellow Cotswold stone in the 15th century when Queen Elizabeth I was instigating a network of coaching inns throughout the country, The Wild Duck is as attractive inside as it is outside. Décor and furnishings are rich and elegant, fine old oil portraits adorn the walls, large open log fires enhance the welcoming ambience in winter, windows look out over a secluded garden that is perfect for al fresco dining in summer. Though old in years, the Inn has all modern comforts and amenities. Each individually decorated bedroom is en suite and has facilities to suit the most discerning visitor. Some of the rooms are on the ground floor, 2 have four poster beds. Guests can enjoy a chat over drinks in a cosy bar or oak panelled lounge before eating in style in the award winning dining room. Traditional British and European menus offer superb seasonal dishes. In winter, specialities include game and fresh fish, which is delivered overnight from Brixham, Devon. All dishes are complemented by the extensive and excellent wine list. Within a mile of the Inn is Cotswold Water Park with 80 lakes providing fishing and a range of water sports. Racing at Cheltenham and polo at Cirencester Park are nearby.

Our inspector loved: *The superb selection of wines on offer at this lovely Inn full of ambience and character.*

Directions: Leave the M4 at junction 7 and follow Cirencester signs. Before the town turn right at Kemble and follow the signs to Ewen.

Web: www.johansens.com/wildduck
E-mail: wduckinn@aol.com
Tel: 01285 770310
Fax: 01285 770924

Price Guide:
single £60
double/twin £80
suite £100

THE NEW INN AT COLN

COLN ST-ALDWYNS, NR CIRENCESTER, GLOUCESTERSHIRE GL7 5AN

In days of yore, when Queen Elizabeth I was giving royal assent to the import of tobacco from the new-found Americas, she was also initiating a travel boom in England, by instigating a network of coaching inns after the pattern already set on the Continent. One of the Cotswold inns that her initiative helped to create was The New Inn at Coln St-Aldwyns on Akeman Street, the old Roman Road, leading East out of Cirencester. The New Inn at Coln, though old in years, is today utterly new in spirit, winning ever fresh awards for food and hospitality – its two Rosettes being in permanent flower as a second Queen Elizabeth reigns. One of its recent acquisitions was becoming Johansens Most Excellent Traditional Inn 1999. Since Brian and Sandra-Anne Evans took over in 1992, The New Inn At Coln has blossomed and the considerable skills of the kitchen add a gastronomic dimension to the charm and comfort of the ancient but cleverly modernised bedrooms – perfect accommodation for an idyllic week in the Cotswolds, a useful stopover or as a timely resting place after a fine dinner. For the business-minded, there is a charming meeting room. Close to this picturesque Cotswolds base are Stratford-upon-Avon, Bath, Oxford and Cheltenham and within healthy walking distance is Bibury with its photogenic Arlington Row.

Our inspector loved: *The cosy homely feel of this lovely inn with its open fires.*

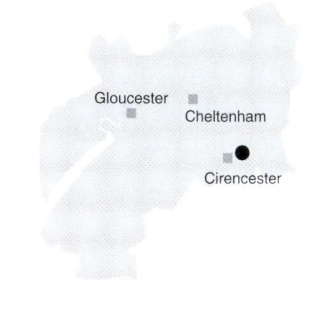

Directions: From Burford (A40), take B4425 to Bibury, turn left after Aldsworth.

Web: www.johansens.com/newinnatcoln
E-mail: stay@new-inn.co.uk
Tel: 01285 750651
Fax: 01285 750657

Price Guide:
single £80–£95
double £110–£140

THREE CHOIRS VINEYARDS ESTATE
NEWENT, GLOUCESTERSHIRE GL18 1LS

Directions: from the A40 take B4125 to Newent. Follow brown heritage signs to vineyard.

Web: www.johansens.com/threechoirs
E-mail: ts@threechoirs.com
Tel: 01531 890223
Fax: 01531 890877

Price Guide:
single £65
double £85

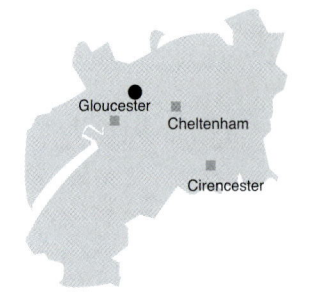

Three choirs is a 70 acre vineyard in the heart of the Gloucestershire countryside, and a rising star in English wine making. New this year are eight beautifully appointed bedrooms in an idyllic location perched high on the vine terraces overlooking the estate below. Each has a private patio that catches the evening sun, and a perfect spot to sip a chilled glass of wine chosen from the day's tasting. Comfortable beds and invigorating power showers will ensure a good night's sleep and refreshing start to the next day's lesson in vine cultivation! The emphasis at Three Choirs is on informality and the local staff offer the warmest of welcomes and cater for your every need during your stay. A wide-ranging menu of delicious and beautifully presented food accompanies the wines with tempting dishes like "Tartlet of avocado pear, tomato and cured ham with Single Gloucester cheese" and "Spiced fillets of Black Bream with marinated vegetables and Coriander cream", and there is a good choice of vegetarian dishes. In addition to the wine tasting tour and exhibition on site, there is the Three Choirs Music Festival and Eastnor Castle to visit, and golf and riding can all be arranged nearby.

Our inspector loved: Sitting on the terrace overlooking the vineyard drinking a glass of our own English wine.

THE WHITE HART INN

51 STOCKPORT ROAD, LYDGATE, SADDLEWORTH, GREATER MANCHESTER OL4 4JJ

Idyllically located in the village of Lydgate, this 18th century Inn retains its quaint historical charms and enjoys panoramic views over Manchester and the Cheshire Plains. Friendly and informal, the Hotel offers an extremely warm welcome and is popular with locals and visitors to the area alike for its award winning dishes and child friendly restaurant. Individually decorated deluxe bedrooms are designed with emphasis on quality, attention to detail and luxury for a truly comfortable stay. All are appointed with up-to-date facilities and guests have access to full business services. Splendid hills, beautiful valleys and wild windswept moors surround the Saddleworth area of Greater Manchester, a favourite with walkers, ramblers and photographers. Guests can watch the world go by in undisturbed peace from a boat on the Huddersfield Narrow Canal, which is now fully restored. Castleshaw Fort boasts a history that goes as far back as the Roman times and there are many museums, art galleries and cultural centres to explore. Awarded 'The International Wine and Food Society of Great Britain - Restaurant of the Year 2002,' 'One of nine Commended Restaurants in The Good Food Guide 2002,' 'One of six Notable Newcomers in The Which? Hotel Guide 2002,' 'The AA Pub Guide 2002 Pick of the Pubs for Greater Manchester.'

Our inspector loved: *The charm and friendliness of this Inn, placed on the edge of Saddleworth Moors.*

Directions: From the M62 jct. 22, A672 towards Saddleworth at Denshaw turn left taking right hand fork onto A6052 to Delph. After Delph turn right onto A62 towards Oldham. After 1.6 miles immediately turn left after the Star Inn and follow road to crossroads, go straight over and The White Hart is 50 yards on the left.

Web: www.johansens.com/whitehartinn
E-mail: bookings@thewhitehart.co.uk
Tel: 01457 872566
Fax: 01457 875190

Price Guide:
single £62.50–£68.50
double/twin £90–£98.50

New Mill Restaurant

NEW MILL ROAD, EVERSLEY, HAMPSHIRE RG27 0RA

Directions: The New Mill is situated just off the A327 (Reading to Farnborough Road), north of Eversley Village and south of Arborfield Cross. Watch for the brown signs.

Web: www.johansens.com/newmillhants
E-mail: info@thenewmill.co.uk
Tel: 0118 973 2277
Fax: 0118 932 8780

Price Guide:
Grill Room circa £25
Riverside Restaurant circa £35

Dating back to the days of William I and the Domesday Book, the Mill became a restaurant in 1972, and since then a great deal of sympathetic restoration work has been carried out to preserve the charm and character of this enchanting listed building. Its idyllic setting on the banks of the River Blackwater make it the perfect location for any special occasion. Within the oldest part of the Mill, the Grill Room serves lunch and dinner in an informal atmosphere, or if the weather is good, al fresco on the patio. A number of rooms are available for private dining, meetings and parties of up to 120, while the Riverside Restaurant offers panoramic views over the river banks and gardens. Head chef Colin Robson-Wright and his team create excellent menus with the finest ingredients, and in winter drinks can be taken by the open log fire. The New Mill has gained a reputation locally as 'the place' for weddings, and has three rooms licensed for civil ceremonies. Its service is comprehensive, offering packages for any size reception, as well as endless ideas on catering, photography, flowers, cakes and marquee hire.

Our inspector loved: The waterlillies, the weir and the wine list.

New Park Manor

LYNDHURST ROAD, BROCKENHURST, NEW FOREST, HAMPSHIRE SO42 7QH

Escape from the pressures of a hectic lifestyle in this grade II listed former hunting lodge of Charles II which dates from the 16th century. The house stands within its own clearing in the heart of the New Forest, yet is easily accessed from the main Lyndhurst/Lymington road. All bedrooms boast fine views of the surrounding parklands and forest and are individually decorated, in-keeping with the historic nature of the house. The New Forest rooms are contemporary in style and even have LCD TV screens in the bathrooms! Wandering ponies and wild deer can be viewed from the Hotel and on the many walks and paths that run through the forest. The Hotel has its own Equestrian Centre, with BHS trained stable crew, heated outdoor pool and tennis courts. It affords a perfect starting point from which to explore the surrounding countryside and to visit the nearby coast and sailing of the Solent. The new, lively Polo Bar (the Hotel has its own polo field!) offers a light menu throughout the day whilst the romantic restaurant provides a more extensive menu serving traditional British cuisine with a continental twist. The views from the New Forest room, with its picture windows, provides a wonderful setting for parties and functions, which are tailor-made to suit personal requirements.

Our inspector loved: *Its own riding stables and the opportunity to see deer from the windows.*

Directions: New Park Manor is ½ mile off the A337 between Lyndhurst and Brockenhurst easily reached from M27 junction 1.

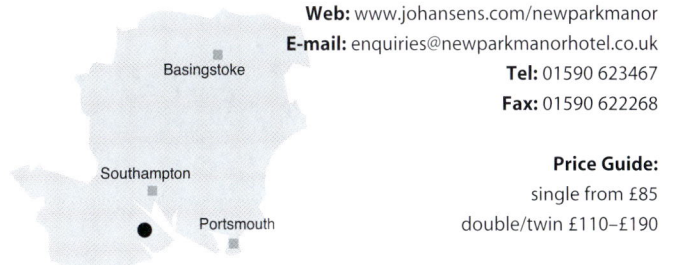

Web: www.johansens.com/newparkmanor
E-mail: enquiries@newparkmanorhotel.co.uk
Tel: 01590 623467
Fax: 01590 622268

Price Guide:
single from £85
double/twin £110–£190

Thatched Cottage Hotel & Restaurant

16 BROOKLEY ROAD, BROCKENHURST, NEW FOREST, HAMPSHIRE SO42 7RR

Directions: M27, Jct1, drive south on A337 through Lyndhurst, in Brockenhurst turn right before level crossing.

Web: www.johansens.com/thatchedcottagebrockenhurst
E-mail: sales@thatchedcottage.co.uk
Tel: 01590 623090
Fax: 01590 623479

Price Guide:
single from £70
double £90–£160
suite £150–£170

This enchanting thatched cottage was built in 1627 and only became a hotel in 1991. The Matysik family has over 120 years of hotel experience between them and this is reflected in the careful transformation that has taken place. Set in one of the prettiest villages in the heart of the New Forest, modernisation for the comfort of guests has not detracted from its original charm. The individually decorated double bedrooms each have a special feature for example, a four-poster bed, Turkish steam shower or open hearth gas fireplace. A cosy beamed lounge is idyllic for pre/after-dinner drinks. An elegant tea garden is presented with lace table cloths and sun parasols. Memorable services include a superb late breakfast, Champagne cream tea and gourmet wicker hampers. In the evening, exquisite culinary delights are freshly prepared by the culinary team on show in their open country kitchen. The menu offers luxurious ingredients harmoniously combined with flair and imagination. "A dining experience difficult to surpass" set in a unique and relaxing ambience by romantic candlelight. An authentic Japanese celebration menu can be prearranged. Places to visit nearby: include the Home of Lord Montagu and his National Motor Museum, Rothschild's Exbury Gardens and the yachting town of Lymington.

Our inspector loved: Watching the chefs create their gastronomic treats in the open plan kitchen.

WHITLEY RIDGE COUNTRY HOUSE HOTEL

BEAULIEU ROAD, BROCKENHURST, NEW FOREST, HAMPSHIRE SO42 7QL

Set in five acres of secluded parkland in the heart of the New Forest, this privately owned Georgian house was once a Royal hunting lodge visited by the Queen Mother. Today it has the ambience of a true country house with the accent on relaxation. The bedrooms are individually decorated, some have a two person steam cabin and a Hydrotherapy bath, and most have lovely views over open forest. The public rooms are similarly luxurious and elegant and log fires burn on cool evenings. Dining is always a pleasure and the two AA Rosette restaurant offers a daily changing table d'hôte menu, together with a high standard of à la carte choices and a well balanced and imaginative vegetarian menu. The wine selection includes wines from traditional areas and interesting choices from further afield. Guests can relax in the grounds or enjoy a game of tennis. Some of the country's best woodland walks are directly accessible from the gardens. Whichever pastime you choose, Whitley Ridge guarantees a restful and enjoyable stay. A number of stately homes, including Broadlands and Wilton House, are within easy reach. Lord Montague's Motor Museum, Buckler's Hard and historic Stonehenge are also within driving distance.

Our inspector loved: The charming rooms and the unique forest setting of this gracious and hospitable house.

Directions: M27 junction 1. Situated on the B3055, Brockenhurst – Beaulieu.

Web: www.johansens.com/whitleyridge
E-mail: whitleyridge@brockenhurst.co.uk
Tel: 01590 622354
Fax: 01590 622856

Price Guide:
single from £65
double £108–£134
suite £144

GORDLETON MILL INN

SILVER STREET, HORDLE, NR LYMINGTON, NEW FOREST, HAMPSHIRE SO41 6DJ

Directions: M27, junction 1. A337 south for 11 miles near Lymington after the railway bridge and mini roundabout turn sharp right before Toll House Inn, head towards Hordle and inn is on right after about 1½ miles.

Web: www.johansens.com/gordletonmill
E-mail: bookings@gordleton-mill.co.uk
Tel: 01590 682219
Fax: 01590 683073

Price Guide:
double/Twin £70–£90
suite £115

Tucked away in the verdant countryside between the New Forest National Park and the sea lies this idyllic ivy-clad 17th century rural hideaway. Immaculately restored to its former glory, yet boasting every modern convenience, the Gordleton Mill must now be considered one of the most tasteful of Hampshire's many fine inns. The landscaped gardens epitomise rustic charm, and visitors weary of their hectic urban lifestyles will surely find peace in the garden and mill pond with its charming sluice gates. The inn is no less immaculate inside. The intimate restaurant, overlooking the river and serving succulent fare, is simply a delight. The individually designed bedrooms, some of which have whirlpools, are extremely comfortable. The new owners, a charming couple, are only too happy to direct visitors to some of the many nearby attractions, which include the Cisterian Abbey at Bealieu and and the more contemporary yacht ports of Hamble Point and Hythe Marina Village. The villages of Sway, Brockenhurst and Bucklers Hard - with their bustling pubs – are also worth a visit.

Our inspector loved: The restaurant terrace above the millstream - jolly ducks and leaping trout.

Westover Hall

PARK LANE, MILFORD-ON-SEA, HAMPSHIRE SO41 0PT

Set on the edge of the New Forest and with stunning views over Christchurch Bay and towards the Needles rocks, this small hotel is an absolute gem recently acknowledged by 3 AA Red Stars. Built in 1897 by the renowned architect Arnold Mitchell, it is an impressive example of late Victorian style with beautiful stained glass windows, oak panelling and ceilings decorated in high relief. Each of the 12 en suite bedrooms is individually decorated and furnished with antique pieces to ensure a careful blend of modern day luxury and historic family-house atmosphere. The award-winning restaurant is a source of great pride and has wonderful views across the Solent to the Isle of Wight. The emphasis is firmly on freshness with the majority of ingredients being sourced locally, particularly the fish but also wild mushrooms and game. The newly created and delightfully intimate private dining room shares the view and an unusual feature of the hotel is its own beachhut. The key attractions of the New Forest are all accessible from here – historic Beaulieu with its motor museum, and the delightful Bucklers Hard (Nelson's boatyard), as well as day trips to the Isle of Wight from Lymington.

Our inspector loved: *The family's true dedication to stylish comfort and quality - and one of the nicest views in all Britain.*

Directions: Leave M3/M27 at Jct1, then A337 to Everton. Turn left onto B3058 to Milford-on-Sea.

Web: www.johansens.com/westoverhall
E-mail: info@westoverhallhotel.com
Tel: 01590 643044
Fax: 01590 644490

Price Guide:
single £70–£85
double/twin £145–£180
suite £200

THE NURSE'S COTTAGE

STATION ROAD, SWAY, LYMINGTON, HAMPSHIRE SO41 6BA

Directions: From M27 Jct1 take A337 to Brockenhurst and then B3055 signed to New Milton. The Nurse's Cottage is next door to Sway Post Office.

Web: www.johansens.com/nursescottage
E-mail: nurses.cottage@lineone.net
Tel: 01590 683402
Fax: 01590 683402

Price Guide:
single £62.50–£72.50
double £105

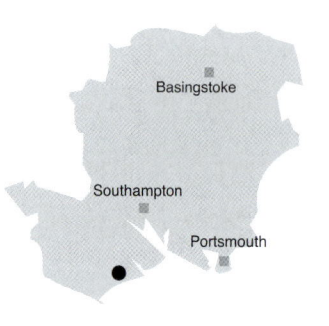

This remarkable little house is centrally situated in a quiet village on the southern edge of the New Forest. For nearly 70 years home to Sway's successive District Nurses, it is now a three-bedroom hotel. The level of visitor provision cannot fail to impress, and chef proprietor Tony Barnfield's dedication to guests' comfort and enjoyment of their stay ensures an exceptional level of repeat visits. A worthy winner of the 'Best Breakfast in Britain' award, the hotel guarantees a good start to the day. At dinner, Tony and his young team offer both 'Classic British' and 'House Speciality' menu choices, served with style in the newly expanded dining room/conservatory overlooking the garden. The award-winning wine list with over 60 bins puts much larger hotels to shame and surprises with many in half bottles and no less than 15 by the glass. All bedrooms are on the ground floor and have CD and video players and refrigerators housing complimentary fruit juices, mineral water and fresh milk. Fruit, biscuits and Beaulieu chocolates add to the pampered feeling. The sparkling bright and warm bathrooms offer a generous array of toiletries. No smoking throughout. Places of interest nearby include the National Motor Museum at Beaulieu, Rothschild's Exbury Gardens and the yachting town of Lymington.

Our inspector loved: *The absolute commitment to guest satisfaction.*

Langrish House

LANGRISH, NR PETERSFIELD, HAMPSHIRE GU32 1RN

Standing in 12 acres of beautiful mature grounds including a picturesque lake, Langrish House combines the welcoming ambience of a traditional country house with the facilities expected from a modern hotel. Extended by the present owners' forbears in 1842, it opened as a hotel in 1979 and remains very much a family home. Today, new life is being breathed into the house by Nigel and Robina Talbot-Ponsonby whose family portraits and heirlooms adorn the rooms. Each of the bedrooms overlooks the grounds, giving guests ample opportunity to savour Langrish's peace and tranquillity. All are fully equipped with en suite bathrooms, direct dial telephones, colour televisions and many thoughtful touches. The Garden Room Restaurant, affords glorious views of the lawns and surrounding countryside. Fresh regional produce features in the superb cuisine, which has won the house an AA Star for fine dining. Langrish House is an ideal venue for wedding receptions and business conferences and offers dining facilities for up to 100 people. This is an excellent base for touring the Hampshire countryside and the New Forest. Gilbert White's Selbourne, Jane Austen's Chawton, Goodwood and Cowdray Park are also close by.

Our inspector loved: *The plump bunnies on the lawns and the lake in the wood.*

Directions: Follow A272 from the M3/A31 at Winchester (16 miles) or from A3 at Petersfield (3 miles). Langrish House is signposted from the village on the road to East Meon.

Web: www.johansens.com/langrishhouse
E-mail: frontdesk@langrishhouse.co.uk
Tel: 01730 266941
Fax: 01730 260543

Price Guide:
single £63–£72
double £96–£104
suite £120

THE STEPPES

ULLINGSWICK, NR HEREFORD, HEREFORDSHIRE HR1 3JG

Directions: A mile off A417 Gloucester–Leominster, signed Ullingswick. Turn right at phone box in centre of village.

Web: www.johansens.com/steppes
E-mail: info@steppeshotel.co.uk
Tel: 01432 820424
Fax: 01432 820042

Price Guide:
single from £45
double from £80

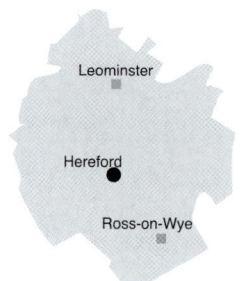

A Grade II listed 14th century yeoman's house, The Steppes is located in Ullingswick, a Domesday Book hamlet set in the Wye Valley. The gleaming whitewashed exterior conceals a host of original features. Cobble and flag-flooring, massive oak timbers and an inglenook fireplace were part of the ancient dairy and cider-making cellars, which form the splendid cellar bar and lounge. Winner of the Johansens 1996 "Value for Money Award", the ambience of this non–smoking house has been applauded by The Sunday Telegraph, The Guardian and The Independent newspapers – all of which praise the enthusiasm and hospitality of owners Henry and Tricia Howland and, in particular, Tricia's cooking. The candlelit dinners are compiled from medieval recipes, revived local dishes, Mediterranean delicacies and French cuisine. The interesting breakfast menu is complemented by generous service. Exceptionally high standard en suite accommodation is provided in either the Tudor Barn or Courtyard Cottage, both located within the grounds. Closed December and January. Places of interest nearby include River Wye (salmon fishing), Black Mountains, Malvern Hills (Elgar's birthplace), Welsh Marches, Gloucester and Worcester. Riding can be arranged.

Our inspector loved: The oak framed buildings and cellar bar - homecooked food and friendly welcome.

THE FEATHERS HOTEL
HIGH STREET, LEDBURY, HEREFORDSHIRE HR8 1DS

Situated in the enchanting, unspoilt market town of Ledbury, with its cobbled streets and narrow lanes, the 16th century Feathers Hotel is an Elizabethan Coaching Inn that proudly dominates the High Street. The Hotel oozes character whilst original beamed walls and ceilings, antiques and stylish décor create a sense of timeless elegance. 19 individually appointed en suite bedrooms maintain a traditional feel and offer all modern facilities ensuring maximum quality and comfort. Quills Restaurant offers quiet, refined dining and the extremely popular Fuggles Brasserie serves irresistible, award winning modern cuisine. An extremely indulgent afternoon tea of home-made cakes and scones can be enjoyed in the reception lounge, which has a huge open fireplace and cosy chairs. To relax and unwind guests can make use of the Leisure Spa which has a wonderful indoor heated swimming pool, jacuzzi, steam room, gym and solarium, also a fully-qualified fitness trainer is available to create a personal fitness programme. Conference facilities with a private bar overlooking the garden have equipment of the highest quality. Visitors will delight in the ancient parish church of the town and a few minutes drive away is the beautiful walking country of the Malvern Hills.

Our inspector loved: Its historical Elizabethan features.

Directions: From the M4, come off on the A419 to Gloucester. Continue on the A417 to Ledbury. From the M50 leave at junction 2. Ledbury is 4 miles.

Web: www.johansens.com/feathersledbury
E-mail: mary@feathers–ledbury.co.uk
Tel: 01531 635266
Fax: 01531 638955

Price Guide:
single £73.50
double £95

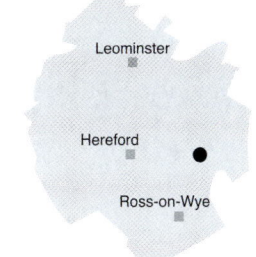

WILTON COURT HOTEL

WILTON, ROSS-ON-WYE, HEREFORDSHIRE HR9 6AQ

Offering abundant peace and tranquillity on the banks of the River Wye, this property is a true gem, surrounded by walled gardens with mature shrubs, sloping lawns and an enchanting river. Leaded windows and stone mullions are some of the many vestiges of the hotel's 15th century origins. Affording a view of either the gardens or the river, the recently refurbished en suite bedrooms are well-appointed, complete with trouser press, hardryer, alarm clock radio, tea and coffee making facilities, direct dial telephones and colour televisions. Guests may dine in the cosy bar, with its warm fire in winter, the light Conservatory with its view of the gardens or enjoy meals alfresco. The very best of fresh local produce is used wherever possible. Sports enthusiasts will be pleased with the local facilities which include canoeing, salmon fishing on the River Wye, horse-riding, ballooning, tennis, cycling, bowling and golf. The hotel has ample car parking and is within walking distance from the bustling streets of Ross on Wye with its 16th century market place. Tintern Abbey, The Malvern Hills, the Forest of Dean and The Cotswolds are some of the many areas that are worth exploring.

Our inspector loved: *The wonderful river view and cosy atmosphere.*

Directions: From the M50, exit at junction 4 and turn into Ross at the junction of A40 and A49. Take the first right turning before the Wye River Bridge. The hotel is on the right facing the river

Web: www.johansens.com/wiltoncourthotel
E-mail: info@wiltoncourthotel.com
Tel: +44 (0)1989 562569
Fax: +44 (0)1989 768460

Price Guide:
single £55–£75
double £80–£105
suite £100–£135

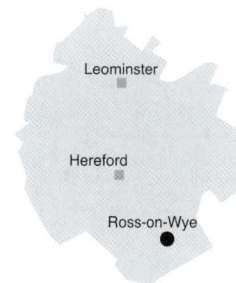

GLEWSTONE COURT

NR ROSS-ON-WYE, HEREFORDSHIRE HR9 6AW

Glewstone Court is set in three acres of fruit orchards, lawns and flower-beds. It is a refreshingly un-stuffy establishment, although secluded, it is only three miles from Ross-on-Wye. Furnishings and an eclectic collection of antiques, bric a brac and books reflect the relaxed, hospitable personality of the owners. Most country pursuits can be arranged, including canoeing, fishing and riding. This is marvellous walking country, alternatively guests may wish to simply laze around in front of the log fires or on fine days, recline out in the garden. Christine's food is always innovative and reflects a love of good fresh local ingredients. Organic and free-range products are used as much as possible on both the restaurant and bistro menus. Featuring both modern and traditional British dishes, the cuisine is always prepared and served with care and attention to detail. Now in their 17th year, accolades awarded include an AA Rosette for good food and the AA Courtesy & Care award. The bedrooms are comfortable and individually decorated. Each has en suite facilities, a hospitality tray, soft bathrobes, direct dial phone and colour television. Closed Christmas Day and Boxing Day. Places of interest nearby include Ross-on-Wye, Hay-on-Wye, the Welsh Marches, Hereford Cathedral and the Brecon Beacons. Bargain breaks available all year round.

Our inspector loved: *This beautiful house with interesting features.*

Directions: From M50 junction 4 follow A40 signposted Monmouth. 1 mile past Wilton roundabout turn right to Glewstone; the Court is ½ mile on left.

Web: www.johansens.com/glewstonecourt
E-mail: glewstone@aol.com
Tel: 01989 770367
Fax: 01989 770282

Price Guide:
single £45-£60-£75
double £75-£90-£105

REDCOATS FARMHOUSE HOTEL AND RESTAURANT

REDCOATS GREEN, NEAR HITCHIN, HERTS SG4 7JR

Directions: Leave A1(M) at junction 8 for Little Wymondley. At mini-roundabout turn left. At T-Junction go right, hotel is on left.

Web: www.johansens.com/redcoatsfarmhouse
E-mail: sales@redcoats.co.uk
Tel: 01438 729500
Fax: 01438 723322

Price Guide:
single £73–£98
double £101–£111

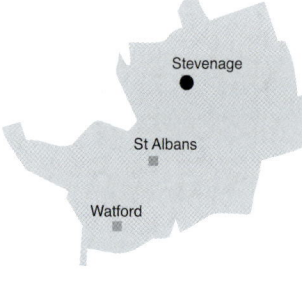

This 15th-century farmhouse has been in the Butterfield family for generations, and in 1971, Peter and his sister converted it into a hotel. They preserved its traditional character of original beams, exposed brickwork and inglenook fireplaces and furnished it in a comfortable and inviting fashion. Redcoats is set in tranquil gardens in the middle of rolling countryside yet not far from the A1(M). There are three dining rooms; the Oak Room with beams, oak panelling and log fires in winter, has 15th-century charm, whilst the elegant Victorian Room offers a more subtle ambience. This is the perfect location for small wedding parties and smaller conferences and business meetings requiring more privacy than a corporate environment. Largest of all is the conservatory with its friendly bustle, also affording views of the beautiful gardens. Redcoats has an excellent reputation for its cuisine, which uses predominantly local produce, and a wine list which is as wide-ranging geographically as it is in prices. Redcoats is close to several historic houses including Knebworth House, Hatfield House, Luton Hoo and Woburn Abbey and Wildlife Park. The Roman city of St Albans, the traditional market town of Hitchin and Cambridge University are all within a 30-minute drive.

Our inspector loved: The great character with so many of the orignal features retained and spacious conservatory restaurant in contrast.

Rylstone Manor

RYLSTONE GARDENS, SHANKLIN, ISLE OF WIGHT PO37 6RE

Neil Graham and Alan Priddle are the proud owners of this hidden gem uniquely located in 4½ acres of tranquil gardens on the fringe of Shanklin. Just two minutes walk away through the gardens are the promenade and beach and the manor gardens enjoy stunning views out across Shanklin Bay. An atmosphere of comfort and relaxation is engendered in the stylish day rooms where afternoon tea and a good book are just the thing on inclement days. In the restaurant, Neil prepares a nightly table d'hôte menu with an eagle eye on the best available produce and an expert's touch in its preparation. Poached fillet of salmon, roast loin of lamb and breast of duck are served with imaginative, simple sauces. Both the restaurant and bedrooms are designated non-smoking; no children under 16 are taken; and dogs are not permitted. Rylstone Manor is truly a haven of peace, in a delightfully protected environment. For the more active, water sports, fishing, riding and golf can all be arranged. In addition to being a walkers' paradise, the island has many other manor houses and gardens to visit. Nearby are the thatched cottages of Shanklin Old Village, Queen Victoria's Osborne House, Carisbrook Castle and Rylstone Gardens Countryside Centre.

Our inspector loved: The house party atmosphere in this truly hospitable house.

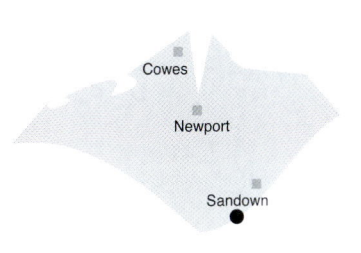

Directions: Just off the A3055 Sandown to Ventnor road in Shanklin Old Village, follow signs directly into Rylstone Gardens.

Web: www.johansens.com/rylstonemanor
E-mail: rylstone@dialstart.net
Tel: 01983 862806
Fax: 01983 862806

Price Guide:
single from £56
double from £118

HOWFIELD MANOR

CHARTHAM HATCH, NR CANTERBURY, KENT CT4 7HQ

Directions: From A2 London–Dover road, follow signs for Chartham Hatch after the Gate Service Station, then follow straight on for 2¼ miles. The hotel is on the left at Junction with A28.

Web: www.johansens.com/howfield
E-mail: enquiries@howfield.invictanet.co.uk
Tel: 01227 738294
Fax: 01227 731535

Price Guide:
single £79.50
double/twin £99–£115

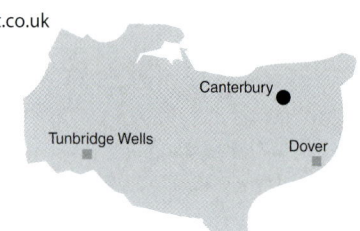

Set in the heart of England's garden county and surrounded by five acres of attractive landscaped gardens, Howfield Manor has a fine tradition of hospitality dating back to 1181. Within easy reach of the motorway network, it is located just south of the great cathedral city of Canterbury. It has been owned and run for many years by the Towns family and is a popular local wedding venue. Furnished in a blend of modern and traditional décor, the bedrooms are individually appointed and are equipped with colour televisions, direct dial telephones and other thoughtful extras. Originally part of the Priory of St. Gregory, vestiges of the hotel's historic past include the authentic priest hole and the ferned ancient well under the floor of the Old Well Restaurant which was the main source of water for the monks who lived here 800 years ago. Today, an extensive menu created with the very best of fresh, local produce is served alongside an excellent and carefully compiled wine list. Howlett's Zoo Park, Leeds and Dover Castles, Rye with its charming cobbled streets and the gardens at Sissinghurst are only a short drive away. Special weekend breaks are available.

Our inspector loved: The ease of access to the heart of Canterbury.

THE GEORGE HOTEL
STONE STREET, CRANBROOK, KENT TN17 3HE

History, character and true Kentish hospitality go hand in hand at this charming inn in the heart of a pleasant and busy little town which features many 18th century houses and a medieval church with the honorary title of 'Cathedral of the Weald'. The George is a Grade II* listed building with references back to 1300 when it is reputed that Edward I stayed here. Queen Elizabeth I was also entertained at the George when she visited the town in 1573. She was presented with a silver cup bearing the arms of the Cinque Ports by the townsfolk in the upstairs beamed Big Room. This is still in use today and reached by a magnificent oak staircase. Owners Douglas and Sue have supervised an excellent refurbishment which has culminated in an agreeable combination of modern facilities with traditional furnishings. Guests have the choice of seven en suite bedrooms, each tastefully and comfortably furnished. Some have four poster beds and one a Jacuzzi. The restaurant 'brooks' offers atmosphere and charm. Its centrepiece is a huge, beautifully preserved 600-year-old open fireplace that was once the 'workhorse' of this former kitchen. Fresh local produce is used in the preparation of delicious menus. Sissinghurst Gardens, Leeds, Hever and Bodiam Castles are all close by.

Our inspector loved: Its typical country town High Street setting - locals popping in and out all the time.

Directions: Exit the M20 at Junction 7 and take the A229 South.

Web: www.johansens.com/georgecranbrook
E-mail: georgecranbrook@aol.com
Tel: 01580 713348
Fax: 01580 715532

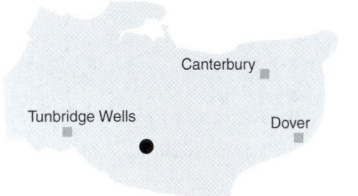

Price Guide:
single from £60
double/twin from £90–£125

Wallett's Court

WEST CLIFFE, ST MARGARET'S-AT-CLIFFE, DOVER, KENT CT15 6EW

Directions: From A2 roundabout immediately north of Dover take A258 signposted Deal. After 1 mile turn right and the Court is on the right.

Web: www.johansens.com/wallettscourt
E-mail: wc@wallettscourt.com
Tel: 01304 852424
Fax: 01304 853430

Price Guide:
single £75–£115
double £90–£150

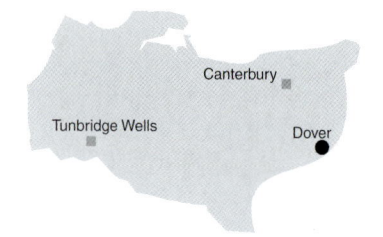

This listed Grade II house, recorded in The Domesday Book as 'The Manor of Westcliffe', was transformed by the Oakley family who discovered it in ruins in the late 70s. The result is a charming property, enveloped in a relaxing atmosphere and set in landscaped grounds near to The White Cliffs of Dover. The beautifully appointed bedrooms are comfortable and well-equipped with an array of modern conveniences. They are located in either the main house or barn conversion, the most recent of which also features an indoor swimming pool and leisure facilities. Fitness enthusiasts may use the steam room, sauna, spa pool, tennis courts and croquet lawn. The attractive restaurant, awarded 3 AA Rosettes, offers imaginative lunch and dinner menus. The dishes change every month to incorporate the fresh seasonal produce. Try the St. Margaret's Bay Lobster served with pilaaf rice and roasted vegetables, Dover Sole Meuniere or Romney Marsh Lamb. The extensive wine list includes a good selection of half-bottles, all acceptably priced. Breakfast is another feast, with farm eggs, sausages made by the nearby butcher and home-made preserves.

Our inspector loved: The super mini gym to work off all that wonderful food!

THE ABBOT'S FIRESIDE HOTEL

HIGH STREET, ELHAM, NEAR CANTERBURY, KENT CT4 6TD

The Abbot's Fireside is situated in the historic village of Elham, south of Canterbury. Built as an inn in 1451, the Grade II listed hotel now offers all comforts to modern travellers. However, the mediaeval character of this building has carefully been maintained. It is one of Kent's best kept Tudor buildings and has an extensive list of famous visitors. The Duke of Wellington used the Abbot's Fireside as his headquarters in preparation for his battle with Napoleon in Waterloo. Charles II and the Duke of Richmond hid in the huge handcarved fireplace. You will be welcomed in a warm and friendly atmosphere. Roaring log fires and exposed beams feature throughout, and all rooms offer en suite bathrooms, colour television, hairdryer and tea and coffee making facilities. Much emphasis is placed on comfort and good food, with patron chef Anton Renac preparing delicious British and international dishes. The hotel is surrounded by breathtaking countryside, and there are several golf courses within close proximity. Visit Canterbury with its Cathedral, Dover Castle, Sissinghurst and Leeds Castle. Ten minutes from the Channel Tunnel, a 10 minute drive from Dover.

Our inspector loved: The tiny secret courtyard, just right for a glass of wine and a book.

Directions: M20 junction 11 or 12 or A2 exit Barham.

Web: www.johansens.com/abbotsfireside
E-mail: info@abbotsfireside.com
Tel: 01303 840265
Fax: 01303 840852

Price Guide:
double/twin £60–£95

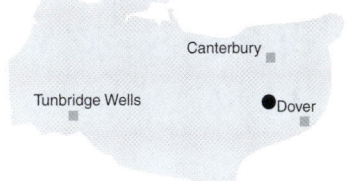

RINGLESTONE INN AND FARMHOUSE HOTEL

'TWIXT HARRIETSHAM AND WORMSHILL, NR MAIDSTONE, KENT ME17 1NX

Directions: Leave M20 at Jct8. Head north off A20 through Hollingbourne, turn right at water tower crossroads to Doddington.

Web: www.johansens.com/ringlestoneinn
E-mail: bookings@ringlestone.com
Tel: 01622 859900
Fax: 01622 859966

Price Guide: (room only)
single from £89
double from £99

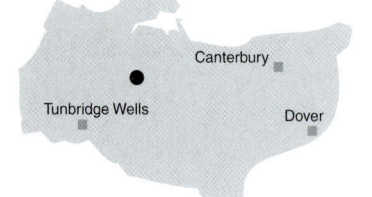

Truly traditional is the welcome that awaits visitors as they step back in time into this delightfully unspoilt, medieval, lamplit tavern. Built in 1533 as a hospice for monks, the Ringlestone became one of the early Ale Houses around 1615 and little has changed since. Its delights include original brick and flint walls and floors, massive oak beams, inglenooks, old English furniture and eight acres of idyllic gardens. There are three en suite bedrooms and a separate cottage at a charming farmhouse just opposite the inn, all furnished in a style totally in keeping with expectations for a stay in this beautiful escapists' spot. Spacious farmhouse dining and reception rooms are also available for private and corporate functions. Full of character and candlelight ambience with sturdy, highly polished tables made from the timbers of an 18th century Thames barge, the Ringlestone has a reputation for excellent English cooking and features in many food guides. The buffet lunch features a variety of country recipes and a traditional roast is served on Sundays. The diverse evening menu includes unusual and interesting pies and local trout, complemented by their extensive wine list and a wide range of English country fruit wines. Leeds Castle is nearby.

Our inspector loved: *The unbelievably quiet and remote setting in unspoilt countryside.*

ROMNEY BAY HOUSE
COAST ROAD, LITTLESTONE, NEW ROMNEY, KENT TN28 8QY

This spectacular house was built in the 1920s for the American actress and journalist, Hedda Hopper, by the distinguished architect, Sir Clough Williams-Ellis. The gracious drawing room overlooks the English Channel, panoramically surveyed through the telescope in the first floor library. There is access to the beach, a tennis court, croquet lawn and golf course. A 5 minute drive to Lydd airport and you can fly to Le Touquet for lunch. The owners have completed an impressive refurbishing programme. Upstairs, designated non-smoking, the charming en suite bedrooms are furnished with antiques. Wonderful cream teas can be enjoyed on the terrace in the sun-lit sea air, a traditional four-course dinner is served most nights and guests will strongly approve of the short but excellent wine list. Less than 20 minutes drive from the Channel Tunnel Terminal. There is so much history in Romney Marsh, renowned years ago for its smuggling. Caesar landed here in 55BC at Port Lympne and the famous Cinque Ports stretch along the coast. Canterbury Cathedral is within easy driving distance. Littlestone Golf Courses adjoin the hotel and windsurfing is popular.

Our inspector loved: The unspoilt dramatic coastal location and the boxer dogs.

Directions: From New Romney head for the coast by Station Road leading to Littlestone Road – pass the miniature railway station – at the sea, turn left and follow signs for Romney Bay House for about a mile.

Web: www.johansens.com/romneybayhouse
Tel: 01797 364747
Fax: 01797 367156

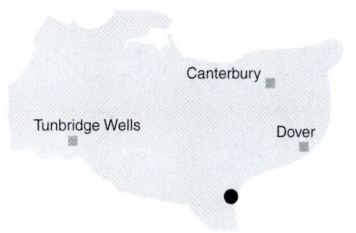

Price Guide:
single £65–£100
double £80–£150

Ye Horn's Inn

HORN'S LANE, GOOSNARGH, NR PRESTON, LANCASHIRE PR3 2FJ

A striking black-and-white timbered building standing at a crossroads in lovely rolling countryside, Ye Horn's radiates charm and atmosphere. Built in 1782 as a coaching inn, the hotel has been run by the Woods family for 40 years. Today it is expertly managed by Elizabeth Jones, her brother Mark Woods and his wife Denise, offering first-rate accommodation for both business visitors and the holiday-maker. The 6 spacious bedrooms, all en suite, are in the adjoining barn – a recent conversion – and are stylishly furnished. All offer tea and coffee-making facilities, trouser press and hairdryer. Oak beams, sumptuous carpets and in winter, open fires, combine to create a mood of cosy, relaxed hospitality throughout. The restaurant has earned a fine reputation for its delicious traditional cuisine, prepared wherever possible from fresh, local produce and served in the main dining room or the 'snug' next to it. Specialities include home-made soup, roast duckling, roast pheasant and a truly addictive sticky toffee pudding. Full English or Continental breakfasts are available. Chingle Hall, a haunted house, the Ribble Valley, the Forest of Bowland and Blackpool are all nearby.

Directions: Exit M6 Jct32, take A6 north to first traffic lights. Turn right onto B5269 signposted Longridge, to just past Goosnargh village shop. Where the road veers sharply right, continue straight ahead into Camforth Hall Lane: the hotel is signed after a few minutes.

Web: www.johansens.com/yehornsinn
E-mail: enquiries@yehornsinn.co.uk
Tel: 01772 865230
Fax: 01772 864299

Price Guide:
single £55–£60
double £70–£80

Our inspector loved: The cosy bars in this historic picturesque inn.

TREE TOPS COUNTRY HOUSE RESTAURANT & HOTEL

SOUTHPORT OLD ROAD, FORMBY, NR SOUTHPORT, LANCASHIRE L37 0AB

The Former Dower House of Formby Hall, Tree Tops, still retains the elegance of a bygone age, set in five acres of lawns and woods. Over the last 19 years, Lesley Winsland has restored the house to its true glory and has installed all the modern conveniences sought after by today's visitor. Spacious accommodation is available in well-appointed en suite lodges with all the facilities a discerning guest would expect. An outdoor-heated swimming pool has direct access to the sumptuously decorated Cocktail Lounge. Rich, dark leather seating, onyx-and-gilt tables and subtle lighting all contribute to the overall ambience, complemented by a truly welcoming and efficient staff. The restaurant and conservatory have been totally refurbished, cleverly incorporating some 21st-century ideas. A new menu offers a wonderful blend of traditional and modern, English and International cuisine. Table d'hôte, à la carte and lunchtime snacks are available, using only the freshest of local produce. Southport with its sweeping sands and famous Lord Street shopping centre is nearby. Ten golf courses including six championship courses are within a 5 mile radius.

Our inspector loved: The newly restyled restaurant with the modern International dining experience.

Directions: From M6 take M58 to Southport to end of motorway. Follow signs to Southport on A565. Bypass Formby on dual carriageway; as it changes to single carriageway, turn right at traffic lights to Tree Tops.

Web: www.johansens.com/treetopscountryhouse
Tel: 01704 572430
Fax: 01704 572430

Price Guide:
single £53–£75
double £90–£130

THE INN AT WHITEWELL

FOREST OF BOWLAND, CLITHEROE, LANCASHIRE BB7 3AT

Directions: From M6 take Jct32; follow A6 towards Garstang for ¼ mile. Turn right at first traffic lights towards Longridge, then left at roundabout; follow signs to Whitewell and Trough of Bowland.

Web: www.johansens.com/innatwhitewell
Tel: 01200 448222
Fax: 01200 448298

Price Guide:
single £63–£80
double £87–£110
suite £125

An art gallery and wine merchant all share the premises of this friendly, welcoming inn, the earliest parts of which date back to the 14th century. It was at one time inhabited by the Keeper of the 'Forêt' – the Royal hunting ground, and nowadays it is not uncommon for shooting parties to stay or drop in for lunch. Set within grounds of three acres, the inn has a splendid outlook across the dramatically undulating Trough of Bowland. All bedrooms, including the four new luxury rooms in the coach house, have been attractively furnished with antiques and quality fabrics. All have hi-tech stereo systems and most have video players. The high quality à la carte menu, created by head chef Jamie Cadman, features predominately English country recipes such as seasonal roast game, home-made puddings and farmhouse cheeses. Good bar meals and garden lunches are also offered. 8 miles of water is available to residents from the banks of the River Hodder, where brown trout, sea trout, salmon and grayling can be caught. Other sports can be arranged locally. Browsholme Hall and Clitheroe Castle are close by and across the river there are neolithic cave dwellings.

Our inspector loved: *The luxury antique baths and the wine shop in the reception.*

Abbots Oak

WARREN HILLS ROAD, NEAR COALVILLE, LEICESTERSHIRE LE67 4UY

This Grade II listed building is on the edge of Charnwood Forest, with 19 acres of gardens, woodland and unusual granite outcrops where guests can stroll or play croquet and tennis. Inside is the most spectacular carved oak panelling and stained glass – indeed the staircase goes to the top of the tower from where it is possible to look out over five counties. The house has four bedrooms available for the use of guests, three of which are en suite. There is a gorgeous drawing room and elegant dining room. Dinner is served en famille by candlelight. The menu is therefore not extensive and the wine list short but good. After dinner enjoy a game of snooker in the superb billiard room. Mid-week it is ideal for businessmen with meetings in Loughborough or Leicester. There is excellent golf nearby, and shooting can be arranged. Further afield are Stratford-upon-Avon, Warwick Castle and Rutland Water. Donington Park race circuit is 15 minutes away.

Our inspector loved: The lovely drawing room with its doors overlooking the gardens.

Directions: From the M1, take the A511 towards Coalville. At the first roundabout, take the 3rd exit to Loughborough. At the traffic lights, turn left. Abbots Oak is 1¼ miles opposite the Bulls Head pub. From the A42, take the A511 towards Coalville. At the 4th roundabout turn left and take the 2nd right, then right at T-junction. Abbots Oak is 50 yards on the right.

Web: www.johansens.com/abbotsoak
Tel: 01530 832 328
Fax: 01530 832 328

Price Guide:
single £50–£70
double £60–£90

THE OLD MANOR HOTEL

11-14 SPARROW HILL, LOUGHBOROUGH, LEICESTERSHIRE LE11 1BT

Overlooking the ancient churchyard of All Saints parish church at the heart of old Loughborough, the Old Manor Hotel is a treasure trove of history. It was rebuilt in the 1480s and later remodelled by Edward, First Lord Hastings of Loughborough, Lord Chamberlain to Queen Mary Tudor. Today it is a lovely hotel, full of interesting furnishings and superb fabrics. Alongside many antiques, some of the fine furniture has been beautifully made by the owner. The Old Manor has undergone many alterations and renovations over the centuries. Today it has all modern comforts but retains a number of original features. These include extensive exposed beams and timberwork. The décor is individual, rich and earthy throughout with an emphasis on comfort and an atmosphere of total friendliness. The Old Manor is an entirely non-smoking house. Although recently developed into a hotel the building has been a restaurant in the ownership of Roger Burdell for more than 16 years. His menus are thoughtfully planned. The food is simple but innovative with an Italian influenced style. Places of interest include Charnwood Forest, Donnington Park Motor Racing Circuit, Rutland Water, Nottingham Castle and the National Watersports Centre.

Directions: From A6 South. At traffic lights past Jarvis Hotel, (Kings Head), turn right onto Baxter Gate. At traffic lights past Beacon Bingo turn left onto Sparrow Hill. The Old Manor Hotel is the first main building on the right hand side.

Web: www.johansens.com/oldmanorloughborough
E-mail: bookings@oldmanor.com
Tel: 01509 211228
Fax: 01509 211128

Price Guide:
single £75–£97.50
double £95–£150

Our inspector loved: The individual style of the bedrooms and attention to detail.

Sutton Bonington Hall

MAIN STREET, SUTTON BONINGTON, LOUGHBOROUGH, LEICESTERSHIRE LE12 5PF

Large, green wrought-iron gates open onto a long drive which leads visitors through expansive landscaped gardens to this elegant, red brick hotel just four miles from the M1. Sutton Bonington Hall is of the Queen Anne period and abounds in character and charm. Despite renovations and refurbishment over the years, it retains many original features which combine gracefully with modern comforts. The emphasis is on country house style and homeliness with owners Henry and Ali Weldon offering a friendly welcome and attentive service. Guests may relax in three superb reception rooms, which include a large conservatory. In keeping with the Hall's history the bedrooms have retained their original names: Lady Elton's Room with a comfortable seating area, The Dressing Room, The Round Room and The Oriental Room all with four-poster beds, and The Garden Room with twin beds. The Attic, with twin beds, sink, but no bathroom, is ideal for children. Breakfast is served in an intimate dining room; dinner can be had by arrangement. Places of interest nearby include Charnwood Forest, Donington Park Motor Racing Circuit, Rutland Water, Nottingham Castle and Belvoir Castle.

Our inspector loved: *The beautiful gardens of this wonderful family home.*

Directions: Exit M1 at junction 24 and follow A6 towards Loughborough, Kegworth and then Sutton Bonington. Pass village church and the Hall is on your left.

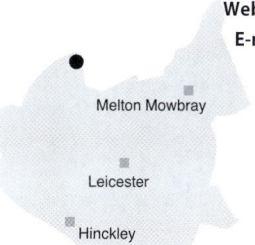

Web: www.johansens.com/suttonboningtonhall
E-mail: enquiries@sutton-bonington-hall.com
Tel: 01509 672355
Fax: 01509 674357

Price Guide:
single £80–£110
double £120–£150

BARNSDALE LODGE

THE AVENUE, RUTLAND WATER, NR OAKHAM, RUTLAND, LEICESTERSHIRE LE15 8AH

Situated in the ancient county of Rutland, amid unspoiled countryside, Barnsdale Lodge overlooks the rippling expanse of Rutland Water. After nine years, the expansion is finally complete and guests are invited to enjoy the hospitality offered by hosts The Hon. Thomas Noel and Robert Reid. A restored 17th century farmhouse, the atmosphere and style are distinctively Edwardian. This theme pervades throughout, from the courteous service to the furnishings, including chaises-longues and plush, upholstered chairs. The 45 en suite bedrooms, mostly on the ground floor, including two superb rooms specifically designed for disabled guests, evoke a mood of relaxing comfort. Traditional English cooking and fine wines are served. The chef makes all the pastries and cakes as well as preserves. Elevenses, buttery lunches, afternoon teas and suppers are enjoyed in the garden, conservatory, courtyard and à la carte dining rooms. There are 5 conference rooms and facilities for wedding receptions and parties. Interconnecting bedrooms, a baby-listening service and safe play area are provided for children. Robert Reid has strived to maintain the friendly intimacy of the lodge and is often on hand, offering advice and suggestions. Belvoir and Rockingham Castles are nearby. Rutland Water, a haven for nature lovers, offers several water sports. A Health Spa is planned for 2003.

Directions: The Lodge is on A606 Oakham–Stamford road.

Web: www.johansens.com/barnsdalelodge
E-mail: barnsdale.lodge@btconnect.com
Tel: 01572 724678
Fax: 01572 724961

Price Guide:
single £69
double/twin £89
junior suite £109.50

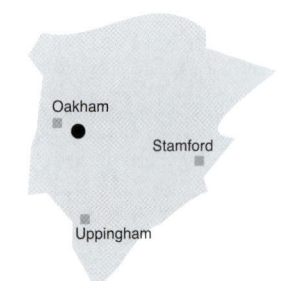

Our inspector loved: *This very popular country hotel has affected many waistlines with its homemade pastries and preserves....and that includes the inspector!*

THE LEA GATE INN

LEAGATE ROAD, CONINGSBY, LINCOLNSHIRE LN4 4RS

Possibly the oldest inn in Lincolnshire, the Lea Gate dates back to 1542. With an abundance of oak beams, inglenook fireplaces, and even a priest hole, it has lost none of its olde worlde charm and has a welcoming atmosphere with as many as five fires blazing on chilly days! The 8 light and spacious bedrooms have a refreshing, airy feel with attractive furnishings and elegant canopied beds, and there is one four-poster. All bathrooms – some with jacuzzi baths – are stylish and modern. Some of the bedrooms overlook the charming gardens which have been recently re-designed around a large Koi pool and waterfall, whilst the gardens still retain features from the past like the ancient Yew tree – said to be as old as the inn itself. The Lea Gate Inn has a reputation for its fine food, which guests may take in any of the bars or in the restaurant. A wide variety of traditional and continental dishes are availabe, including some "Lea Gate Specialities", and local Lincolnshire sausages. RAF Coningsby's Battle of Britain Flight Aircraft is within striking distance, as is the National Trust's Tattershall Castle and Lincoln Cathedral; or guests can explore the beautiful Lincolnshire wolds and local historic towns.

Our inspector loved: *The real comfort & character together with excellent bedrooms.*

Directions: From Lincoln take the A153 towards Horncastle and Skegness. At Coningsby take the B1192.

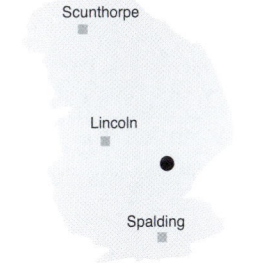

Web: www.johansens.com/leagateinn
E-mail: enquiries@theleagateinn.co.uk
Tel: 01526 342370
Fax: 01526 345468

Price Guide:
single £49.50
double £65–£90

WASHINGBOROUGH HALL

CHURCH HILL, WASHINGBOROUGH, LINCOLN LN4 1BE

Directions: From Lincoln City Centre, go down Broadgate (a dual carriage way) and over Pelham Bridge. At the lights take the B1188 towards Branston, take the first left down the B1190 to Washingborough. In Washingborough turn right at the mini roundabout along Church Hill. Washingborough Hall is on the left hand side.

Web: www.johansens.com/washingboroughhall
E-mail: washingborough.hall@btinternet.com
Tel: 01522 790340
Fax: 01522 792936

Price Guide:
single £65–£80
double £85–£99.50

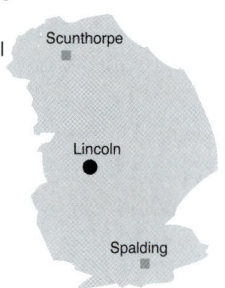

This 2 hundred year old listed Georgian Manor House is hidden amongst 4 acres of secluded grounds, containing many mature trees and colourful borders. During the summer months, its main lawns are an ideal place for relaxing with a drink or playing croquet, whilst in winter guests can recline in the lounge in front of a roaring fire cared for by the attentive and friendly staff. All 14 bedrooms are individually styled and furnished to a very high standard with en suite bathrooms, tea and coffee making facilities, hairdryer, trouser press and many other amenities. In contrast to its traditional façade and interior the Hotel has been modernised to cater for the requirements of the 21st century guest; a Computer Lounge with a high specification computer with complimentary Internet access and other software is available. Overlooking the gardens, the Wedgewood dining room offers the highest quality of fresh local produce, an extensive wine list and well-stocked bar. Places of interest nearby include the city of Lincoln with its magnificent 11th century cathedral and castle. Aircraft buffs should visit The Battle of Britain Memorial Flight and The Aviation Heritage Centre.

Our inspector loved: The peaceful village location, yet only about 3 miles from the historic city of Lincoln.

THE CROWN HOTEL

ALL SAINTS PLACE, STAMFORD, LINCOLNSHIRE PE9 2AG

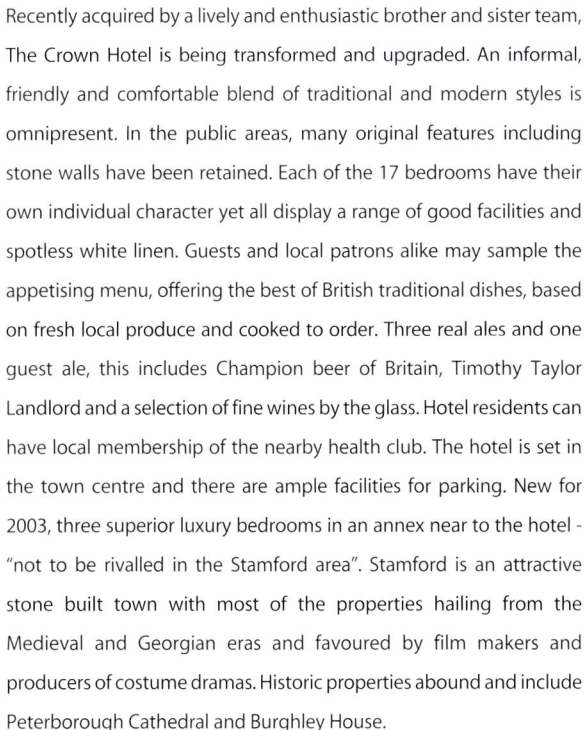

Recently acquired by a lively and enthusiastic brother and sister team, The Crown Hotel is being transformed and upgraded. An informal, friendly and comfortable blend of traditional and modern styles is omnipresent. In the public areas, many original features including stone walls have been retained. Each of the 17 bedrooms have their own individual character yet all display a range of good facilities and spotless white linen. Guests and local patrons alike may sample the appetising menu, offering the best of British traditional dishes, based on fresh local produce and cooked to order. Three real ales and one guest ale, this includes Champion beer of Britain, Timothy Taylor Landlord and a selection of fine wines by the glass. Hotel residents can have local membership of the nearby health club. The hotel is set in the town centre and there are ample facilities for parking. New for 2003, three superior luxury bedrooms in an annex near to the hotel - "not to be rivalled in the Stamford area". Stamford is an attractive stone built town with most of the properties hailing from the Medieval and Georgian eras and favoured by film makers and producers of costume dramas. Historic properties abound and include Peterborough Cathedral and Burghley House.

Our inspector loved: The entrance porch, which was decked with Hyacinths and fresh spring flowers.

Directions: The town is signed from the A1.

Web: www.johansens.com/crownstamford
E-mail: thecrownhotel@excite.com
Tel: 01780 763136
Fax: 01780 756111

Price Guide:
single £60
double £75–£95

OAK LODGE HOTEL
80 VILLAGE ROAD, BUSH HILL PARK, ENFIELD, MIDDLESEX EN1 2EU

Directions: From M25, exit at Jct25 onto A10 south. Turn right at 11th set of traffic lights signposted into Church Street, right again at next lights into Village Road. Oak Lodge is 200 yards on the right.

Web: www.johansens.com/oaklodge
E-mail: oaklodge@f.smail.net
Tel: 020 8360 7082

Price Guide:
single £79.50
double £94–£135

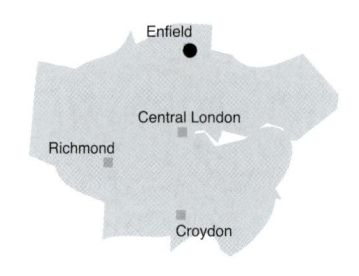

Oak Lodge is just nine miles from central London with excellent road and rail connections and conveniently placed for each of the capital's five airports. The small hotel, awarded an ETB 2 Star Silver Award, offers a warm welcome with charm and old-fashioned hospitality. Each en suite bedroom is individually and imaginatively furnished, and with all the facilities found in larger rooms. A superb new mini executive suite is now available. Traditional English cuisine complemented by an exceptionally good wine list is served in the intimate restaurant, three times an AA Rosette winner, which opens out onto a delightful evergreen garden. For after-dinner relaxation a pianist regularly entertains guests in a romantic Noel Coward style in the hotel's elegant lounge. Enfield has excellent shopping facilities and preserves the atmosphere of the country town it once was. There are many fine old houses, particularly in Gentlemen's Row, where the 19th-century author Charles Lamb lived. Other attractions include Forty Hall, built in 1632 for Sir Nicholas Raynton, Lord Mayor of London, now a cultural centre and museum, and the ruins of a Roman amphitheatre.

Our inspector loved: *The warm welcome and magnificent display of spring flowers.*

MERSYSIDE - BIRKENHEAD (OXTON)

NEW

THE BERESFORD
1 BERESFORD ROAD, OXTON, WIRRAL CH43 1XQ

Originally a Victorian ship owner's residence, with its own tower and surrounded by beautiful landscaped gardens, this magnificent Hotel is perfect for a relaxing stay. The tastefully refurbished character rooms are decorated in an elegant classical style in-keeping with the period of the building and have either large Queen Anne baroque or four poster beds. All the rooms have a wonderful spa bath to unwind in. Tony Dominguez and his staff will cater for your every need in the Hotel's excellent restaurant, which serves delectable traditional English and Continental cuisine. Guests will enjoy a nightcap in the extremely comfortable lounge. A qualified trainer will be delighted to set up a training programme in the fully-equipped techno-gym suite, which also has 2 squash courts, steam room and a sunbed. The Wirral area has a variety of things to offer from a Beatles tour in Liverpool to the hustle and bustle of Birkenhead with its ferries and historic warships, markets, galleries and museums. Wirral County Park has badgers, foxes and hedgerows alive with butterflies in the summer or the clay cliffs. Birdwatchers will delight in the peregrine falcons, which hunt along the coastal cliffs or the numerous migratory and wading birds in Hilbre Island Nature Reserve.

Our inspector loved: Tony Dominguez who looked after me during dinner.

Directions: From the M53, junction 3 towards Birkenhead turn left at the lights into Holm Lane. At the top of the hill turn left into Talbot Road, then right at lights into Gerald Rd, right into Shrewsbury Rd, 2nd left into Palm Grove. The Beresford is 400yards on the left, junction of Beresford Rd & Palm Grove.

Web: www.johansens.com/beresford
Tel: 0151 651 0004
Fax: 0151 652 4684

Price Guide:
single £75–£120
double/twin £90–£160
suite £160

THE WHITE HORSE

BRANCASTER STAITHE, NORFOLK PE31 8BW

Directions: The White Horse is situated on the A149 coast road between Hunstanton and Wells.

Web: www.johansens.com/whitehorsebrancaster
E-mail: reception@whitehorsebrancaster.co.uk
Tel: 01485 210262
Fax: 01485 210930

Price Guide:
single £48–£68
double £48–£96

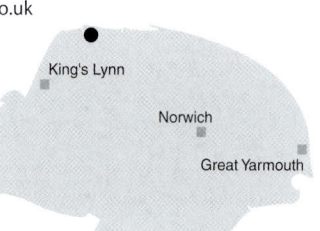

Commanding dramatic views of the Norfolk coast, this welcoming and hospitable Inn is an ideal base for sailors, walkers, birdwatchers and sea-lovers alike. Its friendly atmosphere is perfectly complemented by excellent service, good food and a charming seaside ambience. Newly refurbished, the interior with its scrubbed pine furniture and old sepia prints provides a glimpse of the pleasures to come. The spacious, airy bedrooms are originally and innovatively designed and located in total harmony with the landscape; each has its own patio with flowerbeds and tidal marsh view. New for 2003, seven en suite rooms in the main building, including 'the room at the top', a split-level accommodation with viewing balcony. Also, a new guest lounge and dining area adjoining the Conservatory restaurant all with stunning tidal marsh views. In fact, the award winning restaurant is gaining quite a reputation in the area for its imaginatively prepared food. With freshly caught mussels and oysters the seasonal speciality of the house. The grounds of The White Horse adjoin the Norfolk Coastal path and stunning tidal marsh which, with its many rare species of sea birds, is a paradise for ornithologists. Nearby, visitors will undoubtedly enjoy the horseracing at Fakenham, the Queen's country house at Sandringham, and Holkham Hall. Seasonal breaks available.

Our inspector loved: The clever architecture offering views to the sea.

VERE LODGE
SOUTH RAYNHAM, FAKENHAM, NORFOLK NR21 7HE

Quietly scattered among eight acres of grounds, Vere Lodge offers a selection of spacious, comfortable and well-equipped self-catering cottages that suit any sized family. Some cottages have open fireplaces and their own private garden areas, while all offer microwaves, dishwashers, fridges and electrical appliances. A great deal of care has gone into making the cottages as homely as possible, with pictures and floral arrangements adding thoughtful finishing touches. There is a superb indoor leisure centre with a large heated swimming pool, sauna, solarium and games room, while the peaceful surroundings are a paradise for children. Each morning everybody gathers on the lawn for the animals' breakfast time, offering the opportunity to feed tame rabbits, goats, donkeys and ponies, then throughout the day they can enjoy the toddlers' playground, croquet lawn, football area, tennis court and Enchanted Wood. Further afield the delightful, unspoilt landscape of Norfolk has much to offer with its beaches, innumerable castles and stately homes, bird and wildlife sanctuaries and racing at Fakenham. Upon return to Vere Lodge, the availability of home cooked frozen dishes takes the stress out of the evening meal. Short breaks available.

Our inspector loved: *That this a home from home with an excellent indoor leisure centre.*

Directions: From Swaffham take A1065 towards Fakenham. After 11 miles enter South Raynham. 100 yards past village sign turn left and continue 400 yards.

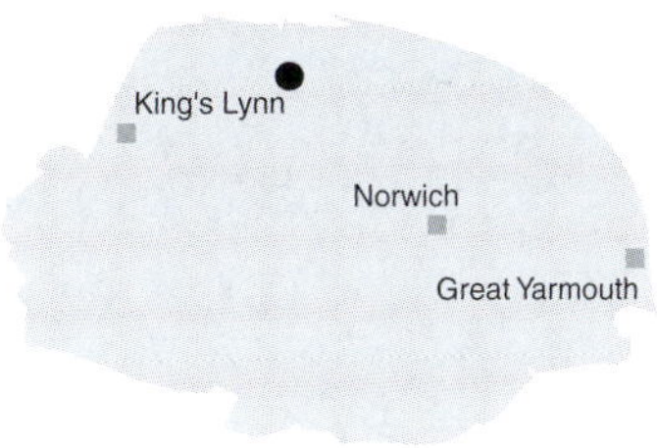

Web: www.johansens.com/verelodge
E-mail: major@verelodge.co.uk
Tel: 01328 838261
Fax: 01328 838300

Price Guide: (excluding VAT) £273–£1209 per week.

THE MANOR HOUSE

BARSHAM ROAD, GREAT SNORING, NORFOLK NR21 0HP

Directions: Great Snoring is three miles north-east of Fakenham from A148. The Manor House is on the Barsham Road, behind the church.

Web: www.johansens.com/manorgreatsnoring
E-mail: gtsnoringmanorho@aol.com
Tel: 01328 820597
Fax: 01328 820048

Price Guide:
house rate from £850 per night

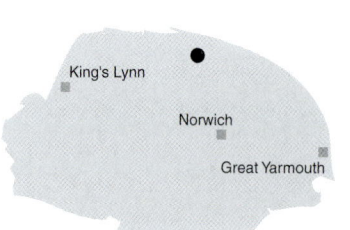

Exclusively yours for up to sixteen guests, the Manor House is an ideal venue to join with friends, family or colleagues whatever the occasion, for one night or longer. Relaxed informality and friendly, personal service are the ideals behind this gracious country house, which has welcomed guests since 1978, and which allows you to get away from the stresses of modern life, yet offers high modern standards. The Manor House nestles behind the village church, standing in 1.5 acres of mature gardens amidst the unspoilt countryside of North Norfolk, only 15 minutes from the Heritage coast, Burnham Market and Holt. The magnificent architecture of this Grade II* listed building provides an impressive sense of history. The dining room is a wonderful example with its heavy oak beams and original stone mullion windows. Norfolk is a haven for wildlife and rare birds on the marshes and inland waterways; it boasts the most beautiful skyscapes and bright starry nights across the villages and beaches, and it harbours a wealth of history in a plethora of hidden houses, mansions, halls and churches. Golf, sailing and horse riding also feature highly on the agenda. Facilities for small conferences are available.

Our inspector loved: *The chance to live like The Lord of the Manor, whether it be a celebration or business.*

CALDECOTT HALL
FRITTON, GREAT YARMOUTH, NORFOLK NR31 9EY

Caldecott Hall stands in the heart of a beautiful 400-acre country estate, surrounded by manicured lawns and varicoloured flower and shrub beds. Views from its sparkling, white-framed, Georgian-style windows sweep from historic Viking burial grounds to the woodland of Waveney Forest. From the moment visitors enter the attractively decorated reception hall with its splendid tartan carpeting they experience the welcoming atmosphere that is the hallmark of Judith Collen's proprietorship. The eight luxury en suite bedrooms have been individually styled from what was formally a Victorian country residence. Each is equipped to a high standard, and most have panoramic views. The Caldecott Suite boasts an Italian style four-poster bed and Jacuzzi bathroom. Guests can enjoy delightful cuisine in an elegant restaurant or more informal meals in a relaxing bar lounge which is warmed by an open fire during colder months. For golf enthusiasts there is an excellent 18-hole golf course, a challenging 9 hole Par 3 course and a 20-bay floodlit driving range in the grounds supported by a resident PGA professional, Pro Shop and clubhouse. The estate is also home to the Redwings Horse Sanctuary. Historic Norwich, Beccles, Bungay and Southwold are within easy reach and the beaches of Great Yarmouth are just four miles away.

Directions: From A12 take A143 towards Beccles.

Web: www.johansens.com/caldecotthall
E-mail: caldecotthall@supanet.com
Tel: 01493 488488
Fax: 01493 488553

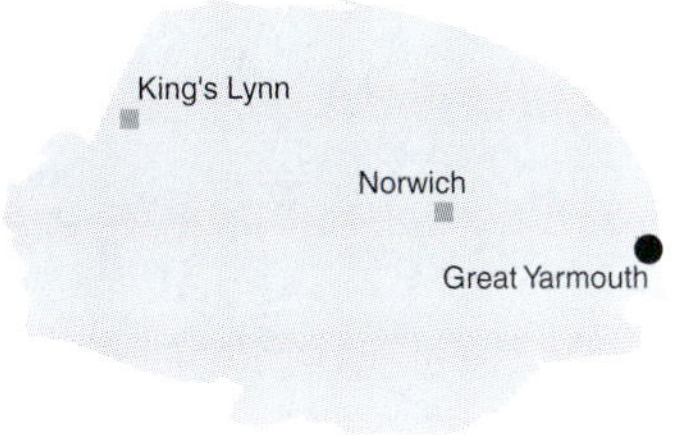

Price Guide:
double/twin £70–£95

Our inspector loved: *The peaceful views.*

NORFOLK - HARLESTON

NEW

J.D. Young

2-4 MARKET PLACE, HARLESTON, NORFOLK IP20 9AD

Directions: From the A14 at Bury St Edmunds, take the A143 signposted Great Yarmouth. The Hotel is approximately 7 miles from Diss.

Web: www.johansens.com/jdjoung
E-mail: info@jdyoung.co.uk
Tel: 01379 852822
Fax: 01379 855370

Price Guide:
single £55
double/twin £60–£90

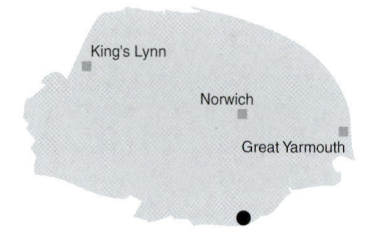

Centrally located on the Market Square, J.D. Young is steeped in history and retains all of its original character. The superb refurbishment of this 16th century Hotel has created an excellent combination of traditional ambience with stylish and comfortable furnishings to suit the modern guest. Oak-panelled and richly wallpapered walls highlight the beauty of the colourful oil paintings and unique design of the Hotel's décor. Uncluttered, peaceful bedrooms have light, relaxing colour schemes, natural wood, hand-finished furniture and freshly styled bathrooms. Many famous historic characters such as Winston Churchill and the artist, Sir Alfred Munnings (who paid many of his bills by donating a painting) have enjoyed the Hotel's hospitality. The spacious bar, which has a wonderful open fire in the winter, is still a favourite with the locals and serves local real ale and tantalizing cocktails for the more adventurous. A delightful lounge and bar area is placed at one end of the dining room and offers a tempting à la carte menu. Harleston, which is mentioned in the Doomsday Book, is an interesting town full of historic buildings, riddled with alleys and passages; there is a market every Wednesday. There are numerous fishing lakes, a golf course and many pleasant walks in the area, such as Angles Way to be enjoyed.

Our inspector loved: *The rich yet mellow colours of the contemporary furnishings complementing the magnificent traditional oil paintings.*

THE VICTORIA AT HOLKHAM

PARK ROAD, HOLKHAM, WELLS-NEXT-THE-SEA, NORFOLK NR23 1RG

Owned by the Earl of Leicester and part of the beautiful Holkham Estate, the Victoria at Holkham has been totally refurbished with eye-catching and original décor. Fascinating, beautifully crafted furniture, hand painted murals, accessories and fabrics from the East (an amusing slant on the Victoria and Empire theme) adorn the spacious public areas, which are light and airy with stunning views stretching over the countryside to the sea. A romantic touch is provided by an abundance of fresh flowers and candles whilst the warm, exotic and plush atmosphere is enhanced by an open fire on colder days. Luxurious bedrooms are individually decorated to original themes, and dramatic bathrooms make use of natural materials such as slate. The traditional Tap Bar is perfect for a relaxing drink, and the restaurant, overlooking the terrace and landscaped gardens with a safe play area for children, has gained a reputation for its fine fish and game specialities made from fresh local and seasonal ingredients. The beautiful beach of Holkham is within walking distance, and places of interest include the Bygones Museum, bird sanctuaries, gift shops and potters, horse racing at Fakenham, Holkham Hall, Sandringham, Blickling Hall and Walsingham. Seasonal breaks available.

Our inspector loved: *That the entire decor is based on furniture, fabrics & objects from the exotic east.*

Directions: The hotel is situated on A149 between Hunstanton and Cromer.

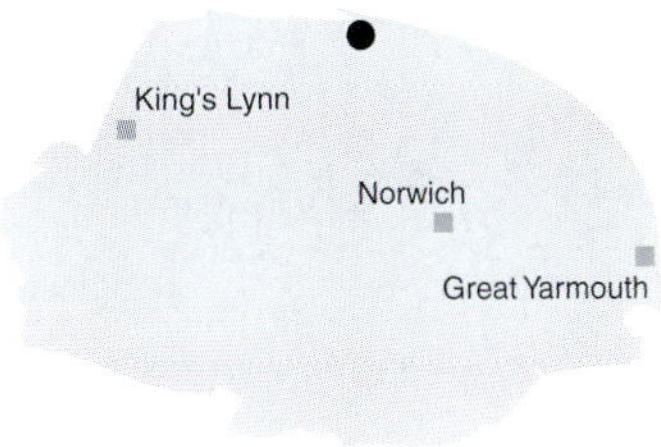

Web: www.johansens.com/victoriaholkham
E-mail: victoria@holkham.co.uk
Tel: 01328 711008
Fax: 01328 711009

Price Guide:
single £80–£105
double/twin £100–£130

THE ROMAN CAMP INN

HOLT ROAD, AYLMERTON, NORWICH, NORFOLK NR11 8QD

Directions: The inn is on the A148, midway between Holt and Cromer

Web: www.johansens.com/romancampinn
E-mail: romancamp@lineone.net
Tel: 01263 838291
Fax: 01263 837071

Price Guide:
single £52
double/twin £80-£88.

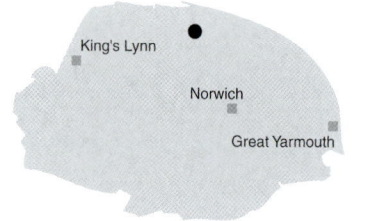

This inn, situated between Sheringham and Cromer close to Norfolk's highest point, Beacon Hill, is steeped in history. Beyond its attractive garden there is a wide expanse of sea, miles of coast, heather and bracken, farms, fields, marshes and medieval churches. The atmosphere is that of a fine old-fashioned rural inn. There is original leaded glass, Latin inscriptions, a restaurant with panoramic countryside views and a ground floor lounge, lovely pictures and sculptures. In the original part of the house, which was built in 1900, the bedrooms are individually styled and some have spa baths. Those in a newer part have a more standardised but equally comfortable style. All are en suite, quiet and have every modern comfort; some overlook the garden and two have been designed for the convenience of disabled visitors. Superb cuisine is served in the stylish conservatory. In summer, drinks and bar food can be enjoyed on the patio or in one of the garden houses. A short drive away are Wolterton Hall, Norwich, Mannington Hall, Blickling Hall with its interesting furniture and gardens, and the National Trust's Felbrigg Estate with walled garden, lake, woods and 17th century hall. Also worth visiting are the Blakeney and Cley marshes and the Norfolk Shire Horse Centre. Special breaks available.

Our inspector loved: The panoramic views from the first floor restaurant.

Felbrigg Lodge

AYLMERTON, NORTH NORFOLK NR11 8RA

Jill and Ian Gillam have created this charming Lodge with the aim of providing the highest possible standards of accommodation in North Norfolk in a setting of total quiet and relaxation. Evoking an informal and welcoming ambience, the Lodge provides complete freedom for guests to mix with others or to seek solitude. Here time has stood still. Nothing disturbs over 50 different species of birds and other wildlife amongst rolling lawns and specimen trees and shrubs. Felbrigg Lodge enjoys an unrivalled position just outside the Felbrigg Hall estate, a 17th century house owned by the National Trust. Approached by a long drive, the eight acres of grounds are totally secluded. The rooms, which are all at ground level, are situated around the gardens to take the greatest advantage of the view and landscape. All are sumptuously decorated with flair and imagination and have luxurious en suite bathrooms. Full English breakfasts and candlelit dinners are served in the converted stables. Jill is an enthusiastic cook and uses the best local produce. Guests may relax in the privacy of their own rooms, wander at leisure through the gardens, play croquet, take afternoon tea in the summer house or swim in the heated indoor pool. A small, well-equipped gym is provided for the more energetic.

Our inspector loved: *The comfort and careful attention to detail of the bedrooms and location in the garden.*

Directions: Please ring the Lodge for detailed directions and brochure.

Web: www.johansens.com/felbrigglodge
E-mail: info@felbrigglodge.co.uk
Tel: 01263 837588
Fax: 01263 838012

Price Guide:
single from £82
double £110
suite £140

PETERSFIELD HOUSE HOTEL

LOWER STREET, HORNING, NR NORWICH, NORFOLK NR12 8PF

Directions: From Norwich ring road, take A1151 to Wroxham. Cross bridge, turn right at Hoveton on A1062 to Horning; hotel is beyond centre of the village

Web: www.johansens.com/petersfieldhouse
E-mail: reception@petersfieldhotel.co.uk
Tel: 01692 630741
Fax: 01692 630745

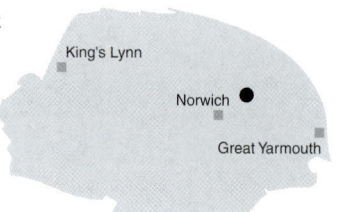

Price Guide:
single from £60
double from £80

Petersfield House Hotel is set back from one of the most attractive reaches of the River Bure in the area known as the Norfolk Broads. The original property was built in the twenties on a prime site as a large private residence in two acres of gardens with its own moorings on a grassy bank of the river. Today it is a secluded family run hotel whose reputation is based on traditional comfort and hospitality. Guests can be sure of receiving personal attention at all times. The bedrooms are bright and welcoming – most rooms overlook the well-kept landscaped gardens which feature an ornamental pond, a putting green and a flintstone moon gate. Varied fixed-price and extensive à la carte menus are served in the restaurant where a list of over 60 wines provides an ideal accompaniment. Regular Saturday night dinner-dances are held with the hotel occupying one of the choicest positions on the Norfolk Broads. Sailing is the popular local pastime and open regattas are held during the summer. Golf is within easy driving distance. Other local attractions include Norwich with its famous art gallery and "Ten Ancient Monuments" and Blickling Hall with its interesting furniture and gardens.

Our inspector loved: *The location in a pretty village on the side of the Norfolk Broads.*

Congham Hall

GRIMSTON, KING'S LYNN, NORFOLK PE32 1AH

Dating from the mid-18th century, this stately Manor House is set in acres of parkland, orchards and gardens. The conversion from country house to luxury hotel in 1982 was executed with care to enhance the elegance of the classic interiors. The hotel's renowned herb garden grows over 700 varieties of herb, many are used by the chef to create modern English dishes with the accent on fresh local produce and fish from the local Norfolk markets. The hotel's hives even produce the honey for your breakfast table. The beautiful flower displays, home-made pot pourri and roaring log fires blend together to create a welcoming and relaxing atmosphere. Congham Hall is the ideal base from which to tour the spectacular beaches of the north Norfolk coastline, Sandringham, Burnham Market and Holkham Hall.

Our inspector loved: *The wonderful herb garden.*

Directions: Go to the A149/A148 interchange northeast of King's Lynn. Follow the A148 towards Sandringham/Fakenham/Cromer for 100 yards. Turn right to Grimston. The hotel is then 2 miles on the left.

Web: www.johansens.com/conghamhall
E-mail: reception@conghamhallhotel.co.uk
Tel: 01485 600250
Fax: 01485 601191

Price Guide:
single from £99
double/twin from £150
suites from £230

The Great Escape Holiday Company

DOCKING, KINGS LYNN, NORFOLK PE31 8LY

Directions: All properties are within easy reach of A149 coast road.

Web: www.johansens.com/greatescape
E-mail: bookings@thegreatescapeholiday.co.uk
Tel: 01485 518717
Fax: 01485 518937

Price Guide:
From £295–£5950

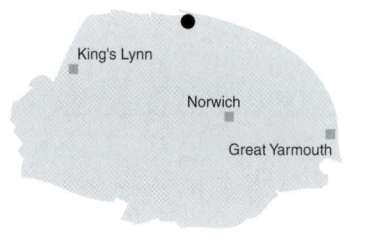

The north-west Norfolk coast, sweeping towards the Wash consists mainly of a long stretch of sand and low cliffs, exposed saltings and tidal inlets. There are picturesque little harbours and villages, an abundance of birdlife and marshland stretching from King's Lynn westwards into Lincolnshire. It is a place of peace where one can believe that time stands still. Scattered along the coastline are a variety of unique and charming Great Escape holiday homes, all of which can help the visitor unwind from the pressures of everyday life. There are grand country houses, particularly attractive for corporate gatherings, charming and secluded little cottages, fascinating period houses and airy barn conversions. Some have large gardens leading down to the marshes, and boats are available for use. Others have a sunny patio, a studio or stables waiting for riding guests. The common denominator is the quality and style of décor, furnishings and service. After a personal welcome guests are provided with wine and the ingredients for a simple meal. White bed and bath linen together with first-class maid service ensure a perfect home-from-home environment. Daily staffing can be arranged. Ready to serve meal service and wine delivery. Short breaks available.

Our inspector loved: *The personal service which is superb.*

Beechwood Hotel
CROMER ROAD, NORTH WALSHAM, NORFOLK NR28 0HD

The combination of an elegant, spacious, ivy-clad house, surrounded by well laid-out gardens, dating back to 1800, with a lovely ambience generated by the proprietors' warm welcome and the attentive staff has created a very special country house hotel in East Anglia. For many years residents in North Walsham knew it as the doctors' house, during these years it had an enviable society guest list headed by Agatha Christie, who was a regular visitor over a thirty year period and the Sheikh of Iraq. The bedrooms are delightful, with big windows, individually decorated and filled with traditional and antique furniture. The comfortable drawing room is well supplied with books and magazines and residents enjoy the lounge/bar. The atmosphere in the 2 AA rosette restaurant reflects the contentment of diners appreciating a menu that includes classic English dishes and the Head Chef's Steven Norgate personal suggestions, incorporating the excellent local produce available, together with fine wines, many from the New World, selected by the owners. Holder of 2 AA Red Stars, a English Tourist Council Gold Award and winner of the 1999 Johansens Most Excellent Value for Money Award.

Our inspector loved: *The wonderful hospitality and lovely interiors including the new Lounge/Bar.*

Directions: Leave Norwich on B1150, driving 13 miles to North Walsham. Pass under the railway bridge, then left at the first traffic lights and right at the next set, finding the hotel 150m on the left.

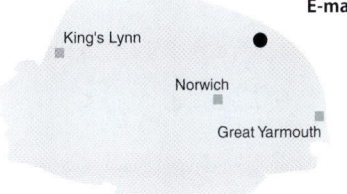

Web: www.johansens.com/beechwood
E-mail: enquiries@beechwood-hotel.co.uk
Tel: 01692 403231
Fax: 01692 407284

Price Guide:
single £65–£90
double £90–£150

Elderton Lodge Hotel & Langtry Restaurant

GUNTON PARK, THORPE MARKET, NR NORTH WALSHAM, NORFOLK NR11 8TZ

Quietly grazing red deer, proudly strutting pheasants and cooing wood pigeons provide memorable awakening viewing to guests gazing from their bedroom windows over the vast and tranquil Gunton Park that is the scene of this 18th century, Grade II listed hotel. Standing in the heart of unspoiled countryside yet only four miles from the coast, the impressive Elderton Lodge Hotel & Langtry Restaurant, with its own six acres of mature gardens, was once the Shooting Lodge and Dower House to Gunton Hall Estate. Gunton Hall, home of the Barons of Suffield, was a favoured retreat for Lillie Langtry, the celebrated Victorian beauty, who according to legend entertained Edward VII here when he was Prince of Wales. Bedrooms are attractive and comfortable, the bar informal and welcoming and the excellent cuisine featuring local game and seafood specialities – fit for a King, not only the Prince of Wales. This is an ideal venue for civil weddings and dinner parties. The cathedral city of Norwich, National Trust properties including Blickling Hall, Felbrigg Hall, Sheringham Park and the Heritage Coast and Norfolk Broads National Park are nearby.

Directions: Leave Norwich on A1151. Join A149 towards Cromer and the hotel is on the left prior to entering Thorpe Market.

Web: www.johansens.com/eldertonlodge
E-mail: enquiries@eldertonlodge.co.uk
Tel: 01263 833547
Fax: 01263 834673

Price Guide:
single £50–£70
double £80–£115

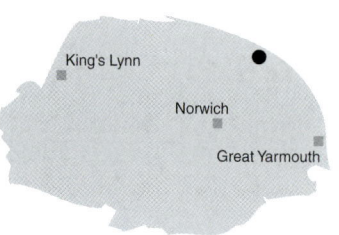

Our inspector loved: *The red deer, which really are an inspirational sight.*

The Beeches Hotel And Victorian Gardens

2–6 EARLHAM ROAD, NORWICH, NORFOLK NR2 3DB

With three acres of English Heritage Victorian Gardens, this hotel offers a warm welcome and an exceptionally high standard of comfort in a relaxed and informal atmosphere. The 3 separate Grade II listed Victorian mansions have been beautifully restored, extended and attractively decorated and are collectively known as the Beeches. When the houses were built in the mid-1800s, an idyllic Italianate garden was created in the deep hollow it overlooks. In 1980, this 'secret' garden, now known as The Plantation Garden, was rediscovered. It is being restored to its former glory and guests are free to wander through this enchanting and extraordinary reminder of our Victorian heritage with its ornate Gothic fountain and amazing terraces. All bedrooms feature charming individual décor, separate modern facilities and are non smoking. A varied selection of tempting dishes, which have won an AA Rosette for their quality, daily table d'hôte and seasonal à la carte is cooked to order and served in the airy Restaurant overlooking a delightful patio garden. Residents and diners can enjoy pre-dinner drinks in the comfortable lounge bar. The Norfolk coast and Broads are within easy reach.

Our inspector loved: *The welcoming family & staff and the beautiful gardens.*

Directions: From the A11 take the ring road west, turn onto the B1108 (Earlham Road) to city centre. The hotel is next to Roman Catholic cathedral.

Web: www.johansens.com/beechesnorwich
E-mail: reception@beeches.co.uk
Tel: 01603 621167
Fax: 01603 620151

Price Guide:
single £59–£79
double £76–£94

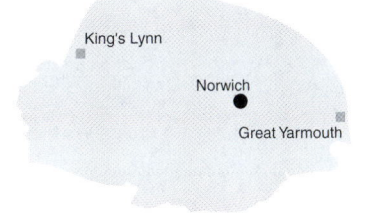

THE NORFOLK MEAD HOTEL

COLTISHALL, NORWICH, NORFOLK NR12 7DN

Directions: On reaching Norwich take outer ring road to B1150 signposted North Walsham. After Horstead/Coltishall bridge, bear right on the B1354, signposted Wroxham. Entrance signposted on right just before church.

Web: www.johansens.com/norfolkmead
E-mail: info@norfolkmead.co.uk
Tel: 01603 737531
Fax: 01603 737521

Price Guide:
single £70–£90
double £85–£140

This elegant Georgian manor house, dating back to 1740, sits on a quiet edge of the Norfolk Broads, standing in 12 acres of lovely gardens and rolling lawns which sweep down to the River Bure. Guests can stroll down to the water to catch a glimpse of a kingfisher or heron and enjoy the variety of birdlife. The owners Don and Jill Fleming have added a host of personal touches to create a homely atmosphere, the fragrance of fresh flowers pervades the hotel. The delightful restaurant, overlooking the gardens and the river, offers a constantly changing menu thoughtfully selected by the chef to utilise the abundance of local produce, which includes fish caught off the Norfolk coast, game from the local estates, vegetables and herbs from the gardens. An extensive wine list has been carefully selected. Relax with a drink before dinner in the bar, where a log fire burns in winter and French windows open onto the old walled garden in the summer. Sport facilities include a well-stocked fishing lake, off-river mooring and a 60ft pool. Situated only 7 miles from the centre of Norwich and 12 miles from the coast, the Norfolk Mead is well-situated for both business and leisure.

Our inspector loved: The airy, romantic decor of the bedrooms.

THE STOWER GRANGE
SCHOOL ROAD, DRAYTON, NORFOLK NR8 6EF

The Stower Grange, built of mellow Norfolk bricks under Dutch pantiles, dates back to the 17th century. In former times it was a gracious rectory. Today it offers travellers a peaceful retreat – the gardens have fine lawns with inviting shade provided by the mature trees – yet the property is only $4\frac{1}{2}$ miles from the commercial and historic centre of Norwich. Stower is owned by Richard and Jane Fannon; the atmosphere is friendly and informal. In cooler months open fires add to the welcome. There are eight spacious individually-decorated bedrooms with en suite facilities, including two with a pine four-poster bed for those in a romantic mood. The Blue Restaurant, locally renowned as a 'special place' to dine, and looks directly on to the gardens. The imaginative cooking of Chef Mark Smith ensures good eating from the individually priced menus. The restaurant closes on Sunday evenings, however, residents can enjoy a steak and salad in the Lounge Bar. Places of interest nearby include Norwich, Norfolk Broads, various historic houses including Sandringham, the Norfolk Coast and horseracing at Fakenham. Seasonal breaks are available.

Our inspector loved: *That it is so easy to reach the town centre for business, tourism and shopping.*

Directions: From A11, turn left on to inner ring road and proceed to the ASDA junction with A1067 Norwich–Fakenham Road. Approximately 2 miles to Drayton turn right at the Red Lion public house. After 80 yards bear left. The Stower Grange is on the right.

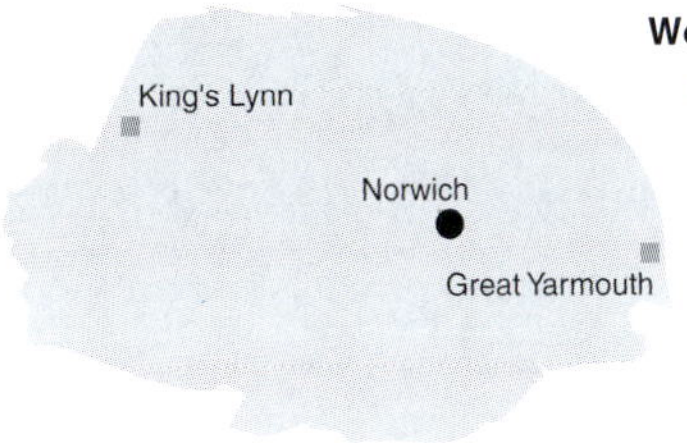

Web: www.johansens.com/stowergrange
E-mail: enquiries@stowergrange.co.uk
Tel: 01603 860210
Fax: 01603 860464

Price Guide:
single £65
double £85
four-poster £120

The Old Rectory

103 YARMOUTH ROAD, NORWICH, NORFOLK NR7 0HF

Chris and Sally Entwistle extend a warm and hospitable welcome and the promise of fine personal service to guests at the Old Rectory. Dating back to 1754, their delightful Grade II listed Georgian home, clad with Wisteria and Virginia Creeper, stands in an acre of mature gardens on the outskirts of Norwich overlooking the River Yare. The spacious and well-furnished bedrooms, both in the hotel and the adjacent Coach House, offer quality, comfort and style. After a busy day, guests may unwind over a pre-dinner drink in the elegant Drawing Room, enhanced by a roaring log fire during the winter and choose from a prix-fixe menu. The tempting AA rosette awarded dishes are changed daily and are freshly prepared to order. The Wellingtonia Room and the Conservatory, overlooking the sun terrace and gardens, are excellent venues for business meetings and private luncheons or dinners. The Old Rectory is an ideal base from which to explore the historic city of Norwich, the Norfolk Broads, the beautiful Broadlands countryside and the Norfolk Coast.

Our inspector loved: *The friendly hospitality from Chris & Sally and the very comfortable accommodation.*

Directions: Follow the A47 Norwich bypass towards Great Yarmouth. Take the A1042 exit and follow the road into Thorpe St Andrew. Bear left onto the A1242 and the hotel is approximately 50 yards on the right after the first set of traffic lights.

Web: www.johansens.com/oldrectorynorwich
E-mail: enquiries@oldrectorynorwich.com
Tel: 01603 700772
Fax: 01603 300772

Price Guide:
single £66–£76
double £85–£100

NORFOLK - OVINGTON (SWAFFHAM)

NEW

BROVEY LAIR

CARBROOKE ROAD, OVINGTON, THETFORD, NORFOLK IP25 6SD

Situated in the picturesque, largely undiscovered Breckland countryside of rural Norfolk, Beverly Hills meets the Pacific Rim in this modern and luxurious location. Belonging more to Sunset Boulevard than Carbrooke Road, Brovey Lair is informal and fun with bright, spacious rooms and a refreshingly homely atmosphere. Its minimalist décor and superbly designed interior complement the elegant furnishings. The conservatory style restaurant, called The Café at Brovey Lair, is considered to be one of the best in Norfolk. Seated at a glass bar surrounding the open plan kitchen guests can chat to chef-patron, Tina Pemberton, while they watch her create a fusion of gastronomic tastes by combining the spiciness of the Orient and Caribbean with flavours of the Mediterranean. Guests can even help design their meal by phone when booking a table. Overlooking stunning views of lawns, fishponds and a backdrop of trees floodlit by night, are two terraced rooms with super-king beds and state-of-the-art bathrooms. Understated décor and subtle colour-coordination create a relaxing haven of peace and tranquillity. Away-day meetings of up to 16 delegates can be arranged. Norwich, Sandringham, the Broads, Thetford Forest and Norfolk's spectacular Heritage coastline are all less than an hour away from Brovey Lair, described locally as a "little piece of paradise".

Our inspector loved: The unusual entrance lobby with its fabulous water feature and eye-catching paintings.

Directions: Allowing 2 hours from north London take the M11 to jnc.9 then A11 towards Norwich. Just north of Thetford turn left onto the A1075 towards Watton. Ovington is a right turn ½ mile north of Watton. (a detailed map is on the web site).

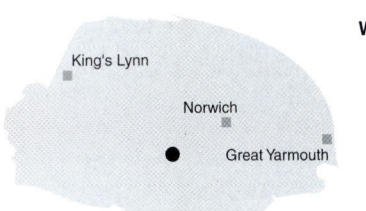

Web: www.johansens.com/broveylair
E-mail: bookings@broveylair.co.uk
Tel: 01953 882706
Fax: 01953 885365

Price Guide:
double £110

151

Broom Hall Country Hotel

RICHMOND ROAD, SAHAM TONEY, THETFORD, NORFOLK IP25 7EX

Directions: Half mile north of Watton on B1077 towards Swaffham.

Web: www.johansens.com/broomhall
E-mail: enquiries@broomhallhotel.co.uk
Tel: 01953 882125
Fax: 01953 882125

Price Guide:
single £58;
double £85–£145

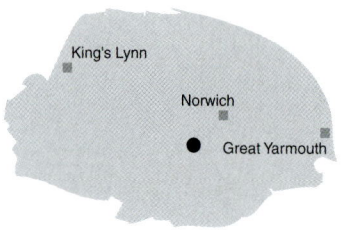

Situated in 15 acres of mature gardens and parkland Broom Hall is a charming Victorian country house offering peace and tranquillity. Airy and spacious bedrooms each individually furnished and most offering lovely views provide guests with both comfort and a range of modern amenities. A feature of the public rooms are the ornate ceilings and in the lounge a large open fire can be enjoyed in the winter months. An indoor heated swimming pool is available for guests' use. Fresh vegetables, from Broom Hall's own garden when in season, and many old fashioned desserts ensure that dinner, overseen by head chef Steven Wright, in the dining room overlooking the garden is an enjoyable occasion. Small conferences can be arranged and the entire house can be 'taken over' for your family reunion or celebration. Seasonable breaks are available. Places of interest nearby include Norwich, Cambridge, Ely and Bury St Edmunds. Sandringham and many National Trust properties, Thetford Forest, Norfolk Broads and coastline offering nature reserves and bird sanctuaries are also within easy reach.

Our inspector loved: *The fragrant gardens.*

THE WINDMILL AT BADBY

MAIN STREET, BADBY, DAVENTRY, NORTHAMPTONSHIRE NN11 6AN

The Windmill Inn Hotel was first established as an inn in the 17th century and is situated in the heart of the pretty village of Badby. A traditional thatched country pub, complete with log fires, The Windmill offers good food and a range of cask-conditioned ales. The owners, with their extensive experience of hotel and pub management, have plenty of ideas for regular activities. Winter Sportsmen's Dinners and theme nights with entertainment are popular events. The en suite bedrooms provide comfortable accommodation and the whole hotel is ideally suitable for house party weekends from 12–14 guests. Under the skilled eye of Gavin Baxter the award-winning kitchen prepares a varied range of freshly cooked dishes. The sumptuous menu includes a delicious traditional Sunday Luncheon, which offers excellent value for money. Stilton mushrooms, chargrilled Cajun chicken, steak and kidney pie and poached salmon with new potatoes are amongst the many highly recommended specialities. Weddings, functions and business meetings and conferences are catered for with ease. Places to visit include Althorp, Sulgrave Manor (home of the Washingtons), Bleinheim Palace, Silverstone Circuit, Warwick and Stratford-upon-Avon.

Directions: Situated in the centre of Badby, a village located off the A361, three miles south of Daventry on the Banbury road.

Web: www.johansens.com/windmillatbadby
E-mail: user@windmillinn.fsnet.co.uk
Tel: 01327 702363
Fax: 01327 311521

Price Guide:
single £55
double £65–£79

Our inspector loved: The ambience of the locals bar.

THE FALCON HOTEL

CASTLE ASHBY, NORTHAMPTONSHIRE NN7 1LF

Directions: Exit M1 junction 14 northbound or 15 southbound. Follow the signs to A428 where Castle Ashby and The Falcon are clearly signposted, six miles south-east of Northampton.

Web: www.johansens.com/falcon
Tel: 01604 696200
Fax: 01604 696673

Price Guide:
single from £87.50
double/twin from £105

Six miles south of Northampton, in the heart of the Marquess of Northampton's estate, The Falcon is a delightful country cottage hotel, secluded and tranquil, minutes away from the rambling acres of Castle Ashby House. The owners have invested energy and enthusiasm into transforming this once modest place into a haven of comfort, excellent food and attentive service. Bedrooms are beautifully furnished, cosy cottage style and the bathrooms have been recently upgraded. Lunch and dinner, which are created where possible from seasonal, home-grown produce, are served in the intimate restaurant which overlooks a lawn with willow trees. The excellent value-for-money cuisine, modern English in flavour, is prepared by chef Harvey Jones. A fixed-price menu costs £23.95, including coffee and petits fours. There is also an interesting à la carte selection. The extensive wine list can be studied by guests at their leisure over preprandial drinks by a glowing log fire. Walk in the grounds of Castle Ashby estate. Further afield, visit Woburn, Althorp, Silverstone, Bedford and Stratford.

Our inspector loved: *Walking round Micheal's vegetable and flower garden.*

WAREN HOUSE HOTEL
WAREN MILL, BAMBURGH, NORTHUMBERLAND NE70 7EE

"To visit the North East and not to stay here, would be foolish indeed". So says one entry in a visitors book that is filled with generous and justified praise for this delightful traditional country house which lives up to all its promises and expectations and beyond. The hotel is set in six acres of gardens and woodland on the edge of Budle Bay Bird Sanctuary overlooking Holy Island and two miles from the majestic Bamburgh Castle. The owners, Anita and Peter, do not cater for children under 14, so they are able to offer a rare commodity of peace and tranquillity even during the busy summer months. Throughout the hotel, the antique furnishings and the immaculate and well-chosen décor evoke a warm, friendly and charming ambience. Seated in the candlelit dining room, surrounded by family pictures and portraits, guests can select dishes from the daily changing menu and wines from over 250 bins. There is a boardroom for executive meetings. Dogs by prior arrangement. Special short breaks available all year. The Farne Islands are just a boat trip away; Bamburgh, Alnwick and Dunstanburgh Castles and Holy Island are nearby. Waren House is open all year. Special breaks available.

Our inspector loved: *This delightful small hotel on the heritage coast overlooking Budle Bay.*

Directions: There are advance warning signs on the A1 both north and south. Take B1342 to Waren Mill. Hotel (floodlit at night) is on south-west corner of Budle Bay just two miles from Bamburgh.

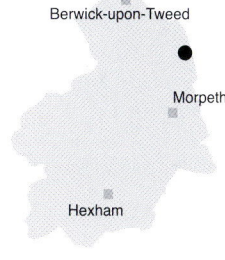

Web: www.johansens.com/warenhouse
E-mail: enquiries@warenhousehotel.co.uk
Tel: 01668 214581
Fax: 01668 214484

Price Guide:
single £90–£110
double £120–£140
suite £165–£195

THE BLUE BELL HOTEL

MARKET PLACE, BELFORD, NORTHUMBERLAND NE70 7NE

Directions: Midway between Berwick and Alnwick, about 14 miles south of Berwick and two minutes from A1. From A1 turn off at Belford/Wooler junction to join the B6349. The hotel is situated in the centre of the village.

Web: www.johansens.com/bluebell
E-mail: bluebel@globalnet.co.uk
Tel: 01668 213543
Fax: 01668 213787

Price Guide:
single £34–£74
double £76–£98

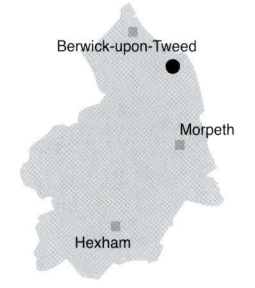

This beautifully restored old coaching inn stands in the centre of Belford, near the old Market Cross. The sophisticated Georgian-style interiors are decorated to complement the original features. Luxurious bedrooms provide every modern comfort and are all unique. There is an elegant residents' lounge and two bars, well stocked with fine malts, rare brandies and vintage ports. The hotel also has three acres of walled terraced grounds, with a putting lawn and an organic vegetable and herb garden. The emphasis is on freshness with fruit and vegetables from the hotel gardens, combined with an excellent supply of fresh local produce such as Cheviot lamb, Tweed salmon and Craster kippers, creating a range of delicious seasonal dishes. Frequently changing à la carte and table d'hôte menus are served in the garden restaurant, which is furnished with locally crafted tables. For a more simple but substantial menu, try the Buttery. There is much to discover along Northumberland's scenic coastline – the Farne Islands, Lindisfarne and Berwick-upon-Tweed are among the many interesting attractions. Sporting activities which can be enjoyed locally include shooting, fishing, riding and golf.

Our inspector loved: The informal and relaxing old coaching inn - by the cobbled Market Cross.

THE OTTERBURN TOWER

OTTERBURN, NORTHUMBERLAND, NE19 1NS

The Otterburn Tower is a magnificent sight. A thick, stone walled fortress, tall and solid with shoulder high ramparts and arrow-slit windows that look out over beautiful Northumberland and National Park countryside. Standing in 32 acres of formal terraced gardens and lush woodland, The Otterburn Tower has witnessed centuries of history. It was built in 1076 as a defence against marauding Scots by a cousin of William the Conqueror. Reminders of its turbulent past remain but once guests have strolled through its imposing, arched entranceway topped by a carved heraldic shield they find comfortable and relaxing surroundings with the warmth of a family home. Elegant public rooms have luxurious furnishings and blazing log fires in winter. Seventeen spacious, en suite guest rooms, some with four-poster beds and large open fireplaces, are individually designed and offer superb comfort and views over the grounds. One of the fireplaces is listed and depicts scenes from the Battle of Otterburn in 1388 when Scots forces lost their leader while defeating the English. Dining at The Otterburn Tower is a delight creating imaginative and tasty lunch and dinner menus using the finest local produce. Places of interest nearby include Hadrian's Wall, Holy Island and Bamburgh Castle. Special breaks available.

Our inspector loved: *This stunning castlegated hotel in the border rivers.*

Directions: From Newcastle take A696 to Otterburn.

Web: www.johansens.com/otterburntower
E-mail: reservations@otterburntower.co.uk
Tel: 01830 520620
Fax: 01830 521504

Price Guide:
single £60–£70
double £90–£170
suite £170

COCKLIFFE COUNTRY HOUSE HOTEL

BURNT STUMP COUNTRY PARK, BURNT STUMP HILL, NOTTINGHAMSHIRE NG5 8PQ

Directions: Exit M1 at junction 26 and take the A60 north from Nottingham.

Web: www.johansens.com/cockliffe
E-mail: enquiries@cockliffehouse.co.uk
Tel: 01159 680179
Fax: 01159 680623

Price Guide:
single from £95
double from £105

This is Robin Hood country and Cockliffe is situated in the heart of it, six miles north of Nottingham. A lovely, unusually designed 17th century house with turreted-style corners it stands in two acres of colourful, mature gardens adjacent to the open spaces of Burnt Stump Country Park. Dane and Jane Clarke rescued the house from disrepair five years ago and are proud of their renovations and refurbishments, many of which are in keeping with original features. Décor and furnishings throughout are elegant and tasteful and most rooms afford splendid views over the garden. The ten bedrooms are individually designed and comfortably appointed to reflect the needs of discerning guests. All are Jacuzzi en suite, with thoughtful touches, period furniture and adorned with beautiful curtain fabrics carefully chosen by Jane Clarke. Chef-Patron Dane Clarke produces an excellent and imaginative menu using local fish and game when in season served in the attractive restaurant, adjoining the cocktail bar which is popular with guests for pre-meal drinks and after dinner coffee. A conference room with high-tech facilities is available. Golf, fishing, riding and fitness and leisure can be arranged locally. Places of interst nearby include Nottingham and its castle, Sherwood Forest, 12th century Newstead Abbey and Southwell Minster with its medieval carvings, the earliest of their kind in England.

Our inspector loved: *The very stylish bedrooms with their superb bathrooms.*

THE COTTAGE COUNTRY HOUSE HOTEL

EASTHORPE STREET, RUDDINGTON, NOTTINGHAM NG11 6LA

Roses and honeysuckle ramble over the walls of The Cottage Country House Hotel, a unique restoration of 17th-century cottages; it lies tucked away in the village of Ruddington, yet only a few minutes drive from the bustling city of Nottingham. It is the imaginative concept of the designer proprietors, and with its private, gated courtyard and walled garden it has won three major awards, including the Conservation Award for the best restoration of an old building in a village setting. Christina and Tim Ruffell are proud of their attention to detail; they engaged local leading craftsmen to renovate and refurbish the hotel in keeping with its original features. Providing quality, style and comfort in tranquil surroundings, all rooms are individually designed and furnished to reflect the needs of discerning guests. The bedrooms are all en suite with thoughtful extra touches. The hotel offers two superb honeymoon suites. The excellent restaurant serves contemporary international cuisine and fine wines. There are two sitting rooms, one with an original inglenook fireplace, a terrace bar overlooking the enclosed courtyard and fountain, and a second terrace leading into the garden. Golf, tennis and water sports are within easy reach.

Our inspector loved: *The lovely cottage style courtyard garden with its water feature.*

Directions: Ruddington is 3 m S of Nottingham on A60 Loughborough road. The hotel is situated at the heart of the village.

Web: www.johansens.com/cottagecountryhouse
Tel: 01159 846882
Fax: 01159 214721

Price Guide:
single from £79
double from £95
suite from £110–£150

THE LAMB INN

SHEEP STREET, BURFORD, OXFORDSHIRE OX18 4LR

Directions: Sheep Street is off the main street in Burford. Burford is 20 miles west of Oxford.

Web: www.johansens.com/lambinnburford
Tel: 01993 823155
Fax: 01993 822228

Price Guide:
single £70–£85
double £110–£130

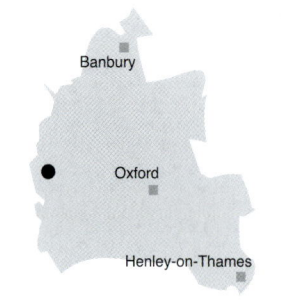

The Lamb Inn, in the small Cotswold town of Burford, is everyone's idea of the archetypal English inn, where it is easy to imagine that time has slipped back to some gentler age. The inn is set in a quiet location with a pretty walled garden. To step inside is to recapture something of the spirit of the 14th century: flagged floors, gleaming copper, brass and silver reflect the flicker of log fires and the well-chosen antiques all enhance the sense of history here. The bedrooms, which have recently been refurbished, offer comfortable accommodation, with oak beams, chintz curtains and soft furnishings. Guests can enjoy the best of British cooking. Dinner, chosen from a three-course table d'hôte menu, is taken in the candlelit pillared dining room and might include such dishes as fresh grilled sardines with lime butter sauce, followed by roast tenderloin of pork wrapped in smoked bacon with a blue cheese cream sauce. Light lunches are served in the bar or in the garden. On Sundays, a traditional three-course lunch is served. Packed lunches and hampers can be provided. The inn is near the heart of the town, where guests can browse through antiques shops or laze by the waters of the River Windrush. Burford is within easy reach of Oxford, Cheltenham, Stow-on-the-Wold and the many attractive Cotswold villages.

Our inspector loved: The transformation of the inn into a very stylish property with super bedrooms.

THE GEORGE HOTEL

HIGH STREET, DORCHESTER-ON-THAMES, OXFORD OX10 7HH

In the heart of the Thames Valley lies The George. Dating from the 15th century, it is one of the oldest inns in the country. In the days of the stage coach, it provided a welcome haven for many an aristocrat including the first Duchess of Marlborough, Sarah Churchill. However, more recent times have seen famous guests of a different hue such as author D H Lawrence. The buildings of the George Hotel have changed little since their heyday as a coaching inn. It retains all the beauty and charm of those days, whilst offering every modern amenity. All rooms are en suite and furnished with fine antiques; the décor suits the requirements of modern times whilst maintaining the spirit of the past. Only the freshest and finest produce is used for the daily changing menu. The imaginative cuisine, awarded AA Rosettes, is beautifully presented and delicious. The beamed dining room provides a delightful setting in which to enjoy an excellent meal, served by friendly, professional staff. Dorchester-on-Thames provides easy access to the Cotswolds, Blenheim Palace and Oxford, Stratford-upon-Avon, Henley, Windsor. Guests can go for beautiful walks and enjoy cultural and sporting activities. Excellent meeting facilities for up to 36 in the Stable Suite and two smaller rooms each for up to 8 people.

Our inspector loved: *This lovely coaching inn with its traditional bar.*

Directions: On A4074, 9 miles south of Oxford.

Web: www.johansens.com/georgedorchester
Tel: 01865 340404
Fax: 01865 341620

Price Guide:
single £65
double £85
four poster £97

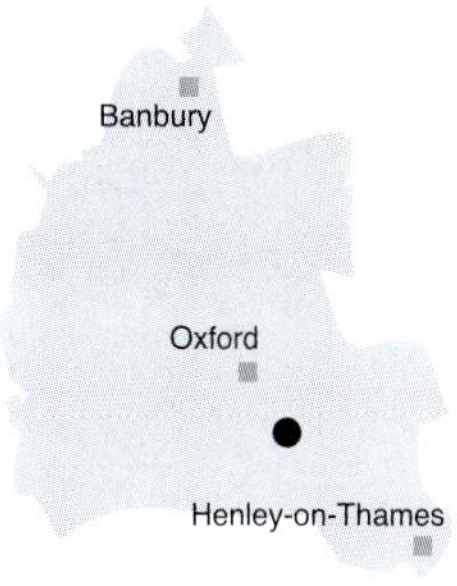

HOLCOMBE HOTEL

HIGH STREET, DEDDINGTON, NR WOODSTOCK, OXFORDSHIRE OX15 0SL

Conveniently located a few miles north of the city of Oxford, this delightful 17th-century high quality hotel is family-run and set in a pretty Cotswold village. It offers personalised attention and traditional hospitality and has a relaxed and friendly atmosphere. Each of the 17 bedrooms is tastefully appointed and has its own distinctive character, offering every amenity and comfort. Holcombe Hotel is known locally for its superb French classical and traditional English cuisine. It is highly recommended and is recognised with an AA Red Rosette and RAC awards. Great care is taken in creating original and beautifully presented food. Excellent wines and Italian menu are served in the Picasso Wine Bar & Bistro. The Holcombe has been in the resident ownership of Chédly and Carol Mahfoudh since 1988, during which time they have received 5 awards, including the AA Courtesy and Care Award 1993, one of only 15 hotels out of 4,000. The Cotswolds, Stratford, Woodstock and Oxford and Bicester Shopping Village "Bond Street at a 50% discount" and many National Trust properties are nearby. Golfing arranged at two excellent 18-hole golf courses.

Our inspector loved: *The fabulous food.*

Directions: Deddington is on A4260, 6 miles south of Banbury M40 J11. Follow A4260 to Adderbury; hotel is on the right at traffic light. M40 J10: follow A43, then B4100 to Aynho, then B4031 to Deddington.

Web: www.johansens.com/holcombe
Tel: 01869 338274
Fax: 01869 337167

Price Guide:
single £75–£85
double £92–£112

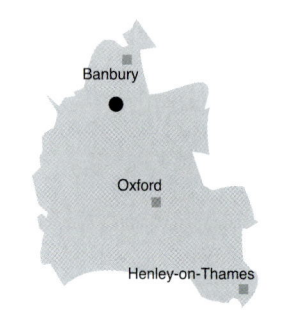

FALLOWFIELDS

KINGSTON BAGPUIZE WITH SOUTHMOOR, OXON OX13 5BH

Fallowfields, once the home of Begum Aga Khan, dates back more than 300 years. It has been updated and extended over past decades and today boasts a lovely early Victorian Gothic southern aspect. The house is set in two acres of gardens, surrounded by ten acres of grassland. The guests' bedrooms, which offer a choice of four poster or coroneted beds, are large and well appointed and offer every modern amenity to ensure maximum comfort and convenience. The house is centrally heated throughout and during the winter months, there are welcoming log fires in the elegant main reception rooms. The cuisine is mainly British, imaginative in style and presentation and there is a good choice of menus available. The walled kitchen garden provides most of the vegetables and salads for the table and locally grown and organic produce is otherwise used wherever possible. Fallowfields is close to Stratford, the Cotswolds, Stonehenge, Bath and Bristol to the west, Oxford, Henley on Thames, the Chilterns and Windsor to the east. Heathrow airport is under an hour away.

Our inspector loved: *Watching the chef hand pick the asparagus for her starter from the organic garden.*

Directions: Take the Kingston Bagpuize exit on the A420 Oxford to Swindon. Fallowfields is at the west end of Southmoor, just after the Longworth sign.

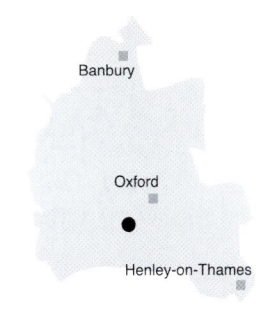

Web: www.johansens.com/fallowfields
E-mail: stay@fallowfields.com
Tel: 01865 820416
Fax: 01865 821275

Price Guide:
single £115–£125
double £122–£155

THE JERSEY ARMS

MIDDLETON STONEY, OXFORDSHIRE OX25 4AD

Directions: Between junctions 9 & 10 of the M40 on the B430 10 miles north of Oxford. From junction 9 take the Oxford Road, Middleton Stoney is signposted 1 mile down. From junction 10 Middleton Stoney is signposted as you leave the slip road.

Web: www.johansens.com/jerseyarms
E-mail: jerseyarms@bestwestern.co.uk
Tel: 01869 343234
Fax: 01869 343565

Price Guide:
single £84
double £96

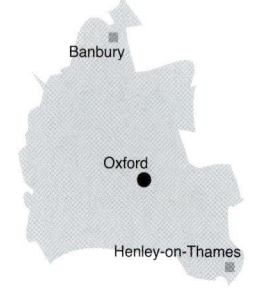

Near Oxford, the city of dreaming spires, in the country of sparkling streams and gentle green pastures, The Jersey Arms occupies a site rich in history. As far back as 1241, the inn was listed as providing William Longsword 'for 25 men of Middleton, necessaries as food and drink'. It thrived in the days of coach-and-horse long-distance travel and in 1823 was a key posting house for cross-country traffic. Today, The Jersey Arms has been honed into a retreat of comfort and peace. An informal air is created with old beams, antique flintlocks and simple, elegant furnishings. Bedrooms, all with private access, vary in size, while blending the charm of the past with modern décor. Facilities include hairdryers, colour TV and telephone. Cuisine of exceptional quality is prepared from the freshest local ingredients and the menu is changed according to season. Diners can sit in the Bar or Restaurant or, in fine weather, in the secluded courtyard garden. Relax first with an apéritif in the elegant lounge. Oxford, Woodstock, Blenheim Palace, Towcester and Cheltenham racecourses and Silverstone Racetrack. Heathrow airport is an hour away by car.

Our inspector loved: *The fresh new décor given to the inn bedrooms with their bright fresh colours.*

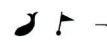

OXFORDSHIRE - OXFORD (MINSTER LOVELL)

THE MILL & OLD SWAN
MINSTER LOVELL, NR. BURFORD, OXFORDSHIRE OX29 5RN

Minster Lovell is one of the most picturesque Doomsday Book villages on the River Windrush and The Mill and Old Swan one of the loveliest and most glorious of picture postcard hotels. It stands regally on a beautiful, 60 acre bankside estate offering an attractive and historical blend of Cotswold stone and half-timbering dating back to the 1350's. This atmospheric and charming hotel features oak beams and crackling log fires, a place in bygone years where shepherds watered their flocks and slaked their own thirst here while journeying to fairs. Retainers of Richard III also slept at the Inn while he was entertained at the nearby, now ruined, manor house. A painted mural of 'The Sun in Splendour' Richard's badge, was discovered under plaster in a bedroom and can now be seen over the fireplace of the former brew house, now the Swan Restaurant. Centuries old coins, hand forged nails, iron latches, ornate hinges and other relics of those days occasionally turn up today and many are on display. Superb and imaginative cuisine can be enjoyed in an elegant restaurant which has gained a high reputation or in an intimate private dining room. Each of the 63 guest rooms is decorated and furnished to the highest standard and comfort. A gym, sauna, fishing, shooting, tennis and badminton are available. Extensive corporate event facilities are available.

Our inspector loved: Sitting by the river taking tea.

Directions: Exit the M40 at junction 8 or 9 and take the A40 or A34 respectively towards Oxford. Follow signs for Cheltenham and approximately 14 miles after Oxford take the sliproad signposted to Carterton, Minster Lovell.

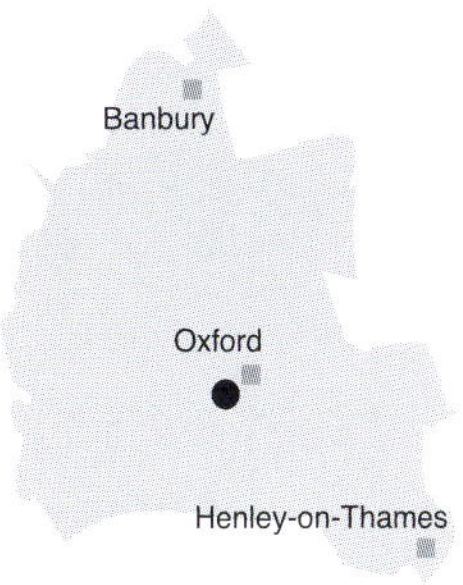

Web: www.johansens.com/milloldswan
E-mail: themill@initialstyle.co.uk
Tel: 01993 774441
Fax: 01993 702002

Price Guide:
single £45
double/twin £60–£120
suites £120

THE SHAVEN CROWN HOTEL

HIGH STREET, SHIPTON UNDER WYCHWOOD, OXFORDSHIRE OX7 6BA

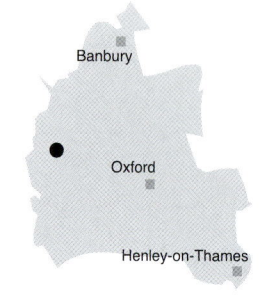

Built of honey-coloured stone around an attractive central courtyard, The Shaven Crown Hotel dates back to the 14th century, when it served as a monks' hospice. The proprietors have preserved the inn's many historic features, such as the medieval hall with its ancient timbered roof. This is now the residents' lounge. Each of the bedrooms has en suite facilities and has been sympathetically furnished in a style befitting its own unique character. Rooms of various style and sizes are available, including a huge family room and ground-floor accommodation. Dining in the intimate, candlelit room is an enjoyable experience, with meals served at the tables, beautifully laid with fine accessories. The best ingredients are combined to create original dishes with a cosmopolitan flair. The table d'hôte menu offers a wide and eclectic choice with a daily vegetarian dish among the specialities. An imaginative selection of dishes is offered every lunchtime and evening in the Monks bar. The Shaven Crown is ideal for day trips to the Cotswolds, Oxford, Stratford-upon-Avon and Bath. There are three golf courses and tennis courts close by. Trout fishing and antiques hunting are popular activities in the area.

Our inspector loved: The courtyard garden.

Directions: Take the A40 Oxford-Cheltenham road. At Burford follow the A361 towards Chipping Norton. The inn is situated directly opposite the village green in Shipton-under-Wychwood.

Web: www.johansens.com/shavencrown
Tel: 01993 830330
Fax: 01993 832136

Price Guide:
single £65
double £95–£130

THE LAMB INN

SHIPTON-UNDER-WYCHWOOD, OXFORDSHIRE OX7 6DQ

Skirted by the River Evenlode and in an 'Area of Outstanding Beauty' the village of Shipton-under-Wychwood is one of the prettiest in the Cotswolds. It takes its name from the old English meaning 'sheep town' and in 1086 was listed as a royal manor in the Doomsday Book. Most of Shipton dates from the 17th century. Houses and cottages are built from the pale golden local stone and many buildings have interesting architectural features and uniquely styled interiors. None more so than The Lamb Inn, a beautiful, historic inn unlike any other. It has a superb restaurant, a chef with an International reputation, an extensive and unrivaled wine list and a bar offering exciting drinks and cocktails rarely found outside the leading restaurants and bars of London. But it is the 5 luxurious, double guest rooms created by interior designer, Jean Harrod, that are truly exceptional. Each is beautifully furnished with an individual exotic theme and room names reflect the quality of the experience guests can expect to enjoy. Leopard Hills, for example, is sheer opulence, taking its styling cues from safaris that inn owner and world traveller, Simon Clifton, has taken in South Africa. A four poster bed is complete with mosquito net and room fabrics reflect the patterns of native weavers.

Our inspector loved: The attention to detail and use of the very best quality fabrics and furnishings.

Directions: Just off the A361, approximately 4 miles north-east of Burford and 23 miles from Oxford.

Web: www.johansens.com/lambshipton
E-mail: info@thelambinn.net
Tel: 01993 830465
Fax: 01993 832025

Price Guide:
double £119–£149

THE KINGS HEAD INN & RESTAURANT
THE GREEN, BLEDINGTON, NR KINGHAM, OXFORDSHIRE OX7 6XQ

The award-winning Kings Head Inn and Restaurant is peacefully located beside a traditional village green, complete with a babbling brook inhabited by friendly ducks. During the summer months Morris dancers and musicians can regularly be seen in action on the green performing the Bledington Dances. The building has always served as a hostelry and much of its medieval character remains. With its exposed stone walls, original beams, inglenook fireplace and old settles, the Kings Head fulfils everyone's anticipations of a traditional English inn. The attractive timbered bedrooms, are all furnished to complement with full facilities. The carefully compiled menu is changed regularly and is backed up by a selection of fine wines. Excellent inventive bar food is served at lunchtimes and in the evenings together with a changing selection of real ales. The Kings Head Inn is situated in the heart of the Cotswolds, within easy reach of Oxford, Stratford-upon-Avon, Cheltenham and Blenheim.

Our inspector loved: The ambience of this lovely old inn.

Directions: Take the A44 Oxford–Woodstock road to Chipping Norton, then the B4450 to Bledington; or take the Oxford–Burford road to Stow-on-the-Wold and join the B4450. Nearest motorway M40 junction 11.

Web: www.johansens.com/kingshead
E-mail: kingshead@orr-ewing.com
Tel: 01608 658365
Fax: 01608 658902

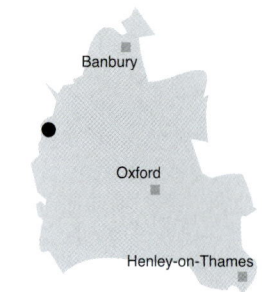

Price Guide:
single £50
double £70–£85
four poster £90

STRETTON HALL

ALL STRETTON, CHURCH STRETTON, SHROPSHIRE SY6 6HG

Set within the beautiful south Shropshire countryside, and just a mile north of the small town of Church Stretton, this elegant Georgian house retains many original features, such as fireplaces, oak panelling and the staircase. The interior is classically furnished with a modern twist, and complemented by fresh flowers and thoughtful touches. Proprietors Charlie and Frances Baker-Vilain have a warm, relaxed style and manner, and this permeates the house itself. The lounge and bar provide the perfect environment in which to enjoy morning coffee, afternoon tea, an evening drink or simply the peace and quiet of the surroundings. In winter a roaring fire warms a cold day, while in summer the lawns, colourful flowers, mature trees and wildlife are an idyllic backdrop. Stretton Hall's award-winning Lemon Tree restaurant is renowned for its superb menus which incorporate fresh local produce such as beef from Pulverbatch, Lamb from Acton Scott and eggs from the Clun Valley. The twelve attractive en suite bedrooms benefit from views across either the Long Mynd or Caer Caradoc. Guests can request the four-poster bedroom as well as more personal home comforts such as hot water bottles, cots and baby monitors. Places of interest nearby are Ludlow, Telford, Shrewsbury, Ironbridge and the Severn Valley Railway.

Our inspector loved: *Its informal family atmosphere.*

Directions: Situated just off A49 Ludlow to Shrewsbury Road.

Web: www.johansens.com/strettonhall
E-mail: enquiries@strettonhall.co.uk
Tel: 01694 723224
Fax: 01694 724365

Price Guide:
single £50
double/twin £80–£130

Pen-Y-Dyffryn Hall Hotel

RHYDYCROESAU, NR OSWESTRY, SHROPSHIRE SY10 7JD

Directions: From A5 and Oswestry town centre take B4580 west towards Llansiln for approximately 3 miles. After a sharp bend turn left in village.

Web: www.johansens.com/penydyffryn
E-mail: stay@peny.co.uk
Tel: 01691 653700
Fax: 01691 650066

Price Guide:
single £72
double £88–£125

From the moment you drive up to this picturesque, silver-stone Georgian Hotel you realise that you're somewhere special. Pen-Y-Dyffryn Hall is a gem in a spectacular setting with lush green pastures, gently sloping hillsides and dramatically rising mountains. It's a region of unspoilt natural beauty where falcons and buzzards rule the skies and badgers and foxes roam below. Built in 1845 as a rectory for an eccentric Celtic scholar, the listed Hall stands 1,000 feet up the last hill in Shropshire between Chester and Shrewsbury. Family run, it combines tranquility, superb comfort, unobtrusive hospitality and good food with an unpretentious atmosphere and enchanting charm. The tastefully decorated and furnished bedrooms have all modern amenities, several have spa baths. The best feature, however is the glorious views over the garden to the nearby Welsh mountains. For guests preferring an extra touch of seclusion there are 4 bedrooms in an adjacent Coach House with their own stone-walled private patios. During cooler months log fires burn in the lounge and restaurant where superb, adventurous cuisine has earned the Hotel a prestigious AA 2 Rosettes food award. Trout fishing nearby, 4 National Trust properties and 6 golf courses are within easy reach.

Our inspector loved: The blissful situation.

THE HUNDRED HOUSE HOTEL

BRIDGNORTH ROAD, NORTON, NR SHIFNAL, TELFORD, SHROPSHIRE TF11 9EE

Character, charm and a warm, friendly atmosphere are guaranteed at this family-run, award-winning inn, situated only 45 minutes' drive from Birmingham International Airport. The bedrooms are attractively furnished with antiques and feature country-style patchwork bed linen and drapes; all guest rooms are fully equipped. There are pretty gardens with a pond, gazebo and herb garden. A special tariff is offered for mid-week and weekend breaks. The inn enjoys a growing reputation for its varied, interesting à la carte and table d'hôte menus. Home-made English fare such as steak pies and game is offered alongside continental dishes and sweets range from delicate sorbets to traditional favourites like treacle tart. Bar meals are served daily, together with a number of real ales. Early booking is recommended as the restaurant is very popular locally. Awarded Michelin Bib Gourmand 1999, 2 AA Rosettes for the past 6 years and the 2002 Good Hotel Guide Cesar award. Severn Valley Railway, Midland Motor Museum, Weston Park, Ironbridge Gorge and Telford are within easy reach. Shifnal's cottages inspired Charles Dickens' Old Curiosity Shop.

Our inspector loved: *The Swing*

Directions: Norton is on the A442 Bridgnorth-Telford road.

Web: www.johansens.com/hundredhousetelford
E-mail: hundredhouse@lineone.net
Tel: 01952 730353 or 0845 130 0607
Fax: 01952 730355

Price Guide:
single £69
double £99–£125

SHROPSHIRE - WEM

SOULTON HALL

NR WEM, SHROPSHIRE SY4 5RS

Directions: M54 to end, then take A5 to junction with A49. Go north on A49, then join B5065 west to Wem.

Web: www.johansens.com/soultonhall
E-mail: j.ashton@soultonhall.fsbusiness.co.uk
Tel: 01939 232786
Fax: 01939 234097

Price Guide:
single £38–£49
double £76–£99

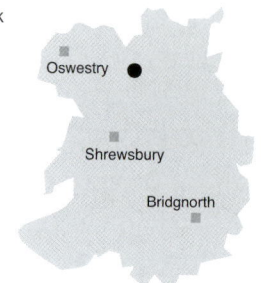

Historic and imposing Soulton Hall stands in 550 acres of beautiful Shropshire parkland two miles east of the ancient market town of Wem. Dating from the 15th and 17th centuries, this Tudor brick built manor, with a magnificent pillared courtyard and beautiful walled garden, retains much of the grandeur and character of those bygone days, enhanced with all modern facilities. Ann and John Ashton, descendants of the Protestant Lord Mayor of London who bought Soulton in 1556, have created a hotel of warmth whilst retaining many of the unique features in the four spacious bedrooms in the house. The two more modern bedrooms in the coach house are equally comfortably and provide total privacy. Ann Ashton presides in the kitchen where her skills in traditional English cooking are enhanced by imagination and flair. Specialities might include hand-raised game pie or butter baked salmon served with saffron oil. The restaurant is open to non residents for dinner. There is a congenial bar and ample parking space. Hawkstone Country Park, Hodnet Hall and Gardens, Grinshill, Nescliffe Hill, Ironbridge and Shrewsbury. Chester, Stoke and Worcester are within easy reach.

Our inspector loved: The warmth of welcomegiven by John and Ann ancient home.

172

Compton House

TOWNSEND, AXBRIDGE, SOMERSET BS26 2AJ

This delightful 17th century Manor House is a real find. With wonderful views across the Somerset Levels to Glastonbury Tor it is a real gem of a hotel, immaculately designed with a unique character and atmosphere. Steeped in English history parts of the Hotel date back to Elizabethan times and there is an abundance of oak panelling, elegant mouldings and wonderful fireplaces. With just 5 carefully designed bedrooms, this is an ideal place for a memorable and intimate wedding or even to visit the historic towns nearby. Wells, with its magnificent cathedral is only 10 miles away, Bath is just 45 minutes away, whilst Cheddar with its fascinating gorge and King Alfred's Saxon palace is just 2 miles down the road. A carefully planned and daily changing menu ensures dinner is a delight at the close of a day's sightseeing whilst every care is taken to ensure that individual requirements and preferences are adhered to.

Our inspector loved: *All the wonderful surprises that greets one when walking through the front door.*

Directions: From the M5 take junction 22, the A38 towards Bristol. After 6 miles turn right onto the A371 to Cheddar/Wells. Compton House is ½ mile on your right, west of Axbridge.

Web: www.johansens.com/comptonhouse
E-mail: info@comptonhse.com
Tel: 01934 733944
Fax: 01934 733945

Price Guide:
single £50-£60
double/twin £80-£100

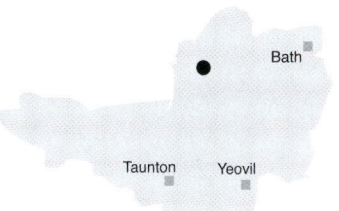

SOMERSET - BATH (WOOLVERTON)

NEW

WOOLVERTON HOUSE
WOOLVERTON, NR BATH, SOMERSET BA3 6QS

Directions: From M4 exit 17 take A350 and then A361 for Woolverton – or on A36 halfway between Bath and Warminster.

Web: www.johansens.com/woolvertonhouse
E-mail: mail@bathhotel.com
Tel: 01373 830415
Fax: 01373 831243

Price Guide:
single £44–£55
double £55–£90

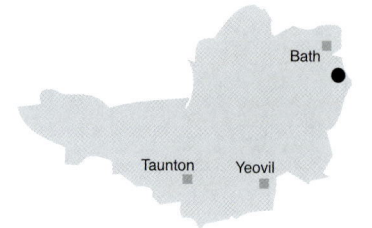

This early 19th century house, built originally as a rectory for the 'United Parishes of Woolverton & Rode', has been sympathetically converted and restored to become an elegant English country house. It is set in over 2½ acres of grounds and commands scenic views over the 'glebe lands' on which the parson traditionally had grazing rights. Today Woolverton House has been developed by its present-day hospitable owners into a retreat where the emphasis is on heritage, history and nature. The gardens are full of colour and also include a narrow gauge steam railway. All the bedrooms are pleasantly decorated and furnished with private bathrooms en suite. They are fully equipped with colour television, direct dial telephone, hospitality tray, trouser press, hairdryer and minibar. Both the dining room and drawing room have log fires in the cooler months and the conservatory bar is pleasant all year. The restaurant is beautifully furnished in excellent taste with food and wines to match and has been awarded an RAC dining award.

Our inspector loved: *The restaurant which offers exceptional value for money.*

Ashwick Country House Hotel
DULVERTON, SOMERSET TA22 9QD

This small, charming AA Red Star Edwardian Country House stands in six acres of beautiful grounds above the picturesque valley of the River Barle within Exmoor National Park. Sweeping lawns lead to woods and water gardens where guests can relax in summer shade and breathe in sweet scents of wild flowers. Ashwick House offers old world hospitality. Its atmosphere is sunny with flowers in summer and elegantly cosy with candlelight and log fires in winter. The baronial style hall with its long, broad gallery and cheerful log fire, the restaurant opening onto a terrace where breakfast is served and the comfortably furnished lounge offer a peaceful sanctuary not easily found in today's busy world. All bedrooms are spacious and pleasantly decorated, finished with many thoughtful personal touches. Chef-patron Richard Sherwood presents quality cuisine using fresh local produce. Shooting and riding facilities are close by. Magnificent walks on Exmoor from the hotel. Dunster's Norman Castle and 17th-century Yarm Market, Exmoor Forest, many National Trust houses and gardens are nearby.

Our inspector loved: The idyllic peaceful rural location.

Directions: From the M5, exit at junction 27 onto the A361 to Tiverton. Take the A396 north until joining the B3222 to Dulverton and then the B3223 signposted Lynton and Exford. After a steep climb drive over a second cattle grid and turn left to Ashwick House.

Web: www.johansens.com/ashwickcountryhouse
E-mail: ashwickhouse@talk21.com
Tel: 01398 323868
Fax: 01398 323868

Price Guide: (including dinner)
single £80–£86
double £140–£152

THE CROWN HOTEL

EXFORD, EXMOOR NATIONAL PARK, SOMERSET TA24 7PP

Directions: Exit M5 Jct25, follow A358 towards Minehead. At Bishops Lydard join B3224 and follow signs to Exford.

Web: www.johansens.com/crownexford
E-mail: info@crownhotelexmoor.co.uk
Tel: 01643 831554
Fax: 01643 831665

Price Guide:
single £55
double/twin £95–£110

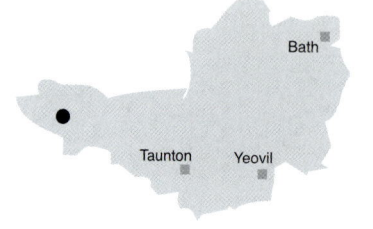

The warmest and friendliest of welcomes awaits guests at this small coaching inn. Almost three hundred years old, the Crown Hotel is situated in the Exmoor National Park, surrounded by wonderful countryside, from coastline to valleys, streams and moorland, populated with red deer, ponies, amazing birdlife and salmon. Owners Hugo and Pam Jeune are planning to refurbish this lovely inn to the standard of their previous hotel, The Rising Sun in Lynmouth. Guests can enjoy its comfort in every season – coolness in summer, warmth in winter. There is a lively bar, patronised by the locals, for drinks or informal meals ordered from the extensive menu, or guests may prefer an apéritif in the extremely comfortable lounge before entering the delightful 2 Rosettes dining room for a beautifully presented evening meal from the seasonal menu. Only the freshest of local produce is used, and good wines complement every delicious meal, which includes home-made bread. After dinner guests may wish to stroll in the water garden. Wild life Land-Rover safaris, riding over the moor and clay pigeon shooting can be arranged. Stabling and livery are available. Order a packed lunch and walk the moor or visit Lynmouth and Porlock. Special breaks are available throughout the year.

Our inspector loved: *The wonderful moorland village location and first class cuisine.*

THE OLD RECTORY

CRICKET MALHERBIE, ILMINSTER, SOMERSET TA19 0PW

Set in the tiny hamlet of Cricket Malherbie and surrounded by peaceful countryside, The Old Rectory is a delightful country house with Strawberry Hill Gothic windows, a thatched roof and weathered hamstone walls. The flagstoned hall leads guests through to the enchanting sitting room, adorned with exquisite carved oak beams and exuding a tranquil atmosphere. The five bedrooms are peaceful and furnished in a very tasteful manner, some with Gothic windows and all overlooking the gardens. Well-equipped and offering every possible comfort, the rooms include en suite bathrooms and showers. This is a totally non-smoking property. The dining room is beautifully presented with large shuttered windows affording views of the lawns on both sides of the house. Guests sit at the grand table in dinner-party fashion and indulge in the daily-changing four-course menu. Produce from the vegetable garden and local fish and game feature highly in the inspired dishes. Bath, Stonehenge, Wells and Glastonbury are ideal destinations for day trips, whilst Montacute House, Barrington Court and Yeovilton Air Museum are all close by.

Our inspector loved: *The welcome, the superb presentation and the totally relaxing atmosphere.*

Directions: The nearest motorway is M5. Exit at junction 25, join A358 towards Chard at A303 roundabout take the Chard exit again onto A358. Drive through the village of Donyatt, turn left for Ilminster and then right for Cricket Malherbie.

Web: www.johansens.com/oldrectoryilminster
E-mail: TheOldRectory@malherbie.freeserve.co.uk
Tel: 01460 54364
Fax: 01460 57374

Price Guide:
single from £50
double from £80

ANDREW'S ON THE WEIR

PORLOCK WEIR, PORLOCK, SOMERSET TA24 8PB

A haven of peace and tranquillity, guests staying at Andrew's On The Weir are offered a quite exceptional experience. In an idyllic location overlooking the picturesque Porlock Weir, and with views reaching to Wales, this Georgian Manor house has been recently taken over by Chef Patron Andrew Dixon and its fine cuisine is already attracting considerable interest. Awarded 3 AA Rosettes after just seven months of business, the restaurant, with its new private dining room, is really putting Andrew's On The Weir on the map, and with a strong patronage of local farmers and suppliers, guests are assured of true West Country fayre! A delight to the eye as well as the palate, the cuisine is imaginative and unusual with such tempting dishes as "Terinne of duck confit, duck breast and duck liver with Exmoor girolle mushrooms" or "Porlock weir sea bass, tian of aubergine confit, potatoes & tomato butter sauce". The bedrooms are delightful, and will provide a restful night's sleep, prior to sampling the stunning breakfast menu, and any dietary requirements are met with maximum creativity. The restaurant is closed Sunday night and all day Monday, but bed and breakfast is available. Places of interest nearby include Dunster's Norman castle, Lynmouth's picturesque harbour, and beautiful Exmoor.

Directions: Exit M5 at junction 25 and join A358 to Minehead. Then take A39 to Porlock and onto Porlock Weir.

Web: www.johansens.com/andrewsontheweir
E-mail: information@andrewsontheweir.co.uk
Tel: 01643 863300
Fax: 01643 863311

Price Guide:
single £50–£85
double £65–£100

Our inspector loved: *Apart from the location, the innovative first class cuisine and country house atmosphere.*

Porlock Vale House
PORLOCK WEIR, SOMERSET TA24 8NY

This former hunting lodge positioned in a truly spectacular setting pinioned by the sea and lush forest, offers a welcome friendly, informal and comforting atmosphere to visitors tired of the formality of traditional hotel accommodation. Porlock Vale's extensive gardens are a sight to behold, visitors always cherish fond memories of the lazy summer afternoons spent there in quiet repose. Winter season also sticks in the mind, with the coast and the Bristol channel viewed from the tranquillity of the lounge with its crackling log fire. Visitors dine in a beautiful dining room, where top-notch local fare is served within mouth-watering menus. The delightful bedrooms are all individually styled, commanding views of the ocean, the tastefully laid out gardens or the wooded combe that flanks the hotel. Situated at the heart of the Exmoor National Park, the Porlock Vale House is the ideal base for a walking tour around this region of dramatic beauty. The area is literally awash with quaint traditional villages dotted along the awe-inspiring coast. Famous landmarks, such as the Dunkery Beacon and the Doone Valley, are also close at hand. Midweek special breaks are available.

Our inspector loved: The location within acres of beautiful grounds, yet so coastal.

Directions: Join the A39 and follow the signs to Minehead. When in Porlock Village, pick up the signs for Porlock Weir.

Web: www.johansens.com/porlockvale
E-mail: info@porlockvale.co.uk
Tel: 01643 862338
Fax: 01643 863338

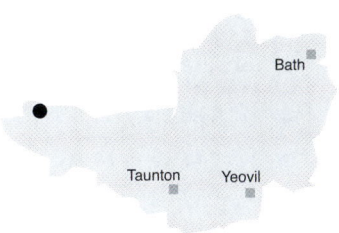

Price Guide:
single £45–£65
double £85–£110

Farthings Hotel & Restaurant

HATCH BEAUCHAMP, SOMERSET TA3 6SG

Directions: Exit M5 Jct25, join A358. Go through Henlade and carry on for approximately one mile, then turn left signed Hatch Beauchamp.

Web: www.johansens.com/farthings
E-mail: farthing1@aol.com
Tel: 01823 480664
Fax: 01823 481118

Price Guide:
single £75–£85
double/twin £105–£115
suites £130

Situated in the delightful village of Hatch Beauchamp, Farthings overlooks a cricket pitch and is surrounded by three acres of beautiful grounds. With a wonderfully relaxing and informal atmosphere it is a place to unwind in a pleasant, non-smoking environment. Owners Stephen and Hilary Murphy have over 20 years experience in welcoming guests, and as chef Stephen creates superb menus, cooked and presented to your choice in the AA Rosette awarded restaurant. Each of the nine spacious en suite rooms is extremely comfortable with excellent facilities, while the self-contained Maple Suite comprises a well appointed bedroom, Regency-style sitting room and modern conservatory with access to the main gardens. Elsewhere in the Hotel, the tasteful lounge and bar with open fires provide a sociable ambience for an evening drink, and in winter an escape from the cold outside. The Hotel has its own fascinating 250-year-old history but there are numerous places to visit nearby including Barrington Court, Forde Abbey and Gardens, Wells Cathedral and the city of Bath. Cheddar Gorge and both the north and south Devon coasts can also be explored from here. Farthings is open over the Christmas period; prices are available on request.

Our inspector loved: The warm friendly inviting atmosphere.

MOUNT SOMERSET COUNTRY HOUSE HOTEL

HENLADE, TAUNTON, SOMERSET TA3 5NB

This elegant Regency residence, awarded 2 Rosettes and 3 stars, stands high on the slopes of the Blackdown Hills, overlooking miles of lovely countryside. The Hotel is rich in intricate craftsmanship and displays fine original features. Its owners have committed themselves to creating an atmosphere in which guests can relax, confident that all needs will be catered for. The bedrooms are sumptuously furnished and many offer views over the Quantock Hills. All of the bedrooms have luxurious bathrooms and some have spa baths. Light lunches, teas, coffees and home-made cakes can be enjoyed in the beautifully furnished drawing room, whilst in the restaurant the finest food and wines are served. A team of chefs work together to create dishes which exceed the expectations of the most discerning gourmet. Adjacent to the Hotel, the President's Health Club, with its large heated indoor pool and fully-equipped gym, is available for use by hotel guests. Places of interest nearby include Glastonbury Abbey, Wells Cathedral and the vibrant city of Exeter.

Our inspector loved: *Driving along the winding approach and finding total comfort within this gracious residence.*

Directions: At M5 exit at junction 25 and join A358 towards Ilminster. Just past Henlade turn right at sign for Stoke St Mary. At T-junction turn left, the hotel drive is 150 yards on the right.

Web: www.johansens.com/mountsomerset
E-mail: info@mountsomersethotel.co.uk
Tel: 01823 442500
Fax: 01823 442900

Price Guide:
single from £95–£125
double/twin from £110–£135
suites £155–£170

LANGLEY HOUSE

LANGLEY MARSH, WIVELISCOMBE, SOMERSET TA4 2UF

Directions: Via M5, South take Jct 26, from the North take Jct 25. The Hotel is on the B3227 about ½ mile North of Wiveliscombe (road signposted as Langley Marsh from the centre of town).

Web: www.johansens.com/langleyhouse
E-mail: info@langleyhousehotel.co.uk
Tel: 01984 623318
Fax: 01984 624573

Price Guide:
single £85–£115
double/twin £110–£135
suites from £165

Secluded and tranquil the Hotel is situated in 4 acres of private gardens, nestled amongst the picturesque Brendon Hills. Steeped in history, this charming Country House was originally built in the 16th century and has been renovated to its present understated Georgian elegance. Good taste exudes from every corner with traditional fabrics, fine antiques and original paintings. The peaceful sitting rooms have roaring log fires, plush sofas and a cosy atmosphere whilst individually appointed bedrooms have all modern conveniences, most boasting lovely views over the gardens. Fresh flowers, reading books, mineral water and hot water bottles make this a home-from-home. 2 AA Rosettes were awarded to the restaurant, which serves prime meat, fresh fish and freshly harvested herbs and vegetables (mainly from their own kitchen garden). The extensive wine list features wines of an impressive quality. A private dining room is available for small meetings. Guests can discover the nearby cliffs, magnificent coastline, wild moorland, sparkling rivers, woods, red deer and ancient villages of Exmoor National Park. Famous gardens in the area include the famous Knightshayes, Stourhead, Bicton, Hestercombe and many others.

Our inspector loved: *The feel of a typical country house which is magical.*

BERYL

WELLS, SOMERSET BA5 3JP

This 19th-century Gothic mansion is a true little gem. Tastefully furnished with antiques, it also offers hospitality of the highest order. The host, Eddie Nowell, is a famous antiques dealer, with showrooms at Beryl. He is also a devoted gardener, his talents being reflected in the 13 acres of parkland which he has restored with great skill. His wife Holly is a charming hostess, and takes pride in the great attention to detail evident throughout the house. Guests are invited to use the honesty bar in the Green Room or enjoy drinks and wines on the lawn in summer. Candlit dinners and house parties are a speciality. There are a host of highly recommended pubs and restaurants within easy reach. The en suite bedrooms have interesting views, with all the requisites for modern comfort. Places of interest nearby include Wells Cathedral (1 mile), Wookey Hole Caves, Cheddar Gorge, Glastonbury Abbey, Longleat House, Stourhead, Farleigh Castle, The Roman Baths at Bath, and many more fascinating places. For more active guests, there is marvellous golf, fishing, riding, excellent walking and a nearby leisure centre.

Our inspector loved: *The absolutely wonderful charming welcome and feeling of belonging.*

Directions: Leave Wells on Radstock Road B3139. Follow the signs to 'The Horringtons' and the 'H' sign for hospital. Opposite the garage turn left into Hawkers Lane, Beryl is signed at the top with a leafy 500 yard drive to the main gate.

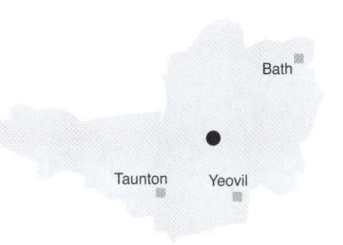

Web: www.johansens.com/beryl
E-mail: stay@beryl-wells.co.uk
Tel: 01749 678738
Fax: 01749 670508

Price Guide:
single £50–£70
double £70–£105

GLENCOT HOUSE

GLENCOT LANE, WOOKEY HOLE, NR WELLS, SOMERSET BA5 1BH

Directions: From the M4, exit at junction 18. Take the A46 to Bath and then follow the signs to Wells and Wookey Hole. From the M5, exit at junction 22. Join the A38 and then the A371 towards Wells and Wookey Hole.

Web: www.johansens.com/glencothouse
E-mail: relax@glencothouse.co.uk
Tel: 01749 677160
Fax: 01749 670210

Price Guide:
single £68–£85
double £90–£120

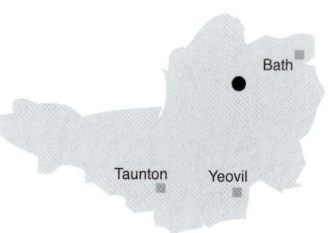

Idyllically situated in 18 acres of sheltered gardens and parkland with river frontage, Glencot House is an imposing Grade II listed Victorian mansion built in grand Jacobean style. It has been sensitively renovated to its former glory to provide comfortable country house accommodation and a homely atmosphere. This elegantly furnished hotel has countless beautiful features: carved ceilings, walnut panelling, mullioned windows, massive fireplaces, antiques and sumptuous chandeliers. The bedrooms are decorated and furnished with period pieces. All have full en suite facilities and splendid views. Many have four-poster beds. Guests can enjoy pleasant walks in the garden, trout fishing in the river, snooker, table tennis, a sauna or a dip in the jet-stream pool. The dining room overlooks the grounds and diverse and delicious fare is served in the restaurant, enriched by beautiful glassware, silver and china. Places of interest include the caves at Wookey Hole, the cathedral town of Wells, the houses and gardens of Longleat, Stourhead and Montacute are all nearby as are Glastonbury, Bath, the Mendip Hills and Cheddar Gorge.

Our inspector loved: Its overall total charm and welcome.

THE WOODBOROUGH INN

SANDFORD ROAD, WINSCOMBE, SOMERSET BS25 1HD

Set in the rolling Mendip Hills, a distinctive ridge punctuated with sinkholes, depressions and rocky outcrops, The Woodborough Inn is the quintessential traditional English inn with beamed ceilings, exposed brickwork and a warm atmosphere. Luxurious bedrooms are individually appointed with elegant furniture, beautiful fabrics and subtle colour schemes for a comfortable, classical style. A unique feature of this Hotel is its skittle alley, ideal for private parties or a fun evening with friends. The inviting, cosy restaurant offers an interesting choice of tempting International dishes and a comprehensive wine list as well as delicious informal bar snacks. Somerset is a land of mystery and many visitors value the peaceful solitude of the area. Cheddar Gorge is spectacular and Wookey Hole, where pagan and Christian legends intermingle, is a breathtaking underground cave carved out by the River Axe. Outdoor activities in the area include walking, cycling, horse riding, bird watching, caving and climbing. Nestled into the foot of the slopes is England's smallest city, Wells, with its beautiful cathedral replete with Gothic carvings, a unique scissors vault to brace the building against shifting medieval foundations and a marvellous chapter house. The sparsely populated windswept Exmoor plateau is a haven for wildlife and its dramatic coastal scenery is a sight not to be missed.

Our inspector loved: The well-appointed, spacious rooms.

Directions: Take the M5, junction 22 then the A38 to Winscombe. Turn left to Sandford and The Woodborough Inn is on the right.

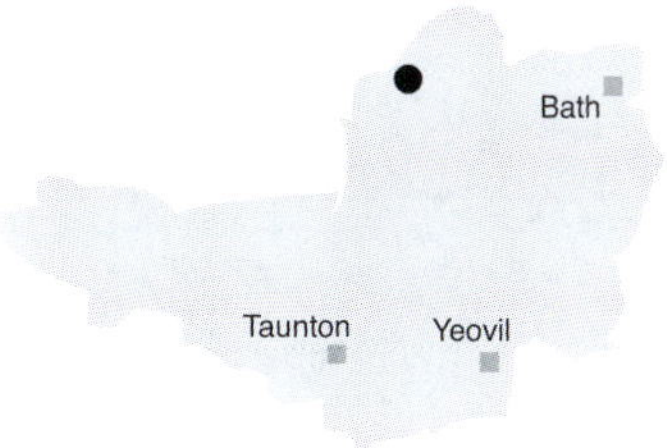

Web: www.johansens.com/woodborough
E-mail: info@woodborough-inn.co.uk
Tel: 01934 844167
Fax: 01934 843862

Price Guide:
single £60
double/twin £70

The Royal Oak Inn

WINSFORD, EXMOOR NATIONAL PARK, SOMERSET TA24 7JE

This immaculate, picturesque thatched Inn dates from the 12th century and sits in the centre of an ancient riverside village on the edge of Exmoor National Park. Lovingly decorated and furnished it combines traditional oak beams and fireplaces with modern facilities. The charming bedrooms are situated either in the Inn itself or in the courtyard area and some feature four poster beds while all have en suite bathrooms. For relaxation 3 lounges and 2 bars are well-appointed with open fires, chintz fabrics and wooden beams. The Inn has won a number of accolades including AA 3 Stars Hotel, an RAC 3 Star Hotel and Dining Award and a 3 Star ETC Hotel Silver Award. Chef, Emma Worsley, prepares high quality English cuisine served in the restaurant with its fine china and glassware. Only the freshest local produce is used to prepare the daily changing country dishes and everything from hams and pies to pâtés and rolls is home-cooked. Proprietor, Charles Steven, can arrange many sporting pastimes for his guests, including riding, fishing, hunting, shooting, golf and adventure walking. The Hotel also provides a comprehensive sightseeing list covering Exmoor National Park and beyond.

Our inspector loved: The picturesque location and enchanting atmosphere.

Directions: Leave the M5 at junction 27 to Tiverton, take the A396 Tiverton to Minehead Road for 20 miles, then turn left to Winsford village.

Web: www.johansens.com/royaloakexmoor
E-mail: enquiries@royaloak-somerset.co.uk
Tel: 01643 851455
Fax: 01643 851009

Price Guide:
single from £80 (annexe)
double £103–£165

CHESTNUT HOUSE

HECTORS STONE, LOWER ROAD, WOOLAVINGTON, BRIDGWATER, SOMERSET TA7 8EQ

This charming 16th-century house is located in the quiet village of Woolavington, tucked away in the heart of Somerset. Proprietors Jonathan and Christine Brinkman pride themselves on offering total comfort and relaxation for leisure and business guests alike. Chestnut House has recently undergone a major refurbishment, but manages to retain all its character throughout, from cosy wood burning fires in winter to the lovely gardens for basking in during the summer months. The six en suite bedrooms are enchanting and tasteful with superb facilities including colour television and fluffy bathrobes. Every evening Jonathan serves tempting meals in the Garden Room overlooking the beautifully presented grounds. Daily changing menus usually consist of five courses and are freshly prepared using the finest local produce. Situated on the edge of the Somerset Levels, Chestnut House acts as an ideal base for some superb walking, and the Lyme Regis coastline is within easy reach, as are Glastonbury, Wells and Bath.

Our inspector loved: *The enchanting atmosphere, charm and absolute value for money.*

Directions: Exit M5 Jct23, then take road signed Street Glastonbury for approximately ½ mile. At T junction turn left, after 1 mile turn left to Woolavington. Go through village, turn left opposite church into Lower Road.

Web: www.johansens.com/chestnut
E-mail: jon@chestnuthouse.freeserve.co.uk
Tel: 01278 683658
Fax: 01278 684333

Price Guide:
single from £58
double £82.25–£88

YE OLDE DOG & PARTRIDGE

HIGH STREET, TUTBURY, BURTON-UPON-TRENT, STAFFORDSHIRE DE13 9LS

Directions: Leave the M1 at junction 23A or the M6 at junction 15. Follow the A50 exiting at the junction for the A511 Burton-upon-Trent (Foston/Scropton/Hatton) and pick up the signs for Tutbury. The Hotel is on the High Street.

Web: www.johansens.com/yeoldedogandpartridge
Email: info@dogandpartridge.net
Tel: 01283 813030
Fax: 01283 813178

Price Guide:
single £65
double £85–£100

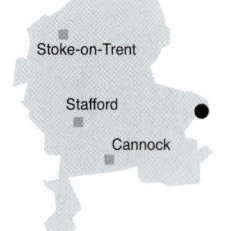

Ye Olde Dog & Partridge has entertained travellers since the time of the "Tutbury Bull Run" 400 years ago. Steeped in history, the village boasts its own castle as well as many shops and road links are excellent for those wishing to explore the sights of Derbyshire and Staffordshire with both the A50 and A38 less than 10 minutes away. The Hotel set within its own delightful mature gardens, has 29 bedrooms and conference facilities. Whilst retaining the charm of a bygone era, the bedrooms deliver the standard expected of a modern hotel. The heritage rooms boast air conditioning, digital televisions and many more quality features. In addition to the superb accommodation facilities, there is the opportunity to dine in either of the first class restaurants. The Carvery offers traditional English fare accompanied by the sound of the grand piano. The upbeat Brasserie restaurant provides a combination of classic and contemporary dishes that personifies this beautiful Hotel. Guests are also entitled to use the leisure facilities of Branston Golf & Country Club at no extra charge (Green fee rates available on application). For those wishing to explore, the Hotel provides an ideal base for local attractions within easy access such as the Peak District, Uttoxeter Race Course, Donington Race Track, Alton Towers and many National Trust properties such as Chatsworth House and Calke Abbey.

Our inspector loved: The historic rooms.

OAK TREE FARM

HINTS ROAD, HOPWAS, NR TAMWORTH, STAFFORDSHIRE B78 3AA

This peaceful little gem of a retreat is a rural oasis situated down a country road in the pretty village of Hopwas within short distance of Tamworth, Lichfield and Birmingham. Bordering the River Tame, it is surrounded by an area rich in history and culture and brimming with activity. Oak Tree Farm's charm is complemented by a gentle atmosphere which eases away any stress. Owner Sue Purkis provides a hospitable and helpful yet unobtrusive service that has earned Oak Tree Farm an enviable reputation and the five diamond qualification by the Premier Selected alongside the Gold Rose award by the England Tourist Board. Throughout the hotel, furnishings and the immaculate décor evoke a friendly ambience. Creature comforts are plentiful in the 7 en suite, non-smoking bedrooms which include comfortable sofas, colour television, trouser press, iron and courtesy tray. Some of the rooms are in an adjoining L-shaped wing and a waterbed is now situated in one the rooms. Breakfast is served in an elegant and light dining room. Facilties include a small heated indoor swimming pool and steam room but outside there are numerous country and woodland walks to be taken; guests can visit Drayton Manor Theme Park, Middleton Hall, the National Exhibition Centre, Lichfield Cathedral, Warwick Castle and Twycross Zoo.

Our inspector loved: *The waterbed. A property full of surprises.*

Directions: From M42 Jct10 take A5, then A51 towards Tamworth, then A51 Lichfield. Stay on A51 until you enter the village of Hopwas. Take first left into Hints Road.

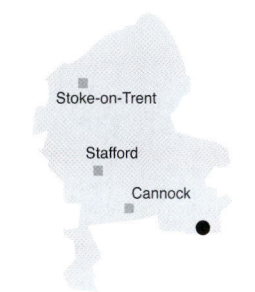

Web: www.johansens.com/oaktree
Tel: 01827 56807
Fax: 01827 56807

Price Guide:
single £57–£90
double/twin £75–£100

CLARICE HOUSE

HORRINGER COURT, HORRINGER ROAD, BURY ST. EDMUNDS SUFFOLK IP29 5PH

Directions: About 1 mile outside Bury St. Edmunds, situated on the A143 towards Haverhill.

Web: www.johansens.com/clarice
E-mail: enquire@clarice–bury.fsnet.co.uk
Tel: 01284 705550
Fax: 01284 716120

Price Guide:
single £55-£70
double/twin £80-£90

Clarice House is a residential spa housed within a beautifully refurbished Neo Jacobean mansion. Set within 20 acres of Suffolk countryside its grounds include ancient woodland and a protected site of scientific interest. Inside, an air of calm relaxation pervades. Guests are welcomed in the large lounge with lovely panelling and carved wood whilst informal meals are served in the bar. The excellent restaurant is open to residents and non-residents alike. For those choosing to stay for bed and breakfast, bedrooms are comfortable and well-appointed with luxurious en suite bathrooms. A variety of Spa Break packages are available which also include dinner and of course full use of the spa facilities, prices start from £115 per person. The gym comprises hi-tech equipment with computerised personal programme management. There is a team of dedicated instructors and a full programme of classes run daily. A beautiful 20 metre indoor swimming pool leads into a spa bath, steam room and sauna. The suite of beauty salons offer a huge range of indulgent treatments from the more traditional facials, manicures and pedicures to holistic treatments such as reflexology, reiki and Indian head massage. The Hotel is within easy reach of the racing at Newmarket, the university city of Cambridge and glorious Constable country. Fly fishing and clay pigeon shooting can also arranged.

Our inspector loved: The combination of modern comfort within the period surroundings.

THE SUFFOLK GOLF & COUNTRY CLUB

FORNHAM ST GENEVIEVE, BURY ST EDMUNDS, SUFFOLK IP28 6JQ

Situated in 150 acres and ideally located for both the business and leisure traveller, The Lodge at The Suffolk Golf & Country Club is an immaculate, modern hotel lying just minutes from the bustling town of Bury St. Edmunds and the A14. The Genevieve 18 hole golf course was built in 1967 and has rapidly gained a reputation for being one of the prettiest in East Anglia due to the River Lark meandering through the course and the abundance of lofty, shady trees providing many challenging holes. The Hotel was purpose-built and each of the 41 en suite bedrooms are spacious with a light and airy ambience and are pleasantly furnished and well-equipped, many with stunning views over the golf course. The lounge bar has a large balcony with commanding views over the course making this an ideal place for relaxing meals or drinks during the summer. Guests can enjoy the indoor pool with spa, sauna and steam room as well as the air-conditioned gym. A beauty and hair salon are due to open late 2002. There is much to see in this area: Newmarket Racecourse is easily reached and Thetford Forest is great walking territory. Bury St. Edmunds has a delightful Abbey and gardens and Cambridge, Norwich and the Suffolk coast are within easy access. Golf breaks and full conference and function facilities are available. Ample parking is on site.

Directions: From the A14 head west towards Bury St. Edmunds and follow the A1101 towards Mildenhall.

Web: www.johansens.com/suffolkgolfclub
E-mail: thelodge@the-suffolk.co.uk
Tel: 01284 706777
Fax: 01284 706721

Price Guide:
single £62
double/twin £75–£90

Our inspector loved: The great views from the lounge bar and balcony.

THE WHITE HORSE INN

HOLLOW HILL, WITHERSFIELD, HAVERHILL, SUFFOLK CB9 7SH

The White Horse Inn is the ideal choice of venue for both pleasure and business. Set in the beautiful Suffolk countryside, only 12 miles south of Cambridge, it is just a short drive from East Anglia's many attractions and business centres. Guests are assured of a warm, personal welcome from Bernard and Cherry Lee and their excellent staff. The original character of this charming inn has been carefully retained and with its intimate corners and open fires, there is always somewhere cosy to escape to and relax with a magazine or book. The bedrooms are situated in the renovated Suffolk Cart Lodge, fronted by a pretty garden. The style is light and airy, with country pine furnishings lending a modern but homely feel to the surroundings. On the ground floor, 2 four-poster suites, open onto their own gardens. A growing reputation for superb food means that it is essential for guests to book a table for dinner. The excellent wine list offered here is renowned and the ales are similarly applauded. Small meetings and private functions can be held during the daytime. A marquee is now available for functions up to 60 guests. Among the many places of interest nearby are the Newmarket and Saffron Walden. The inn is ETB 4 Diamonds Highly Commended.

Our inspector loved: *That this hotel is both cosy and welcoming.*

Directions: From M11, junction 9, take A11 in direction of Newmarket and turn onto A1307. Withersfield is signed after Horse Heath.

Web: www.johansens.com/whitehorsecambridge
Tel: 01440 706081
Fax: 01440 706081

Price Guide:
single £52.50
double from £89.50
honeymoon suite £95

THE GEORGE
THE GREEN, CAVENDISH, SUDBURY, SUFFOLK CO10 8BA

Located on the edge of the village green, this charming restaurant and bar captures the traditional spirit of south Suffolk's quintessential medieval villages, whose colour washed cottages and ancient woodlands have inspired some of Britain's greatest painters. Parts of the building date back to the 16th century and wooden beams, exposed brickwork, large open fireplaces and antique furniture are beautifully blended with soft, mellow colour schemes to create a comfortable, cosy ambience. In contrast, the handsome bar has a contemporary design and a large display of the finest wines. From the bar the kitchen is just in view, where it is possible to catch a glimpse of Jonathan Nicholson, once the head chef of 2 Conran restaurants in London, preparing good, wholesome and fresh classical dishes with a modern twist. Meals are complemented by a well-chosen, good value wine list from around the world. In the summer months, the outdoor shaded eating area is a cool oasis. The George is an excellent venue for small functions, parties and business events. There are plenty of antique shops, historic houses and churches to explore and walking or cycling through the picturesque countryside is sublime. Newmarket Racecourse is nearby and a fun day out.

Our inspector loved: *Jonathan's sheer enthusiasm and watching him personally making the bread rolls.*

Directions: Take the M11, junction 8 and follow the A120 east to Braintree. Take the A131 to Sudbury A134 to Long Melford then the A1092 to Cavendish.

Web: www.johansens.com/georgecavendish
E-mail: reservations@georgecavendish.co.uk
Tel: 01787 280248
Fax: 01787 280248

THE PLOUGH INN

BROCKLEY GREEN, NR HUNDON, SUDBURY, SUFFOLK CO10 8DT

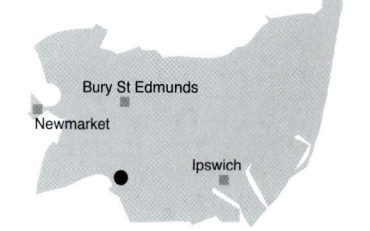

The Plough is a typical, charming, early 19th century inn commanding superb, panoramic views from its windows over the beautiful Stour Valley and five acres of immaculate grounds. Old beams, exposed soft red brickwork, solid, heavy furniture and comfortable sofas and chairs contribute to the inn's welcoming ambience. Under the current refurbishment programme each of the bedrooms will be themed after a local place of interest or beauty. The intimate, attractive bar is a restful delight offering an imaginative choice of bar meals and a good selection of traditional ales. Simms restaurant is highly regarded locally and serves superb English style cuisine. The Plough's peaceful rural location belies the presence of the many areas of interest within a short distance. Cycles are available for those seeking to explore the delightful picture-postcard villages nearby and landscape immortalised by painter John Constable. Within a 30 minutes drive there is the historic market town of Bury St Edmunds, the medieval wool towns of Lavenham and Long Melford, Constable's birthplace at Sudbury, Cambridge, Ely, Newmarket and the Imperial War Museum at Duxford.

Our inspector loved: The views, which are as amazing as they are unexpected.

Directions: From M11 Jct9 follow A11 to A1307 (towards Haverhill). Turn left onto A143 and after 2 miles turn right to Kedington, then follow signs to Clare.

Web: www.johansens.com/ploughinnclare
Tel: 01440 786789
Fax: 01440 786710

Price Guide:
single from £55
double from £75

Thornham Hall & Restaurant

THORNHAM MAGNA, NR. EYE, SUFFOLK IP23 8HA

Although of modern construction, the Hall retains the elegant proportions and style of its Tudor, Georgian and Victorian predecessors. Guests have exclusive use of a beautiful drawing room, study and breakfast room, which include fine porcelain, portraits and open fires; the study features a satellite/TV. The Hall is an ideal location for private house parties and small functions and provides a totally flexible service. The restaurant, which has disabled facilities, is situated in the old coach-house and is adjoined by a terrace. Here, as in the rest of the house, fresh flowers abound and the atmosphere is informal and welcoming. Food is pure country house cuisine and wonderful local game dishes regularly appear on the menu. The property is surrounded by stunning flower gardens and parkland. The Hall's Victorian walled orchard and 13 miles of walks are now open to the public. There is also a tennis court on the estate available for guests to use. Nearby wool towns such as Lavenham and Long Melford are well worth a visit as are the villages of Thornham Magna and especially Thornham Parva with its 9th century thatched church and medieval triptych. The Suffolk coast is just a short drive away.

Our inspector loved: The strutting peacocks and the large collection of Oriental pictures contrasting with traditional portraits.

Directions: From the A14 between Ipswich and Bury St. Edmunds take the A140 and follow signposts to Thornham Magna, the Hall is beyond the church.

Web: www.johansens.com/thornham
E-mail: lhenniker@thornhamhall.com
Tel: 01379 783314
Fax: 01379 788347

Price Guide:
single £50
double/twin £80

STANHILL COURT HOTEL

STAN HILL ROAD, CHARLWOOD, NR HORLEY, SURREY RH6 0EP

Directions: Charlwood is north-west of the airport off the M23/A23 via Hookwood or Lowfield Heath. Go through Charlwood and follow signs towards Newdigate.

Web: www.johansens.com/stanhillcourt
E-mail: enquiries@stanhillcourthotel.co.uk
Tel: 01293 862166
Fax: 01293 862773

Price Guide:
single from £110
double £125–£200

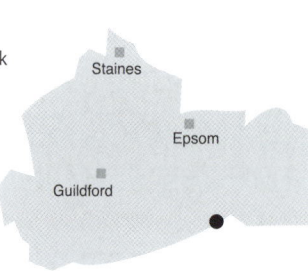

Built in 1881 in the Scottish Baronial style, Stanhill Court Hotel is set in 35 acres of ancient wooded countryside and offers total peace and tranquillity. It boasts an original Victorian walled garden and amphitheatre available for concerts or corporate presentations and events. These facilities are further enhanced by the rebuilding of the Orangery, offering further accommodation for events/conferences and banqueting. The hotel is traditionally furnished to provide an intimate, warm and comfortable atmosphere, with pitch pine panelling throughout the hall, minstrels gallery and barrel roof. There is a wide choice of bedrooms, all decorated and furnished to the same high standards and offering a full range of facilities. Restaurant 1881 serves a superb à la carte menu which is international in flavour and complemented by an excellent range of regional and vintage wines. A choice of vegetarian dishes is always included and old-style, personal service is guaranteed. Versatile conference facilities include meeting rooms and six function rooms. Stanhill Court Hotel has a renowned reputation for wedding receptions, family celebrations and social gatherings. Voted Most Romantic Hotel by the AA, awarded a RAC Blue Ribbon and Michelin listed.

Our inspector loved: The stained glass and the stairway.

Chase Lodge

10 PARK ROAD, HAMPTON WICK, KINGSTON-UPON-THAMES, SURREY KT1 4AS

Chase Lodge is situated in a quiet conservation area of architectural merit adjacent to Bushy Park. Originally built in 1870 as an artisan's house, the Lodge is now a very successful, bustling small hotel run by its owners, Nigel and Denise Stafford-Haworth and their young staff. The interiors have been designed to a high standard, with particular regard to the bijou nature of the building and with well chosen items of furniture complementing bold décor and fabrics. The bedrooms are cosy and the most recently refurbished bathrooms all feature either a jacuzzi bath or a steam shower. The conservatory style restaurant, with its cane furniture and marble topped tables, looks onto the tiny courtyard garden. Its proximity to many major events in the English social season makes Chase Lodge an outstanding choice for value: Wimbledon tennis; the Oxford and Cambridge Boat Race; horse racing at Kempton Park, Epsom Downs, Sandown Park and Royal Ascot; rugby at Twickenham; and the now annual flower show at Hampton Court. Central London with its shops and theatres is a short train ride away. Other places of interest nearby are Richmond and Syon Park, Windsor Castle, Ham House and Kew Gardens.

Our inspector loved: Its individual character and the imaginative use of space within a tiny town house setting.

Directions: From the M3 (junction 1) or Kingston take the A308. At western end of Kingston Bridge is the Hampton Wick roundabout, take the White Hart exit into High Street (A310), then left at The Forresters into Park Road.

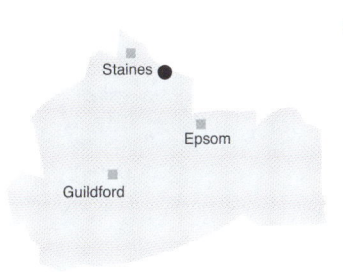

Web: www.johansens.com/chaselodge
E-mail: info@chaselodgehotel.com
Tel: 020 8943 1862
Fax: 020 8943 9363

Price Guide:
single from £65
double from £75

HORTON GRANGE COUNTRY HOUSE HOTEL

BERWICK HILL, PONTELAND, NEWCASTLE UPON TYNE, NE13 6BU

Directions: Exit A1 at A19 Tyne Tunnel. Take 1st exit from roundabout and one mile ahead turn left to Ponteland and Dinnington. The hotel is two miles further up on the right hand side.

Web: www.johansens.com/hortongrange
E-mail: andrew@horton-grange.co.uk
Tel: 01661 860686
Fax: 01661 860308

Price Guide:
single £79-90
double £85-£95

This hotel is "a small oasis," tucked away within tree-lined grounds; this certainly seems an apt description although "little gem" could possibly also apply. The Victorian house has been carefully maintained and now offers nine carefully appointed suites, five of which are in the main house and four in the garden rooms. The interior style is one of classic mixed with contemporary and makes clever use of checks and stripes with pretty florals, and greenery. The Japanese garden is a triumph and a key focal point for the Hotel – indeed the light and airy conservatory dining room gives guests delightful views over the garden and was also mentioned by our inspector as a highlight of her stay. Here, the cuisine reflects the style of the Hotel taking classic dishes and refreshing them with a modern twist resulting in an exciting menu that is adaptable to all tastes. Newcastle airport is only a short drive away and the city centre lies within 8 miles and has a vast array of shops and nightlife although the surrounding scenery and coastlines are extremely pretty and comparatively undiscovered.

Our inspector loved: This small oasis on the outskirts of Newcastle.

CLARENDON HOUSE

OLD HIGH STREET, KENILWORTH, WARWICKSHIRE CV8 1LZ

Set in the heart of England, in the verdant conservation area of Kenilworth, Clarendon House is steeped in a most interesting history. Dating back to 1430, the original timber-framed 'Castle Tavern' is ever present and is still supported by the old oak tree around which it was built. Whilst there has recently been a complete refurbishment of this property, vestiges of the past and traditional features have still been retained, such as the many cottage-style bedrooms. All of the rooms are well-equipped with satellite televisions and modem/fax sockets and furnished in an elegant style. For those seeking an air of romance and sentiment, there are two rooms with four-poster beds and a luxurious suite. Open day and night, the bar and brasserie form the very heart of this establishment. Offering a deliciously versatile menu, prepared with fresh, seasonal produce, the brasserie serves everything from hearty British meals to delicate seafood platters. A list of carefully chosen fine wines has been compiled with the flavours in mind. With its good function rooms and conference facilities, the hotel is an ideal venue for private dining, business meetings and special occasions such as intimate weddings. Budding thespians will be pleased with the proximity of Stratford-upon-Avon.

Our inspector loved: The cosy lounge in which to sit quietly and read.

Directions: The nearest motorway is the M40, exit at junction 15.

Web: www.johansens.com/clarendonhouse
E-mail: info@clarendonhouse.com
Tel: 01926 857668
Fax: 01926 850669

Price Guide:
single £49.50–£55
double £79.50–£90
suite £110

GLEBE FARM HOUSE

LOXLEY, WARWICKSHIRE CV35 9JW

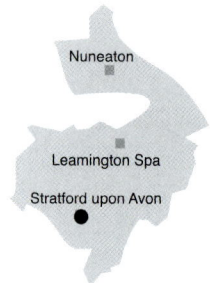

The pleasure of staying at this delightful country house is like that of visiting a private home. Just three miles from historic Stratford-upon-Avon and eight miles from Warwick, Glebe Farm is surrounded by a superb expanse of secluded lawned garden which opens on to 30 acres of beautiful farmland where one can ramble and enjoy the sounds and sights of local wildlife. Owner Kate McGovern is an accomplished cook and her dinners, served in the attractive surroundings of a conservatory overlooking the gardens, will tempt every palate. Whenever possible fresh organic produce from the kitchen garden are used. Kate is a talented water colour artist and many of her paintings adorn the walls throughout the house which is furnished and decorated with immaculate taste. There are four pretty en suite bedrooms with four-poster beds and television and tea and coffee facilities. From all bedrooms and the lounge there are splendid views of the countryside. Local sporting activities include golf, shooting and riding. The country house is an ideal base for visiting Shakespeare's Stratford-upon-Avon, Warwick's imposing castle, Ragley Hall, Birmingham N.E.C., the Heritage Motor Museum and the Cotswolds.

Directions: From the M40, exit at junction 15. Join the A429 and follow the signs to Wellsbourne, then Loxley. Glebe Farm is on the right as you leave Loxley.

Web: www.johansens.com/glebefarmhouse
E-mail: scorpiolimited@msn.com
Tel: 01789 842501
Fax: 01789 842501

Price Guide:
single £75
double £100–£115
suite from £130

Our inspector loved: The superb food – all prepared from their own organic produce, home cooked on the Aga by Kate.

THE GRANVILLE
124 KINGS ROAD, BRIGHTON BN1 2FA

You only have to take one step through the front door to realise, and appreciate, that this Regency sea front property is a place for the style aware. The Granville has been created and furnished with considerable flair – it is a unique little hotel that offers guests a most attractive alternative to the many larger establishments that crowd the sea front. It is situated at the heart of Regency Brighton overlooking the sea and the once splendid Edwardian West Pier. The hotel has been awarded three stars by the AA and the English Tourism Council. Its new owners have begun a programme of sensitive and appropriate refurbishment. The majority of the 24 en suite bedrooms are not large but they are quite distinctive and the feature rooms include sumptuous bathrooms. Many have fabulous sea views. Among them is the romantic, pale pink and white Brighton Rock Room, the opulent Noel Coward Room with its art-deco bathroom, the huge late-Victorian four-poster bed and marble fireplaces of the Balcony Room and the Marina Room with a water bed. Breakfast is the only meal served by the hotel but guests have a wide and cosmopolitan choice of restaurants for evening dining within just a few minutes walk.

Our inspector loved: The sea views, the Brighton bustle and the boldly themed rooms.

Directions: The Granville is on the north side of Kings Road opposite the West Pier.

Web: www.johansens.com/granville
E-mail: granville@brighton.co.uk
Tel: 01273 326302
Fax: 01273 728294

Price Guide:
single from £55
double £85–£165

EAST SUSSEX - RYE

NEW

THE HOPE ANCHOR HOTEL

WATCHBELL STREET, RYE, EAST SUSSEX TN31 7HA

Dating back to the mid-18th century, The Hope Anchor was featured in Malcolm Saville's children's books and with its beautiful old timbers, nooks and crannies and secret passages it possesses immense character and charm. An enviable position in one of Rye's most enchanting and interesting cobbled streets means it boasts stunning views across the harbour, Romney Marsh, Camber Castle and the rivers Brede and Rother. 12 individually furnished bedrooms offer a range of single, double and family accommodation and all are en suite with tea and coffee making facilities. The Hotel comprises of two bars, a lounge and an excellent restaurant that welcomes residents and non-residents alike. Menus portray an imaginative use of fresh, seasonally available local ingredients. Rye itself was described as, "about as perfect as a small town can get," by the Daily Telegraph in 1997 and landmarks such as Mermaid Street, Church Square, St. Mary's Church, Lamb House and the 13th century Ypres Tower are all within a few minutes stroll.

Our inspector loved: Its quiet setting in the cobbled heart of Rye.

Directions: From the A268 circumnavigate Rye clockwise via the A259. Turn right by the Heritage Centre and straight up Mermaid Street. Turn right into West Street, right into Church Square and right again into Watchbell Street. The Hope Anchor is at the end of the street.

Web: www.johansens.com/hopeanchor
E-mail: info@hotel-rye.freeserve.co.uk
Tel: 01797 222216
Fax: 01797 223796

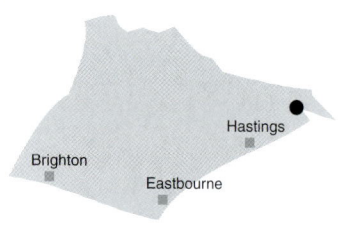

Price Guide:
single from £50
double/twin £85–£120

HOOKE HALL

HIGH STREET, UCKFIELD, EAST SUSSEX TN22 1EN

Uckfield lies on the borders of Ashdown Forest, near the South Downs and resorts of Brighton and Eastbourne and 40 minutes from Gatwick Airport. Hooke Hall is an elegant Queen Anne town house, the home of its owners, Juliet and Alister Percy, who have carried out extensive renovations. The comfortable bedrooms are individually decorated to a high standard with private facilities. In the panelled study guests can relax and enjoy sampling the excellent range of malt whiskies on offer from the well-stocked 'Honesty Bar'. There are several restaurants within easy walking distance of the hotel and further choices only minutes away by car. Within easy reach are Leeds, Hever and Bodiam Castles, Penshurst Place and Battle Abbey. The gardens of Sissinghurst, Nymans, Great Dixter, Sheffield Park, Wakehurst Place and Leonardslee are no distance nor is Batemans, Rudyard Kipling's home. Glyndebourne Opera is only 15 minutes by car. There are several English vineyards nearby to be visited. Hooke Hall is closed for Christmas.

Our inspector loved: *The 'home from home' atmosphere in a fine Queen Anne building.*

Directions: From M25 take the exit for East Grinstead and continue South on the A22 to Uckfield. Hooke Hall is at the northern end of the High Street.

Web: www.johansens.com/hookehall
E-mail: a.percy@virgin.net
Tel: 01825 761578
Fax: 01825 768025

Price Guide:
single from £60
double from £85

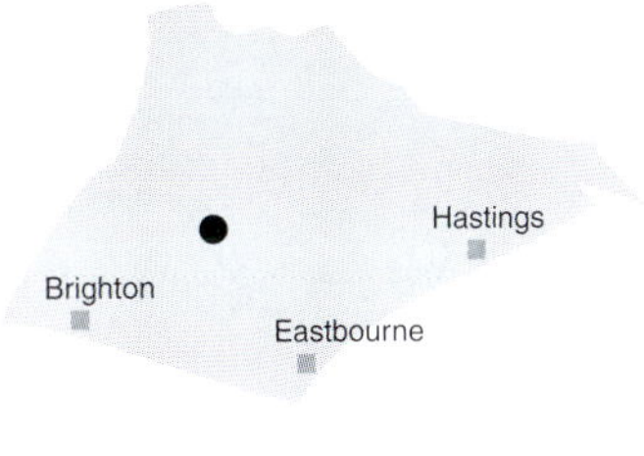

WEST SUSSEX - ARUNDEL (BURPHAM)

BURPHAM COUNTRY HOUSE HOTEL

OLD DOWN, BURPHAM, NR ARUNDEL, WEST SUSSEX BN18 9RJ

Directions: The Hotel is signposted on the A27 east of Arundel railway bridge. Turn off here and follow this road for 2½ miles.

Web: www.johansens.com/burphamcountryhouse
E-mail: burphamchh@ukonline.co.uk
Tel: 01903 882160
Fax: 01903 884627

Price Guide:
single from £58.50
double £87–£130

This charming country house hotel nestles in a fold of the Sussex Downs – perfect for a stress remedy break. New owners Ann McCawley and Paul Michalski are upgrading the ten en-suite bedrooms with stylish furnishings and delightful bathrooms. A lovely old world garden surrounds the hotel. Drinks before dinner can be enjoyed by the open fire in the comfortable Cocktail Lounge. A good wine list is available with most countries represented. A fine new conservatory addition to the dining room makes a quite delightful setting in which to enjoy the excellent award-winning cuisine of Stephen Piggott. The Hotel has won a Silver award from the English Tourist Board for quality and the most prestigious Johansens 1999 award for 'Most Excellent Service'. Special breaks are offered throughout the year. Golf, riding, fishing and sailing are all available in the locality. Racing at Goodwood and Fontwell. Burpham has a beautiful and historic Norman church, while Arundel, with its Wildfowl Sanctuary and renowned Castle, is three miles away. The coast lies within six miles.

Our inspector loved: The excellent refurbished bedrooms and bathrooms.

THE MILL HOUSE HOTEL

MILL LANE, ASHINGTON, WEST SUSSEX RH20 3BX

This charming Grade II listed building exudes warmth and character. Vestiges of the past are evident throughout the country house, and the original paintings adorning the walls and the antiques in the public rooms form a lasting testament to its 17th century past. Following extensive renovation in 1997, the house combines the charm and attentive service associated with bygone days with the modern facilities of the present. The enthusiastic owners, Simon and Maria Hudson, and their gracious staff provide a helpful yet unobtrusive service. The bedrooms, some of which have recently been refurbished, are simple yet stylish. Gastronomes will be impressed with the excellent cuisine which is complemented by a good selection of wines, liqueurs and Cognacs. The menu includes the ever popular griddled fillet steak with a rustique camembert and mixed peppercorn crust, served with a rich port sauce presented on wild mushrooms. Accommodating up to 30 people, the private dining room is ideal for small conferences and meetings and for private dining. Heritage enthusiasts will be delighted with the situation of this property as Parham House and Arundel Castle and Cathedral are within easy reach. Popular daytime excursions include trips to the pleasant beaches of Chichester and Brighton.

Our inspector loved: *The polished terracotta tiles and quaint guest lounge.*

Directions: Ashington is west of the A24 and north of the junction with the A283. If travelling from the North, follow the large brown sign.

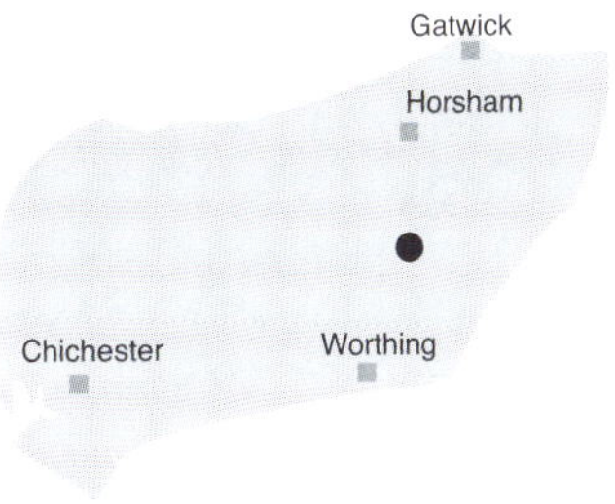

Web: www.johansens.com/millhousehotelashington
E-mail: ashingtonmill@aol.com
Tel: 01903 892426

Price Guide:
single from £49
double from £79–£89

THE OLD TOLLGATE RESTAURANT AND HOTEL

THE STREET, BRAMBER, STEYNING, WEST SUSSEX BN44 3WE

An original Tollhouse centuries ago, travellers now look forward to stopping here and paying their dues for wonderful hospitality. Part of the old building is still in evidence with newer additions attractively blending. There are some splendid suites, even a four-poster, which are excellent value and delightful bedrooms, some of which are reached across the courtyard. The hotel is a popular meeting place for visitors and locals alike, with friendly staff adding to the welcoming ambience. The restaurant has built up a fine reputation, extending far beyond Sussex. It has a magnificent award-winning carvery and sumptuous cold table. Breakfast, lunch and dinner are all catered for at various price structures according to the number of courses consumed. Soups and broths, fresh and smoked fish, roasts and casseroles, pies and puddings and vegetarian dishes are in abundance. A secluded garden suntrap has been newly created. Bramber is famous for its Norman Castle and spectacular views over the South Downs. Brighton, with its shops, beach and Pavilion is an easy drive away, as is Worthing. Sporting activities nearby include riding, golf and fishing.

Directions: Bramber is off the A283 between Brighton and Worthing, easily accessed from the A24 or A27.

Web: www.johansens.com/oldtollgatebrighton
E-mail: otr@fastnet.co.uk
Tel: 01903 879494
Fax: 01903 813399

Price Guide: (room only)
single from £75
double £75–£125
suite £105

Our inspector loved: what everybody loves - the finest twice a day buffet in the south.

CROUCHERS COUNTRY HOTEL & RESTAURANT

BIRDHAM ROAD, APULDRAM, NEAR CHICHESTER, WEST SUSSEX PO20 7EH

This former farmhouse, set just ½ a mile from the Yacht Basin and 2 miles from the centre of Chichester, has been re-styled into a fine country hotel and awarded 3 AA stars for its 18 bedrooms, good food and most attentive service. The new, spacious open-plan ground floor impresses guests the moment they arrive at reception and the bedrooms, most of which are located in the converted coach house and barn, do not disappoint. However, it is the newly designed public areas which will excite approval: the bar and lounge areas and the fine new 60 seat restaurant have transformed Crouchers. Dishes, freshly prepared from the very finest ingredients and the inspiration of Chef Gavin Wilson, have already won the first Rosette recognition. Meals are complemented by a carefully constructed and interesting wine list, reflecting the family's connections with South Africa. Crouchers Country Hotel will delight those wishing merely to relax and escape the pressures of a hectic lifestyle. In the summer months a tranquil ambience envelopes the courtyard as guests sip chilled drinks and laze in the sun.

Our inspector loved: *The very relaxed atmosphere in the Restaurant.*

Directions: From the M27, junction 12, take the A27 to Chichester and then the A286 south towards The Witterings. Crouchers Country Hotel is on the left.

Web: www.johansens.com/crouchersbottom
Email: info@crouchersbottom.com
Tel: 01243 784995
Fax: 01243 539797

Price Guide:
single from £60
double £85–£120

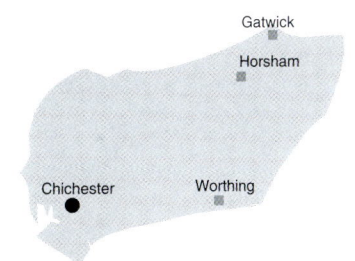

FORGE HOTEL

CHILGROVE, CHICHESTER, WEST SUSSEX PO18 9HX

Set in the folds of the Downs, six miles from the Cathedral City of Chichester, this charming tiny brick and flint hotel could easily be your dream hideaway in the country. Once the blacksmith's cottage, the original building has been sensitively restored and extended. The comfortable bedrooms reflect an understated intimate style. Owner and classically trained chef Neil Rusbridger, prepares meals to delight his guests, who eat together around one big table. Only the very best of ingredients will feature on the ever changing, seasonal menus. Most produce will be sourced locally and much will be organic. Guests will also be welcomed at Neil's new wine bar in Chichester called The Dining Room. For eight or nine people meeting up or travelling together, this is the perfect house party location. Places of interest nearby include West Dean Gardens, Petworth House, Uppark, Goodwood House, Chichester Festival Theatre and Cathedral, Fishbourne Roman Palace, the Weald and Downland Museum. There is horse racing at 'Glorious Goodwood', the Festival of Speed and the Revival Meeting for motor sport enthusiasts; antique hunting at Petworth and Midhurst, and sailing at Chichester harbour.

Directions: Between Petersfield and Chichester on B2141. At Chilgrove take road in front of the White Horse.

Web: www.johansens.com/forgehotel
E-mail: reservations@forgehotel.com
Tel: 01243 535333
Fax: 01243 535363

Price Guide:
single from £49
double/twin £98–£145

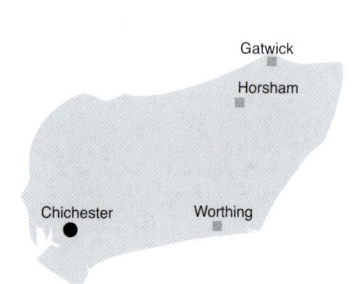

Our inspector loved: *The clever marriage of old and new in this warm and welcoming timbered house.*

THE CHEQUERS AT SLAUGHAM

SLAUGHAM, NR HANDCROSS, WEST SUSSEX RH17 6AQ

Set in this attractive conservation village, The Chequers at Slaugham is a delightful hostelry offering a warm welcome, good accommodation and acclaimed cooking. All five of the guest rooms are appointed to a high standard, each with a host of amenities that include remote-control television, trouser press, radio alarm, hairdryer and refreshments. All have four poster beds and some have spa or double baths. The public rooms are given over mainly to dining areas, however, there is a comfortable residents' lounge. The Chequers' culinary reputation has gone from strength to strength. The menu caters for all tastes but majors on outstanding seafood dishes with manager Ray Charman personally buying direct from the London market. Depending upon availability, the menu may include wing of skate, halibut, monkfish, fresh crab, lobster, plaice, lemon sole, scallops, salmon and richly flavoured fish soups. Guests can also dine in the conservatory restaurant with outstanding views of the Sussex countryside. The Chequers is conveniently located just ten minutes from Gatwick and is easily accessible from London. It is also well placed for visiting the stately homes and gardens of Surrey and Sussex.

Our inspector loved: *This long-time favourite eaterie which never disappoints.*

Directions: From the main London- Gatwick-Brighton road (A23), exit 2 miles south of Handcross.

Web: www.johansens.com/chequersatslaugham
Tel: 01444 400239/400996
Fax: 01444 400400

Price Guide:
single from £60
double from £85

THE HALF MOON INN

KIRDFORD, NEAR PETWORTH, WEST SUSSEX RH14 0LT

Directions: Just off the A272 between Billinghurst and Petworth. Kirdford is signposted from there.

Web: www.johansens.com/halfmoon
E-mail: halfmooninn.kirdford@virgin.net
Tel: 01403 820223
Fax: 01403 820224

Price Guide: (including dinner) double from £120

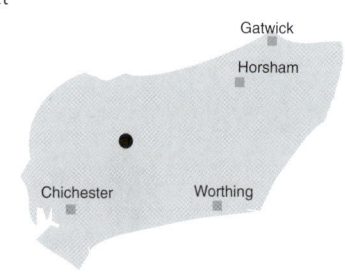

Situated in the heart of the beautiful West Sussex countryside, this lovely 17th century Inn has been proudly and lovingly restored and is the essence of charm with its red tiles, climbing roses and air of quaint cosiness. The low beamed ceilings and curved bar are combined with modern décor to create an inviting atmosphere of spaciousness and sophistication. Well-known for its delicious, well presented cuisine, the head chef delivers a 'great British menu with a twist.' His imaginative dishes are created using only the finest quality meat, fish and vegetables and there are plenty of vegetarian and healthy options. The pub serves excellent lagers and cask ales as well as an extensive list of wines. The Inn is happy to cater for all special events with a tailor-made menu, flowers and cakes. Newly refurbished bedrooms have a shared bathroom. There is an abundance of country walks in the area and The Half Moon Inn is the ideal base to explore the surrounding villages. Petworth House is nearby, a magnificent mansion set in a beautiful deer park, immortalised in Turner's paintings and contains the National Trust's finest collection of works by artists such as Turner, Van Dyck, Reynolds and Blake.

Our inspector loved: The up-to-date interior for a stylish experience in the heart of unspoilt countryside.

RUDLOE HALL

LEAFLY LANE, NEAR BOX, WILTSHIRE SN13 0PA

This beautiful Victorian Country House lies in an unrivalled position on the crest of Box Hill with views reaching across some 6 miles towards Bath. The surrounding countryside is delightful and great care has been taken to ensure that Rudloe Hall is more like an old Victorian home than a hotel and that it is a romantic and welcoming refuge after a day's sightseeing in the area. The elegant features of a bygone era have been preserved at Rudloe and in some of the bedrooms guests will have the luxury of bathing in a Victorian roll top bath in front of a roaring fire and sleeping in an elegant four poster bed. Open fires are a key feature in the Hotel and are regularly lit in both the public rooms and the bedrooms whilst candlelight is also used to create an intimate atmosphere in which to enjoy a romantic dinner accompanied by fine wines. There is a great deal to enjoy in the surrounding area; with Bath being only a short drive away, there is great walking on the doorstep in the Woodland Trust's Box Valley.

Our inspector loved: The Tower suite with its own roof-spa bathing.

Directions: Leave the M4 at junction 17 and take the A350 to Chippenham. Follow the A4 Bath signs through Chippenham bypass. and Rudloe Hall is on the left 1 mile after leaving Pickwick (on the outskirts of Corsham).

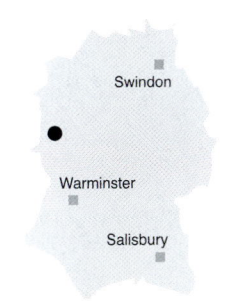

Web: www.johansens.com/rudloehall
E-mail: mail@rudloehall.co.uk
Tel: 01225 810555
Fax: 01225 811412

Price Guide:
single £85-£159
double/twin £119-£225
suite £300

THE OLD MANOR HOTEL

TROWLE, BRADFORD-ON-AVON, WILTSHIRE BA14 9BL

Directions: The Hotel is on the A363 towards Trowbridge, 1½ miles from Bradford-on-Avon.

Web: www.johansens.com/oldmanorbath
E-mail: romanticbeds@eastnet.co.uk
Tel: 01225 777393
Fax: 01225 765443

Price Guide:
single £59.50–£78
double/twin £78–£100
suite £125

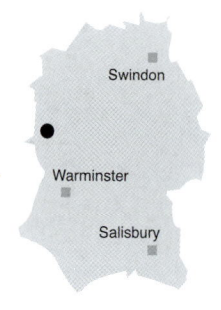

Set on Trowle Common, only 8 miles from the centre of Bath, a Doomsday Book site in the heart of Wiltshire, this magnificent Grade II listed farmhouse is of outstanding historical interest with a combination of medieval and Queen Anne architecture. Surrounded by 4 ½ acres of farmland and picture perfect gardens, The Old Manor exudes a sense of idyllic rural charm and peace. The main buildings, barns and stables have been lovingly converted into bedrooms and are built around an extremely pretty courtyard. Romantic, spacious bedrooms and heavily beamed suites have uninterrupted views over open fields and are decorated with stunning antiques, huge comfortable beds (some four poster) and glorious furnishings. Open fires complement the cosy atmosphere of the public areas, where ease and comfort are sublime. Delicious home-cooked meals are served in the restaurant, which was converted from the original milking parlour and boasts a large stone fireplace. Bird lovers will be astonished by the abundance of kestrels, sparrowhawks, buzzards, herons and wild duck in the area. The Hotel is also the perfect base for walking the lovely Kennet and Avon Canal path with its slow moving barges and picturesque views. Bradford-on-Avon is nearby with its Saxon church (900AD), tithe barn, period streets and buildings as well as Lacock Abbey where Harry Potter was filmed.

Our inspector loved: *The large, spacious suites across the courtyard.*

WIDBROOK GRANGE

TROWBRIDGE ROAD, BRADFORD-ON-AVON, NR BATH, WILTSHIRE BA15 1UH

Widbrook Grange, the home of resident owners Jane and Peter Wragg, is an elegant 250 year old Georgian Country House set in 11 acres of gardens and fields near the Kennet and Avon canal just outside the medieval town of Bradford-on-Avon. It nestles in peaceful rolling countryside yet is only 17 minutes from the Georgian City of Bath. The house was originally built as a model farm. In the surrounding courtyard the stables and barns have been imaginatively renovated to include some of the 20 well-appointed bedrooms, an indoor heated swimming pool and small gymnasium. The informal Medlar Tree Restaurant serves award winning British regional cuisine using local ingredients complimented by an interesting selection of new and old world wines. The purpose built Manvers Conference Suite, with its magnificent 18 foot oak boardroom table is ideal for meetings, training seminars and private dining. Widbrook welcomes its guests with an atmosphere of warmth and informality, the service being attentive yet unobtrusive. Two golf clubs are a short drive away and horse riding; fishing and cycle and boat hire can be arranged. Other places of interest nearby include Longleat, Stonehenge and Laycock Abbey.

Our inspector loved: *The informal, personal and friendly service and lovely indoor swimming pool.*

Directions: From Bradford-on-Avon take the A363 Trowbridge Road. Widbrook Grange is 200 metres on the right after the Kennet and Avon canal bridge.

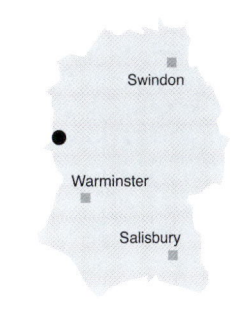

Web: www.johansens.com/widbrookgrange
E-mail: stay@widbrookgrange.com
Tel: 01225 864750/863173
Fax: 01225 862890

Price Guide:
single £95–£105
double £110–£120
four poster £125-£140
family rooms from £140

HINTON GRANGE

NR. HINTON, DRYHAM, WILTSHIRE SN14 8HG

Directions: 15 to 20 minutes away from Bath and Bristol.

Web: www.johansens.com/hintongrange
Email: mail@hintongrange.co.uk
Tel: 0117 937 2916
Fax: 0117 937 3285

Price Guide:
single £85
double/twin £119–£225

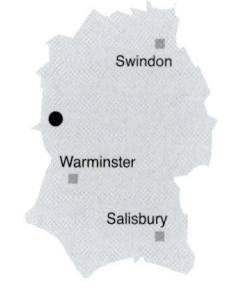

Originally built in 1614 and extended in 1750, Hinton Grange nestles beneath a hill within the famous Anglo Saxon Battle of Dyrham site. Today, the Hotel provides a hopelessly romantic, if somewhat slightly eccentric, retreat with its low doors and beams, old stone walls and frayed rugs. Converted barns house some of the best bedrooms and open fires are a feature throughout, providing the warmest welcome even on the coldest days. All of the rooms are individually decorated with four poster beds and comfy olde worlde furnishings. Some have screened Victorian bathing alcoves with cast iron baths, and dinner can also be served privately in a candlelit, fireside setting. Cuisine at the Hotel has an excellent reputation and daily changing menus are prepared using the finest and freshest ingredients. A choice of restaurants include: the Inglenook; the smaller Crofters Nookery; and the tropical Georgian Conservatory, while pre-dinner drinks can be enjoyed in the snug sitting rooms adorned with antiques. Hinton adjoins the National Trust estate and stately home of Dyrham Park and the renowned Cotswold Way Walk meanders close to the house. Other nearby places of interest include Castle Combe and Laycock and the Hotel itself offers croquet, fishing and Pitch and Putt.

Our inspector loved: *This romantic retreat in lovely grounds.*

STANTON MANOR

STANTON SAINT QUINTIN, NR CHIPPENHAM, WILTSHIRE SN14 6DQ

A wide, columned entranceway welcomes visitors to this attractive stone-built Hotel standing in 7 acres of beautiful grounds in the delightful Wiltshire village of Stanton Saint Quintin. The original house was listed in the Domesday Book, was once owned by Lord Burghley, chief minister to Queen Elizabeth I, and was rebuilt in 1840. Stanton Manor has recently been completely refurbished by owners Duncan and Linda Hickling, who are on hand to ensure that a friendly and attentive service is extended to guests. Modern facilities and comforts combine easily and unobtrusively with those of the past, which include magnificent Tudor fireplaces and stone flooring. The en suite bedrooms are spacious and individually designed with toning fabrics and comfortable furniture. Some have four poster beds, antique brass beds or king-size pine beds. Head Chef, Wendy White, and her team take pride in creating traditional British cuisine with flare and quality, which is immaculately served in the elegant and light Burghley Restaurant, overlooking the grounds. Light snacks can be enjoyed in the cosy, copper and brass hung bar decorated with motor racing, rugby and horse racing memorabilia.

Our inspector loved: The rooms with garden views.

Directions: Exit the M4 at junction 17 and join the A429 towards Cirencester. After approximately 200 yards, turn left to Stanton Saint Quintin. Stanton Manor is on the left in the village.

Web: www.johansens.com/stantonmanor
E-mail: reception@stantonmanor.co.uk
Tel: 01666 837552
Fax: 01666 837022

Price Guide:
single £65–£95
double £85–£135

THE GEORGE INN

LONGBRIDGE DEVERILL, WARMINSTER, WILTSHIRE BA12 7DG

A warm welcome awaits guests to this friendly inn. All rooms have been refurbished, and there is a public bar as well as a cosy residents lounge with a good selection of books and games to while away a lazy afternoon. The inn can cater for conferences, weddings and parties and has a skittles alley. The welcoming Kingston Restaurant and the Longbridge Bar, which are both warmed by an open fire, serve an excellent à la carte menu and a good selection of mouthwatering home-cooked dishes that might include tender lamb shank braised in a rich red wine and redcurrant jus or oven-baked Dover sole with lemon and herb butter. Outside the Riverside Garden, which is set in two acres of gardens and has plenty of car parking, is a popular venue during the warmer months. Active guests can explore the surroundings on foot or by bicycle, whilst golf and fishing can also be arranged. The George Inn is the ideal base from which to explore nearby Longleat and Bath, Stourhead, Wookey Hole Caves, Stonehenge and Wardour Castle.

Our inspector loved: The cleanliness and standard of accommodation - home from home.

Directions: From the A303 take the A350 towards Warminster; the George is on the left. From the A36 take the A350 towards Shaftesbury; the George is on the right.

Web: www.johansens.com/georgewarminster
Tel: 01985 840396
Fax: 01985 841333

Price Guide:
single £40
double/twin £60–£95
family room £75

THE MILL AT HARVINGTON

ANCHOR LANE, HARVINGTON, EVESHAM, WORCESTERSHIRE WR11 8PA

From the first glimpse of Simon and Jane Greenhalgh's elegant brochure one is aware that The Mill at Harvington is very special. This delightful small country hotel set on the bank of the Avon is in the heart of England with easy access to the West, The Cotswolds, Wales and, of course, Shakespeare country. From inside the welcoming and graceful reception rooms, which are brightened by big open fires in the winter, there are views over the extensive gardens and the river. The high standards of hospitality and service are evident throughout. The en suite bedrooms, located in the main building and the superb annexe extension are beautifully furnished with all the modern comforts including hairdryer, colour television, tea and coffee facilities. The restaurant has won 2 AA Rosettes for its delicious cuisine, and an excellent wine list accompanies the menu, which makes maximum use of local and seasonal produce, fish and game, reflecting the owners' belief that dining well must be high on the agenda for a successful visit. Light meals are served in the Chestnut Tree bistro and on the riverside patio in summer. Guests take away memories of spectacular countryside, superb meals, immaculate service, charming surroundings and perfect hosts.

Our inspector loved: The lovely riverside location.

Directions: The Mill can be reached by a roadbridge over A46 opposite Harvington village, off Evesham–Bidford road.

Web: www.johansens.com/millatharvington
E-mail: millatharvington@aol.com
Tel: 01386 870688
Fax: 01386 870688

Price Guide:
single £65–£88
double/twin £109–£131

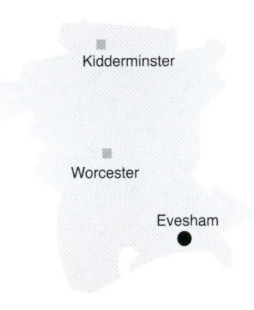

THE MOUNT PLEASANT HOTEL

BELLE VUE TERRACE, MALVERN, WORCESTERSHIRE WR14 4PZ

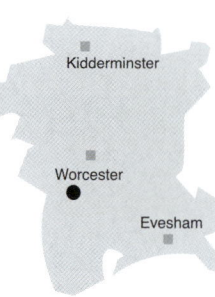

Malvern has hills. Not for climbing, but for walking; easy enough for anyone who is reasonably fit. They provide superb views westwards towards Hereford and Wales and eastwards over the patchwork countryside of Worcester. The Mount Pleasant Hotel is perched on the slopes of these hills in celebrated composer Sir Edward Elgar country. It is an impressive red brick Georgian building that commands a spectacular 30 mile outlook from sparkling, white-framed windows across Malvern Priory and the Vale of Evesham. There is countryside at the gate and central Malvern, with its specialist shops, art galleries, theatre, restaurants and popular attractions on the doorstep. Each of the 14 comfortable and individually decorated bedrooms offer a high standard of facilities and owners, Julie and Alan Josey, pride themselves in providing a relaxing and welcoming atmosphere throughout the Hotel. They are also proud of their local reputation for the cuisine served both in the elegant Number 50 Restaurant and of the quality bistro dishes served in the less formal Auberge Brasserie, which is open from 10.30am to 10.30pm daily. Wines are a particular speciality with trophy winning selections from local vineyards appearing alongside old and new world favourites. Over 30 wines and champagnes are available by the glass. Pets are greeted with a welcoming bowl of water and biscuit.

Directions: Malvern is approximately 8 miles from junctions 7 and 8 of the M5. Take the A449 out of town towards Ledbury.

Web: www.johansens.com/mountpleasant
E-mail: mountpleasanthotel@btinternet.com
Tel: 01684 561837
Fax: 01684 569968

Price Guide:
single £58
double/twin £88
superior double £98

Our inspector loved: The stunning view from the front facing rooms.

THE WHITE LION HOTEL

HIGH STREET, UPTON-UPON-SEVERN, NR MALVERN, WORCESTERSHIRE WR8 0HJ

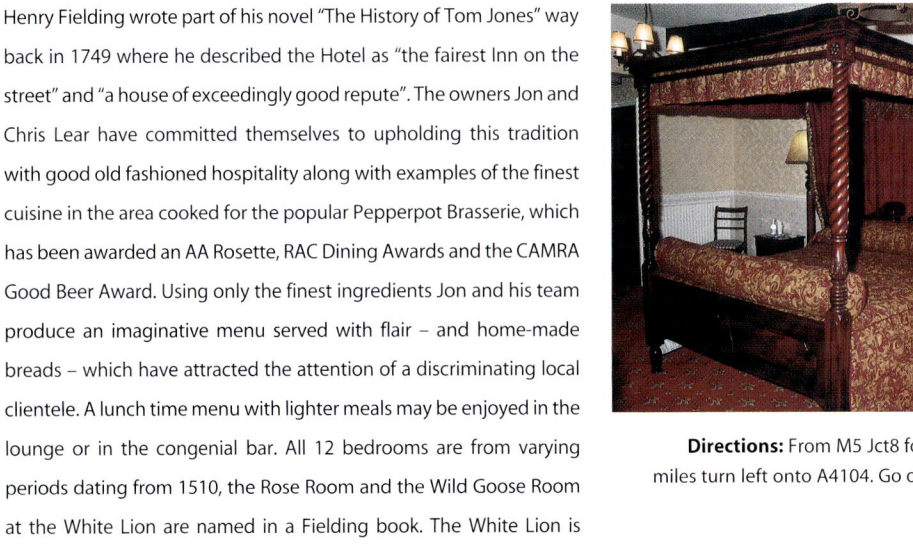

Henry Fielding wrote part of his novel "The History of Tom Jones" way back in 1749 where he described the Hotel as "the fairest Inn on the street" and "a house of exceedingly good repute". The owners Jon and Chris Lear have committed themselves to upholding this tradition with good old fashioned hospitality along with examples of the finest cuisine in the area cooked for the popular Pepperpot Brasserie, which has been awarded an AA Rosette, RAC Dining Awards and the CAMRA Good Beer Award. Using only the finest ingredients Jon and his team produce an imaginative menu served with flair – and home-made breads – which have attracted the attention of a discriminating local clientele. A lunch time menu with lighter meals may be enjoyed in the lounge or in the congenial bar. All 12 bedrooms are from varying periods dating from 1510, the Rose Room and the Wild Goose Room at the White Lion are named in a Fielding book. The White Lion is central for visiting The Malvern Hills, The Three Counties Show Ground, the market town of Ledbury, Tewkesbury's Norman Abbey, Worcester, Cheltenham and Gloucester. The Cotswolds, Black Mountains and Stratford-Upon-Avon are all within an easy drive.

Our inspector loved: The friendly atmosphere.

Directions: From M5 Jct8 follow M50. Exit at Jct1 onto A38 north. After 3 miles turn left onto A4104. Go over the bridge, turn left, then right. Parking is at the rear of the hotel.

Web: www.johansens.com/whitelionupton
E-mail: reservations@whitelionhotel.demon.co.uk
Tel: 01684 592551
Fax: 01684 593333

Price Guide:
single £55–£75
double £85–£110.
Multiple days negotiable

THE AUSTWICK COUNTRY HOUSE HOTEL & RESTAURANT

AUSTWICK, VIA LANCASTER, NORTH YORKSHIRE LA2 8BY

Directions: Austwick is midway between Skipton and junction 36 of the M6 and on the A65.

Web: www.johansens.com/austwick
E-mail: austwick@aol.com
Tel: 015242 51224
Fax: 015242 51796

Price Guide:
single £45–£85
double/twin £90–£120

Standing in 2 acres of peaceful, landscaped gardens in the heart of the Yorkshire Dales National Park is this fine Georgian Country House Hotel and Restaurant which oozes character, charm and the friendliest of hospitality. It is an ideal location for those wishing to enjoy dramatic scenery, spectacular walks, tranquillity and the freshest of country air. Surrounding the unspoilt village of Austwick is some of the most sensational limestone scenery in Europe, including the Ingleborough Cave with its dazzling stalagmites and stalagatites. Close by are the 3 famous peaks of Whernside, Pen-y-ghent and Ingleborough, and within a short walk of the nearby market town of Settle are caves which have yielded finds from pre-history. Guests at the Austwick Hotel can relax after walking and sightseeing tours in a comfortable bar and lounge, warmed in winter by open log fires or enjoy a quiet nap in their bedroom. There is a choice of 11. Each is en suite, individually designed, delightfully decorated and like the remainder of the building, beautifully furnished with English and Oriental antiques. Chef Richard Price produces excellent Anglo-French cuisine in the award-winning restaurant, complemented by an extensive wine-list. Special breaks available.

Our inspector loved: The warm and friendly welcome.

NORTH YORKSHIRE - AYSGARTH (WENSLEYDALE)

Stow House Hotel

AYSGARTH, LEYBURN, NORTH YORKSHIRE DL8 3SR

Tall, charming and attractive this stone-built former Victorian Vicarage stands impressively in 2 acres of mature grounds. It is a 10 minute walk from famous Aysgarth Falls in the heart of beautiful Wensleydale, watered by the Ure, the most open and wooded of the Yorkshire Dales. Built in 1876 for Fenwick William Stow, Rural Dean of Wensleydale and over the years lovingly and sympathetically restored, it has 9 en suite bedrooms, all individually decorated and furnished with every comfort. 2 luxury guest rooms, one with a four poster, are slightly larger and offer panoramic views over the Dale although all rooms have a lovely outlook. There is a cosy bar and a comfortable lounge which opens onto a garden that features an impressive selection of trees dating from the mid 19th century and a stunning view towards Bishopdale. Excellent meals can be enjoyed in the intimate dining room and chef, Michael Sullivan, uses the freshest of local produce. A croquet lawn and lawn tennis court are available during the summer months. Stow House specialises in house-parties where guests are able to take over the whole hotel for their own special celebration. There are wonderful walks direct from the door and the area abounds in historic castles, abbeys and stately homes. There are 3 golf courses locally.

Our inspector loved: The giant Redwood tree in the garden.

Directions: Stow House is situated on the A684 at the edge of the village of Aysgarth, which is midway between Leyburn and Hawes.

Web: www.johansens.com/stowhouse
E-mail: info@stowhouse.co.uk
Tel: 01969 663635

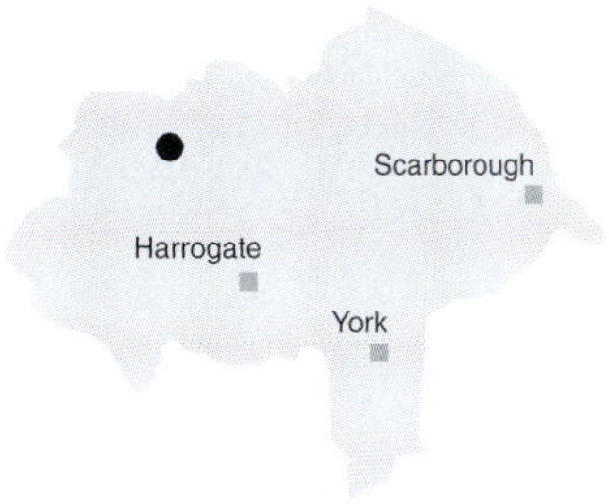

Price Guide:
single £42–£47
double/twin £68–£78

THE RED LION

BY THE BRIDGE AT BURNSALL, NEAR SKIPTON, NORTH YORKSHIRE BD23 6BU

Directions: Burnsall is north of Skipton on B6160 between Grassington and Bolton Abbey. The inn is in the village centre by the bridge.

Web: www.johansens.com/redlionburnsall
E-mail: redlion@daelnet.co.uk
Tel: 01756 720204
Fax: 01756 720292

Price Guide:
single £54–£80
double £107–£130

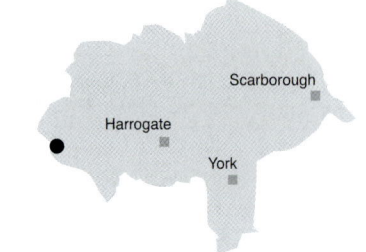

Beamed ceilings, creaky floors and log fires in winter greet you at this former 16th century Ferryman's Inn on the banks of the River Wharfe in the picturesque Yorkshire Dales village of Burnsall. Owned and run by the Grayshon family, it is surrounded by glorious open countryside. Guests can step out for numerous walks straight from the front door. The hotel is actually on the "Dalesway". The bedrooms are all slightly different yet traditionally furnished, many with antiques and most have wonderful views over the village green, river and Burnsall Fell. The restaurant has been awarded an AA Rosette for serving food that is delicious and varied, imaginatively cooked and well-presented. Table d'hôte dishes such as local rabbit braised in ale and served with herb dumplings, or partridge with apricot seasoning and game chips, are complemented by international wines. Special half-board terms and winter warmer breaks are available. Bolton Abbey and Priory, the historic market town of Skipton with its medieval castle and the Settle to Carlisle Railway. The Red Lion has private fishing on the River Wharfe, 7 miles of trout and grayling fishing and offers partridge and pheasant shooting over 3000 acres on the nearby Grimwith Estate. Skipton and Ilkley golf courses are 11 miles away. Two self-catering cottages are also available.

Our inspector loved: The River Wharfe which runs past the hotel.

THE BLUE LION

EAST WITTON, NR LEYBURN, NORTH YORKSHIRE DL8 4SN

Heather moorlands, waterfalls, limestone scars and remote valleys surround the picturesque village of East Witton – the gateway to Wensleydale and Coverdale. The Blue Lion, a 19th century coaching inn, has much to entice visitors to its doors – lovely individually furnished bedrooms, welcoming public rooms with original flagstone floors and open fires, plus delicious food. Private functions for up to 45 people can be accommodated. Head Chef, John Dalby, provides an ample selection of well-compiled, innovative dishes with a frequently changing menu. Some interesting choices such as breast of chicken filled with blue wensleydale cheese, fillet of sea bass with roast fennel and tapenade sauce are regularly available. The wine list that accompanies the menus offers a vast array of excellent wines from all over the world. The dining room is attractively decorated with candle-light creating an intimate atmosphere. In the bar there is a fine selection of hand-pulled traditional beers as well as an extensive menu of freshly prepared meals served at lunchtime and dinner. The spa towns of Ripon and Harrogate are within easy driving distance and well worth a visit. Jervaulx Abbey and many castles are in the area. There is an all-weather tennis court in the village.

Our inspector loved: The traditional stone flagged bar.

Directions: A6108, eight miles north of Masham and five miles south of Leyburn.

Web: www.johansens.com/bluelion
E-mail: bluelion@breathemail.net
Tel: 01969 624273
Fax: 01969 624189

Price Guide:
single £54–£75
double £69–£95

HOB GREEN HOTEL AND RESTAURANT

MARKINGTON, HARROGATE, NORTH YORKSHIRE HG3 3PJ

Set in 870 acres of farm and woodland this charming 'country house' hotel is only a short drive from the spa town Harrogate and the ancient city of Ripon. The restaurant has an excellent reputation locally with only the finest fresh local produce being used, much of which is grown in the hotel's own garden. The interesting menus are complemented by an excellent choice of sensibly priced wines. All twelve bedrooms have been individually furnished and tastefully equipped to suit the most discerning guest. The drawing room and hall, warmed with log fires in cool weather, are comfortably furnished with the added attraction of fine antique furniture, porcelain and pictures. Situated in the heart of some of Yorkshire's most dramatic scenery, the hotel offers magnificent views of the valley beyond from all the main rooms. York is only 23 miles away. There is a wealth of cultural and historical interest nearby with Fountains Abbey and Studley Royal water garden and deer park a few minutes' drive. The Yorkshire Riding Centre is in Markington Village. Simply relax in this tranquil place where your every comfort is catered for. Special breaks available.

Directions: Turn left signposted Markington off the A61 Harrogate to Ripon road, the hotel is one mile after the village on the left.

Web: www.johansens.com/hobgreen
E-mail: info@hobgreen.com
Tel: 01423 770031
Fax: 01423 771589

Price Guide:
single £85–£95
double/twin £100–£125
suite £130

Our inspector loved: The large vegetable and herb garden.

THE BOAR'S HEAD HOTEL

THE RIPLEY CASTLE ESTATE, HARROGATE, NORTH YORKSHIRE HG3 3AY

Imagine relaxing in a luxury hotel at the centre of a historic private country Estate in England's incredibly beautiful North Country. The Ingilby family who have lived in Ripley Castle for 28 generations invite you to enjoy their hospitality at The Boar's Head Hotel. There are 25 luxury bedrooms, individually decorated and furnished, most with king-size beds. The Restaurant menu is outstanding, presented by a creative and imaginative kitchen brigade and complemented by a wide selection of reasonably priced, good quality wines. There is a welcoming bar serving traditional ales straight from the wood and popular bar meal selections. When staying at The Boar's Head, guests can enjoy complimentary access to the delightful walled gardens and grounds of Ripley Castle, which include the lakes and a deer park. A conference at Ripley is a different experience – using the idyllic meeting facilities available in the castle, organisers and delegates alike will appreciate the peace and tranquillity of the location which also offers opportunities for all types of leisure activity in the Deer Park.

Our inspector loved: The pretty, historic village of Ripley.

Directions: Ripley is very accessible, just 10 minutes from the conference town of Harrogate, 20 minutes from the motorway network, and Leeds/Bradford Airport, and 40 minutes from the City of York.

Web: www.johansens.com/boarsheadharrogate
E-mail: reservations@boarsheadripley.co.uk
Tel: 01423 771888
Fax: 01423 771509

Price Guide:
single £99–£120
double £120–£140

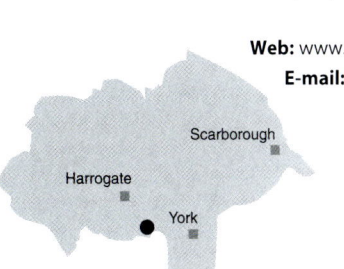

ROOKHURST COUNTRY HOUSE HOTEL

WEST END, GAYLE, HAWES, NORTH YORKSHIRE DL8 3RT

Directions: Take A684 Sedbergh–Bedale road. At Hawes take Gayle Lane to Gayle. At the top of the lane turn right and the hotel is 300 yards further on the right.

Web: www.johansens.com/rookhurst
E-mail: rookhurst@lineone.net
Tel: 01969 667454
Fax: 01969 667128

Price Guide: (including dinner)
single £70–£80
double £130–£160

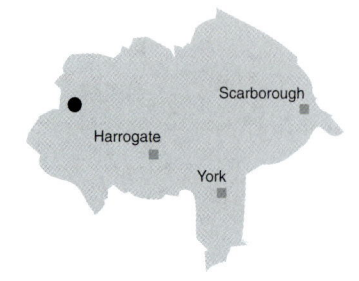

Nestling in the midst of Wensleydale, the front gate of this part-Georgian, part-Victorian country house opens onto the 250 mile-long Pennine Way. The cosy oak-beamed Georgian bedrooms are well-appointed and the more spacious Victorian bedrooms are furnished with four-poster beds whilst the rustic attic is particularly ornate, featuring a half-tester bed. All the bedrooms are en suite. This is a non smoking house. Judith specialises in traditional home-cooked English dishes, made with fresh mostly locally produced ingredients and bakes the bread for Breakfast. An open fire creates a cosy atmosphere in the sitting room, where guests can relax with a drink and enjoy the views over the landscaped garden and fields to the fells. Rookhurst is an ideal base for exploring Herriot country – the Yorkshire Dales are a delight for both serious walkers and strollers. Nearby is the Carlisle to Settle railway and you can be collected from Garsdale Station. Just round the corner is the Wensleydale Creamery, and in Hawes the Upper Dales folk museum. Special breaks available.

Our inspector loved: Seeing the gardens evolve and mature.

THE WHITE SWAN

THE MARKET PLACE, PICKERING, NORTH YORKSHIRE YO18 7AA

This 16th century former coaching inn is full of charm and character. Family-run by an enthusiastic young team with a passion for people, good food and fine wine, The White Swan was redesigned with luxury in mind. All bedrooms are now presented with crisp, clean design complemented by the Buchanan family's collection of beautiful antiques, and the new white bathrooms sparkle and shine. The Suite has the atmosphere of an apartment, and a large Junior Suite is also available. The hotel restaurant is extremely popular with locals because Chef Darren Clemmit really knows about food, spending as much time buying ingredients as preparing his delicious dishes. He prefers food with a simple freshness and real flavours and makes his own stock, sauces, ice cream and most of the bread, with herbs straight from the garden. Small Yorkshire suppliers are used for 75% of the purchases. The wine list features fine Clarets dating back to 1934 and a collection of rare 1963 Port, and the New World is also well represented. The White Swan is situated in one of the prettiest and yet undiscovered parts of the country famous for TV's 'Heartbeat' and nearby Castle Howard. Diverse activities, from microlite flying to trout fishing can be organised. Classic cars are available for hire. Special breaks 3 nights for the price of 2.

Our inspector loved: *The large range of clarets on the extensive wine list.*

Directions: Map available upon request.

Web: www.johansens.com/whiteswan
E-mail: welcome@white-swan.co.uk
Tel: 01751 472288
Fax: 01751 475554

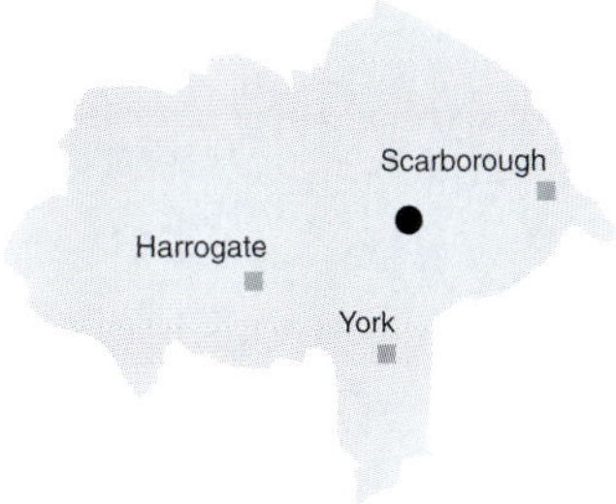

Price Guide:
single £70–£85
double/twin £90–£130
suite £120–£150

Dunsley Hall

DUNSLEY, WHITBY, NORTH YORKSHIRE YO21 3TL

Directions: From A171 Whitby–Teeside road, turn right at signpost for Newholme, three miles north of Whitby. Dunsley is the first turning on the left. Dunsley Hall is one mile further on the right.

Web: www.johansens.com/dunsleyhall
Tel: 01947 893437
Fax: 01947 893505

Price Guide:
single £70–£98
double/twin £112–£165

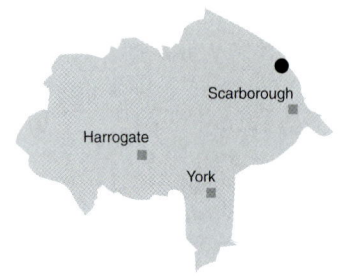

Dunsley Hall stands in four acres of magnificent landscaped gardens in the North Yorkshire Moors National Park and has remained virtually unaltered since being built at the turn of the 20th century. Most of the individually decorated bedrooms, some with four-poster beds, benefit from a fantastic view over the sea, which is only a few minutes walk away, and have rich, luxurious fabrics and fine furniture. All rooms are non-smoking. Mellow oak panelling, a handsome Inglenook carved fireplace and stained glass windows enhance the drawing room's relaxing and restful features. From the Oak Room, Terrace Suite or Pyman Bar, guests can savour the award-winning regional dishes and seafood specialities made from only the freshest of ingredients. There are up-to-date exercise and health facilities available with a fully equipped fitness room, sauna and large indoor pool. Outside are a hard-surface tennis court, a 9-hole putting green and a croquet lawn. Places of interest nearby include Castle Howard, Robin Hood's Bay, the North Yorkshire Moors Steam Railway and the birthplace of Captain Cook. Guests enjoy reduced green fees at Whitby Golf Course.

Our inspector loved: The stained glass windows in the drawing room.

THE SHIBDEN MILL INN

SHIBDEN MILL FOLD, SHIBDEN, HALIFAX, WEST YORKSHIRE HX3 7UL

This charming inn nestles in a delightfully secluded spot in West Yorkshire's Shibden Valley, two miles east of Halifax. Dating from the 17th century, Shibden Mill Inn is a venue of high quality and hospitality. Steeped in history, it has been sympathetically renovated by owners Simon and Caitlin Heaton, who purchased the property in 1998 as an attractive but run-down set of old buildings comprising Shibden Mill. Antiques, fine furnishings and comfortable furniture now abound, and open fires, original beamed ceilings and rafters create a cosy atmosphere. Guests can sip drinks in a friendly bar before enjoying a candlelit dinner in the beamed restaurant where Chef Neil Butterworth offers a varied selection of dishes to satisfy every taste. Winner of the West Yorkshire Dining Pub of the Year 2001. The extensive and superb wine list earned the inn the award of UK Wine Pub of the Year 2000. 12 en suite bedrooms are individually decorated and have all the warmth, style and comfort expected from a good country inn. There is complimentary use of the nearby Swimrite Health and Fitness Club. Guests can explore the Pennines and Brontë country, and the 18th-century Piece Hall and Eureka Children's Museum in Halifax.

Our inspector loved: Eating outside the heated dining garden.

Directions: From M62 Jct26 take A58 towards Halifax. After 5½ miles (passing 4 sets of traffic lights) turn right before Stump Cross Inn into Kell Lane. After ¾ mile turn left down Blake Hill.

Web: www.johansens.com/shibdenmill
E-mail: shibdenmillinn@zoom.co.uk
Tel: 01422 365840
Fax: 01422 362971

Price Guide:
single £55–£70
double/twin £67–£105

THE ROCK INN HOTEL

HOLYWELL GREEN, HALIFAX, WEST YORKSHIRE HX4 9BS

Directions: Leave M62 at Jct24 and follow signs for Blackley for approximately one mile, at the crossroads turn left for Holywell Green. The hotel is ½ mile along on the left.

Web: www.johansens.com/rockinn
E-mail: reservations@rockinnhotel.com
Tel: 01422 379721
Fax: 01422 379110

Price Guide:
single £64–£130
double £64–£130

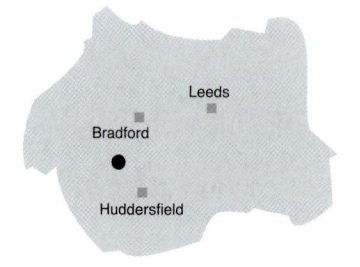

Situated in a tranquil valley, yet midway between the commercial centres of Halifax/Huddersfield and Manchester/Leeds, this superb hostelry offers all the attractions of a traditional wayside inn as well as the sophistication of a first-class hotel. Bedrooms are equipped to luxurious standards being en suite with baths and showers, remote-control satellite TV, mini-bar and tea/coffee making facilities. 12 new deluxe bedrooms. The Victorian-style bar serves a range of hand-pulled ales and is open all day, every day, for meals and drinks. Superb conference facilities are available for up to 200 persons. Palmers is a spacious restaurant, with a dance floor and a light and airy conservatory, opening out on to a large patio, overlooking a delightful rural aspect, where one can dine 'alfresco'. A variety of menus is available all day in any of the dining areas including the two conservatories, ranging from snacks to an á la carte selection and daily blackboard specials. Romantic Brontë country and the spectacular Yorkshire countryside is ideal for rambling. The award-winning Eureka! Museum is a great favourite with families and the immediate area is a golfer's paradise.

Our inspector loved: The new modern bedrooms with King sized beds.

THE WEAVERS SHED RESTAURANT WITH ROOMS

KNOWL ROAD, GOLCAR, HUDDERSFIELD, WEST YORKSHIRE HD7 4AN

Set in the Colne Valley, an area once famous for woollen manufacturing, The Weavers Shed was originally a cloth finishing mill. It was converted to a restaurant 28 years ago and adjoins the Mill Owners residence which comprises of five luxury en suite bedrooms. The fusion of modern and classic influences in the kitchen parallels the blend of styles in the bedrooms. The textile heritage that is omnipresent in West Yorkshire is praised in the accommodation at Weavers Shed as each of the five bedrooms is named after one of the local textile mills. Chef Patron, Stephen Jackson and his team strive to create a welcoming ambience. The excellent menu features Modern British cuisine using predominantly local produce with much of the vegetables, herbs and fruit cultivated in the restaurant's own kitchen garden and orchard. Typical dishes include braised lamb shank with wild mushrooms, mashed roots and parsnip crisps followed by banana tarte tatin with Barbados rum and raisin ice cream.

Our inspector loved: Their own kitchen garden, providing fresh produce daily.

Directions: Leave the M62 at junction 23 eastbound or junction 24 westbound and follow the A640 towards Rochdale crossing over the M62. Turn left into Quebec Road and then go into Golcar Village. The Weavers Shed is through the centre of the village on the left hand side of the road.

Web: www.johansens.com/weaversshed
E-mail: info@weaversshed.co.uk
Tel: 01484 654284
Fax: 01484 650980

Price Guide:
single £45–£55
double £60–£70

PERFECT HOSPITALITY BEGINS

WITH PERFECT FORM.

Classic furniture from Selva is the calling card of exclusive establishments.
By creating uniquely stylish surroundings, Selva spoils
not only your guests, but you, as well: with custom solutions,
creative ideas, and the most modern logistics. We would be happy to make
an appointment for you to visit our hotel furnishings showroom in Bolzano.

SELVA
HOTEL STYLE
A brand of Selva Style International

In UK and Ireland: Lidija Braithwaite - LPB Agencies   16 Lenham Avenue, Saltdean   Brigton, East Sussex BN2 8AE
Tel./Fax 01273 385 255   Mobile: 0771 852 2 746   e-mail: lpbagencies@cwcom.net

Selva AG/SpA, I-39100 Bolzano (Italy), Via Luigi-Negrelli-Straße 4
Tel. 0471 240111   Fax 0471 240211   e-mail: selva@selva.com   www.selva.com

CHANNEL ISLANDS

Recommendations in the Channel Islands appear on pages 234-240

For further information on the Channel Islands, please contact:

Guernsey Tourist Board
PO Box 23, St Peter Port, Guernsey GY1 3AN
Tel: +44 (0)1481 723552
Internet: www.guernseytouristboard.com

Jersey Tourism
Liberation Square, St Helier, Jersey JE1 1BB
Tel: +44 (0)1534 500777
Internet: www.jtourism.com

Sark Tourism
Harbour Hill, Sark, Channel Islands GY9 0SB
Tel: +44 (0)1481 832345
Internet: www.sark-tourism.com

Herm
The White House Hotel, Herm Island via Guernsey GY1 3HR
Tel: +44 (0)1481 722159
Internet: www.herm-island.com

or see **pages 306-309** for details of local attractions to visit during your stay.

Images from www.britainonview.com

La Favorita Hotel

FERMAIN BAY, GUERNSEY, CHANNEL ISLANDS GY4 6SD

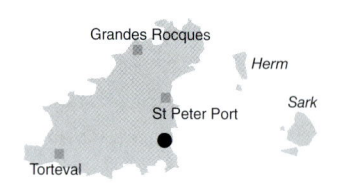

Once a fine private country house, La Favorita retains all the charm and character of those former days. The hotel is comfortable and fully licensed. Set in its own grounds, a few minutes walk from Guernsey's famous Fermain Bay, it enjoys spectacular views over the sea towards Jersey. The bedrooms, all non smoking, are comfortable and provide every modern amenity, including colour television, radio and refreshment tray. Guernsey's mild climate means that it has much to offer out of season and the hotel also has a full range of facilities to satisfy the extra needs of spring, autumn and winter guests, including the indoor pool. La Favorita has an excellent reputation for traditional English cooking and island seafood specialities. The restaurant is strictly no smoking. A coffee shop serves a wide range of lunch dishes and bar suppers for those who enjoy a more informal meal. St Peter Port is within walking distance, whether taking the woodland walk which follows the coastline or the more direct route past Victor Hugo's Hauteville House. Guests can explore the coast of Guernsey and all the island's attractions. Boat trips to Jersey, Alderney, Herm and Sark can easily be arranged.

Directions: Fermain Bay is 10 minutes from the airport and five minutes from St Peter Port on the east coast of Guernsey.

Web: www.johansens.com/lafavorita
E-mail: info@favorita.com
Tel: 01481 235666
Fax: 01481 235413

Price Guide:
single from £48
double from £80

Our inspector loved: *The welcoming staff and Helen's coffee shop puds.*

BELLA LUCE HOTEL & RESTAURANT

LA FOSSE, ST MARTINS, GUERNSEY, GY4 6EB

Dating back in part to the 11th century, The Bella Luce Hotel is a beautiful building that lies in its own grounds amidst some of the prettiest Guernsey scenery. In a very unspoilt part of the island there are gorse cliffs and sandy coves in abundance for both the child or the seasoned rambler to explore and is an ideal location for the fisherman. The Hotel itself has just 31 bedrooms, the majority of which are to be found on the first floor and each is decorated in charming sprig prints and appointed with canopied beds and elegant bathrooms. The gardens are a sun-trap and awash with colour, with an elegant swimming pool area that is the ideal place for rest and relaxation. The dining-room makes a delightful setting for the restaurant that is gaining an excellent reputation throughout the island for its imaginative collection of both English and Continental dishes including a selection of seafood specialities. The Royal Guernsey Golf Club is to be found at nearby L'Ancresse and is home to a picturesque links course and the Manor Riding School and St Martins Tennis School are just 10 minutes walk away. Any guest visiting Guernsey for the first time should take one of the marine trips that run frequently to Herm (3 miles) and Sark (9miles), or even to Jersey and the nearby French coast.

Directions: 5 minutes from the airport and St Peter Port.

Web: www.johansens.com/bellaluce
E-mail: info@bellalucehotel.guernsey.net
Tel: 01481 238764
Fax: 01481 239561

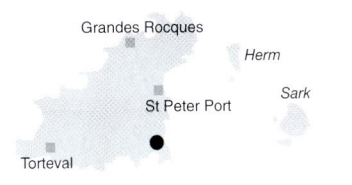

Price Guide:
double £66–£108

Our inspector loved: Its traditional presentation.

CHANNEL ISLANDS - GUERNSEY (ST MARTINS)

Les Douvres Hotel & Restaurant

RUE DE LA MOTTE, ST MARTINS, GUERNSEY GY4 6ER

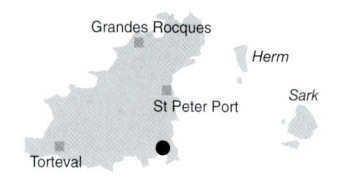

Situated in one of the prettiest parts of the island, Les Douvres is a former 18th century manor house that has been carefully developed into the charming Hotel that it is today. Retaining every scrap of its "olde-worlde" charm has been of paramount importance and it is now a little gem of a Hotel with just 25 bedrooms and an abundance of character. Nestling in the south east corner of the island in the quiet St Martins Parish it is an ideal location for exploring the many coves and bays, or taking cliff top walks. The beamed bar is a haven of traditional hospitality with its horse brasses and blackboards and here guests are invited to mix with the non-residents to enjoy local stories and history. The restaurant has recently been upgraded to 3 star status and offers a table d'hote menu of English and Continental recipes, whilst the Hotel prides itself on its seafood and flambé specialities. Sun-worshippers will enjoy sitting around the swimming pool in the sheltered corner of the gardens and sporting enthusiasts will relish the wealth of pursuits available. The St Martins tennis club and Manor Riding School are within 10 minutes walk, whilst 3 of the island's most beautiful bays: Moulin Huet; Petit Port and Saints, are within easy reach.

Our inspector loved: The locals' bar and the refurbished bedrooms.

Directions: Situated at the top of Saint Bay Valley, Les Douvres is 2 ½ miles from St Peter Port.

Web: www.johansens.com/lesdouvres
E-mail: info@lesdouvreshotel.guernsey.net
Tel: 01481 238731
Fax: 01481 239683

Price Guide:
double/twin £60–£94

THE WHITE HOUSE
HERM ISLAND, GUERNSEY, CHANNEL ISLANDS GY1 3HR

As wards of Herm Island, Adrian and Pennie Heyworth assume responsibility for the well-being of all visitors to their island home which is for all to enjoy at leisure. For an island just 1½ miles long its diversity is remarkable and during a two-hour stroll that takes in its cliff walks, white sandy coves and abundant wildlife no two moments are the same. The magic starts to work from the moment of arrival at the pretty harbour, for in the absence of cars on Herm a tractor laden with guests' luggage chugs up from the jetty to The White House. Here, relaxation is the key, and guests can enjoy afternoon tea or a drink in its succession of homely lounges, in the bar or on the poolside patio. In keeping with a cherished tradition there are no televisions, no clocks nor telephones in the hotel's 39 bedrooms, the best of which have balconies and sea views. Appointments are nonetheless faultless and all include spacious up-to-date private bathrooms. Families are made particularly welcome and high tea is a popular event with younger guests. Seafood plays a prominent part on Chris Walder's wonderful menus: Guernsey lobster, scallops and crab are landed regularly. Self-catering holiday cottages also available.

Our inspector loved: Its unique location - Its own island and its own ferry to take you there.

Directions: Herm is reached by boat from Guernsey.

Web: www.johansens.com/whitehouseherm
E-mail: hotel@herm-island.com
Tel: 01481 722159
Fax: 01481 710066

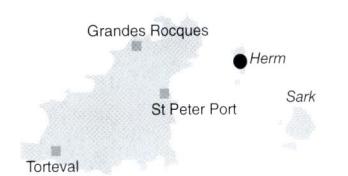

Price Guide: (including dinner)
double/twin £122–£170

Eulah Country House

MONT COCHON, ST. HELIER, JERSEY JE2 3JA

Directions: Immediately west of St Helier, at St Aubin's Bay, Le Mont Cochon runs due north from the A1/A2 coastal road.

Web: www.johansens.com/eulah
E-mail: eulah@jerseymail.co.uk
Tel: 01534 626626
Fax: 01534 626600

Price Guide:
single £120–£180
double/twin £150–£220

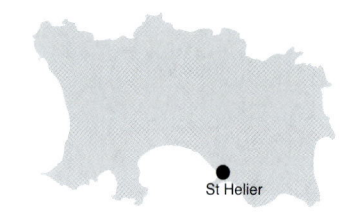

Set amongst beautiful gardens, this attractive and stylish Edwardian House enjoys a unique position overlooking St. Helier and St. Aubins Bay. Formerly a vicarage, the house was refurbished and opened as a small luxury hotel a year ago taking care to maintain the ambience of a comfortable family country home. Most of the bedrooms, three of which are junior suites, have sea views. All are individually furnished with king sized beds, antique furniture, wonderful fabrics and linens as well as satellite television, direct dial telephones, fax and modem points. Luxurious bathrooms include large baths and separate showers decorated with beautiful Spanish and Italian ceramic tiles. The owners of the Hotel pride themselves on offering a homely, personalised service and in the elegant main lounge with its attractive paintings and décor there is an honesty bar where guests can serve themselves. Outside, the gardens, heated swimming pool and sun terrace provide the perfect atmosphere for relaxation. Breakfast, light snacks and refreshments are available and although there is no full restaurant facility staff are more than happy to advise visitors on local cuisine and make bookings at the many excellent nearby restaurants. The heart of St. Helier is just a stone's throw away, as are the beach and beautiful surrounding countryside.

Our inspector loved: The enormous bedrooms, the four poster bath, the sweeping views and its unique character.

LA SABLONNERIE
LITTLE SARK, SARK, CHANNEL ISLANDS GY9 0SD

Owner and manager Elizabeth Perrée considers La Sablonnerie an oasis of good living and courtesy rather than a luxury hotel. It is truly that – and more! It is an hotel of rare quality situated in a time warp of simplicity on a tiny, idyllic island where no motor cars are allowed and life ambles along at a peaceful, unhurried pace . A vintage horse-drawn carriage collects guests from Sark's tiny harbour to convey them in style to the islands' southernmost tip - Little Sark. Crossing la Coupée, a narrow isthmus, guests can enjoy breathtaking views of the coast. Tranquil cosiness, friendliness and sophistication characterise this hotel with its low ceilings and 400 year old oak beams. Opened in 1948 and retaining many of the characteristics of the old farmhouse, La Sablonnerie has been extended and discreetly modernised to provide 22 bedrooms which are charmingly individual in style and offer every amenity. The granite-walled bar, with its open fire, is a comfortable extra lounge where pre-dinner drinks can be enjoyed before sampling the delights of the candlelit restaurant. The hotel has a reputation for superb cuisine. Many of the dishes are prepared from produce grown on its own farm and gardens and enhanced by locally caught lobster and oysters.

Our inspector loved: *Its dedication to the hedonistic pursuits in this improbable location.*

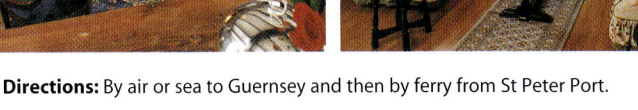

Directions: By air or sea to Guernsey and then by ferry from St Peter Port.

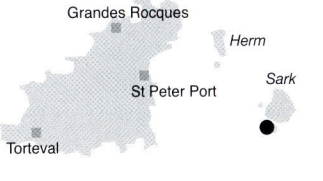

Web: www.johansens.com/lasablonnerie
Tel: 01481 832061
Fax: 01481 832408

Price Guide: (including dinner)
single £78–£85
double/twin £148–£188

Les Rocquettes Hotel

LES GRAVEES, ST PETER PORT, GUERNSEY, CHANNEL ISLANDS GY1 1RN

Originally a country mansion, this much extended hotel provides guests with all the modern amenities in a relaxed and friendly atmosphere. Strolling around the tranquil gardens of Les Rocquettes, guests could easily forget that they are within walking distance of the financial heartland of Guernsey. All 51 en suite bedrooms are comfortably appointed, with several adapted to allow wheelchair access. There is also the choice of two well-equipped self catering apartments which can accommodate either four or six guests. The new Mulberry Health suite boasts state-of-the-art facilities which feature both cardiovascular and toning equipment, as well as a large indoor pool, Jacuzzi and sauna. Light lunches and afternoon teas are enjoyed in the cosy Mulberry Bar or alfresco on the terrace. For those exploring the surrounding areas, a picnic can be provided upon request. In the evening, the Tartan Bar proves as popular with the guests and locals alike for fine fare and good company. There is plenty to do nearby, including walking and cycling along the exquisite Guernsey coastline. Places of interest are the maritime museum at Castle Cornet, Hauteville House, which was the home of Victor Hugo during his exile in Guernsey, and the islands of Herm and Sark.

Our inspector loved: Its atmosphere of family hospitality.

Directions: The hotel is 15 mins from the airport and 5 mins from the ferry port.

Web: www.johansens.com/lesrocquettes
E-mail: rocquettes@sarniahotels.com
Tel: 01481 722146
Fax: 01481 714543

Price Guide:
single £40–£60
double £70–£118

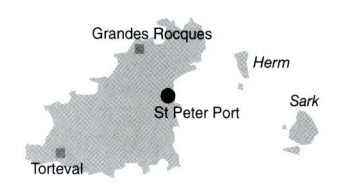

IRELAND – EIRE

Recommendations in Ireland appear on pages 242-251

For further information on Ireland, please contact:

The Irish Tourist Board
St Andrews Church
Suffolk Street
Dublin 2
Tel: +353 (0)1 602 4000
Internet: www.ireland.travel.ie

Northern Ireland Tourist Board
St Anne's Court
59 North Street
Belfast BT1 1NB
Tel: +44 (0)28 9024 6609
Internet: www.nitb.com

or see **pages 306-309** for details of local attractions to visit during your stay.

241

Hyland's Burren Hotel

BALLYVAUGHAN, CO. CLARE

Directions: The Hotel is in the main street of Ballyvaughan, on the N67 from Galway.

Web: www.johansens.com/hylandsburren
E-mail: hylandsburren@eircom.net
Tel: 00 353 65 7077037
Fax: 00 353 65 7077131

Price Guide:
single €70–€95
double/twin €110–€140

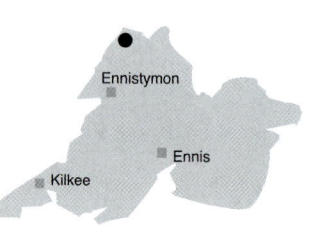

Nestled on the south shore of Galway Bay in the picturesque village of Ballyvaughan, the Hotel is surrounded by the wild splendour of the breathtaking Burren scenery, an artist's haven, reflecting the charm of bygone days. Decorated in a traditional style with emphasis on elegance and comfort; open fireplaces, cosy lounge chairs, bare wood and beautiful antiques create an inviting warmth whilst the patio is the perfect place to relax and enjoy the beautiful views. Fine local seafood, succulent Burren lamb and home-baked cakes are served in the restaurant and a casual bar menu is ideal for a delicious snack. Traditional Irish musicians and storytellers often frequent the Burren Bar, which has a wonderfully enchanting atmosphere. This is a paradise for birdwatchers and a perfect base for exploring the rugged cliffs and unspoilt beaches of County Clare, Connemara and Kerry. The enormous limestone rock plateau that makes up the breathtaking Burren landscape has an abundance of unique alpine and arctic flora. There are numerous fine walks and occasionally a walking weekend is organised. Guests will discover ancient marine fossils, caves, graves, transient lakes, seabirds, larks and cuckoos, golden beaches and many castles and ruins in the area. Golfing enthusiasts will enjoy a round on the famous Lahinch golf course. Trips to the Aran Islands can be arranged.

Our inspector loved: *The situation, in the centre of the village.*

Aberdeen Lodge
53 PARK AVENUE, BALLSBRIDGE, DUBLIN 4, IRELAND

This symbol of classical Edwardian architecture has a prime site in a serene tree-lined avenue in what is often called Dublin's Embassy Belt. Set in its own large formal gardens, Aberdeen Lodge provides high quality accommodation, comfort and service accompanied by all the modern luxuries which visitors to a flourishing capital city would expect today. Every room is an elegant reminder of Edwardian grace and Pat Halpin and his family's renowned hotel experience is evident in the detail of décor and operation. They pride themselves on being able to ensure that the needs of guests are met quickly and efficiently. Each of the tastefully furnished bedrooms is en suite and designed in complete harmony with the house. The spacious suites feature a jacuzzi and period style furniture. The award winning intimate Breakfast Room is complemented by a special menu served between 11am and 10pm, accompanied by a good selection of fine wines from around the world. A sister property, Merrion Hall, enjoys many accolades and is located a short stroll from the new Four Seasons Hotel in Ballsbridge. The Hotel makes an ideal base from which to explore Dublin and enjoy shopping in the famous Grafton Street. As well as many first class golf courses there is horse racing and 2 major marinas along the coast. Lansdowne Road rugby ground is a short walk.

Our inspector loved: The quiet seclusion, so close to the city centre.

Directions: Off Ailesbury Road, Aberdeen Lodge is 7 minutes from the city centre by D.A.R.T. bus. Private car park for guests.

Web: www.johansens.com/aberdeenlodge
E-mail: aberdeen@iol.ie
Tel: 00 353 1 283 8155
Fax: 00 353 1 283 7877

Price Guide:
single €99–€129
double/twin €124–€189
suite €159–€239

ROSS LAKE HOUSE HOTEL

ROSSCAHILL, OUGHTERARD, CO GALWAY, IRELAND

Directions: Ross Lake House is off N59, 14 miles north west of Galway.

Web: www.johansens.com/rosslake
E-mail: rosslake@iol.ie
Tel: 00 353 91 550109
Fax: 00 353 91 550184

Price Guide:
single €100–€110
double €150–€200
suite: €260–€300

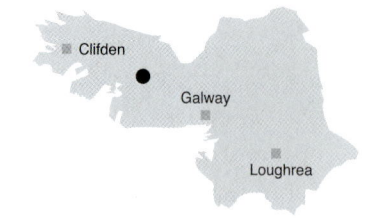

Homeliness and relaxation are the hallmarks of this elegant 19th century hotel situated in the beautiful County Galway countryside unspoilt by the advance of time. It is an attractive old house whose former glory has been carefully and tastefully revived by owners Henry and Elaine Reid. Surrounded by rambling woods and magnificent lawned gardens studded with colourful flowers and evergreen shrubs, Ross Lake was formerly an estate house of landed gentry who prized it for its serenity. The owners pride themselves that the hotel is a haven of peace where recreation comes naturally and service and hospitality are of the highest order. Public rooms are spacious and combine the elegance of an earlier age with modern comforts. The drawing room, is particularly attractive. Comfort and good taste are also reflected in the hotel's 13 bedrooms which are all en suite and offer lovely views over the gardens. Quality Irish food is excellently prepared and presented in the intimate restaurant with dishes enhanced by fresh produce from the Connemara hills, streams and lakes. For the active there is tennis in the grounds, golfing at the Oughterard 18-hole parkland course, game and course fishing. Places of interest nearby include Aughnanure Castle, Kylemore Abbey, Connemara National Park, the Aran Islands, Cliffs of Moher and the Burren.

Our inspector loved: The ideal location from which to explore Connemara.

CARAGH LODGE
CARAGH LAKE, CO KERRY

The breathtaking slopes of Ireland's highest mountain range, McGillycuddy Reeks, rise majestically above this elegant Victorian hotel whose award-winning gardens run gently down to Caragh Lake. Less than a mile from the spectacular Ring of Kerry, Caragh Lodge offers an unsurpassed blend of luxury, heritage, tranquillity, hospitality and service. A member of Ireland's Blue Book, it has won an RAC Blue Ribbon in 1999 and Gold Ribbon in 2000 & 2001 and the Johansens Country House Award in 1999. All bedrooms are en suite and decorated with period furnishings and antiques, with the converted garden rooms looking over magnificent displays of magnolias, camellias, rhododendrons, azaleas and rare subtropical shrubs. The dining room overlooks the lake and Mary Gaunt prepares menus of the finest Irish food, including fresh salmon, succulent Kerry lamb, garden-grown vegetables and home-baked breads. Open mid-April to mid-October. The gardens conceal a sauna chalet. Salmon and trout swim in the lake and two boats are available for angling guests. Ghillies or permits for fishing in the two local rivers can be arranged. There are local golf courses where tee off times can be organised.

Our inspector loved: The award winning gardens that sweep down to the lake.

Directions: From Killorglin travel on N70 towards Glenbeigh and take second road signposted for Caragh Lake. At lake turn left, Caragh Lodge is on your right.

Web: www.johansens.com/caraghlodge
E-mail: caraghl@iol.ie
Tel: 00 353 66 9769115
Fax: 00 353 66 9769316

Price Guide:
single €130
double €180–€230
suite €325

245

EMLAGH HOUSE

DINGLE, CO KERRY, IRELAND

Directions: Dingle is situated on the N86, 32 miles from Tralee and 40 miles from Killarney. Emlagh House is a 5 minute walk from Dingle town centre and harbour.

Web: www.johansens.com/emlagh
E-mail: info@emlaghhouse.com
Tel: 00 353 66 915 2345
Fax: 00 353 66 915 2369

Price Guide:
single from €140
double/twin from €200

Beautifully located on the picturesque Dingle Peninsula, Emlagh House is a quiet Georgian-style country house hotel set within lovely landscaped gardens. Purpose-built to create luxury with outstanding quality and standards the house, displays a fine, original Irish art collection. Exceeding the needs of every discerning traveller, attentive staff create a friendly, informal atmosphere with a personal touch. The private drawing room with views over the garden and harbour has an intimate serenity enhanced by an open fireplace, books and games. Individually decorated bedrooms feature the delightful theme of native Irish wild flowers with luxurious en suite bathrooms and all modern conveniences; some have patios and harbour views. Drinks are available in the friendly Honour Bar whilst the bright conservatory breakfast room serves freshly prepared dishes using local ingredients. Famous for its sandy beaches, stunning scenery and numerous archaeological sites, the Dingle Peninsula is the perfect getaway. Guests may enjoy breathtaking walks, eco tours, bird watching and fishing, whilst horse riding, golf and water sports, are all nearby. Dingle has an abundance of boutique shops, arts and crafts, galleries and excellent restaurants. Rental of the entire house is available.

Our inspector loved: *The outstanding Irish art collection and luxurious finish in this purpose-built house.*

Gorman's Clifftop House & Restaurant

GLAISE BHEAG, BALLYDAVID, DINGLE PENINSULA – TRALEE, CO KERRY

Surrounded by dramatic mountains, cliffs, coves and sandy beaches, the serenity of the Dingle Peninsular is breathtaking. Probably the most westerly establishment in Europe, the quiet Gorman's Clifftop House is a peaceful getaway from the hustle and bustle of daily life with an extremely welcoming atmosphere. Gorman's Restaurant features large picture windows with stunning views over Ballydavid Head, Three Sisters and the Atlantic Ocean – the perfect place to watch the sunset on a summer evening. A successful combination of hospitality, comfort and friendly service enhances the excellent cuisine which includes home-made brown bread, fresh wild salmon chowder and an extensive international wine list. Well appointed, spacious bedrooms with tasteful décor and handmade pine furniture have views of the ocean and mountains. Ideal for hiking, the hotel is situated on the Dingle Way long distance walking route. Other activities are golf on Dingle championship course, horse riding, fishing and cycling. Guests can explore the Gallarus Oratory, the oldest place of Christian worship in Western Europe, and there are plenty of archaeological sites in the area.

Our inspector loved: *The clifftop view and fresh Irish fayre.*

Directions: Go through Dingle Harbour to roundabout west of town, straight across the road signposted An Fheothanach; hotel is eight miles from roundabout. There is a v on the road after about five miles – keep left here.

Web: www.johansens.com/gormans
E-mail: gormans@eircom.net
Tel: 00 353 66 9155162
Fax: 00 353 66 9155162

Price Guide:
single €80–€110
double/twin €110–€160
suite €185

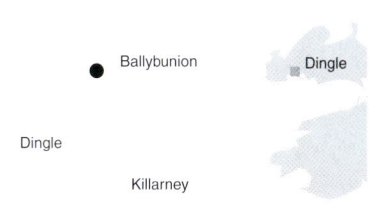

KILLARNEY ROYAL HOTEL

COLLEGE STREET, KILLARNEY, CO KERRY, IRELAND

Directions: In the centre of Killarney off the N22.

Web: www.johansens.com/killarneyroyal
E-mail: royalhot@iol.ie
Tel: 00 353 64 31853
Fax: 00 353 64 34001

Price Guide:
single €120–€220
double/twin €230–€320
suite €250–€350

Joe and Margaret Scally's charming Victorian town house is the older sister of the larger property, Hayfield Manor in Cork. Located in the heart of bustling Killarney the Hotel is the perfect base for golfers and touring South West Ireland. Surrounded by Killarney National Park with its lakes, mountains and gardens, giant rhododendrons and tropical plants grow in abundance. The owners pride themselves in their hospitality and 24 hour personal service that ensures guests enjoy the Hotel's charm and grace. Nothing is taken for granted once the visitor steps through the shining black entrance door into the black and white tailed lobby. Each individually designed bedroom has unique features, is delightfully decorated, furnished with fine antiques and has a comfortable sitting area and lovely marble bathroom. All rooms are air-conditioned. The elegant dining room offers innovative cuisine complemented by a selection of wines from a well-stocked cellar. Numerous challenging golf courses are in the vicinity as well as an almost endless variety of outdoor pursuits. Fishing, shooting, riding and day trips to such attractions as the Ring of Kerry, Dingle peninsula and the Lakes of Killarney can be arranged. Killarney National Park, Muckross House and Gardens, Ross Castle, St. Mary's Cathedral and Demesne are nearby.

Our inspector loved: *This Victorian Townhouse with modern air conditioned comfort.*

COOPERSHILL HOUSE

RIVERSTOWN, CO SLIGO

Winner of Johansens 1995 Country House Award, Coopershill is a fine example of a Georgian family mansion. Home to seven generations of the O'Hara family since 1774, it combines the spaciousness and elegance of an earlier age with modern comforts. Public rooms are furnished in period style with gilt-framed portraits, hunting trophies and antiques. Six of the bedrooms have four-poster or canopy beds and all have private bathrooms. Dinner is served by candlelight in the elegant dining room, where good cooking is complemented by a wide choice of wines. Open log fires and personal attention from owners Brian and Lindy O'Hara help to create the warm atmosphere and hospitality that typify Coopershill. Out of season the house is open to parties of 12 to 16 people at a special rate. Tariffs are reduced if guests stay for three consecutive nights or more. The River Arrow winds through the 500-acre estate and boating, trout and coarse fishing are available. Shooting is not permitted, leaving the abundant wildlife undisturbed. There is an excellent hard tennis court and also a croquet lawn. There are marvellous mountain and lakeside walks to enjoy in the area. Closed 1st November to 1st April.

Our inspector loved: The atmosphere that could only be created by a family that built the house 7 generations ago.

Directions: Leave N4 Sligo–Dublin road at Drumfin follow signs for Coopershill. One mile on, turn left.

Web: www.johansens.com/coopershillhouse
E-mail: ohara@coopershill.com
Tel: 00 353 71 65108
Fax: 00 353 71 65466

Price Guide:
single €97–€118
double €156–€198

Cashel Palace Hotel
MAIN STREET, CASHEL, CO TIPPERARY

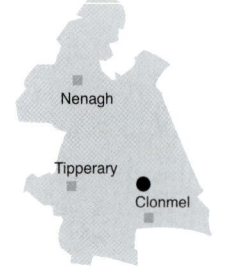

This magnificent and luxurious 18th century Hotel stands in the shadow of the famous Rock of Cashel. In the heart of a heritage town surrounded by a wealth of historical sites, Cashel Palace built in 1730 was for Archbishop Theophilus Bolton, it is a jewel of late Queen Anne and early Georgian style. Described as, "A place of notable hospitality," in Loveday's Tour of 1732, Cashel Palace Hotel's beauty is enhanced by 28 acres of walled gardens which include a private walk to the Rock of Cashel and 2 Mulberry Trees planted in 1702 to commemorate the coronation of Queen Anne. Lovingly restored with great attention its character and integrity has been preserved. The spacious bedrooms of the main house echo the style and elegance of the 18th century and are individually furnished to the highest standards. The recent restoration of the Mews House, across the courtyard from the main house, has afforded the Hotel 10 beautifully appointed en suite bedrooms. The tradition of fine food, in the relaxed ambience of the Bishops Buttery, specialises in lighter modern Irish cuisine with classical influences. Local leisure activities include pony trekking, horse riding, golf, tennis, trout and salmon fishing. Cashel is an ideal base from which to tour Munster and the south east and is within easy reach of Cahir Castle, the Devil's Bit Mountain and Holy Cross.

Directions: Cashel is on the junction of the N8 and N74.

Web: www.johansens.com/cashelpalace
E-mail: reception@cashel-palace.ie
Tel: 00 353 62 62707
Fax: 00 353 62 61521

Price Guide:
single €171
double €253
suite €349

Our inspector loved: *The tranquil walled garden and private walk to the famous 'Rock of Cashel'.*

KILMOKEA COUNTRY MANOR & GARDENS

KILMOKEA – GT. ISLAND, CAMPILE, CO WEXFORD

Kilmokea is a gracious 18th-century Georgian stone rectory nestled on the shores of the River Barrow. This oasis of tranquillity is surrounded by 7 acres of stunning landscaped gardens overflowing with flowers; the air is filled with delightful fragrance and the old walls of the formal garden encircle rare and tender species from around the world. An old wooden door leads into the woodland gardens, home to a display of exotic plants with colourfully bordered winding paths and peaceful pools. An Italian loggia and pool with stone pillars is brimming with iris and roses whilst proud peacocks parade their magnificent plumage. The Hotel has been recently restored with rich colours complementing the welcoming ambience. The individually decorated bedrooms are comfortable with views over the gardens. Cream teas, lunches, freshly baked bread and salads are served in the spacious conservatory, whilst organic homegrown produce will tempt your palate in the elegant dining room. Guests can relax in the cosy drawing room warmed by a log fire, go horse riding, deep-sea fishing, practise watersports or play golf at numerous excellent golf courses nearby. New for 2003, tennis courts, a sauna and a gym will complement the rooms for aromatherapy massage.

Our inspector loved: *The 7 acres of rare specimen trees and shrubs in the garden.*

Directions: From Dublin drive to New Ross. Take R733 past JFK "Arboretum". After 1 mile, drive through 'S' bend then take right turning towards Great Island and Kilmokea Gardens.

Web: www.johansens.com/kilmokea
E-mail: kilmokea@indigo.ie
Tel: 00 353 51 388109
Fax: 00 353 51 388776

Price Guide: (per person)
€70–€125
single supplement €25

Hildon Ltd., Broughton, Hampshire SO20 8DQ, ☎ 01794 - 301 747, Fax 01794 - 301 718
e-mail: hildon@hildon.com – www.hildon.com

SCOTLAND

Recommendations in Scotland appear on pages 254-277

For further information on Scotland, please contact:

Visit Scotland
23 Ravelston Terrace, Edinburgh EH4 3TP
Tel: +44 (0)131 332 2433
Internet: www.visitscotland.com

or see **pages 306-309** for details of local atractions to visit during your stay.

Images from www.britainonview.com

253

Maryculter House Hotel

SOUTH DEESIDE ROAD, MARYCULTER, ABERDEEN AB12 5GB

Directions: 8 miles from the city centre and rail station and 11 miles from the airport, take the B9077.

Web: www.johansens.com/maryculter
E-mail: info@maryculterhousehotel.com
Tel: 01224 732124
Fax: 01224 733510

Price Guide:
single £65–£85
double/twin £90–£110

Situated on the banks of the famous River Dee, this collection of buildings is steeped in Scottish history. Dating back to the 12th century, clearly documented through King John, Bonnie Prince Charlie and even the Titanic disaster this was at one time the homeland of the Knights Templar, who gave pilgrims protected passage on their way to the holy land. The house became a hotel shortly after World War II and has been undergoing a programme of refurbishment for the past couple of years. An abundance of natural stone and exposed fireplaces, with tall beamed ceilings that convey a theatrical style, the Hotel has been carefully enhanced by stylish decoration to create a winning combination of modern luxury with period detail. A perfect setting for weddings and functions, the grounds sweep down to the water's edge, whilst the informality of the poacher's bar is ideal for mid-winter retreats. An extensive and imaginative collection of menus combines the very best of local dishes with a modern twist and special dietary requirements are eagerly accommodated. Scottish history becomes a compelling part of a stay at Maryculter House and close to Aberdeen city centre which is also prime fishing territory.

Our inspector loved: *The progress this hotel has made under fresh control and looks forward to the further planned improvements.*

BALGONIE COUNTRY HOUSE

BRAEMAR PLACE, BALLATER, ROYAL DEESIDE, ABERDEENSHIRE AB35 5NQ

In the heart of one of Scotland's most unspoilt areas, on the outskirts of the village of Ballater, lies Balgonie House. Winner of the 1997 Johansens Country House Award for Excellence. This Edwardian-style building is set within four acres of mature gardens and commands wonderful views over the local golf course towards the hills of Glen Muick beyond. Balgonie's nine bedrooms are each named after a fishing pool on the River Dee. They are individually decorated and furnished and most offer lovely outlooks from their windows. Amenities include private bathrooms, colour television and direct-dial telephones. At the heart of the hotel is the dining room, offering superb Scottish menus: including fresh salmon from the Dee, succulent local game, high quality Aberdeen Angus beef and seafood from the coastal fishing ports and vintage wine chosen from an excellent list. Balgonie has won the coveted Taste of Scotland Prestige Award for its cuisine, also 2 AA Red Star and 2 Rosettes. The village of Ballater, a 5-minute walk away, is a thriving community. As suppliers to the Queen, many of its shops sport Royal Warrant shields. This is an ideal centre for golf, hillwalking, sightseeing and touring. Balmoral Castle is within easy reach, as are both the Malt Whisky Trail and Castle Trail.

Our inspector loved: *A relaxed retreat with a highly personal style. Oh that all hotels do not have such immaculate upkeep!*

Directions: Upon entering Ballater from Braemar on the A93, Balgonie House is signposted on the right.

Web: www.johansens.com/balgoniecountry
E-mail: balgoniech@aol.com
Tel: 013397 55482
Fax: 013397 55482

Price Guide:
single £75
double £125

CASTLETON HOUSE HOTEL

GLAMIS, BY FORFAR, ANGUS DD8 1SJ

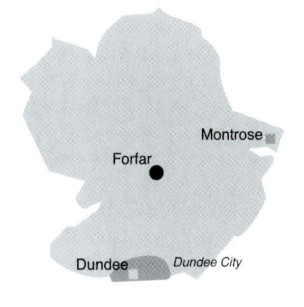

This elegant Edwardian hotel lies in the beautiful vale of Strathmore, a lush enclave beneath the Angus glens. Built in 1902, it stands on the site of a 12th-century fortification, the surrounding ditch being presumed to be a former defensive moat. Recently completely refurbished by its new owners, it now has an ambience of relaxed elegance where attention to detail and personal service are paramount. Each of the six bedrooms has been individually furnished, whilst the Regency four-poster suite has an additional dressing room housed in the turret. Guests may dine in the beautiful period dining room or the more informal conservatory; in either location a carefully planned menu of local ingredients with a winning combination of traditional and contemporary dishes is served. Glamis Castle is just three miles away and a must for every visitor. The family home of the late Queen Mother, it is surprisingly free of rope restricted areas and has a number of family photographs as well as two resident ghosts! Dundee and Perth are within easy driving distance and Blairgowrie lies just 15 minutes away. Beyond Rosemount lies the route to the Highlands for true historians and the more adventurous.

Our inspector loved: *Newly refurbished with experienced, new proprietors who are setting enviable standards with their food, comfort and service.*

Directions: From Edinburgh, take M90 Jct11; take A90 through Dundee, then A928 to Glamis, left on to A94. 3 miles on right.

Web: www.johansens.com/castletonhouse
E-mail: hotel@castletonglamis.co.uk
Tel: 01307 840340
Fax: 01307 840506

Price Guide:
single £95
double/twin £120
four-poster £1750

BALLACHULISH HOUSE
BALLACHULISH, ARGYLL PH49 4JX

Steeped in Scottish history, and proud of its origins, Ballachulish House has recently undergone an extensive refurbishment programme. No expense has been spared to ensure the ambience is one of total comfort and luxury, whilst retaining every scrap of the character of this 17th-century laird's house. Once home to the Stewarts of Ballachulish, this is the scene of the famous Red Fox murder, and later the subject of Robert Louis Stevenson's "Kidnapped", and fans of Scottish history will love to visit this significant landmark. The welcome here is one of the warmest to be found and a reassuring indicator of what is to follow. A traditional piper heralds the start of dinner, and the chef carefully prepares an innovative fusion of classic French cooking teamed with some wonderful local fayre, awarded 2 AA Rosettes. All of the seven en suite bedrooms have been carefully designed to afford views of the garden, loch or hill; and with elegant furnishings and plenty of space this is a place of total tranquillity and relaxation. Mull and Skye are accessible for day trips, while Glencoe, Ben Nevis and Fort William are all nearby. A ghillie is provided for salmon fishing, or a guide for intrepid hill walkers, perhaps followed by a trip to the nearby Nevis distillery for a wee dram.

Directions: A82 to Ballachulish and then A828 under Ballachulish Bridge and first left.

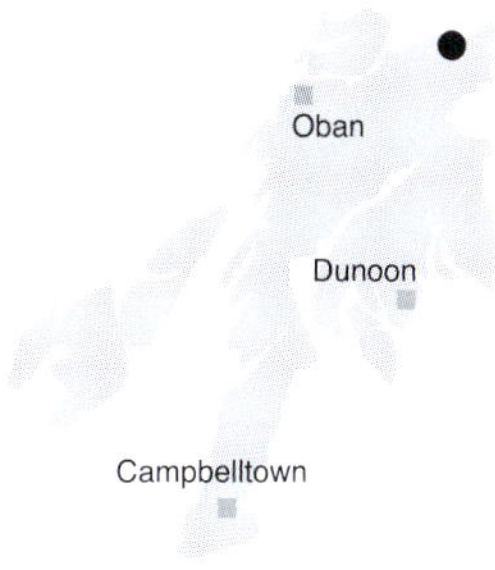

Web: www.johansens.com/ballachulish
E-mail: mclaughlins@btconnect.com
Tel: 01855 811266
Fax: 01855 811498

Price Guide:
double/twin £60–£140
suites £60–£140

Our inspector loved: *Personal service that will be hard to beat.*

ARGYLL & BUTE - CARDROSS (NR LOCH LOMOND)

KIRKTON HOUSE

DARLEITH ROAD, CARDROSS, ARGYLL & BUTE G82 5EZ

Directions: Cardross is on the A814 between Dumbarton and Helensburgh. Darleith Road is at west end of village, signed at road junction.

Web: www.johansens.com/kirktonhouse
E-mail: johan@kirktonhouse.co.uk
Tel: 01389 841951
Fax: 01389 841868

Price Guide:
single £40-£49.50
double/twin £60-£80

For peace, tranquility and old world charm this lovely, converted 18th century farmhouse would be difficult to beat. Built around an attractive courtyard it stands in two acres of grounds above the north Clyde village of Cardross, 18 miles west of Glasgow. The locality has myriad scenic, historical and architectural areas of interest and Kirkton House is an ideal base from which to visit Loch Lomond, the Trossachs, the west highlands and islands. An RAC Little Gem Scottish award winner, the hotel has an informal, relaxed ambience and friendly but unobtrusive personal service. Décor and furnishings throughout are homely and comfortable with the public rooms boasting original stone walls and rustic fireplaces. Two of the six attractive bedrooms are on the ground floor. All are centrally heated and have every amenity from private bath and/or shower to television, telephone and refreshment tray. Extensive Scottish breakfasts are prepared to order and superb dinners are served at oil lamplit tables in the intimate dining room. The daily, varied menus are extensive with a three or four course meal available from £22.50 per person. Golf is available locally from Monday to Friday. Closed December and January.

Our inspector loved: The way a family home was skillfully converted into a small hotel.

BARCALDINE HOUSE
BARCALDINE, OBAN, ARGYLL PA37 1SG

In 1709 'Red Patrick' of Barcaldine commissioned the mason, James Duff, to build Barcaldine House for his large family. Since then it has been home to 7 generations of the Campbell family and witness to many extraordinary historical events in Argyll and indeed Scotland's turbulent past. Located on the edge of Barcaldine Forest it sits at the foot of Ben Vreck and overlooks Loch Creran. Beautiful landscaped gardens provide easy access to miles of forest walks and spectacular views across the Loch, the Morvern Coast and the mountains of Glencoe. Each of the Hotel's en suite bedrooms are elegantly furnished with thoughtful little luxuries. The day starts with a traditional Scottish breakfast and in the evening dinner is served in the magnificent dining room. An à la carte menu features contemporary dishes created by using fresh local produce, while an extensive wine list includes wines from all over the world. Guests can take coffee in the drawing room or make the most of the vaulted oak panelled billiard room and enjoy a game of snooker. As the principal town and ferry port of Argyll, Oban offers numerous cruises to islands such as Iona, Mull and the Outer Hebrides. Other activities in the area include sailing, riding, loch fishing, climbing and gliding. Short breaks available.

Directions: From Oban follow the A828 to Benderloch, then continue north for just over 4 miles to the village of Barcaldine and follow the signpost to the right for Barcaldine House.

Web: www.johansens.com/barcaldine
E-mail: barcaldine@breathe.co.uk
Tel: 01631 720219
Fax: 01631 720219

Price Guide:
single £60–£90
double/twin £70–£90

Our inspector loved: *The immense character of this old house.*

THE FROG AT PORT DUNSTAFFNAGE

DUNSTAFFNAGE MARINA, CONNEL, BY OBAN, ARGYLL PA37 1PX

Directions: The Frog is 2 ½ miles north of Oban on the A85.

Web: www.johansens.com/thefrog
E-mail: frogenqs@aol.com
Tel: 01631 567005
Fax: 01631 571044

Price Guide: (room only)
double/twin £45–£65

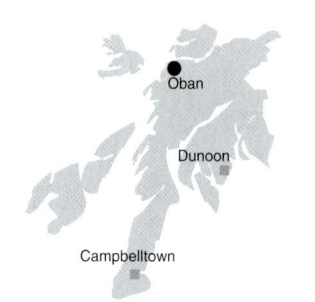

Located on the Dunstaffnage Marina and overlooking the bay and castle, The Frog is an ideal stop-over for weekend travellers or budding sailors, as many local yachtsmen live nearby. Stuart and Linda Byron concentrate on creating a casual, relaxed atmosphere for their guests as well as those who enjoy the bars and restaurant on a regular basis. Made up of converted old farm buildings, the Hotel acts as a jolly meeting place and on its ground floor is where the eating happens. An all day food service provides breakfast through to dinner and a good selection of bar snacks and novelty children's dishes. Menus combine the best quality of local produce and as expected, feature a wide variety of fresh seafood. The bars serve an impressive range of draught, bottled beers, malt whiskies, wines and spirits. 7 non smoking en suite bedrooms were added to The Frog in 2001, each equipped with satellite colour television, direct dial telephones, bath and power shower. Rooms, though not huge, are full of character with quirky crooked ceilings and all new furnishings. Accommodation is comfortable but fairly basic, as reflected in the excellent price. Nearby attractions include Dunstaffnage Castle, 'Gannet' diving, angling, scenic trips and the Oban Distillery.

Our inspector loved: If you are keen on sailing you are right in the middle of it here.

LOCH MELFORT HOTEL & RESTAURANT

ARDUAINE, BY OBAN, ARGYLL PA34 4XG

Spectacularly located on the west coast of Scotland, the Loch Melfort Hotel is a quiet hideaway on Asknish Bay, with the awe-inspiring backdrop of woodlands and the magnificent mountains of Argyll. Friendly staff attend to every need and there is a warm, welcoming atmosphere. Spacious bedrooms are lavishly appointed with bold bright fabrics, comfortable furnishings and have large patio windows overlooking the islands of Jura, Shuna and Scarba. The award winning restaurant, which has breathtaking views stretching as far as the eye can see, is perfect for a romantic meal. Guests may feast on the sumptuous fresh local fish, shellfish and meat complemented by an extensive selection of fine wines. There is also a mouth-watering array of home-made desserts, delicious ice creams and Scottish cheeses. Skerry Bistro serves informal meals, lunches, suppers and afternoon teas. Outdoor activities include fishing, sailing, riding, windsurfing, walking and mountain biking. Visitors can explore the nearby islands and local places of interest include Mull, Kilchoan Castle, Castle Stalker and the stunning Dunstaffnage Castle (home of Clan Campbell). The Arduaine Gardens, situated adjacent to the Hotel, are extremely beautiful and home to a diversity of plants and trees from all over the world. The Marine Sanctuary and Landmark Forest Heritage Park are well worth a visit.

Directions: Loch Melfort Hotel is situated 19 miles south of Oban on the A816.

Web: www.johansens.com/lochmelfort
E-mail: reception@lochmelfort.co.uk
Tel: 01852 200233
Fax: 01852 200214

Price Guide: (including dinner)
double/twin £118-£174

Our inspector loved: The super views.

ROYAL HOTEL

TIGHNABRUAICH, ARGYLL, SCOTLAND PA21 2BE

Directions: From Dunoon take A885 and A815 north to Strachur. Turn onto B836 across to A886, then A8003 to Tighnabruaich.

Web: www.johansens.com/royalhotelargyll
E-mail: info@royalhotel.org.uk
Tel: 01700 811239
Fax: 01700 811300

Price Guide:
single £69–£100
double/twin £78–£140

Standing regally on the water's edge of the Kyles overlooking Argyll's breathtakingly beautiful and unspoilt coast, the Royal Hotel is a unique oasis. Its location in one of Scotland's wildest and most spectacular settings south of the Highlands belies its proximity to civilisation: Glasgow is just an hour's drive away. Family-owned and run, the hotel has been a landmark to visiting yachtsmen and country lovers seeking tranquillity for more than 150 years. Guests with their own boat can go sailing from the hotel's slipway. Owners Roger and Bea McKie offer splendid hospitality and the most attentive and personal service. Each of the hotel's eleven individually furnished bedrooms offers the highest standard of comfort and provides superb panoramic views of the rugged coastline and the Island of Bute. There are tastefully decorated bars with open fires and an excellent restaurant where discerning diners can enjoy the beautifully presented cuisine. Jumbo prawns, clams, lobsters, mussels, oysters and fish are offloaded at the hotel daily by local fishermen. Venison, pheasant, and rabbit are stalked locally. As well as enjoying good walking and bird watching country, guests can go windsurfing and play golf, or visit Mount Stuart on Bute, Ostel Bay, Kilmartin and Inveraray Castle.

Our inspector loved: This haven amongst some of Scotland's finest scenery.

WESTERN ISLES HOTEL
TOBERMORY, ISLE OF MULL, ARGYLLSHIRE PA75 6PR

With its warming, welcoming whiskies and log fires, delightful décor, elegant furnishings, superb scenic views and the cleanest of air to inhale this is a haven of relaxation, well-being and friendliness that welcomes guests time and time again. Built in 1883 for the proprietor of the estate Mish-Nish in Mull, Western Isles Hotel rises majestically against the skyline overlooking the beautiful Sound of Mull and Tobermory with its liberal sprinkling of sailing craft. It is considered one of the best views in the Hebridean Islands and is popularly enjoyed from the Hotel's sun-trap patio whilst taking afternoon tea or sipping an evening aperitif before delighting in superb cuisine served in the serenity of a classical dining room. The Hotel has been host to the rich and famous and to many events in history. These range from use as a second world war allied H.Q. to the setting for films such as 'I Know Where I'm Going'. Western Isles Hotel has such charm, good taste, style, service and atmosphere that upon first entering its reception hall guests immediately feel as if they have stepped back to the elegance of a previous era. Every room, fitment, furnishing and facility is a delight. Guest rooms and the conservatory are particularly attractive and comfortable. An excellent base for island exploring and wildlife and birdlife enthusiasts.

Our inspector loved: *The views over Tobermory and the Sound of Mull: must be amongst the best in Scotland.*

Directions: By ferry from Oban to Craignure, Lochaline to Fishnish, Kilchoan to Tobermory.

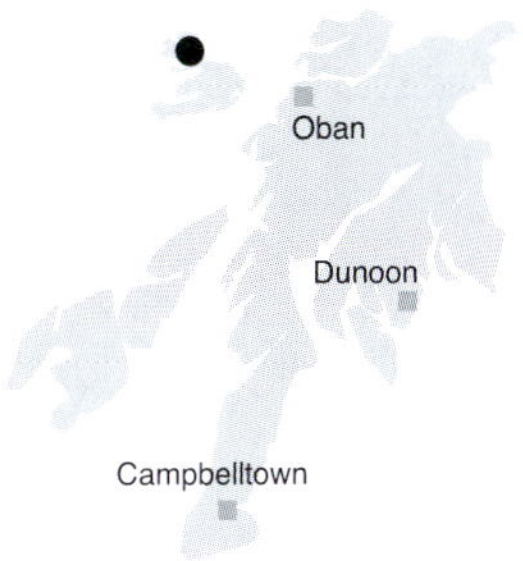

Web: www.johansens.com/westernisles
E-mail: wihotel@aol.com
Tel: 01688 302012
Fax: 01688 302297

Price Guide:
double £85–£196

FERNHILL HOTEL

HEUGH ROAD, PORTPATRICK, DG9 8TD

Perfectly located amongst beautifully landscaped, secluded gardens with resplendent views over the bustling yacht and fishing village of Portpatrick to the sea, Fernhill is a cosy and friendly Hotel offering a warm welcome. A huge picture window in the light and airy lounge proudly displays the breathtaking scenery and on a clear day it is possible to see the coast of Ireland, some 21 miles away. 3 elegant bedrooms are decorated with warm colours and expertly chosen fabrics to create a sense of quiet luxury. Some bedrooms have balconies and the Garden House, which comfortably sleeps 8, has a sunny porch and benefits from all the Hotel's facilities. The Stables House has an extremely spacious four poster suite and uninterrupted views over the gardens, village and sea. A mouth-watering choice of fresh, locally caught lobster as well as Scottish beef, game and poultry are on the menu, which the chef changes every day. The Hotel's attractive cocktail bar is ideal for pre-dinner drinks or a relaxing get-together with friends. Only a few minutes walk away, Portpatrick's quaint craftshops and harbourside pubs are wonderful to explore or guests may simply sit and watch the boats go by. For golf lovers, there is a superb local golf course nearby.

Directions: Portpatrick is situated just off the A75 from Carlisle or the A77 from Prestwick Airport.

Web: www.johansens.com/fernhill
E-mail: info@fernhillhotel.co.uk
Tel: 01776 810220
Fax: 01776 810596

Price Guide: (per person including dinner) single/double/twin from £67

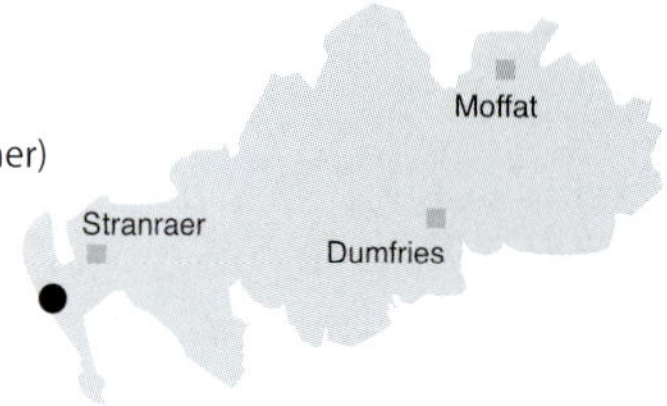

Our inspector loved: The superb clifftop views high above the fishing village of Portpatrick.

CORRIEGOUR LODGE HOTEL

LOCH LOCHY, BY SPEAN BRIDGE, INVERNESS-SHIRE PH34 4EB

Set amid nine contrasting acres of mature woodland and garden, Corriegour Lodge commands outstanding views over Loch Lochy. Formerly a Victorian hunting lodge, it enjoys one of the finest settings in the 'Great Glen' – an area steeped in history. Enclosed within the grounds is a small lochside beach complete with jetty. Christian and son Ian place the accent on guests' relaxation and comfort – the service is friendly and nothing is too much trouble. Each bedroom is immaculately decorated, well appointed and most have views of the loch. Gate Lodge self-catering accommodation is also available. The Loch View Conservatory Restaurant has splendid views of the boats sailing across Loch Lochy on their way through the Caledonian Canal. A Taste of Scotland establishment, the hotel serves fine Scottish cuisine and tasty home-baked breads. The excellent wine list is very reasonably priced. Corriegour Lodge is STB 4 Stars and also a member of Taste of Scotland and represents exceptionally good value for money, especially for a stay of three or seven nights. Open at weekends only from November to February, fully open March to October and between Christmas and New Year. Places of interest include Loch Ness, Ben Nevis and Castle Urquhart.

Our inspector loved: Chef, Ian Drew's interesting food, complemented by the spectacular views down the Great Glen from every restaurant table.

Directions: 17 miles north of Fort William on the A82, on the south side of Loch Lochy, between Spean Bridge and Invergarry on the way to Skye.

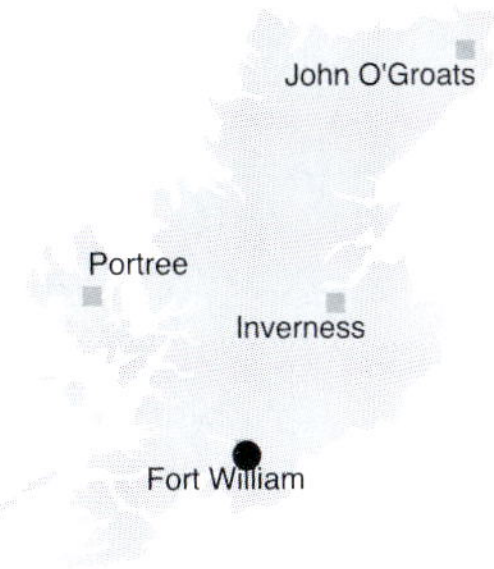

Web: www.johansens.com/corriegour
E-mail: info@corriegour-lodge-hotel.com
Tel: 01397 712685
Fax: 01397 712696

Price Guide:
single £55.50–£59.50
double/twin £111–£118

Culduthel Lodge

14 CULDUTHEL ROAD, INVERNESS, INVERNESS-SHIRE IV2 4AG

Directions: Take the B851 out of Inverness. Culduthel Road is a continuation of Castle Street and the Lodge is less than half a mile from the city centre on the right.

Web: www.johansens.com/culduthellodge
E-mail: johansens@culduthel.com
Tel: 01463 240089
Fax: 01463 240089

Price Guide:
single £45–£75
double £80–£105
suite £105

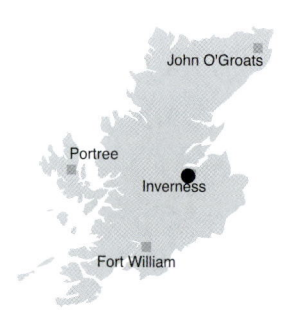

This beautifully appointed hotel, just a few minutes walk from the town centre, is a Grade II Georgian residence set in its own grounds and offering splendid views of the River Ness and surrounding countryside. Great emphasis is placed on providing good food, comfort and a quiet, friendly atmosphere. On arrival in their rooms, guests are greeted with fresh fruit, flowers and a small decanter of sherry. Each bedroom is individually decorated and furnished to a high standard of comfort and provides every modern amenity including a cd/cassette player. Delicious, freshly prepared food is presented by a table d'hôte menu which offers choices at each course, including Scottish fare and local produce. A carefully selected range of wines is available to complement the appetising and nourishing meals. Inverness is a good base for guests wishing to tour the Highlands and the north and west coasts. The Isle of Skye, Royal Deeside and the splendours of the Spey Valley are within a day's travel.

Our inspector loved: An unobtusive gem of a hotel, many rooms having a splendid outlook over the river and city.

HOTEL EILEAN IARMAIN

SLEAT, ISLE OF SKYE IV43 8QR

Hotel Eilean Iarmain stands on the small bay of Isle Ornsay in the South of Skye with views over the Sound of Sleat. The hotel prides itself on its log fires, inventive cooking and friendly staff. 1997/8 accolades include the RAC Restaurant Award, RAC Merit Award for Hospitality, Comfort and Restaurant, AA Rosette for Restaurant, AA Romantic Hotel of Great Britain and Ireland Award, Les Routiers Corps d'Elite Wine Award and Macallan Taste of Scotland, runner-up Hotel of the Year Award. There are 12 individually decorated bedrooms and four light and airy suites, each with a double bedroom and cosy sitting room with a sofa bed. Log fires warm the reception rooms and the wood-panelled dining room where candle-lit dinners can be enjoyed overlooking the bay and the island of Ornsay. The menu features game when in season and fresh seafood landed at the pier. Premier cru clarets feature on the extensive wine list, and a large selection of malt whiskies includes local Poit Dhubh and Talisker. Clan MacDonald Centre, Armadale Castle and Talisker Distillery are close by. Sports include sea-fishing, shooting and walking.

Our inspector loved: *This delightful, informal hostelry, quite magically situated, unpretentious food, charming staff and lovely fresh bright rooms.*

Directions: The hotel is in Sleat, between Broadford and Armadale on A851. 20 mins from Skye Bridge; 15 mins from Mallaig Armadale Ferry and Lochalsh railway station.

Web: www.johansens.com/eileaniarmain
E-mail: hotel@eilean-iarmain.co.uk
Tel: 01471 833332
Fax: 01471 833275

Price Guide:
single from £90
double from £120
suites £180–£200

THE LODGE ON THE LOCH

ONICH, NEAR FORT WILLIAM, HIGHLANDS PH33 6RY

Directions: Approximately 14 miles south west of Fort William on A82.

Web: www.johansens.com/lodgeontheloch
E-mail: reservations@freedomglen.co.uk
Tel: 01855 821237
Fax: 01855 821463

Price Guide:
single £69.50–£105
double/twin £139–£210

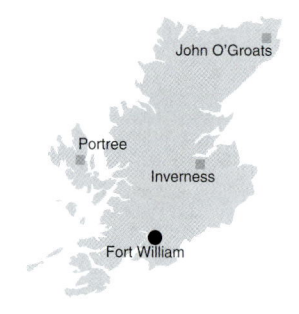

Brushed by the warmth of the Gulf Stream and with outstanding mountain, loch and sea views, this delightful and charming classical Scottish Hotel is an idyllic Highland retreat from the noise and stress of modern life. Seclusion and serenity, comfort and luxury are the Lodge's hallmarks, together with panoramic vistas stretching across the sea south to Argyll and west to the heights of Morvern. Beautifully decorated and furnished lounges offer guests total and peaceful relaxation. Bedrooms are superb, they are individually designed with tasteful décor, stylish furnishings and every facility sought by the discerning visitor. One features a colourful mural wrapping the room in romantic highland scenes and a bathroom with a window-positioned bath-with-a-view and hydrotherapy steam shower. Another has a large and low Japanese-style bed resting amid calming colours, driftwood and shells with a stunning mirrored bathroom and a freestanding 2 person bath. Dining in the elegant restaurant, which overlooks the lochside garden, is an experience to savour. The 5 course daily changing gourmet Taste of Scotland menu is excellently prepared by German chef Dieter Hoffman-Rollauer with every dish handcooked to order. An extensive wine list is reasonably priced. Service is friendly and nothing is too much trouble.

Our inspector loved: The inimitable décor, loch-side position, overall feel and the attentions of the indefatigable hosts Jamie and Jackie Burns.

PORTLAND ARMS HOTEL

LYBSTER, CAITHNESS KW3 6BS

Within the land of the Picts, Vikings, crofters and fisherfolk, the recently refurbished Portland Arms Hotel, with its welcoming atmosphere, is the perfect place to unwind. The 22 stylish en suite bedrooms are tastefully decorated with subtle co-ordinated fabrics and equipped with all modern amenities. The new bar and restaurant are an excellent addition to the hotel, and guests may feast on a superb traditional menu of mouth-watering dishes using only fresh local produce. All diets are catered for and the home-made puddings are delicious. After the meal, guests can relax in the spacious and comfortable lounge. Surrounded by tranquillity and outstanding natural beauty, the hotel is set amongst dramatic coastlines, big skies, unspoilt beaches and abundant birdlife, giving guests a host of activities to choose from. Explore the moorland wilderness, picturesque harbours and historical ruins in this idyllic location. Outdoor pursuits include trout fishing, sea angling, walking, golfing, riding, deer stalking, game hunting, bird watching and discovering the Flow Country for a day with a ranger. Places of interest are the Caithness Glass Visitor Centre and local potteries. There are wildlife cruises from John O' Groats and many museums to wander through.

Our inspector loved: *The totally unexpected and pleasant surprise on entering this tastefully rejuvenated roadside inn for the first time.*

Directions: In the centre of Lybster Village on the A99, 12 miles south of Wick.

Web: www.johansens.com/portlandarms
E-mail: info@portlandarms.co.uk
Tel: 01593 721721
Fax: 01593 721722

Price Guide:
single £48–£58
double £72.50–£90

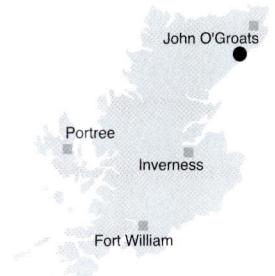

THE PEND

5 BRAE STREET, DUNKELD, PERTHSHIRE PH8 0BA

Directions: From A9, turn off into Dunkeld. Brae Street is off the Main Street.

Web: www.johansens.com/pend
E-mail: molly@thepend.sol.co.uk
Tel: 01350 727586
Fax: 01350 727173

Price Guide:
single £50
double to £100

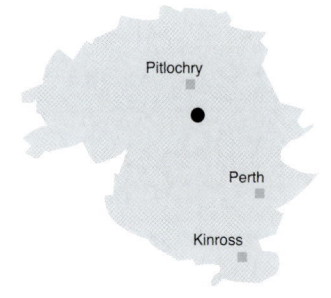

Set in the heart of Perthshire, this charming Georgian house has preserved most of its original features while displaying many modern amenities. The three bedrooms are decorated in a tasteful manner and are complemented by antique furniture. Two bathrooms are currently available for the guests' use. The elegant sitting room is enhanced by a beautiful fireplace and soft furnishings. Continental cuisine and traditional Scottish fare are served in the room at breakfast and dinner. Three or four-course dinners of uncompromising standards are offered accompanied by the small but interesting and award-winning wine list. The range of activities available nearby is extensive and includes many outdoor pursuits. Guests wishing to indulge in the breathtaking Scottish landscape will enjoy abseiling, mountaineering, rock-climbing or simply rambling. For the less adventurous, there are castles, museums, theatres and shops to visit or peruse. Personal itineraries and quotations are designed to suit the needs of the group or individual.

Our inspector loved: *This gem of a small town hotel, with its lovely furnishings, attentive and personal care and charming owners.*

Ardeonaig

SOUTH LOCH TAY SIDE, BY KILLIN, PERTHSHIRE FK21 8SU

The Ardeonaig is a relaxed and informal hotel and restaurant set in ten acres of grounds on the south shore of Loch Tay. Commanding superb views of the magnificent Ben Lawers, the hotel is situated amongst some of the most breathtaking scenery in Scotland. Good hospitality and excellent service offered by the friendly staff adds to the inviting ambience of the hotel. Careful attention to detail and the use of subtle colours in each of the individually decorated bedrooms result in a peaceful and restful abode with all modern conveniences. There are sitting rooms with open fires, a quiet bar area and a library with views over the loch, which all create a calm and harmonious environment. The Chef specialises in classically based French cuisine using Scottish produce sourced as local as possible. The menu is complemented by an excellent selection of fine wines and Scottish malt whiskies. Guests can take a leisurely stroll along the secluded loch shore or explore the many castles, museums, highland games, distilleries, gardens and historical sights nearby. Other activities include fishing (gillies are available) and exploring the loch by boat, golf, horse-riding and trekking, deer stalking, game hunting and bird watching.

Our inspector loved: *A delightful, small hotel having progressed from simple origins, offering an intimate ambiance, excellent cuisine and attention to detail.*

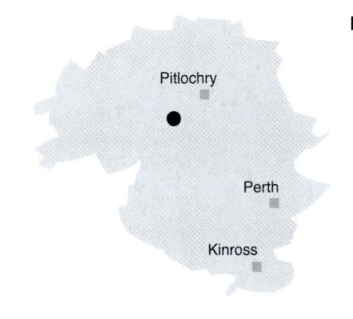

Directions: On South Loch side seven miles from Killin and nine miles from Kenmore.

Web: www.johansens.com/ardeonaig
E-mail: ardeonaighotel@btinternet.com
Tel: 01567 820400
Fax: 01567 820282

Price Guide:
single £75
double £100

THE FOUR SEASONS HOTEL

ST FILLANS, PERTHSHIRE PH6 2NF

Directions: Take the A85 west from Perth.

Web: www.johansens.com/fourseasons
E-mail: info@thefourseasonshotel.co.uk
Tel: 01764 685333
Fax: 01764 685444

Price Guide:
single £70
double £85–£110

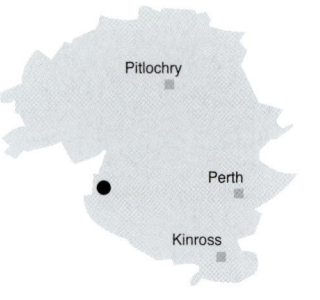

This rambling, white hotel is delightfully situated on the eastern edge of Loch Earn, which has been described as the jewel in the crown of Perthshire lochs. All around is unspoiled Southern Highland landscape, steep hillsides and towering, rugged mountains whose lower slopes are covered with deep green woodland. It is an area of scenic splendour, about 30 miles west of the historic city of Perth. The Four Seasons Hotel, under owner Andrew Low, is excellent in every way and superb value for money. The furnishings and décor throughout the hotel are in simple yet tasteful and open fires and several lounges add to the interior charm. Talented chef John Sherry creates sumptuous, imaginative and traditional cuisine featuring the best local produce. The bedrooms are beautifully proportioned and cosy. All are on the first floor and each has a private bathroom and home from home comforts. Six fully equipped chalets on the hillside behind the hotel are suitable for families with one or two children or for those visitors seeking extra privacy. When not enjoying the magnificent views and changing colours from the hotel's south facing terrace, guests can enjoy walking at Ben Vorlich or visiting the picturesque Southern Highlands villages.

Our inspector loved: *What a pleasant, friendly and relaxed hotel with excellent value for money cooking.*

Parklands Hotel & Acanthus Restaurant

ST. LEONARD'S BANK, PERTH, PH2 8EB

Beautiful panoramic views over and beyond Perth's peaceful South Inch Park impart a distinctive country feel to this attractive, classical, grey-stone Town House with huge ground floor bay windows and a colourful garden. There is a friendly and welcoming ambience throughout this mid-19th century building, formerly the home of the City's Lord Provost, Parklands has been sympathetically restored and refurbished over the years to ensure that it is to the taste of today's discerning hotel guest. All bedrooms are spacious and have en suites, each is individually decorated and furnished with all home comforts. Front facing, superior class rooms are particularly large and one has a jacuzzi installed. The attractive, award-winning restaurant offers an elegant, yet informal atmosphere, in which to enjoy an excellent and attentively served dinner, complemented by an extensive and reasonably priced wine-list. Only the freshest produce is used to create meals of originality and finesse. Guests can relax and enjoy the scenic views whilst enjoying breakfast, or the innovative menu in Parkland's bright and airy Colourist Bistro and Bar, whose walls are decorated with pictures of the Scottish Colourists. Alternatively the picturesque surroundings can be savoured on the shaded patio.

Our inspector loved: *The understated nature of this hotel, set apart from the town's bustle, well-run with strong emphasis on the cuisine.*

Directions: On entering the town from Edinburgh on the A90, take the inner ring road. The Hotel is 200 yards on the left.

Web: www.johansens.com/parklands
E-mail: parklands.perth@virgin.net
Tel: 01738 622451
Fax: 01738 622046

Price Guide:
single £79
double/twin £99–£115

KNOCKENDARROCH HOUSE

HIGHER OAKFIELD, PITLOCHRY, PERTHSHIRE PH16 5HT

Directions: On entering Pitlochry from the south via Atholl Road, pass Bells distillery on you right, then pass under the railway bridge; 100 yards turn right into East Moulin Road; after 200 yards take 2nd left into Higher Oakfield. Knockendarroch House is 300 yards on the left.

Web: www.johansens.com/knockendarrochhouse
E-mail: info@knockendarroch.co.uk
Tel: 01796 473473
Fax: 01796 474068

Price Guide: (including dinner)
single £64–£81
double £92–£126

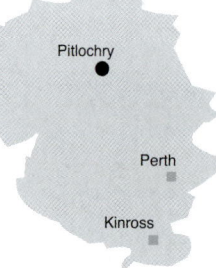

Now a listed building, this elegant 19th-century Victorian mansion with its grand three-storey high peaked tower stands imposingly on a plateau within the picturesque town of Pitlochry offering visitors superb views over the beautiful Tummel Valley. It is surrounded by landscaped gardens and framed by ancient oak trees which give Knockendarroch its name – from the Gaelic, meaning Hill of Oaks. Owned and run by Tony and Jane Ross, Knockendarroch House is a totally non-smoking property and has a reputation for its hospitality amid beautiful Highland scenery. Historic sights and castles abound and the battle-famed pass of Killiecrankie lies just a few miles to the north. Each of the 12 en suite bedrooms is spacious and equipped with every comfort from television to electric blanket. First floor premier rooms have magnificent southerly or westerly views, two of the second-floor standard rooms have balconies. In the elegant restaurant, the finest local produce is the base of the expertly prepared menus and guests can enjoy a complimentary glass of sherry prior to dining. During the Pitlochry theatre season the restaurant opens from 6pm and the hotel runs a courtesy bus to and from the evening performances.

Our inspector loved: *The panoramic position, a landmark overlooking Pitlochry and Tummel valley, this well run hotel gives great value.*

THE LAKE HOTEL
PORT OF MENTEITH, PERTHSHIRE FK8 3RA

The Lake Hotel is set in a splendid sheltered position on the banks of the Lake of Menteith in the Trossachs. Its lawn runs down to the edge of the lake, which in winter months often freezes over. When this happens, it is not unusual for locals to bring out their skates for a skim over the ice. Guests are assured of all the amenities of an STB 3 Star Highly Commended hotel. A programme of refurbishment has been completed, so the interiors have fresh decoration and furnishings. All bedrooms have en suite facilities and the details that will make your stay comfortable. There is an elegant lounge and a large conservatory from which the vista of lake and mountains is stunning. The à la carte and table d'hôte menus present a varied choice of imaginatively prepared dishes. The table d'hôte menus are particularly good value: start with chicken & herb terrine with sun dried tomato dressing, followed by sorbet, then after a main course of grilled halibut with spinach, saffron potatoes and an orange & aniseed sauce, enjoy a Drambuie parfait with raspberry coulis before your coffee and home-made petits fours. Special rates are available for mini-breaks of two nights or more. Inchmahome Priory, Loch Lomond and Stirling Castle are nearby.

Our inspector loved: *The beautiful view over the water.*

Directions: Situated on the A81 road, south of Callander and east of Aberfoyle, on the northern banks of the Lake of Menteith.

Web: www.johansens.com/lakehotel
E-mail: enquiries@lake-of-menteith-hotel.com
Tel: 01877 385258
Fax: 01877 385671

Price Guide: (including dinner)
single £65–£112
double £110–£204

BOWFIELD HOTEL & COUNTRY CLUB

HOWWOOD, RENFREWSHIRE PA9 1LA

Directions: From the M8 towards Glasgow Airport, take the A737 (Irvine route). The Hotel is signposted from the A737.

Web: www.johansens.com/bowfield
E-mail: enquiries@bowfieldcountryclub.co.uk
Tel: 01505 705225
Fax: 01505 705230

Price Guide:
single £75
double/twin £120

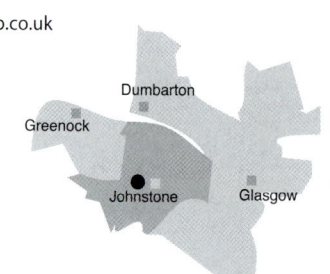

Deceptively just 15 minutes from Glasgow International Airport, Bowfield Country Club is tucked away in the rolling Renfrewshire hills and seemingly a world away from the hustle and bustle of city life. A haven of peace and tranquillity, the Country Club offers a full spa with steam, sauna and beautiful swimming pool, as well as a comprehensive Health and Beauty Suite. There are 17 golf courses within 25 miles of the Hotel and the famous Ayrshire links are within an hour's drive, as well as fishing, sailing and some great walking country. Each of the 23 en suite bedrooms is decorated in cottage style and the emphasis is placed on informality with newspapers and magazines in the lounge, and a light and friendly atmosphere in the Club Bar where light suppers and snacks are served. The Country Club prides itself on using locally produced ingredients complemented by a fine wine selection and the private conference facilities are conducive to a real "get away from it all" atmosphere. Loch Lomond is only 35 minutes away by car, Kyles of Bute and the picturesque isles of Millport and Arran are accessible from the port at the nearby river Clyde.

Our inspector loved: *A real getaway into the country yet close proximity to Glasgow.*

Culzean Castle – The Eisenhower Apartment

MAYBOLE, AYRSHIRE KA19 8LE

Situated in the heart of one of Scotland's most magnificent country parks and dramatically perched on a cliff top with breathtaking views, Culzean Castle is the ideal base for a golfing trip in an area that boasts some of Scotland's finest links courses. The Eisenhower Apartments is a presidential retreat for guests bored with 5 star hotels. The 6 bedroom upper floor of Culzean was retained for General Eisenhower when the Castle was handed over to the National Trust for Scotland in 1945. Now, guests can enjoy the style and comfort once reserved for the General and his family. Guests staying in the apartments can either enter the Castle through the impressive armoury at the front door or use the private lift at the side door. When you arrive on the top floor you feel like entering a rather splendid home and the friendly welcome from Jonathan and Susan Cardale simply amplifies this feeling. Whether you are travelling on your own, as a couple or maybe wishing to book all the rooms for that special party, the Castle will make you feel most welcome. Guests have access to the complete Castle during opening hours and can explore the 560 acre country park with its woodlands, deer park, newly recreated Victorian Vinery and exotic pagoda.

Our inspector loved: *The completely different experience. This is one hotel where you can really feel like the Lord of the Manor. Spectacular property with spectacular views.*

Directions: From Glasgow, take the A77 towards Ayr. Culzean Castle is 12 miles south of Ayr on the A719.

Web: www.johansens.com/culzeancastle
E-mail: culzean@nts.org.uk
Tel: 01655 884455
Fax: 01655 884503

Price Guide:
single £140–£265
double £200–£375

THE WHITE COMPANY
LONDON

Elegant Toiletries and Guest Amenities available exclusively from Pacific Direct

Email: sales@pacificdirect.co.uk   www.pacificdirect.co.uk   Worldwide Sales Telephone (+44) 1234 347 140   USA Toll Free 1-877-363-4732

---

exceed your guests' expectations – luxury toiletries and amenities from **pacific direct**

Pacific Direct

www.pacificdirect.co.uk

international telephone:
(+44) 1234 347 140

e-mail sales@pacificdirect.co.uk

USA office:
call toll free 1-8777-363-4732

e-mail pdirectusa@aol.com

Furniture supplied by Victoria House (+44) 01234 320000

WALES – CYMRU

Recommendations in Wales appear on pages 280-300

For further information on Wales, please contact:

Wales Tourist Board
Brunel House, 2 Fitzalan Road, Cardiff CF24 0UY
Tel: +44 (0)29 2049 9909
Web: www.visitwales.com

North Wales Tourism
Tel: +44 (0)1492 531731
Web: www.nwt.co.uk

Mid Wales Tourism
Tel: (Freephone) 0800 273747
Web: www.mid-wales-tourism.org.uk

Tourism South & West Wales
Tel: +44 (0)1792 781212

or see **pages 306-309** for details of local atractions to visit during your stay.

Images from www.britainonview.com

THE GREAT HOUSE

HIGH STREET, LALESTON, BRIDGEND, WALES CF32 0HP

Directions: From M4 exit at junctions 35 or 37.

Web: www.johansens.com/greathouse
E-mail: enquiries@great-house-laleston.co.uk
Tel: 01656 657644
Fax: 01656 668892

Price Guide:
single £60–£90
double £85–£135

This is a superb example of charming Elizabethan architecture, delightfully situated overlooking an ancient church in the pretty conservation village of Laleston. Dating back to around 1550, the Grade II listed Great House with its beautiful walled garden is said to have been a gift from Queen Elizabeth I to the Earl of Leicester and used by him as a hunting lodge. Owners Stephen and Norma Bond bought Great House as a dilapidated shell in 1985 and have beautifully restored the building to its original condition, with modern comforts. Numerous interesting features include stone archways, mullioned windows, inglenook fireplaces, huge oak beams, a unique stone and wood spiral staircase. The stone arch above the cocktail bar fireplace is the single largest unbroken span of stone in Wales. Guestrooms are in the main house with two garden suites in converted stables, all with an individual personality reflecting the warmth and character throughout the house. Each is en suite and furnished with every modern comfort. Chef Neil Hughes produces imaginative, award-winning cuisine in the 2 AA Rosette restaurant, with its relaxed elegant ambience. Places of interest nearby include Margam Country Park, Sker House and St Fagans Welsh Folk Museum, Cardiff.

Our inspector loved: *The outstanding restoration of this magical Elizabethan building providing superb accommadation and comfort.*

Inn At The Elm Tree

ST BRIDES WENTLOOGE, NR NEWPORT NP10 8SQ

This is a warm, welcoming and extremely relaxing place. Situated in a little known coastal village just a 15 minutes drive from Cardiff and Newport, the Inn at the Elm Tree is described by owners Mike and Patricia Thomas as a 21st century Inn with traditional values. Surrounded by the flat river meadows of the Seven Estuary it is an ideal venue in which to escape from the noise and pressures of everyday life. Peace and tranquility abound in an area of special scientific interest teems with bird and wildlife, offering protection to rare and varied flora and fauna. The Inn's bedrooms are excellent; designed to the highest standards of quality and comfort, homely and appealing whilst offering every facility, plus personal touches and little luxuries characteristic of a leading Hotel. They have king-sized beds, iron and brass beds and four-posters, beamed ceilings, chunky pine furniture and rocking chairs. 2 ground-floor rooms can be booked as a family suite with its own entrance. The intimate, AA Rosette award-winning candlelit restaurant with adjoining Café Bar, which opens onto a Tropical Courtyard, serves traditional favourites alongside the varied and seasonal European cuisine. Open fires burn during cooler months. Golf, horse riding, clay shooting, sea, trout and course fishing are all nearby.

Our inspector loved: the warm and welcoming atmosphere created by the owners with an abundance of extra personal touches throughout.

Directions: From Newport, exit M4 at junction 28 and take B4239 for approximately 3 miles.

Web: www.johansens.com/elmtree
E-mail: inn@the-elm-tree.co.uk
Tel: 01633 680225
Fax: 01633 681035

Price Guide:
single £70–£90
double/twin £80–£100

CONRAH COUNTRY HOUSE HOTEL

RHYDGALED, CHANCERY, ABERYSTWYTH, CEREDIGION SY23 4DF

One of Wales' much loved country house hotels, the Conrah is tucked away at the end of a rhododendron-lined drive, only minutes from the spectacular rocky cliffs and sandy bays of the Cambrian coast. Set in 22 acres of rolling grounds, the Conrah's magnificent position gives views as far north as the Cader Idris mountain range. Afternoon tea and Welsh cakes or pre-dinner drinks can be taken at leisure in the quiet writing room or one of the comfortable lounges, where antiques and fresh flowers add to the relaxed country style. The acclaimed restaurant uses fresh local produce, together with herbs and vegetables from the Conrah kitchen garden, to provide the best of both classical and modern dishes. The hotel is owned and run by the Heading family who extend a warm invitation to guests to come for a real 'taste of Wales', combined with old-fashioned, high standards of service. For recreation, guests may enjoy a game of table-tennis in the summer house, croquet on the lawn or a walk around the landscaped gardens. The heated swimming pool and sauna are open all year round. Golf, pony-trekking and sea fishing are all available locally, while the university town of Aberystwyth is only 3 miles away. Closed Christmas.

Directions: The Conrah lies 3 miles south of Aberystwyth on the A487.

Web: www.johansens.com/conrahcountryhouse
E-mail: enquiries@conrah.co.uk
Tel: 01970 617941
Fax: 01970 624546

Price Guide:
single £72–£100
double/twin £110–£145

Our inspector loved: The view from the restaurant.

TAN-Y-FOEL

CAPEL GARMON, NR BETWS-Y-COED, CONWY LL26 0RE

This contemporary bijou style house, built of magnificent Welsh stone has won many accolades as an outstanding small country house that blends finest country elegance with innovative interior design. The intimate reception rooms styled in earth tones offer a calming and tranquil atmosphere. Set in breathtaking surroundings, it commands views of the verdant Conwy Valley and the rugged peaks of Snowdonia. Once inside Tan-y-Foel a "no smoking" policy prevails. Each extremely comfortable bedroom has its own strikingly individual style, thoughtful small touches add to their charm and the bathrooms are delightfully appointed. Celebrated for her impeccable cuisine, Janet, a member of "The Master Chefs of Great Britain," sources the best local produce, fresh fish, Welsh black beef and organically grown vegetables for her creatively composed nightly menus which have been recognised with 3 AA Rosettes. This, combined with an outstanding selection of wines, will ensure an experience to savour. The personal welcome, which perfectly complements the nature of the Pitmans' unique house, has resulted in the Hotel receiving the award of 2 AA Red Stars for exemplary service and the prestigious accolade of 5 Star Country House with the Welsh Tourist Board.

Our inspector loved: Its style; a wonderful place.

Directions: From Chester, A55 to Llandudno, A470 towards Betws-y-Coed. 2 miles south from Llanrwst fork left towards Capel Garmon. Tan-y-Foel is just over a mile uphill on the left.

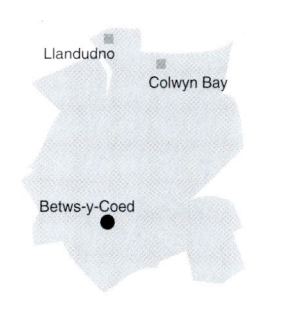

Web: www.johansens.com/tanyfoel
E-mail: enquiries@tyfhotel.co.uk
Tel: 01690 710507
Fax: 01690 710681

Price Guide:
single £99–£105
double £120–£170

CASTLE HOTEL

HIGH STREET, CONWY LL32 8DB

This town house hotel offers everything: history, atmosphere, friendliness, comfort, good food and quality service. The Castle's owners, the Lavin family, along with their friend, partner and Rosette award-winning chef, Graham Tinsley, take hospitality and good food very seriously. Formerly a 15th-century coaching inn, the hotel stands in the World Heritage Centre and mediaeval town of Conwy close to the quay and the ancient castle. Attractively built from local granite and Ruabon brick, it is one of the town's most photographed and popular buildings. Antiques and fine paintings by Victorian artist John Dawson-Watson decorate the interiors, with an excellent collection of his work in Shakespeare's, the hotel's delightful restaurant. Here, Graham creates menus inspired by bygone days but with modern interpretation. Each of the 29 en suite bedrooms has its own character and every home-from-home comfort. One has an ornately carved four-poster bed dated 1570 which Charles I reputedly slept in while on a visit during the Civil Wars. Activities such as sailing, horse riding, golf and cycling can be arranged. Within easy reach are Snowdonia National Park, Bodnant Gardens, Penrhyn Castle, Plas Mawr and Bangor. Meeting facilities.

Our inspector loved: *Its tradition and warmth. A true hostelry.*

Directions: Conwy is beside Llandudno, on the A55 along the north coast of Wales from M56 and Chester.

Web: www.johansens.com/castleconwy
E-mail: mail@castlewales.co.uk
Tel: 01492 582 800
Fax: 01492 582 300

Price Guide:
single £55–£70
double/twin £69–£109
four-poster £89–£119

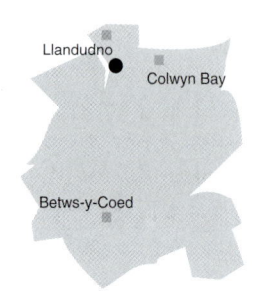

CONWY

SYCHNANT PASS HOUSE
SYCHNANT PASS ROAD, CONWY LL32 8BJ

'This is not a hotel but a home that welcomes guests,' claim owners, Bre and Graham Carrington-Sykes, who have been warmly greeting visitors to Sychnant Pass House since purchasing it in the spring of 1999. They have been so successful in their stylish refurbishment, service, manner and provision of home-from-home comforts that the RAC awarded them a Little Gem award, its highest for guest accommodation and the Booker Prize for Excellence 2002 for best guest house. Sychnant Pass House is idyllically situated in the foothills of Snowdonia National Park just a mile from the medieval town of Conwy, with its Edward I castle and less than 3 miles from a fine, sandy beach. It stands in 2 acres of lawns and wild garden with a small stream running through it. With views of the bordering Pensychant Nature Reserve the house is a delightful haven of relaxation. Inside the attractive, white-faced exterior are all the facilities of a good unstuffy country house. There are spacious sitting rooms, big sofas and large log fires. The bedrooms are beautifully furnished and benefit from superb views. Graham enjoys producing interesting dinner dishes in the intimate restaurant, open Tuesday to Sunday.

Our inspector loved: *The thought and kindness given towards children, and the budgie too!*

Directions: From the A55 take the Conwy turn at Llandudno. Follow signs for the town centre. Pass Conwy Visitor Centre and take the second left into Upper Gate Street. Sychnant Pass House is on the right.

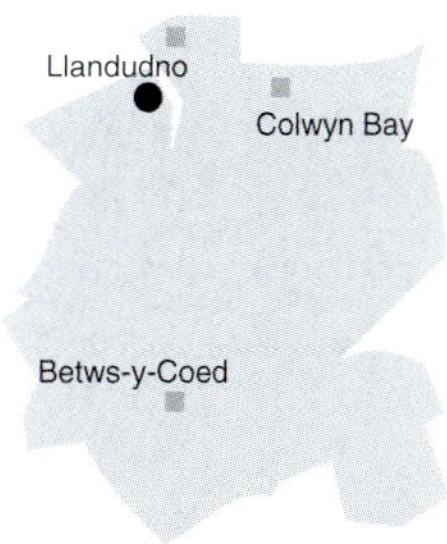

Web: www.johansens.com/sychnant
E-mail: bresykes@sychnant-pass-house.co.uk
Tel: 01492 596868
Fax: 01492 596868

Price Guide:
single from £50
double/twin from £70
suite from £100

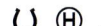

285

The Old Rectory Country House

LLANRWST ROAD, LLANSANFFRAID GLAN CONWY, CONWY LL28 5LF

Directions: On A470, 1/2 mile south of A55 junction, 2 miles from Llandudno Junction Station. 3 hrs from London Euston.

Web: www.johansens.com/oldrectorycountryhouse
E-mail: info@oldrectorycountryhouse.co.uk
Tel: 01492 580611
Fax: 01492 584555

Price Guide:
single £99–£129
double £129–£169

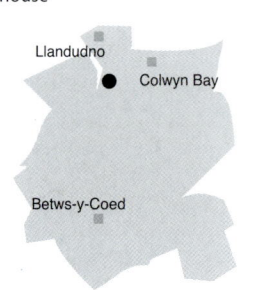

Enjoy dramatic Snowdonian vistas, breathtaking sunsets and views of floodlit Conwy Castle from this idyllic country house set in large gardens overlooking Conwy Bird Reserve. An AOL Top Ten Gourmet Hotel in the UK, The Old Rectory's Michelin Starred Chef, Wendy, is a 'Master Chef of Great Britain' who creates gourmet 3 course dinners combining a lightness of touch and delicacy of flavour with artistic presentation. Awarded 2 AA Red Stars and RAC Gold Ribbon for 'outstanding levels of comfort, service and hospitality' and A.A. 3 Rosettes for food, the Welsh mountain lamb, locally reared Welsh black beef and locally landed fish are on the menu. An award-winning wine list complements her fine cuisine. Antiques and Victorian watercolours decorate the interiors. The luxury en suite bedrooms have draped beds, bathrobes, ironing centres, fresh fruit and flowers. Michael is happy to share his knowledge of Welsh history, and culture and to assist in planning touring routes. Three 18-hole golf courses within 10 minutes drive. Relax in the garden and watch the River Conwy ebb and flow and see why this elegant Georgian home is a 'beautiful haven of peace'. An ideal venue for exclusive small conferences.

Our inspector loved: *The time spent over dinner; every moment was to be relished.*

THE WEST ARMS HOTEL

LLANARMON D C, CEIRIOG VALLEY, NR LLANGOLLEN, DENBIGHSHIRE LL20 7LD

Situated in one of Wales' most beautiful valleys, surrounded by sheep studded hills, woodlands and lush meadows, this is an unforgettable oasis of peace and is well known for its quality of service, heartfelt welcome and relaxed atmosphere. Originally a shelter for cattle drivers, The West Arms became a hotel in 1670 and has been popular with locals and visitors from all parts of the globe since then. Character and warmth oozes from every corner; cosy armchairs are set around beautiful inglenook fireplaces with roaring log fires. Slate floors and ancient timberwork are combined with antiques and harmonious décor to stunning effect. Some of the comfortable bedrooms have low exposed beams and character furniture for an authentic historic impression whilst boasting every modern convenience. Outstanding cuisine is prepared meticulously and creatively by the Hotel's award winning chef, Grant Williams, who uses fresh local ingredients and has even cooked for H.R.H. Prince Charles! Guests can stroll along the Ceiriog River and surrounding countryside or visit the many castles and historical places of interest in the area. Outdoor activities include mountain biking, walking, pony trekking, golf, fishing, microlight flights, caving and potholing. A landscape painting course is offered at the Hotel.

Our inspector loved: *This warm, welcoming, unspoilt Inn situated in a delightful rural area just 20 minutes from civilisation.*

Directions: Take the A5 to Chirk, then the B4500 for 11 miles to Llanarmon DC. Once over the bridge, the Inn is on the right.

Web: www.johansens.com/westarms
E-mail: gowestarms@aol.com
Tel: 01691 600665
Fax: 01691 600622

Price Guide:
single £52.50–£65
double £95–£108
suite £139

PORTH TOCYN COUNTRY HOUSE HOTEL

ABERSOCH, PWLLHELI, GWYNEDD LL53 7BU

Directions: The hotel is two miles from Abersoch on the Sarn Bach road. Watch for bilingual signs – Gwesty/hotel – then the hotel name.

Web: www.johansens.com/porthtocyn
E-mail: porthtocyn.hotel@virgin.net
Tel: 01758 713303
Fax: 01758 713538

Price Guide:
single £52.50–£68.50
double/twin £70–£128

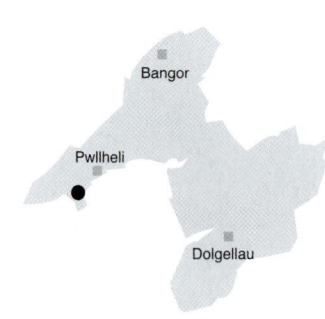

This is a rare country house seaside hotel – family-owned for three generations, the first of whom had the inspiration to transform a row of miners' cottages into an attractive, low white building, surrounded by enchanting gardens, with glorious views over Cardigan Bay and Snowdonia. The Fletcher-Brewer family have created a unique ambience that appeals to young and old alike. Children are welcome; the younger ones have their own sitting room and high tea menu. Nonetheless, Porth Tocyn's charm is appreciated by older guests, with its Welsh antiques and delightful, comfortable sitting rooms. Most of the pretty bedrooms have sea views, some are family oriented and three on the ground floor are ideal for those with mobility problems. All have en suite bathrooms. Enjoy cocktails in the intimate bar, anticipating a fabulous meal, for dining at Porth Tocyn is a memorable experience every day of the week – the menu changes completely every day. Scrumptious dishes and mellow wines are served in great style on antique tables. Lunch is informal, on the terrace or by the pool. Glorious beaches, water sports, golf, tennis, riding and exploring the coast provide activities for all ages.

Our inspector loved: *The atmosphere. Nick and Louise have a truly balanced hotel. They have thought of everything.*

GWYNEDD - BALA

BRYN TEGID COUNTRY HOUSE
BALA, GWYNEDD LL23 7YG

A magical hideaway and country retreat, Bryn Tegid is a fine Victorian house set within 9 acres of private woodland and grounds. Originally built in 1849 for General Jones, it has been restored and lovingly maintained by owner, Rosina Jones, whose unobtrusive yet attentive style means the whole concept is one of being totally pampered. Rosina prefers guests to book by telephone so that she can know a little about them beforehand and discuss dining requirements. As the Hotel does not have a license for alcohol, visitors are encouraged to bring their own wines or champagne which are then decanted and prepared correctly. For those less inclined to bring their own the trust bar is available. Upon arrival, tea and home-made cakes are served and the relaxed breakfast is a delight with smoked salmon omelettes proving to be a favourite among regular guests. The 3 bedrooms are well-appointed with views across Lyn Tegid, the Bala Lake or the gardens. Outside, superb deck loungers are in abundance on the south facing lawns and guests can fish for pike from the Lake, visitors have even been known to wander down to the shore and create a barbecue. With its warm welcome and air of solitude the Hotel is perfect for exclusive hire. One mile from Bala town centre.

Our inspector loved: This true hideaway.

Directions: Drive out from Bala along the A494 towards Dolgellau, pass The Leisure centre on the left, pass a church and cemetery on the left. Continue after the church for ¼ mile and take the first turn right signed Bryn-Tegid.

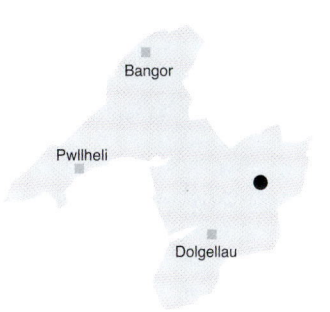

Web: www.johansens.com/bryntegid
E-mail: info@bryntegid.co.uk
Tel: 01678 521645
Fax: 01678 521645

Price Guide:
single/double/twin from £80

GWYNEDD - BARMOUTH

BAE ABERMAW

PANORAMA HILL, BARMOUTH, GWYNEDD LL42 1DQ

From the outside, Bae Abermaw looks solid and traditional but inside the Hotel delivers excitement, particularly in the kitchen where superb feasts are served in a stunning restaurant where each changing menu is a delight and each individual dish is an experience. The service is friendly and the view over the gardens can be enjoyed whilst savouring the evening's past and future gourmet delights. Executive Chef, Martin James, was trained by the renowned Anton Mossiman and formerly worked at Bodysgallen and Hambleton Hall. Martin oversees an enthusiastic and talented corps which includes Head Chef, Kevin Williams, a member of the Welsh Culinary Team whose modern expertise contrasts with Martin's traditional dishes to produce a really exciting menu mix. This typical, dark stone-built Victorian building is situated above Cardigan Bay and has been restored and converted by new owners into a fresh, vibrant, modern hotel of the 21st century whilst retaining the charm and elegance of its past. Features include polished wooden floors, log burning marble and slate fireplaces, simple but tasteful décor, soft, comfortable chairs and sofas. The delightfully designed bar has slate flooring and there is outside seating from where guests can sip their drinks while admiring the sea views. All bedrooms are en suite, have quality furnishings and every modern amenity.

Directions: From Dolgellau take the A496 to Barmouth. At Barmouth turn right, signposted Bae Abermaw.

Web: www.johansens.com/baeabermaw
E-mail: bae.abermaw@virgin.net
Tel: 01341 280550
Fax: 01341 280346

Price Guide:
single £55
double/twin £80

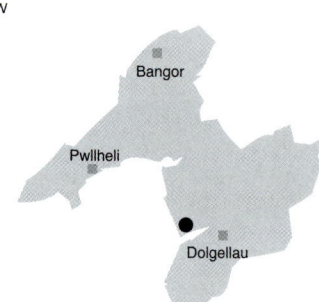

Our inspector loved: Its freshness.

BONTDDU HALL
BONTDDU, NR BARMOUTH, GWYNEDD LL40 2UF

Solid and grey-stoned, with a rampart-topped tower and slim, arched windows, Bontddu Hall looks in every way like a small fairytale castle. Situated in the beautiful Southern Snowdonia National Park, the hotel stands majestically in 4 acres of gardens and woodlands overlooking the picturesque magnificence of the Mawddach Estuary. It is a superb example of Gothic architecture, reflected inside by the grandeur, elegance and tradition of high, beamed ceilings, huge fireplaces, handsome portraits and rich furnishings. Period furniture and Victorian style wallpapers add to the country-house ambience of the bedrooms, each suite named after a past visiting Prime Minister. Each bedroom is en suite, delightfully decorated and has all modern facilities. Four rooms in the Lodge have balconies from which occupants can enjoy mountain views. There are two comfortable lounges and a Victorian-style bar where local artists occasionally exhibit their work. Lunch and dinner are served in the brasserie or on the sun-catching garden terrace. The devoted team of chefs produce traditional cuisine using fresh, local produce in the Mawddach Restaurant.

Our inspector loved: The gothic hall which has been brought back to life.

Directions: Bontddu Hall is on A496 between Dolgellau and Barmouth.

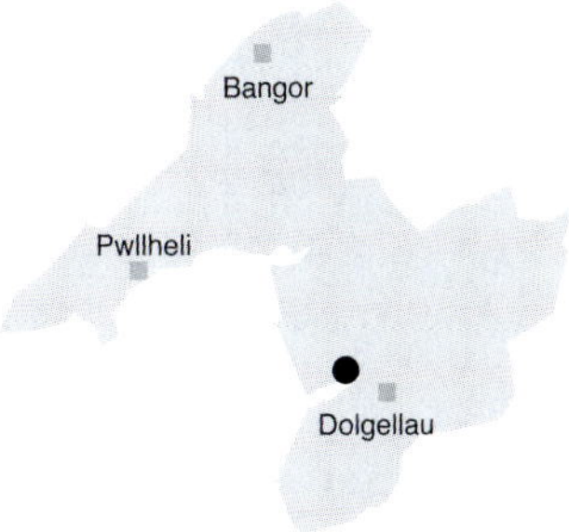

Web: www.johansens.com/bontdduhall
E-mail: reservations@bontdduhall.co.uk
Tel: 01341 430661
Fax: 01341 430284

Price Guide: (including dinner)
single £85–£95
double/twin £130–£170
suite £170–£210

PLAS DOLMELYNLLYN

GANLLWYD, DOLGELLAU, GWYNEDD LL40 2HP

Directions: Plas Dolmelynllyn is off the main A470 Dolgellau– Llandudno road, 5 miles north of Dolgellau.

Web: www.johansens.com/plasdolmelynllyn
E-mail: info@dolly-hotel.co.uk
Tel: 01341 440273
Fax: 01341 440640

Price Guide:
single £60–£70
double £96–£125

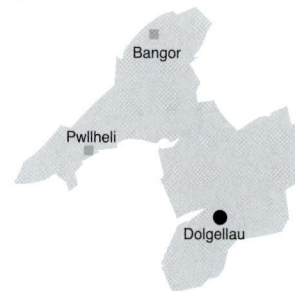

Set in 3 acres of beautifully landscaped gardens with a swift flowing stream and surrounded by mountains and meadows of Snowdonia National Park, the stunning Plas Dolmelynllyn oozes charm and elegance from a bygone era. An avenue of beech trees makes a suitable entrance to this grand Manor House, parts of which date back to the 16th century. 3 large windows in the comfortable sitting room offer a magnificent view of the gardens and over the valley making it the perfect place to relax. Delicious modern British cuisine is lovingly prepared by the Hotel's award winning chef, who offers a wide choice menu catering for all dietary requirements. Individually decorated bedrooms are each named after a local river and are beautifully decorated with relaxing colours and subtle designs. The area offers a wealth of castles and stately homes and guests can walk all day over the Rhinogs or stroll along the estuary without seeing a car or crossing the road. Only a short drive away are Cader Idris and Snowdon, a more strenuous climb for those who want an awe-inspiring adventure. There is a wonderful secluded fishing spot on the River Mawdach and guests staying for 4 nights or more get the fishing free. Dinner, bed and breakfast combined rates and short breaks are available.

Our inspector loved: *The wonderful selection offered at breakfast; delicious and so leisurely.*

Ye Olde Bull's Head

CASTLE STREET, BEAUMARIS, ISLE OF ANGLESEY LL58 8AP

After catching a glimpse of the beautiful Menai Strait viewed from Thomas Telford's famous suspension bridge, a short scenic drive leads to the sailing town of Beaumaris, which was founded in 1295 by Edward I, whose magnificent castle - now a World Heritage site - nestles on the edge of the town. Formerly a staging post on the way to Ireland, the Inn combines the traditional architecture of its past with stunning contemporary décor and sophistication, where quality and comfort is key. Spacious bedrooms are luxurious and feature antique furniture and brass and cast iron bedsteads. Creative, modern British cuisine is lovingly prepared to an extremely high standard using fine local produce and is complemented by a carefully selected wine list. Guests may eat in the elegant, intimate surrounds of the dining room or the equally stylish yet informal Brasserie, which makes use of local stone, slate and oak to create an environment sensitive to its distinguished surroundings. Real ale lovers can enjoy a pint by the open fire in the cosy historic bar. The spectacular and diverse Anglesey scenery is right on the doorstep and most of the coastal area is classified as an 'Area of Outstanding Natural Beauty.' Anglesey boasts an impressive concentration of burial chambers and other places of historic and archaeological interest.

Our inspector loved: This delightful inn, the restaurant upstairs is quite a surprise.

Directions: From Britannia Road Bridge (A5), follow the A545 for approximately 5 miles to Beaumaris.

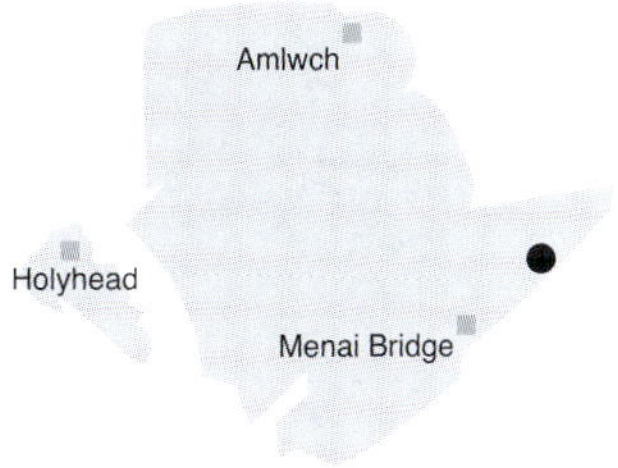

Web: www.johansens.com/yeoldebullshead
E-mail: info@bullsheadinn.co.uk
Tel: 01248 810329
Fax: 01248 811294

Price Guide:
single £57
double/twin £89
four-poster £100

The Bell At Skenfrith

SKENFRITH, MONMOUTHSHIRE NP7 8UH

Directions: Leave the M4 (J24) take the A449 (A40) north. At the roundabout in Monmouth, turn left and then right at the traffic lights torwards Hereford. Travel 4 miles and turn left onto B4521 towards Abergavenny. The Bell is 3 miles on the left.

Web: www.johansens.com/bellskenfrith
E-mail: enquiries@thebellatskenfrith.com
Tel: 01600 750235
Fax: 01600 750525

Price Guide:
single £65–£110
double/twin £85–£140

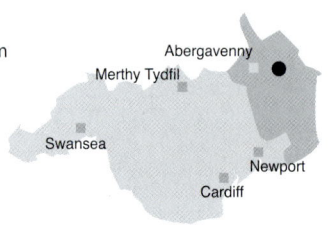

Situated in a tiny picturesque village on the edge of the River Monnow and surrounded by unspoilt Monmouthshire countryside, The Bell, a carefully renovated 17th century coaching inn and recently voted the Best Place to Stay in Wales by the tourist board, is an oasis for visitors. The Inn looks out over the historic arched bridge as well as the old castle ruins and mill. Beautifully designed in a classical style, there are roaring log fires, flagstone floors and stunning oak beams complemented by antiques, sumptuous sofas and tasteful decor. Cosy bedrooms are homely and welcoming with beautiful welsh blankets, crisp linen, all modern amenities and sweeping views over the rolling hills or river. Guests may enjoy an informal meal whilst sipping on a glass of wine or real ale in the relaxed atmosphere of the bistro style bar with its wooden tables and chairs, newspapers and magazines. For a more intimate experience, there is the quiet Williamsburg-style restaurant, which serves stylish, imaginative, contemporary dishes created by the Inn's 2 AA rosetted chef. The Skenfrith area is rich in cultural and historical heritage and is an ideal base for many walks.

Our inspector loved: The huge welcoming log fire, abundance of flowers and the outstanding quality of the decor throughout.

Parva Farmhouse And Restaurant

TINTERN, CHEPSTOW, MONMOUTHSHIRE NP16 6SQ

Surrounded by the glorious, wooded hillsides of the beautiful lower Wye Valley and just a mile from 12th century Tintern Abbey, one of the finest relics of Britain's monastic age, Parva Farmhouse is a homely haven where visitors can relax and forget the pressures of their daily world. This is an ideal spot for country lovers. The River Wye flows just 50 yards from the hotel's small, flower-filled garden, there is an abundance of wildlife and hundreds of tempting walks. Built during the 17th century, Parva today provides every comfort. The bedrooms are well-furnished and most have pretty views across the River Wye. The beamed lounge with its log-burning fireplace, "Honesty Bar" and deep Chesterfield sofas and chairs is the perfect place to relax and chat over the day's happenings. The crowning glory of Parva is the excellent food, home-cooked by chef-patron Dereck Stubbs and served in the AA Rosette Inglenook Restaurant before a 14-foot beamed fireplace. Golf, shooting and riding are close by and there is horse-racing at Chepstow. Two night breaks inclusive of dinner are especially popular and good value for money. Places of interest nearby include Tintern Abbey, castles at Abergavenny and Chepstow, Offa's Dyke, the Royal Forest of Dean, many old ruins and ancient monuments.

Our inspector loved: *The spacious well appointed and tastefully decorated bedrooms with views over the River Wye.*

Directions: Leave M48 at Jct2 and join A466 towards Monmouth. The hotel is on the north edge of Tintern Village.

Web: www.johansens.com/parvafarmhouse
E-mail: Parva_hoteltintern@hotmail.com
Tel: 01291 689411
Fax: 01291 689557

Price Guide:
single £55
double £76–£80

Stone Hall Hotel & Restaurant

WELSH HOOK, HAVERFORDWEST, PEMBROKESHIRE SA62 5NS

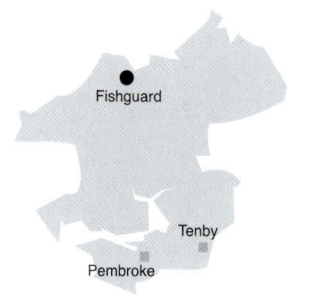

Surrounded by 10 acres of secluded landscaped gardens and mature woodlands near the lovely hamlet of Welsh Hook, stands the charming Stone Hall Hotel. Originally built 600 years ago as a manor house, it was sensitively converted into a country hotel in 1984 where an atmosphere of harmonious historical authenticity is combined with all the comforts of modern-day living for a truly pleasant stay. Care was taken to preserve the original architectural features such as the 14th century slate-flagged floors and large rough-hewn oak beams as well as the impressive 17th century wood panelling and decorative ceilings. 4 comfortable double bedrooms offer spotless and homely accommodation, with delightful views of the landscaped gardens. A superb restaurant serves delectable genuine French cuisine offering an extensive à la carte and table d'hôte menu accompanied by an excellent selection of fine wines. The Hotel is within easy reach of the long sandy beaches of St. Bride's Bay and a walk along the beautiful Pembrokeshire Coastal Path is a must. Outdoor enthusiasts will enjoy the excellent golf, fishing, sailing and horse riding available in the locality. This area is steeped in history and fascinating to explore with Wolf's Castle and St. Bride's Bay within easy reach.

Location: Stone Hall is signposted off the A40. Haverfordwest-Fishguard Road, approximately 6 miles from Fishguard.

Web: www.johansens.com/stonehall
E-mail: mstonehall@aol.co.uk
Tel: 01348 840212
Fax: 01348 840815

Price Guide:
double/twin £85

Our inspector loved: The tranquillity and beauty of the gardens and the tastefully refurbished bedrooms/bathrooms creating an absolute haven.

PETERSTONE COURT

LLANHAMLACH, BRECON, POWYS LD3 7YB

There has been some form of dwelling on the site of this carefully restored Georgian Manor since the early 14th century when it was home to the first Sir John Walbcoffe, head of a family of butchers to their Lord, Bernard Newmarch, a companion to William the Conqueror. Charles I is believed to have stayed here while recruiting Royalist forces during the Civil War. Over the years, the house has been demolished, rebuilt, added to, renovated and refurbished. Now it is a comfortable and tranquil retreat for those attempting to escape the stresses of today's world. Standing impressively in a tiny village on the eastern edge of the Brecon Beacons, Peterstone Court has over the years, collected a string of awards that include merits from the AA, RAC and Welsh Tourist Board. Visitors have a choice of 8 beautifully proportioned period-style guest bedrooms in the main house and 4 charming split-level studios in converted stables. Each has every amenity, together with thoughtful extras such as soft, fluffy dressing gowns and bathroom toiletries to tape and video players. The Hotel has gained a reputation for its traditional cuisine which is complemented by a carefully selected wine list. The Health Club features a gymnasium, sauna, solarium and jacuzzi while outside in the summer there is a heated pool.

Our inspector loved: *The summer dining in the conservatory and winter dining in the attractive dining room.*

Directions: Peterstone Court is located in the village of Llanhamlach, on the A40, 3 miles east of Brecon.

Web: www.johansens.com/peterstonecourt
E-mail: info@peterstone-court.com
Tel: 01874 665387
Fax: 01874 665376

Price Guide:
single £98
double/twin £109–£135

POWYS - CRICKHOWELL (ABERGAVENNY)

GLANGRWYNEY COURT

GLANGRWYNEY, NR CRICKHOWELL, POWYS NP8 1ES

Directions: Glangrwyney is just off the A40 approximately 4 miles north west of Abergavenny.

Web: www.johansens.com/glangrwyneycourt
E-mail: glangrwyney@aol.com
Tel: 01873 811288
Fax: 01873 810317

Price Guide:
single £45-£60
double/twin £45-£90
suite £55-£90

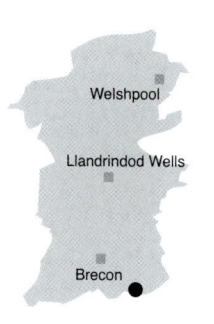

Christina and Warwick Jackson offer visitors a truly warm and friendly welcome to their splendid Georgian house situated in the heart of picturesque gardens and parkland in the scenic Usk Valley of the beautiful Brecon Beacons National Park. Traditional relaxed country house hospitality and comfort make guests feel at home from the moment they step into the impressive entrance hall. Glangrwyney Court is a handsome, majestic, bed and breakfast only hotel with a richly decorated interior that combines superior comfort with a charming lived-in-quality. There are fine antiques and family bric-a-brac, colourful rugs, an elegant curved staircase, a grand piano that isn't just a showpiece and, during winter months, open log fires in the main sitting rooms. All bedrooms have en-suite or private facilities and furnishings and decor that coordinates with the style of the house. The master suite has a king-size bed, en-suite steam shower and luxuriously deep bath whilst one twin room has a Jacuzzi bathroom. All bedrooms have views over the garden and surrounding countryside. There are excellent restaurants nearby. Croquet and boules can be enjoyed in the garden, riding, fishing and shooting can be arranged and there is wonderful walking on the doorstep.

Our inspector loved: The whole atmosphere, wonderful bedrooms; charming.

Norton House Hotel And Restaurant

NORTON ROAD, MUMBLES, SWANSEA SA3 5TQ

A really warm Welsh welcome and home-from-home hospitality are generously offered by this elegant hotel's resident proprietors Jan and John Power together with son Mark. Nothing is too much trouble and they are justly proud of the attentive and friendly atmosphere that pervades the whole hotel Norton House is attractively Georgian in style. It stands in lovely gardens set back from the Mumbles seafront and although not exactly rural it is run as a country house. Décor, furnishings and fabrics throughout are a tasteful delight. The bedrooms all have up-to-date private amenities with four of the more spacious rooms offering four-poster beds. The majority of rooms are in a newer wing and are slightly smaller. Ground floor rooms have easy access from a private terrace. The charming restaurant overlooks the terrace and gardens and chef Mark Comisini has earned a high reputation for tasty and imaginative cuisine with the emphasis on local produce and traditional flavours. Dinner menus are written in Welsh with English translations and include tempting dishes such as Penclawdd cockles and local laverbread and rack of Welsh lamb with black peppercorns and minted sauce. Places to visit nearby include the sandy beaches of the Gower Peninsula, Swansea's maritime quarter and market.

Our inspector loved: *The warm welcome of this traditional family run hotel ; a most comfortable and relaxing retreat.*

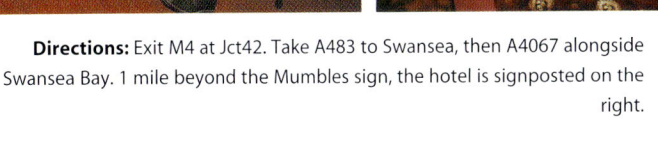

Directions: Exit M4 at Jct42. Take A483 to Swansea, then A4067 alongside Swansea Bay. 1 mile beyond the Mumbles sign, the hotel is signposted on the right.

Web: www.johansens.com/nortonhouse
E-mail: nortonhouse@btconnect.com
Tel: 01792 404891
Fax: 01792 403210

Price Guide:
single £67.50–£79
double £77–£97

VALE OF GLAMORGAN - CARDIFF (PORTHKERRY)

NEW

EGERTON GREY

PORTHKERRY, NR CARDIFF, VALE OF GLAMORGAN

Directions: From the M4, junction 33, take the A4050. Follow airport signs for 10 miles then take the A4226 towards Porthkerry. After 400 yards turn into the lane between 2 thatched cottages, the Hotel is at end of the lane.

Web: www.johansens.com/egertongrey
E-mail: info@egertongrey.co.uk
Tel: 01446 711666
Fax: 01446 711690

Price Guide:
single £89.50–£110
double/twin £95–£110
suite £130

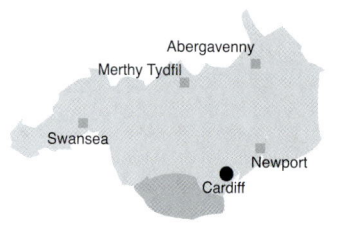

A distinguished former rectory dating from the early 19th century, Egerton Grey was opened as a small luxury hotel in 1998. Tucked away in 7 acres of gardens in a secluded, wooded valley in the Vale of Glamorgan, no other houses or roads are visible; instead guests can savour glorious views towards Porthkerry Park and the sea. The house's historic character has been carefully preserved with interior design that complements its architectural features. An Edwardian drawing room has intricate plaster mouldings, chandeliers, an open fireplace and oil paintings, while a quiet library overlooks the garden. All 10 immaculately presented bedrooms are extremely comfortable and several have Victorian baths and brasswork. The main restaurant, once a billiard room, creates an air of intimacy with its original Cuban mahogany panelling and candlelit tables. Owner's Richard Morgan and Huw Thomas take great pride in presenting high quality cuisine and fine wines. Riding can be arranged and there is a pitch and putt course a short stroll away by the sea. The Welsh Folk Museum, Castle Coch and Cardiff Castle are nearby.

Our inspector loved: *The abundance of personal touches throughout and the extremely warm welcome from Richard and Huw.*

Tchibo,
Awaken the senses...

Fresh ground coffee, and equipment solutions wherever, whenever

Contact

Local Call 0845 600 8244 **Fax** 01372 748196 **E-mail** sales@tchibo.co.uk

Tchibo Coffee International, Tchibo House, Blenheim Road, Epsom, Surrey KT19 9AP www.tchibo.co.uk

Tchibo

MINI LISTINGS GREAT BRITAIN & IRELAND

Condé Nast Johansens are delighted to recommend over 430 properties across Great Britain and Ireland.
These properties can be found in *Recommended Hotels - GB & Ireland 2003*
Call 0800 269 397 or see the order forms on page 285 to order guides.

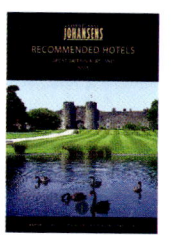

England

The Bath Priory Hotel And Restaurant	Bath & NE Somerset	+44 (0)1225 331922
The Bath Spa Hotel	Bath & NE Somerset	+44 (0)870 400 8222
Combe Grove Manor Hotel & Country Club	Bath & NE Somerset	+44 (0)1225 834644
Homewood Park	Bath & NE Somerset	+44 (0)1225 723731
Hunstrete House	Bath & NE Somerset	+44 (0)1761 490490
The Queensberry	Bath & NE Somerset	+44 (0)1225 447928
The Royal Crescent Hotel	Bath & NE Somerset	+44 (0)1225 823333
The Windsor Hotel	Bath & NE Somerset	+44 (0)1225 422100
Flitwick Manor	Bedfordshire	+44 (0)1525 712242
Moore Place Hotel	Bedfordshire	+44 (0)1908 282000
The Berystede	Berkshire	+44 (0)870 400 8111
The Castle Hotel	Berkshire	+44 (0)870 400 8300
Cliveden	Berkshire	+44 (0)1628 668561
Donnington Valley Hotel & Golf Club	Berkshire	+44 (0)1635 551199
Fredrick's Hotel & Restaurant	Berkshire	+44 (0)1628 581000
The French Horn	Berkshire	+44 (0)1189 692204
Monkey Island Hotel	Berkshire	+44 (0)1628 623400
The Regency Park Hotel	Berkshire	+44 (0)1635 871555
Sir Christopher Wren's House Hotel	Berkshire	+44 (0)1753 861354
The Swan At Streatley	Berkshire	+44 (0)1491 878800
The Vineyard At Stockcross	Berkshire	+44 (0)1635 528770
The Burlington Hotel	Birmingham	+44 (0)121 643 9191
Hotel Du Vin & Bistro	Birmingham	+44 (0)121 200 0600
Hotel Du Vin & Bistro	Birmingham	+44 (0)121 200 0600
Hotel Du Vin & Bistro	Birmingham	+44 (0)121 200 0600
Hotel Du Vin & Bistro	Birmingham	+44 (0)121 200 0600
Hotel Du Vin & Bistro	Birmingham	+44 (0)121 200 0600
New Hall	Birmingham	+44 (0)121 378 2442
Taplow House Hotel	Buckinghamshire	+44 (0)1628 670056
Danesfield House Hotel And Spa	Buckinghamshire	+44 (0)1628 891010

▼

Hartwell House	Buckinghamshire	**+44 (0)1296 747444**
Stoke Park Club	Buckinghamshire	+44 (0)1753 717171
The Haycock	Cambridgeshire	+44 (0)1780 782223
Hotel Felix	Cambridgeshire	+44 (0)1223 277977
The Alderley Edge Hotel	Cheshire	+44 (0)1625 583033
The Chester Crabwall Manor	Cheshire	+44 (0)1244 851666
Crewe Hall	Cheshire	+44 (0)1270 253333
Mere Court Hotel	Cheshire	+44 (0)1565 831000
Nunsmere Hall	Cheshire	+44 (0)1606 889100
Rookery Hall	Cheshire	+44 (0)1270 610016
Rowton Hall Hotel	Cheshire	+44 (0)1244 335262
The Stanneylands Hotel	Cheshire	+44 (0)1625 525225
Budock Vean - The Hotel On The River	Cornwall	+44 (0)1326 252100
Fowey Hall Hotel & Restaurant	Cornwall	+44 (0)1726 833866
The Garrack Hotel & Restaurant	Cornwall	+44 (0)1736 796199

The Greenbank Hotel	Cornwall	+44 (0)1326 312440
Hustyns Hotel & Leisure Club	Cornwall	+44 (0)1208 893700
The Lugger Hotel	Cornwall	+44 (0)1872 501322
Meudon Hotel	Cornwall	+44 (0)1326 250541
The Nare Hotel	Cornwall	+44 (0)1872 501111
Penmere Manor	Cornwall	+44 (0)1326 211411
Rose-In-Vale Country House Hotel	Cornwall	+44 (0)1872 552202
The Rosevine Hotel	Cornwall	+44 (0)1872 580206
St Martin's On The Isle	Cornwall	+44 (0)1720 422090
Talland Bay Hotel	Cornwall	+44 (0)1503 272667
Treglos Hotel	Cornwall	+44 (0)1841 520727
The Well House	Cornwall	+44 (0)1579 342001
Appleby Manor Country House Hotel	Cumbria	+44 (0)17683 51571
The Borrowdale Gates Country House Hotel	Cumbria	+44 (0)17687 77204
The Derwentwater Hotel	Cumbria	+44 (0)17687 72538
Farlam Hall Hotel	Cumbria	+44 (0)16977 46234
Gilpin Lodge	Cumbria	+44 (0)15394 88818
Graythwaite Manor	Cumbria	+44 (0)15395 32001
Holbeck Ghyll Country House Hotel	Cumbria	+44 (0)15394 32375
The Inn on the Lake	Cumbria	+44 (0)17684 82444
Lakeside Hotel On Lake Windermere	Cumbria	+44 (0)8701 541586
Langdale Chase	Cumbria	+44 (0)15394 32201
Lovelady Shield Country House Hotel	Cumbria	+44 (0)1434 381203
Miller Howe	Cumbria	+44 (0)15394 42536
Rampsbeck Country House Hotel	Cumbria	+44 (0)17684 86442
Rothay Manor	Cumbria	+44 (0)15394 33605
The Samling	Cumbria	+44 (0)15394 31922
Sharrow Bay Country House Hotel	Cumbria	+44 (0)17684 86301
Storrs Hall	Cumbria	+44 (0)15394 47111
Tufton Arms Hotel	Cumbria	+44 (0)17683 51593
The Wordsworth Hotel	Cumbria	+44 (0)15394 35592
Callow Hall	Derbyshire	+44 (0)1335 300900
Cavendish Hotel	Derbyshire	+44 (0)1246 582311
East Lodge Country House Hotel	Derbyshire	+44 (0)1629 734474
Fischer's	Derbyshire	+44 (0)1246 583259
The George At Hathersage	Derbyshire	+44 (0)1433 650436
Hassop Hall	Derbyshire	+44 (0)1629 640488
The Izaak Walton Hotel	Derbyshire	+44 (0)1335 350555
The Lee Wood Hotel & Restaurant	Derbyshire	+44 (0)1298 23002
Riber Hall	Derbyshire	+44 (0)1629 582795
Ringwood Hall Hotel	Derbyshire	+44 (0)1246 280077
Risley Hall Country House Hotel	Derbyshire	+44 (0)115 939 9000
Riverside House	Derbyshire	+44 (0)1629 814275
The Arundell Arms	Devon	+44 (0)1566 784666
Buckland-Tout-Saints	Devon	+44 (0)1548 853055
Fairwater Head Country House Hotel	Devon	+44 (0)1297 678349
Gidleigh Park	Devon	+44 (0)1647 432367
Hotel Barcelona	Devon	+44 (0)1392 281000
Hotel Riviera	Devon	+44 (0)1395 515201
Mill End	Devon	+44 (0)1647 432282
Northcote Manor Country House Hotel	Devon	+44 (0)1769 560501
Orestone Manor Hotel & Restaurant	Devon	+44 (0)1803 328098
The Osborne Hotel & Langtry's Restaurant	Devon	+44 (0)1803 213311
The Palace Hotel	Devon	+44 (0)1803 200200
Plantation House Hotel & Matisse Restaurant	Devon	+44 (0)1548 831100
Soar Mill Cove Hotel	Devon	+44 (0)1548 561566
The Tides Reach Hotel	Devon	+44 (0)1548 843466
Watersmeet Hotel	Devon	+44 (0)1271 870333
Woolacombe Bay Hotel	Devon	+44 (0)1271 870388
Bridge House Hotel	Dorset	+44 (0)1308 862200
The Dormy	Dorset	+44 (0)1202 872121
Langtry Manor - Lovenest Of A King	Dorset	+44 (0)1202 553887

302

Mini Listings Great Britain & Ireland

Condé Nast Johansens are delighted to recommend over 430 properties across Great Britain and Ireland. These properties can be found in *Recommended Hotels - GB & Ireland 2003*
Call 0800 269 397 or see the order forms on page 285 to order guides.

Menzies East Cliff Court	Dorset	+44 (0)1202 554545
Moonfleet Manor	Dorset	+44 (0)1305 786948
Norfolk Royale Hotel	Dorset	+44 (0)1202 551521
Plumber Manor	Dorset	+44 (0)1258 472507
The Priory Hotel	Dorset	+44 (0)1929 551666
The Priory Hotel	Dorset	+44 (0)1929 551666
Summer Lodge	Dorset	+44 (0)1935 83424
Headlam Hall	Durham	+44 (0)1325 730238
Seaham Hall Hotel & Oriental Spa	Durham	+44 (0)191 516 1400
Willerby Manor Hotel	East Riding Of Yorkshire	+44 (0)1482 652616
Ashdown Park Hotel And Country Club	East Sussex	+44 (0)1342 824988
Buxted Park Country House Hotel	East Sussex	+44 (0)1825 732711
Dale Hill	East Sussex	+44 (0)1580 200112
The Grand Hotel	East Sussex	+44 (0)1323 412345
Horsted Place Country House Hotel	East Sussex	+44 (0)1825 750581
Newick Park	East Sussex	+44 (0)1825 723633
Powdermills Hotel	East Sussex	+44 (0)1424 775511
White Lodge Country House Hotel	East Sussex	+44 (0)1323 870265
Five Lakes Hotel, Golf, Country Club & Spa	Essex	+44 (0)1621 868888
Greenwoods Estate	Essex	+44 (0)1277 829990
Maison Talbooth	Essex	+44 (0)1206 322367
The Pier At Harwich	Essex	+44 (0)1255 241212
The Bear Of Rodborough	Gloucestershire	+44 (0)1453 878522
Calcot Manor	Gloucestershire	+44 (0)1666 890391
Charingworth Manor	Gloucestershire	+44 (0)1386 593555
The Close Hotel	Gloucestershire	+44 (0)1666 502272
Corse Lawn House Hotel	Gloucestershire	+44 (0)1452 780479
Cotswold House	Gloucestershire	+44 (0)1386 840330
The Grapevine Hotel	Gloucestershire	+44 (0)1451 830344
The Greenway	Gloucestershire	+44 (0)1242 862352
Hotel Kandinsky	Gloucestershire	+44 (0)1242 527788
Hotel On The Park	Gloucestershire	+44 (0)1242 518898
Lords Of The Manor Hotel	Gloucestershire	+44 (0)1451 820243
Lower Slaughter Manor	Gloucestershire	+44 (0)1451 820456
The Manor House Hotel	Gloucestershire	+44 (0)1608 650501
The Noel Arms Hotel	Gloucestershire	+44 (0)1386 840317
The Painswick Hotel	Gloucestershire	+44 (0)1452 812160
The Swan Hotel At Bibury	Gloucestershire	+44 (0)1285 740695
The Unicorn Hotel	Gloucestershire	+44 (0)1451 830257
Washbourne Court Hotel	Gloucestershire	+44 (0)1451 822143
Wyck Hill House	Gloucestershire	+44 (0)1451 831936
Didsbury House	Greater Manchester	+44 (0)161 448 2200
Etrop Grange	Greater Manchester	+44 (0)161 499 0500
Careys Manor Hotel	Hampshire	+44 (0)1590 623551
Chewton Glen	Hampshire	+44 (0)1425 275341
Esseborne Manor	Hampshire	+44 (0)1264 736444
Fifehead Manor	Hampshire	+44 (0)1264 781565
Lainston House Hotel	Hampshire	+44 (0)1962 863588
Le Poussin At Parkhill	Hampshire	+44 (0)23 8028 2944
The Master Builder's House	Hampshire	+44 (0)1590 616253
The Montagu Arms Hotel	Hampshire	+44 (0)1590 612324
Old Thorns Hotel, Golf & Country Club	Hampshire	+44 (0)1428 724555
Passford House Hotel	Hampshire	+44 (0)1590 682398
Rhinefield House Hotel	Hampshire	+44 (0)1590 622922
Stanwell House	Hampshire	+44 (0)1590 677123
Tylney Hall	Hampshire	+44 (0)1256 764881
Allt-Yr-Ynys Hotel	Herefordshire	+44 (0)1873 890307
The Chase Hotel	Herefordshire	+44 (0)1989 763161
Down Hall Country House Hotel	Hertfordshire	+44 (0)1279 731441
Hanbury Manor	Hertfordshire	+44 (0)1920 487722
Pendley Manor Hotel & Conference Centre	Hertfordshire	+44 (0)1442 891891
Sopwell House Hotel, Country Club & Spa	Hertfordshire	+44 (0)1727 864477
St Michael's Manor	Hertfordshire	+44 (0)1727 864444
The Priory Bay Hotel	Isle Of Wight	+44 (0)1983 613146
Chilston Park	Kent	+44 (0)1622 859803
Eastwell Manor	Kent	+44 (0)1233 213000
Rowhill Grange Hotel And Spa	Kent	+44 (0)1322 615136
The Spa Hotel	Kent	+44 (0)1892 520331
Astley Bank Hotel & Conference Centre	Lancashire	+44 (0)1254 777700
The Gibbon Bridge Hotel	Lancashire	+44 (0)1995 61456
Northcote Manor	Lancashire	+44 (0)1254 240555
Quorn Country Hotel	Leicestershire	+44 (0)1509 415050
Stapleford Park Hotel, Spa, Golf & Sporting Estate	Leicestershire	+44 (0)1572 787 522
The George Of Stamford	Lincolnshire	+44 (0)1780 750750
The Olde Barn Hotel	Lincolnshire	+44 (0)1400 250909
The Petersham	London	+44 (0)20 8940 7471
41	London	+44 (0)20 7300 0041
51 Buckingham Gate	London	+44 (0)20 7769 7766
The Academy, The Bloomsbury Town House	London	+44 (0)20 7631 4115
The Ascott Mayfair	London	+44 (0)20 7659 4321
The Athenaeum Hotel & Apartments	London	+44 (0)20 7499 3464
Basil Street Hotel	London	+44 (0)20 7581 3311
The Beaufort	London	+44 (0)20 7584 5252
Beaufort House	London	+44 (0)20 7584 2600
The Cadogan	London	+44 (0)20 7235 7141
Cannizaro House	London	+44 (0)870 333 9124
The Capital Hotel & Apartments	London	+44 (0)20 7589 5171
The Chesterfield Mayfair	London	+44 (0)20 7491 2622
Circus Apartments	London	+44 (0)20 7719 7000
The Cliveden Town House	London	+44 (0)20 7730 6466
The Colonnade, The Little Venice Town House	London	+44 (0)20 7286 1052
The Cranley	London	+44 (0)20 7373 0123
Dolphin Square Hotel	London	+44 (0)20 7834 3800
The Dorchester	London	+44 (0)20 7629 8888
Dorset Square Hotel	London	+44 (0)20 7723 7874
Draycott House Apartments	London	+44 (0)20 7584 4659
The Gallery	London	+44 (0)20 7915 0000
Great Eastern Hotel	London	+44 (0)20 7618 5000
The Halkin	London	+44 (0)20 7333 1000
Harrington Hall	London	+44 (0)20 7396 9696
Kensington House Hotel	London	+44 (0)20 7937 2345
Kingsway Hall	London	+44 (0)20 7309 0909
The Leonard	London	+44 (0)20 7935 2010
The Lexham Apartments	London	+44 (0)20 7559 4444
London Bridge Hotel & Apartments	London	+44 (0)20 7855 2200
The Milestone Hotel & Apartments	London	+44 (0)20 7917 1000
Number Eleven Cadogan Gardens	London	+44 (0)20 7730 7000
Number Sixteen	London	+44 (0)20 7589 5232
One Aldwych	London	+44 (0)20 7300 1000
The Pelham Hotel	London	+44 (0)20 7589 8288

Mini Listings Great Britain & Ireland

Condé Nast Johansens are delighted to recommend over 430 properties across Great Britain and Ireland.
These properties can be found in *Recommended Hotels - GB & Ireland 2003*
Call 0800 269 397 or see the order forms on page 285 to order guides.

Pembridge Court Hotel	London	+44 (0)20 7229 9977
The Queensgate	London	+44 (0)20 7761 4000
The Richmond Gate Hotel And Restaurant	London	+44 (0)20 8940 0061
The Rubens At The Palace	London	+44 (0)20 7834 6600
Twenty Nevern Square	London	+44 (0)20 7565 9555
Warren House	London	+44 (0)20 8547 1777
West Lodge Park Country House Hotel	London	+44 (0)20 8216 3900
The Westbourne	London	+44 (0)20 7243 6008
Barnham Broom	Norfolk	+44 (0)1603 759393
Park Farm Country Hotel & Leisure	Norfolk	+44 (0)1603 810264
Ambassador Hotel	North Yorkshire	+44 (0)1904 641316
The Balmoral Hotel	North Yorkshire	+44 (0)1423 508208
Crathorne Hall	North Yorkshire	+44 (0)1642 700398
The Devonshire Arms Country House Hotel	North Yorkshire	+44 (0)1756 718111
Grants Hotel	North Yorkshire	+44 (0)1423 560666
Hackness Grange	North Yorkshire	+44 (0)1723 882345
Hazlewood Castle Hotel	North Yorkshire	+44 (0)1937 535353
Middlethorpe Hall	North Yorkshire	+44 (0)1904 641241
Monk Fryston Hall Hotel	North Yorkshire	+44 (0)1977 682369
Mount Royale Hotel	North Yorkshire	+44 (0)1904 628856
Rudding Park Hotel & Golf	North Yorkshire	+44 (0)1423 871350
Simonstone Hall	North Yorkshire	+44 (0)1969 667255
Swinton Park	North Yorkshire	+44 (0)1765 680900
The Worsley Arms Hotel	North Yorkshire	+44 (0)1653 628234
Wrea Head Country Hotel	North Yorkshire	+44 (0)1723 378211
Fawsley Hall	Northamptonshire	+44 (0)1327 892000
Whittlebury Hall	Northamptonshire	+44 (0)1327 857857
Linden Hall	Northumberland	+44 (0)1670 50 00 00
Marshall Meadows Country House Hotel	Northumberland	+44 (0)1289 331133
Matfen Hall	Northumberland	+44 (0)1661 886500
Tillmouth Park	Northumberland	+44 (0)1890 882255
Hotel Des Clos	Nottinghamshire	+44 (0)1159 866566
The Bay Tree Hotel	Oxfordshire	+44 (0)1993 822791
Bignell Park Hotel & Restaurant	Oxfordshire	+44 (0)1869 362550
The Cotswold Lodge Hotel	Oxfordshire	+44 (0)1865 512121
Le Manoir Aux Quat' Saisons	Oxfordshire	+44 (0)1844 278881
Phyllis Court Club	Oxfordshire	+44 (0)1491 570500
The Plough At Clanfield	Oxfordshire	+44 (0)1367 810222
The Spread Eagle Hotel	Oxfordshire	+44 (0)1844 213661
The Springs Hotel & Golf Club	Oxfordshire	+44 (0)1491 836687
Studley Priory	Oxfordshire	+44 (0)1865 351203
Weston Manor	Oxfordshire	+44 (0)1869 350621
Westwood Country Hotel	Oxfordshire	+44 (0)1865 735 408
Hambleton Hall	Rutland	+44 (0)1572 756991
The Lake Isle	Rutland	+44 (0)1572 822951
Dinham Hall	Shropshire	+44 (0)1584 876464
Madeley Court	Shropshire	+44 (0)1952 680068
The Old Vicarage Hotel	Shropshire	+44 (0)1746 716497
Prince Rupert Hotel	Shropshire	+44 (0)1743 499955
Bindon Country House Hotel	Somerset	+44 (0)1823 400070
Charlton House And The Mulberry Restaurant	Somerset	+44 (0)1749 342008
Mount Somerset Country House Hotel	Somerset	+44 (0)1823 442500
Ston Easton Park	Somerset	+44 (0)1761 241631
The Swan Hotel	Somerset	+44 (0)1749 836300
The Swan Hotel	Somerset	+44 (0)1749 836300
Thornbury Castle	South Gloucestershire	+44 (0)1454 281182
Charnwood Hotel	South Yorkshire	+44 (0)114 258 9411
Hellaby Hall Hotel	South Yorkshire	+44 (0)1709 702701
Whitley Hall Hotel	South Yorkshire	+44 (0)114 245 4444
Hoar Cross Hall Health Spa Resort	Staffordshire	+44 (0)1283 575671
Swinfen Hall Hotel	Staffordshire	+44 (0)1543 481494
Angel Hotel	Suffolk	+44 (0)1284 714000
Bedford Lodge Hotel	Suffolk	+44 (0)1638 663175
Belstead Brook Hotel	Suffolk	+44 (0)1473 684241
Black Lion Hotel & Restaurant	Suffolk	+44 (0)1787 312356
Hintlesham Hall	Suffolk	+44 (0)1473 652334
The Ickworth Hotel	Suffolk	+44 (0)1284 735350
The Marlborough Hotel	Suffolk	+44 (0)1473 226789
Ravenwood Hall Country Hotel & Restaurant	Suffolk	+44 (0)1359 270345
Seckford Hall	Suffolk	+44 (0)1394 385678
Swynford Paddocks Hotel And Restaurant	Suffolk	+44 (0)1638 570234
Wentworth Hotel	Suffolk	+44 (0)1728 452312
The Angel Posting House And Livery	Surrey	+44 (0)1483 564555
Foxhills	Surrey	+44 (0)1932 704500
Great Fosters	Surrey	+44 (0)1784 433822
Langshott Manor	Surrey	+44 (0)1293 786680
Lythe Hill Hotel & Spa	Surrey	+44 (0)1428 651251
Nutfield Priory	Surrey	+44 (0)1737 824400
Oatlands Park Hotel	Surrey	+44 (0)1932 847242
Pennyhill Park Hotel	Surrey	+44 (0)1276 471774
Woodlands Park Hotel	Surrey	+44 (0)1372 843933
The Vermont Hotel	Tyne & Wear	+44 (0)191 233 1010
Alveston Manor	Warwickshire	+44 (0)870 400 8181
Ardencote Manor Hotel and Country Club	Warwickshire	+44 (0)1926 843111
Billesley Manor	Warwickshire	+44 (0)1789 279955
Ettington Park	Warwickshire	+44 (0)1789 450123
The Glebe At Barford	Warwickshire	+44 (0)1926 624218
Mallory Court	Warwickshire	+44 (0)1926 330214
Nailcote Hall	Warwickshire	+44 (0)2476 466174
Nuthurst Grange	Warwickshire	+44 (0)1564 783972
The Welcombe Hotel And Golf Course	Warwickshire	+44 (0)1789 295252
Wroxall Abbey Estate - Wroxall Court	Warwickshire	+44 (0)1926 484470
Alexander House Hotel	West Sussex	+44 (0)1342 714914
Amberley Castle	West Sussex	+44 (0)1798 831992
The Angel Hotel	West Sussex	+44 (0)1730 812421
Bailiffscourt	West Sussex	+44 (0)1903 723511
Gravetye Manor	West Sussex	+44 (0)1342 810567
The Millstream Hotel	West Sussex	+44 (0)1243 573234
Ockenden Manor	West Sussex	+44 (0)1444 416111
South Lodge Hotel	West Sussex	+44 (0)1403 891711
The Spread Eagle Hotel & Health Spa	West Sussex	+44 (0)1730 816911
Chevin Country Park Hotel	West Yorkshire	+44 (0)1943 467818
Haley's Hotel & Restaurant	West Yorkshire	+44 (0)113 278 4446
Holdsworth House	West Yorkshire	+44 (0)1422 240024
Quebecs	West Yorkshire	+44 (0)113 244 8989
Wood Hall	West Yorkshire	+44 (0)1937 587271
Bishopstrow House	Wiltshire	+44 (0)1985 212312
Howard's House	Wiltshire	+44 (0)1722 716392
Lucknam Park, Bath	Wiltshire	+44 (0)1225 742777
The Manor House Hotel & Golf Club	Wiltshire	+44 (0)1249 782206
The Pear Tree At Purton	Wiltshire	+44 (0)1793 772100

Mini Listings Great Britain & Ireland

Condé Nast Johansens are delighted to recommend over 430 properties across Great Britain and Ireland.
These properties can be found in *Recommended Hotels - GB & Ireland 2003*
Call 0800 269 397 or see the order forms on page 285 to order guides.

Woolley Grange	Wiltshire	+44 (0)1225 864705
The Broadway Hotel	Worcestershire	+44 (0)1386 852401
Brockencote Hall	Worcestershire	+44 (0)1562 777876
Colwall Park	Worcestershire	+44 (0)1684 540000
The Cottage In The Wood	Worcestershire	+44 (0)1684 575859
Dormy House	Worcestershire	+44 (0)1386 852711
The Evesham Hotel	Worcestershire	+44 (0)1386 765566
Salford Hall Hotel	Worcestershire	+44 (0)1386 871300

Channel Islands

The Atlantic Hotel	Channel Islands	+44 (0)1534 744101
Château La Chaire	Channel Islands	+44 (0)1534 863354
Hotel L'Horizon	Channel Islands	+44 (0)1534 743101
Longueville Manor	Channel Islands	+44 (0)1534 725501

Ireland

Dromoland Castle	Clare	+353 61 368144
Hayfield Manor Hotel	Cork	+353 21 4845900
The Davenport Hotel	Dublin	+353 1 607 3500
Merrion Hall	Dublin	+353 1 668 1426
The Merrion Hotel	Dublin	+353 1 603 0600
The Mill Park Hotel	Dublin	+353 73 22880
Stephen's Green Hotel	Dublin	+353 1 607 3600
Killarney Park Hotel	Kerry	+353 64 35555
Parknasilla Hotel	Kerry	+353 64 45122
Sheen Falls Lodge	Kerry	+353 64 41600
Killashee House Hotel	Kildare	+353 45 879277
Mount Juliet	Kilkenny	+353 56 73000
Ashford Castle	Mayo	+353 92 46003
Knockranny House Hotel	Mayo	+353 982 8600
Nuremore Hotel And Country Club	Monaghan	+353 42 9661438
Dunbrody Country House & Restaurant	Wexford	+353 51 389 600
Kelly's Resort Hotel	Wexford	+353 53 32114
Marlfield House	Wexford	+353 55 21124
Hunter's Hotel	Wicklow	+353 404 40106

Scotland

Ardoe House Hotel And Restaurant	Aberdeenshire	+44 (0)1224 860600
Darroch Learg Hotel	Aberdeenshire	+44 (0)13397 55443
Ardanaiseig	Argyll & Bute	+44 (0)1866 833333
Enmore Hotel	Argyll & Bute	+44 (0)1369 702230
Isle of Eriska	Argyll & Bute	+44 (0)1631 720371
Stonefield Castle	Argyll & Bute	+44 (0)1880 820836
Balcary Bay Hotel	Dumfries & Galloway	+44 (0)1556 640217
Cally Palace Hotel	Dumfries & Galloway	+44 (0)1557 814341
The Dryfesdale Hotel	Dumfries & Galloway	+44 (0)1576 202427
Kirroughtree House	Dumfries & Galloway	+44 (0)1671 402141
The Bonham	Edinburgh	+44 (0)131 623 6060
Bruntsfield Hotel	Edinburgh	+44 (0)131 229 1393
Channings	Edinburgh	+44 (0)131 332 3232
The Howard	Edinburgh	+44 (0)131 315 2220
Prestonfield House	Edinburgh	+44 (0)131 668 3346
The Roxburghe	Edinburgh	+44 (0)131 240 5500
The Scotsman	Edinburgh	+44 (0)131 556 5565
The Rusacks	Fife	+44 (0)1334 474321
Strathblane Country House Hotel	Glasgow	+44 (0)1360 770491
Bunchrew House Hotel	Highland	+44 (0)1463 234917
Glenmorangie House At Cadboll	Highland	+44 (0)1862 871671
The Glenmoriston Town House Hotel	Highland	+44 (0)1463 223777
Muckrach Lodge Hotel & Restaurant	Highland	+44 (0)1479 851257
Cuillin Hills Hotel	Highlands	+44 (0)1478 612003
Borthwick Castle	Midlothian	+44 (0)1875 820514
Dalhousie Castle And Spa	Midlothian	+44 (0)1875 820153
Knockomie Hotel	Moray	+44 (0)1309 673146
Ballathie House Hotel	Perth & Kinross	+44 (0)1250 883268
Cromlix House	Perth & Kinross	+44 (0)1786 822125
Dalmunzie House	Perth & Kinross	+44 (0)1250 885224
Gleneagles	Perth & Kinross	+44 (0)1764 662231
Kinfauns Castle	Perth & Kinross	+44 (0)1738 620777
Kinloch House Hotel	Perth & Kinross	+44 (0)1250 884237
The Royal Hotel	Perth & Kinross	+44 (0)1764 679200
Gleddoch House	Renfrewshire	+44 (0)1475 540711
Castle Venlaw	Scottish Borders	+44 (0)1721 720384
Ednam House Hotel	Scottish Borders	+44 (0)1573 224168
The Roxburghe Hotel & Golf Course	Scottish Borders	+44 (0)1573 450331
Enterkine House	South Ayrshire	+44 (0)1292 521608
Glenapp Castle	South Ayrshire	+44 (0)1465 831212
Macdonald Crutherland House Hotel	South Lanarkshire	+44 (0)1355 577000
Forest Hills Hotel	Stirling	+44 (0)1877 387277
Houstoun House	West Lothian	+44 (0)1506 853831
The Norton House Hotel	West Lothian	+44 (0)131 333 1275

Wales

Ynyshir Hall	Ceredigion	+44 (0)1654 781209
Bodysgallen Hall	Conwy	+44 (0)1492 584466
St Tudno Hotel	Conwy	+44 (0)1492 874411
Palé Hall	Gwynedd	+44 (0)1678 530285
Penmaenuchaf Hall	Gwynedd	+44 (0)1341 422129
Portmeirion And Castell Deudraeth	Gwynedd	+44 (0)1766 770000
The Trearddur Bay Hotel	Isle of Anglesey	+44 (0)1407 860301
Llansantffraed Court Hotel	Monmouthshire	+44 (0)1873 840678
Lamphey Court Hotel	Pembrokeshire	+44 (0)1646 672273
Penally Abbey	Pembrokeshire	+44 (0)1834 843033
Warpool Court Hotel	Pembrokeshire	+44 (0)1437 720300
Gliffaes Country House Hotel	Powys	+44 (0)1874 730371
The Lake Country House	Powys	+44 (0)1591 620202
Lake Vyrnwy Hotel	Powys	+44 (0)1691 870 692
Llangoed Hall	Powys	+44 (0)1874 754525
Nant Ddu Lodge Hotel	Powys	+44 (0)1685 379111
Miskin Manor Country House Hotel	Rhondda Cynon Taff	+44 (0)1443 224204

HISTORIC HOUSES, CASTLES & GARDENS

Incorporating Museums & Galleries.
We are pleased to feature over 200 places to visit during your stay at a Condé Nast Johansens recommended hotel.

England

Bedfordshire

Cecil Higgins Art Gallery – Castle Lane, Bedford, Bedfordshire MK40 4AF. Tel: 01234 211222

John Bunyan Museum – Bunyan Meeting Free Church, Mill Street, Bedford, Bedfordshire MK40 3EU. Tel: 01234 213722

Woburn Abbey – Woburn, Bedfordshire MK17 9WA. Tel: 01525 290666

Berkshire

Savill Garden – Windsor Great Park, Berkshire. Tel: 01753 847518

Taplow Court – Berry Hill, Taplow, Nr Maidenhead, Berkshire SL6 0ER. Tel: 01628 591209

Buckinghamshire

Hughenden Manor – High Wycombe, Buckinghamshire HP14 4LA. Tel: 01494 755573

Stowe Landscape Gardens – Stowe, Buckingham, Buckinghamshire MK18 5EH. Tel: 01280 818809

Waddesdon Manor – Waddesdon, Nr Aylesbury, Buckinghamshire HP18 0JH. Tel: 01296 653211

Cambridgeshire

Ely Cathedral – The Chapter House, The College, Ely, Cambridgeshire CB7 4DL. Tel: 01353 667735

King's College – Cambridge, Cambridgeshire CB2 1ST. Tel: 01223 331212

Cheshire

Adlington Hall – Nr Macclesfield, Cheshire SK10 4LF. Tel: 01625 820201

Dorfold Hall – Nantwich, Cheshire CW5 8LD. Tel: 01270 625245

Dunham Massey Hall, Park & Garden – Dunham, Altrincham, Cheshire WA14 4SJ. Tel: 0161 941 1025

Ness Botanic Gardens – Ness, Neston, South Wirral, Cheshire CH64 4AY. Tel: 0151 353 0123

Norton Priory Museum & Gardens – Tudor Road, Manor Park, Cheshire WA7 1SX. Tel: 01928 569895

Tabley House Stately Home – Tabley House, Knutsford, Cheshire WA16 0HB. Tel: 01565 750151

County Durham

Raby Castle – Staindrop, Darlington, County Durham DL2 3AH. Tel: 01833 660207 / 660202

Cornwall

Jamaica Inn Museums – Jamaica Inn Courtyard, Bolventor, Launceston, Cornwall PL15 7TS. Tel: 0156 68 68 38

Cumbria

Holker Hall and Gardens – Cark-in-Cartmel, Nr Grange-over-Sands, Cumbria LA11 7PL. Tel: 01539 558328

Isel Hall – Cockermouth, Cumbria CA13 0QG.

Levens Hall & Gardens – Kendal, Cumbria LA8 0PD. Tel: 01539 560321

Mirehouse & Keswick – Mirehouse, Keswick, Cumbria CA12 4QE. Tel: 01768 772287

Windermere Steamboat Centre – Rayrigg Road, Windermere, Cumbria LA23 1BN. Tel: 01539 445565

Wordsworth House – Main Street, Cockermouth, Cumbria CA13 9RX. Tel: 01900 824805

Derbyshire

Haddon Hall – Bakewell, Derbyshire DE45 1LA. Tel: 01629 812855

Hardwick Hall – Doe Lea, Chesterfield, Derbyshire S44 5QJ. Tel: 01246 850430

Melbourne Hall & Gardens – Melbourne, Derbyshire DE73 1EN. Tel: 01332 862502

Tissington Hall – Tissington, Ashbourne, Derbyshire DE6 1RA. Tel: 01335 352200

Devon

Cadhay – Ottery St Mary, Devon EX11 1QT. Tel: 01404 812432

The Royal Horticultural Society, Garden Rosemoor – Great Torrington, North Devon EX38 8PH. Tel: 01805 624067

Dorset

Abbotsbury Sub Tropical Gardens – Bullers Way, Abbotsbury, Nr Weymouth, Dorset DT3 4LA. Tel: 01305 871387

Chiffchaffs – Chaffeymoor, Bourton, Gillingham, Dorset SP8 5BY. Tel: 01747 840841

Compton Acres – 164 Canford Cliffs Road, Canford Cliffs, Poole, Dorset BH13 7ES. Tel: 01202 700778

Cranborne Manor Garden – Cranborne, Wimborne, Dorset BH21 5PP. Tel: 01725 517248

Deans Court Garden – Deans Court, Wimborne, Dorset BH21 1EE. Tel: 01202 886116

Mapperton – Mapperton, Beaminster, Dorset DT8 3NR. Tel: 01308 862645

Minterne Gardens – Minterne Magna, Dorchester, Dorset DT2 7AU. Tel: 01300 341370

Sherborne Castle – New Road, Sherborne, Dorset DT9 5NR. Tel: 01935 813182

Tolpuddle Museum – Tolpuddle, Dorset DT2 7EH. Tel: 01305 848237

East Riding of Yorkshire

Burton Agnes Hall & Gardens – Burton Agnes, Driffield, East Riding of Yorkshire YO25 4NB. Tel: 01262 490324

East Sussex

Bentley Wildfowl & Motor Museum – Halland, Nr Lewes, East Sussex BN8 5AF. Tel: 01825 840573

Charleston – Firle, East Sussex BN8 6LL. Tel: 01323 811626

Firle Place – The Estate Office, Lewes, East Sussex BN8 6NS. Tel: 01273 858043

Garden and Grounds of Herstmonceux Castle – Herstmonceux Castle, Hailsham, East Sussex BN27 1RN. Tel: 01323 833816

Merriments Gardens – Hurst Green, East Sussex TN19 7RA. Tel: 01580 860666

Pashley Manor Gardens – Ticehurst, East Sussex TN5 7HE. Tel: 01580 200888

Wilmington Priory – Wilmington, Nr Eastbourne, East Sussex BN26 5SW. Tel: 01628 825920

Essex

Hedingham Castle – Bayley Street, Castle Hedingham, Halstead, Essex CO9 3DJ. Tel: 01787 460261

Ingatestone Hall – Hall Lane, Ingatestone, Essex CM4 9NR. Tel: 01277 353010

The Gardens of Easton – Warwick House, Easton Lodge, Essex CM6 2BB. Tel: 01371 876979

The Sir Alfred Munnings Art Museum – Castle House, Dedham, Essex CO7 6AZ. Tel: 01206 322127

Gloucestershire

Chavenage House – Chavenage, Tetbury, Gloucestershire GL8 8XP. Tel: 01666 502329

Cheltenham Art Gallery & Museum – Clarence Street, Cheltenham, Gloucestershire GL50 3JT. Tel: 01242 237431

Frampton Court – Frampton-on-Severn, Gloucestershire GL2 7DY. Tel: 01452 740267

Hardwicke Court – Gloucester, Gloucestershire GL2 4RS. Tel: 01452 720212

Sezincote – Moreton-in-Marsh, Gloucestershire GL56 9AW. Tel: 01386 700444

Greater Manchester

Heaton Hall – Heaton Park, Prestwich, Manchester, Greater Manchester M25 5SW. Tel: 0161 773 1231/ 0161 235 8888

Ordsall Hall Museum – Ordsall Lane, Salford, Greater Manchester M5 4WU. Tel: 0161 872 0251

Salford Museums & Art Gallery – Peel Park, Crescent, Salford, Greater Manchester M5 4WU. Tel: 0161 736 2649

Wythenshawe Hall – Wythenshawe Park, Northenden, Manchester, Greater Manchester M23 0AB. Tel: 0161 998 2331

Hampshire

Avington Park – Winchester, Hampshire SO21 1DB. Tel: 01962 779260

Beaulieu – John Montagu Building, Beaulieu, Hampshire SO42 7ZN. Tel: 01590 612345

Broadlands – Romsey, Hampshire SO51 9ZD. Tel: 01794 505010

HISTORIC HOUSES, CASTLES & GARDENS
Incorporating Museums & Galleries.
www.historichouses.co.uk

Gilbert White's House and The Oates Museum – Selborne, Hampshire GU34 3JH. Tel: 01420 511275

Greywell Hill House – Greywell, Hook, Hampshire RG29 1DG

Hall Farm – Bentworth, Alton, Hampshire GU34 5JU. Tel: 01420 564010

Mottisfont Abbey – Mottisfont, Nr Romsey, Hampshire SO51 0LP. Tel: 01794 340757

Pylewell Park – South Baddesley, Lymington, Hampshire SO41 5SJ. Tel: 01329 833130

The Vyne – The National Trust, Sherborne St John, Basingstoke, Hampshire RG24 9HL. Tel: 01256 881337

Uppark – South Harting, Petersfield, Hampshire GU31 5QR. Tel: 01730 825415

Herefordshire

Eastnor Castle – Eastnor, Ledbury, Herefordshire HR8 1RL. Tel: 01531 633160

Hertfordshire

Ashridge – Ringshall, Berkhamsted, Hertfordshire HP4 1NS. Tel: 01442 843491

Gorhambury – St. Albans, Hertfordshire AL3 6AH. Tel: 01727 855000

Hatfield House, Park & Gardens – Hatfield, Hertfordshire AL9 5NQ. Tel: 01707 287010

Isle of Wight

Deacons Nursery – Moor View, Godshill, Isle of Wight PO38 3HW. Tel: 01983 840750

Kent

Belmont House and Gardens – Belmont Park, Throwley, Nr Faversham, Kent ME13 0HH. Tel: 01795 890202

Cobham Hall – Cobham, Kent DA12 3BL. Tel: 01474 823371

Dickens House Museum – 2 Victoria Parade, Broadstairs, Kent CT10 1QS. Tel: 01843 863453

Finchcocks, Living Museum of Music – Goudhurst, Kent TN17 1HH. Tel: 01580 211702

Graham Clarke Up the Garden Studio – Green Lane, Boughton Monchelsea, Maidstone, Kent ME17 4LF. Tel: 01622 743938

Groombridge Place Gardens & Enchanted Forest – Groombridge, Tunbridge Wells, Kent TN3 9QG. Tel: 01892 861444

Hever Castle & Gardens – Edenbridge, Kent TN8 7NG. Tel: 01732 865224

Leeds Castle – Maidstone, Kent ME17 1PL. Tel: 01622 765400

Mount Ephraim Gardens – Hernhill, Nr Faversham, Kent ME13 9TX. Tel: 01227 751496

Penshurst Place & Gardens – Penshurst, Nr Tonbridge, Kent TN11 8DG. Tel: 01892 870307

Scotney Castle, Garden & Estate – Lamberhurst, Tunbridge Wells, Kent TN3 8JN. Tel: 01892 891081

Smallhythe Place – Smallhythe, Tenterden, Kent TN30 7NG. Tel: 01580 762334

The New College of Cobham – Cobhambury Road, Graves End, Kent DA12 3BG. Tel: 01474 814280

Lancashire

Stonyhurst College – Stonyhurst, Clitheroe, Lancashire BB7 9PZ. Tel: 01254 826345

Townhead House – Slaidburn, Via CLitheroe, Lancashire BBY 3AG

Leicestershire

Hazel Kaye's Garden & Nursery – 1700 Melton Rd, Rearsby, Leicester, Leicestershire LE7 4YR. Tel: 01664 424578

Stanford Hall – Stanford Park, Lutterworth, Leicestershire LE17 6DH. Tel: 01788 860250

Lincolnshire

Burghley House – Stamford, Lincolnshire PE9 3JY. Tel: 01780 752451

London

Burgh House – New End Square, Hampstead, London NW3 1LT. Tel: 020 7431 0144

Dulwich Picture Gallery – Gallery Road, London SE21 7AD. Tel: 020 8299 8711

Handel House Museum – 25 Brook Street, London W1K 4HB. Tel: 020 7495 1685

Imperial War Museum – Lambeth Road, London SE1 6HZ. Tel: 020 7416 5000

▼

Kensington Palace State Apartments – Kensington, London W8 4PX. Tel: 0870 751 5176

Leighton House Museum – 12 Holland Park Road, London W14 8LZ. Tel: 020 7602 3316

National Portrait Gallery – St Martin's Place, London WC2H 0HE. Tel: 020 7306 0055

Pitshanger Manor House – Walpole Park, Mattock Lane, Ealing, London W5 5EQ. Tel: 020 8567 1227

Royal Institution Michael Faraday Museum – 21 Albemarle Street, London W1S 4BS. Tel: 020 7409 2992

Sir John Soane's Museum – 13 Lincoln's Inn Fields, London WC2A 3BP. Tel: 020 7405 2107

Somerset House – Strand, London WC2R 1LA. Tel: 020 7845 4600

St. John's Gate – St John's Lane, Clerkenwell, London EC1M 4DA. Tel: 020 7324 4070

The Fan Museum – 12 Crooms Hill, Greenwich, London SE10 8ER. Tel: 020 8305 1441

The Traveller's Club – 106 Pall Mall, London SW1Y 5EP. Tel: 020 7930 8688

Tower of London – Tower Hill, London EC3N 4AB. Tel: 0870 751 5177

Middlesex

Orleans House Gallery – Riverside, Twickenham, Middlesex TW1 3DJ. Tel: 020 8892 0221

Strawberry Hill House – St. Mary's University College, Strawberry Hill, Waldegrave Road, Twickenham, Middlesex TW1 4SX. Tel: 020 8270 4114

Syon Park – London Road, Brentford, Middlesex TW8 8JF. Tel: 020 8560 0882

Norfolk

Hoveton Hall Gardens – Hoveton, Wroxham, Norfolk NR12 8RJ. Tel: 01603 782798

Walsingham Abbey Grounds – c/o The Estate Office, Little Walsingham, Norfolk NR22 6BP. Tel: 01328 820259 / 820510

Wolterton and Mannington Estate – Mannington Hall, Norwich, Norfolk NR11 7BB. Tel: 01263 584175

North Yorkshire

Castle Howard – York, North Yorkshire YO6 7DA. Tel: 01653 648333

Duncombe Park – Helmsley, York, North Yorkshire YO62 5EB. Tel: 01439 770213

Hovingham Hall – Hovingham, York, North Yorkshire YO62 4LU. Tel: 01653 628771

Ripley Castle – Ripley Castle Estate, Harrogate, North Yorkshire HG3 3AY. Tel: 01423 770152

Sion Hill Hall – Kirby Wiske, Thirsk, North Yorkshire YO7 4EU. Tel: 01845 587206

The Forbidden Corner – The Tupgill Park Estate, Coverham, Middleham, North Yorkshire DL8 4TJ. Tel: 01969 640638

The Royal Horticultural Society Garden Harlow Carr – Crag Lane, Harrogate, North Yorkshire HG3 1QB. Tel: 01423 565418

Thorp Perrow Arboretum & The Falcons of Thorp Perrow – Bedale, North Yorkshire DL8 2PR. Tel: 01677 425323

Yorkshire Garden World – Main Road, West Haddlesey, Nr Selby, North Yorkshire YO8 8QA. Tel: 01757 228279

Northamptonshire

Althorp – Northampton, Northants NN7 4HQ. Tel: 01604 770107

Cottesbrooke Hall and Gardens – Cottesbrooke, Northampton, Northamptonshire NN6 8PF. Tel: 01604 505808

Haddonstone Show Garden – The Forge House, Church Lane, East Haddon, Northamptonshire NN6 8DB. Tel: 01604 770711

Kelmarsh Hall & Gardens – Kelmarsh, Northampton, Northamptonshire NN6 9LT. Tel: 01604 686543

Northumberland

Alnwick Castle – Alnwick, Northumberland NE66 1NQ. Tel: 01665 510777/ 511100

Chillingham Castle – Chillingham, Alnwick, Northumberland NE66 5NJ. Tel: 01668 215359

Chipchase Castle – Chipchase, Wark on Tyne, Hexham, Northumberland NE48 3NT. Tel: 01434 230203

Paxton House & Country Park – Berwick-upon-Tweed, Northumberland TD15 1SZ. Tel: 01289 386291

Seaton Delaval Hall – Seaton Sluice, Whitley Bay, Northumberland NE26 4QR. Tel: 0191 237 1493 / 0786

Oxfordshire

Ditchley Park – Enstone, Chipping Norton, Oxfordshire OX7 4ER. Tel: 01608 677346

Kingston Bagpuize House – Kingston Bagpuize, Abingdon, Oxfordshire OX13 5AX. Tel: 01865 820259

Mapledurham House – Mapledurham, Nr Reading, Oxfordshire RG4 7TR. Tel: 01189 723350

River & Rowing Museum – Mill Meadows, Henley-on-Thames, Oxfordshire RG9 1BF. Tel: 01491 415600

Stonor Park – Stonor, Henley-on-Thames, Oxfordshire RG9 6HF. Tel: 01491 638587

Sulgrave Manor – Manor Road, Sulgrave, Banbury, Oxfordshire OX17 2SD. Tel: 01295 760205

HISTORIC HOUSES, CASTLES & GARDENS
Incorporating Museums & Galleries.
www.historichouses.co.uk

Upton House – Nr Banbury, Oxon OX15 6HT.
Tel: 01295 670266

Wallingford Castle Gardens – Castle Street, Wallingford, Oxfordshire. Tel: 01491 835373

Shropshire

Hawkstone Park & Follies – Weston-under-Redcastle, Shrewsbury, Shropshire SY4 5UY. Tel: 01939 200 611

Hodnet Hall Gardens – Hodnet, Market Drayton, Shropshire TF9 3NN. Tel: 01630 685786

Hopton Court – Kidderminster, Shropshire DY14 0EF. Tel: 01299 270734

Royal Air force Museum – Cosford, Shifnal, Shropshire TF11 8UP. Tel: 01902 376200

Shipton Hall – Shipton, Much Wenlock, Shropshire TF13 6JZ. Tel: 01746 785225

Shrewsbury Castle & Shropshire Regimental Museum – Castle Street, Shrewsbury, Shropshire SY1 2AT. Tel: 01743 358516

Shrewsbury Museum & Art Gallery – Barker Street, Shrewsbury, Shropshire SY1 1QH. Tel: 01743 361196

The Dorothy Clive Garden – Willoughbridge, Market Drayton, Shropshire TF9 4EU. Tel: 01630 647237

Weston Park – Weston-under-Lizard, Nr Shifnal, Shropshire TF11 8LE. Tel: 01952 852100

Somerset

Barford Park – Enmore, Nr Bridgwater, Somerset TA5 1AG. Tel: 01278 671269

Great House Farm – Wells Road, Theale, Wedmore, Somerset BS28 4SJ. Tel: 01934 713133

Milton Lodge Gardens – Old Bristol Road, Wells, Somerset BA5 3AQ. Tel: 01749 672168

Museum of Costume & Assembly Rooms – Bennett Street, Bath, Somerset BA1 2QH. Tel: 01225 477789 / 477785

Orchard Wyndham – Williton, Taunton, Somerset TA4 4HH. Tel: 01984 632309

▼

Roman Baths & Pump Room – Abbey Church Yard, Bath, Somerset BA1 1LZ. Tel: 01225 477785

The American Museum in Britain – Claverton Manor, Bath, Somerset BA2 7BD. Tel: 01225 460503

Staffordshire

Ford Green Hall – Ford Green Road, Smallthorne, Stoke-on-Trent, Staffordshire ST6 1NG. Tel: 01782 233195

Sandon Hall – Sandon, Staffordshire ST18 0BZ. Tel: 01889 508004

Whitmore Hall – Whitmore, Newcastle-under-Lyme, Staffordshire ST5 5HW. Tel: 01782 680478

Suffolk

Ancient House – Clare, Suffolk CO10 8NY. Tel: 01628 825920

Otley Hall – Hall Lane, Otley, Ipswich, Suffolk IP6 9PA. Tel: 01473 890264

Shrubland Park Gardens – Shrubland Estate, Coddenham, Ipswich, Suffolk IP6 9QQ. Tel: 01473 830221

Surrey

Clandon Park – West Clandon, Guildford, Surrey GU4 7RQ. Tel: 01483 222482

Claremont House – Claremont Drive, Esher, Surrey KT10 9LY. Tel: 01372 467841

Goddards – Abinger Common, Dorking, Surrey RH5 6TH. Tel: 01628 825920

Great Fosters – Stroude Road, Egham, Surrey TW20 9UR. Tel: 01784 433822

Hampton Court Palace – East Molesey, Surrey KT8 9AU. Tel: 0870 751 5175

Hatchlands – East Clandon, Guildford, Surrey GU4 7RT. Tel: 01483 222482

Loseley Park – Estate Office, Guildford, Surrey GU3 1HS. Tel: 01483 304440

Merton Heritage Centre – The Canons, Madeira Road, Mitcham, Surrey CR4 4HD. Tel: 020 8640 9387

Painshill Landscape Garden – Portsmouth Road, Cobham, Surrey KT11 1JE. Tel: 01932 868113

The Royal Horticultural Society, Wisley Garden – Nr Woking, Surrey GU23 6QB. Tel: 01483 224234

Warwickshire

Arbury Hall – Nuneaton, Warwickshire CV10 7PT. Tel: 024 7638 2804

Ragley Hall – Alcester, Warwickshire B49 5NJ. Tel: 01789 762090

Shakespeare Houses – The Shakespeare Centre, Henley Street, Stratford-upon-Avon, Warwickshire CV37 6QW. Tel: 01789 204016

West Midlands

Barber Institute of Fine Arts – The University of Birmingham, Edgbaston, Birmingham, West Midlands B15 2TS. Tel 0121 414 7333

Castle Bromwich Hall Gardens – Chester Road, Castle Bromwich, Birmingham, West Midlands B36 9BT. Tel: 0121-749 4100

The Birmingham Botanical Gardens and Glasshouses – Westbourne Road, Edgbaston, Birmingham, West Midlands B15 3TR. Tel: 0121 454 1860

West Sussex

Borde Hill Garden – Balcombe Road, West Sussex RH16 1XP. Tel: 01444 450326

Chichester District Museum – 29 Little London, Chichester, West Sussex PO19 1PB. Tel: 01243 784683

Denmans Garden – Clock House, Denmans, Fontwell, West Sussex BN18 0SU. Tel: 01243 542808

Goodwood House – Goodwood, Chichester, West Sussex PO18 0PX. Tel: 01243 755000

High Beeches Gardens – High Beeches, Handcross, West Sussex RH17 6HQ. Tel: 01444 400589

Leonardslee - Lakes & Gardens – Lower Beeding, Horsham, West Sussex RH13 6PP. Tel: 01403 891212

Weald and Downland Open Air Museum – Singleton, Chichester, West Sussex PO21 4JU. Tel: 01243 811363

West Dean Gardens – West Dean, Chichester, West Sussex PO18 0QZ. Tel: 01243 818210

Worthing Museum & Art Gallery – Chapel Road, Worthing, West Sussex BN11 1HP. Tel: 01903 239999

West Yorkshire

Bramham Park – Estate Office, Bramham Park, Wetherby, West Yorkshire LS23 6ND. Tel: 01937 846000

Harewood House – The Harewood House Trust, Moorhouse. Harewood, Leeds, West Yorkshire LS17 9LQ. Tel: 0113 218 1010

Ledston Hall – Hall Lane, Ledstone, West Yorkshire WF10 2BB. Tel: 01423 523 423

Wiltshire

Charlton Park House – Charlton, Malmesbury, Wiltshire SN16 9DG. Tel: 01666 824389

Hamptworth Lodge – Landford, Salisbury, Wiltshire SP5 2EA. Tel: 01794 390215

▼

Longleat – Warminster, Wiltshire BA12 7NW. Tel: 01985 844400

Salisbury Cathedral – Visitor Services, 33 The Close, Salisbury, Wiltshire SP1 2EJ. Tel: 01722 555120

Sheldon Manor – Nr Chippenham, Wiltshire SN14 0RG. Tel: 01249 653120

The Peto Garden At Iford Manor – Bradford-on-Avon, Wiltshire BA15 2BA. Tel: 01225 863146

Worcestershire

Hagley Hall – Hagley, Worcestershire DY9 9LG. Tel: 01562 882408

Harvington Hall – Harvington, Kidderminster, Worcester DY10 4LR. Tel: 01562 777846

Little Malvern Court – Nr Malvern, Worcestershire WR14 4JN. Tel: 01684 892988

Spetchley Park Gardens – Spetchley Park, Worcester, Worcestershire WR5 1RS. Tel: 01453 810303

Ireland

Co Antrim

Benvarden Gardens – Benvarden Dervolk, Co Antrim BT53 6NN. Tel: 028 2074 1331

Co Cork

Bantry House & Gardens – Bantry, Co Cork. Tel: + 353 2 750 047

Co Down

North Down Heritage Centre – Town Hall, Bangor, Co Down BT20 4BT. Tel: 028 9127 1200

Seaforde Gardens – Seaforde, Downpatrick, Co Down BT30 8PG. Tel: 028 4481 1225

HISTORIC HOUSES, CASTLES & GARDENS

Incorporating Museums & Galleries.
www.historichouses.co.uk

Co Kildare

Japanese Gardens & St Fiachra's Garden – Tully, Kildare Town, Co Kildare. Tel: +353 45 521617

Co Wicklow

Powerscourt Gardens & Waterfall – Powerscourt Estate, Enniskerry, Co Wicklow. Tel: +353 1 204 6000

Scotland

Aberdeenshire

Craigston Castle – Turriff, Aberdeenshire AB53 5PX. Tel: 01888 551228

Angus

Glamis Castle – Glamis, by Forfar, Angus DD8 1RJ. Tel: 01307 840393

Ayrshire

Auchinleck House – Ochiltree, Ayrshire. Tel: 01628 825920
Kelburn Castle and Country Centre – Kelburn, Fairlie (Nr Largs), Ayrshire KA29 0BE. Tel: 01475 568685

▼

Inveraray Castle – Cherry Park, Inveraray, Argyll PA32 8XE. Tel: 01499 302203
Maybole Castle – Maybole, Ayrshire KA19 7BX. Tel: 01655 883765
Sorn Castle – Sorn, Mauchline, Ayrshire KA5 6HR. Tel: 0141 942 6460

Dumfries

Drumlanrig Castle, Gardens and Country Park – Nr Thornhill, Dumfries DG3 4AQ. Tel: 01848 330248

East Lothian

Lennoxlove House – Haddington, East Lothian EH41 4NZ. Tel: 01620 823720

Edinburgh

Dalmeny House – South Queensferry, Edinburgh EH30 9TQ. Tel: 0131 331 1888

Fife

Callendar House – Callendar Park, Falkirk, Fife FK1 1YR. Tel: 01324 503770

Isle of Skye

Armadale Castle, Gardens & Museum of the Isles – Armadale, Sleat, Isle of Skye IV45 8RS. Tel: 01471 844305

Perthshire

Scone Palace – Scone, Perth, Perthshire PH2 6BD. Tel: 01738 552300

Scottish Borders

Bowhill House & Country Park – Bowhill, Selkirk, Scottish Borders TD7 5ET. Tel: 01750 22204
Traquair House – Innerleithen, Peebles EH44 6PW. Tel: 01896 830323

South Lanarkshire

New Lanark World Heritage Site – New Lanark Mills, South Lanarkshire ML11 9DB. Tel: 01555 661345

West Lothian

Hopetoun House – South Queensferry, West Lothian EH30 9SL. Tel: 0131 331 2451
Newliston – Kirkliston, West Lothian EH29 9EB. Tel: 0131 333 3231

Wales

Carmarthenshire

Aberglasney Gardens – Llangathen, Carmarthenshire SA32 8QH. Tel: 01558 668998

Conway

Bodnant Garden – Tal-y-Cafn, Nr Colwyn Bay, Conway LL28 5RE. Tel: 01492 650460

Flintshire

Golden Grove – Llanasa, Nr. Holywell, Flintshire CH8 9NA. Tel: 01745 854452

Gwynedd

Gwydir Castle – Llanrwst, Gwynedd LL26 0PN. Tel: 01492 641687

Monmouthshire

Llanvihangel Court – Llanvihangel Crucorney, Abergavenny, Monmouthshire NP7 8DH. Tel: 01873 890217
Penhow Castle – Penhow, Monmouthshire NP26 3AD. Tel: 01633 400800
Usk Castle – Usk, Monmouthshire NP15 1SD. Tel: 01291 672563

Newport

Fourteen Locks Canal Centre – High Cross, Newport NP10 9GN. Tel: 01633 894802
Newport Museum and Art Gallery – John Frost Square, Newport NP20 1PA. Tel: 01633 840064
Newport Transporter Bridge Visitor Centre – Usk Way, NewPort, South Wales NP20 2JT. Tel: 01633 250322
Tredegar House – Newport NP10 8YW. Tel: 01633 815880

Pembrokeshire

Carew Castle & Tidal Mill – Carew, Nr.Tenby, Pembrokeshire SA70 8SL. Tel: 01646 651782

Powys

The Judge's Lodging – Broad Street, Presteigne, Powys LD8 2AD. Tel: 01544 260650

South Glamorgan

Museum Of Welsh Life – St Fagans, Cardiff, South Glamorgan CF5 6XB. Tel: 029 2057 3500

Continental Europe

Belgium

Kasteel Ooidonk – Ooidonkdreef 9, B9800 Deinze. Tel: 0032 9 282 35 70

France

▼

Château de Chenonceau – 37150 Chenonceaux. Tel: +33 2 47 23 90 07
Chateau Royal D'Amboise – Chateau Royal, B.P. 271, 37403 Amboise. Tel: 00 33 2 47 57 00 98
Floral Park and Chateau of Martinvast – Domaine de Beaurepaire, 50690 Martinvast. Tel: +33 2 33 87 20 80

The Netherlands

Palace Het Loo National Museum – Koninklijk Park 1, 7315 JA Apeldoorn, Holland. Tel: +31 55 577 2400

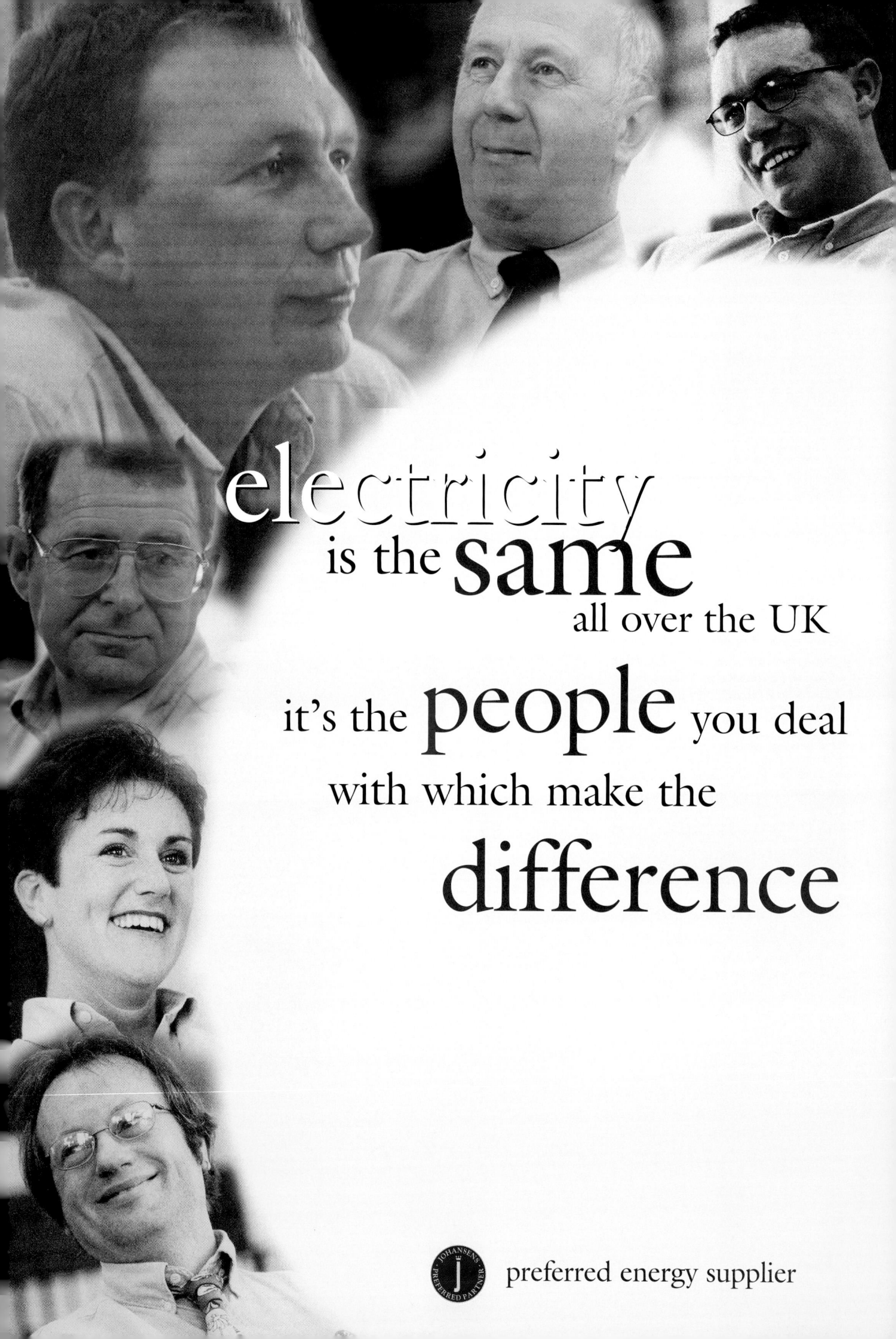

electricity is the same all over the UK

it's the people you deal with which make the difference

JOHANSENS PREFERRED PARTNER

preferred energy supplier

Maverick Energy specialise in the business of electricity supply.

Having been energy consultants and brokers for 7 years we know what you need, and want, in terms of customer care.

To safeguard our beliefs in how the industry could be, we've become a licensed electricity supplier using simple principles. A competitive price offer with straightforward, timely and accurate billing - backed up with solid, tangible customer care.

Doing what needs to be done, by whom, when agreed, as agreed, and keeping you informed is what gives us a 97% annual retention rate of customers.

You will struggle to find a better Energy Team to work with.

Contact us to receive an excellent electricity price for your premises.

maverick
ENERGY

27 Shamrock Way, Hythe Marina Village, Hythe, Hampshire, SO45 6DY.

T **(023) 80 841555**   F **(023) 80 841777**

Email: rachel@maverickenergy.co.uk

Website: www.maverickenergy.co.uk

• CUSTOMER ORIENTATED • RELIABLE • INNOVATIVE • EFFICIENT • FRIENDLY • ENERGETIC • ACCURATE •

Mini Listings North America

Condé Nast Johansens are delighted to recommend over 190 properties across North America, Mexico, Bermuda, The Caribbean, The Pacific. Call 0800 269 397 or see the order forms on page 351 to order guides.

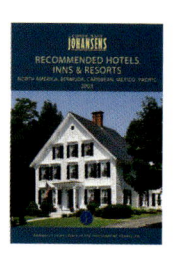

ARIZONA - SEDONA

Canyon Villa Inn
125 Canyon Circle Drive, Sedona, Arizona 86351
Tel: 1 520 284 1226
Fax: 1 520 284 2114

ARIZONA - SEDONA

L'Auberge De Sedona
L'Auberge Lane, PO Box B, Sedona, Arizona 86339
Tel: 1 928 282 1661
Fax: 1 928 282 2885

ARIZONA - TUCSON

Tanque Verde Ranch
14301 East Speedway, Tucson, Arizona 85748
Tel: 1 520 296 6275
Fax: 1 520 721 9426

ARIZONA - TUCSON

White Stallion Ranch
9251 West Twin Peaks Road, Tucson, Arizona 85743
Tel: 1 520 297 0252
Fax: 1 520 744 2786

CALIFORNIA - EUREKA

Carter House
301 L Street, Eureka, California 95501
Tel: 1 707 444 8062
Fax: 1 707 444 8067

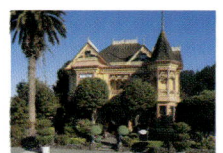

CALIFORNIA - FERNDALE

Gingerbread Mansion Inn
P.O.Box 40; 400 Berding Street, Ferndale, California 95536
Tel: 1 707 786 4000
Fax: 1 707 786 4381

CALIFORNIA - LA JOLLA

The Bed & Breakfast Inn At La Jolla
7753 Draper Avenue, La Jolla, California 92037
Tel: 1 858 456 2066
Fax: 1 858 456 1510

CALIFORNIA - MILL VALLEY

Mill Valley Inn
165 Throckmorton Avenue, Mill Valley, California 94941
Tel: 1 415 389 6608
Fax: 1 415 389 5051

CALIFORNIA - NEWPORT BEACH

Doryman's Inn
2102 West Ocean Front, Newport Beach, California 92663
Tel: 1 949 675 7300
Fax: 1 949 675 9300

CALIFORNIA - PALM DESERT

Shadow Mountain Resort & Club
45750 San Luis Rey, Palm Desert, California 92260
Tel: 1 760 346 6123
Fax: 1 760 346 6518

CALIFORNIA - PALM SPRINGS

Caliente Tropics Resort
411 East Palm Canyon Drive, Palm Springs, California 92264
Tel: 1 760 327 1391
Fax: 1 760 318 1883

CALIFORNIA - PALM SPRINGS

L'Horizon
1050 East Palm Canyon Drive, Palm Springs, California 92264
Tel: 1 760 323 1858
Fax: 1 760 327 2933

CALIFORNIA - PALM SPRINGS

The Willows
412 West Tahquitz Canyon Way, Palm Springs, California 92262
Tel: 1 760 320 0771
Fax: 1 760 320 0780

CALIFORNIA - SAN FRANCISCO

Nob Hill Lambourne
725 Pine Street, San Francisco, California 94108
Tel: 1 415 433 2287
Fax: 1 415 433 0975

CALIFORNIA - SAN FRANCISCO BAY AREA

Gerstle Park Inn
34 Grove Street, San Rafael, California 94901
Tel: 1 415 721 7611
Fax: 1 415 721 7600

CALIFORNIA - SANTA ANA

Woolley's Petite Suites
2721 Hotel Terrace Road, Santa Ana, California 92705
Tel: 1 714 540 1111
Fax: 1 714 662 1643

CALIFORNIA - SANTA BARBARA

Upham Hotel
1404 De La Vina Street, Santa Barbara, California 93101
Tel: 1 805 962 0058
Fax: 1 805 963 2825

CALIFORNIA - SANTA MONICA

The Georgian Hotel
1415 Ocean Avenue, Santa Monica, California 90405
Tel: 1 310 395 9945
Fax: 1 310 451 3374

CALIFORNIA - TIBURON

Waters Edge Hotel
25 Main Street, Tiburon, California 94920
Tel: 1 415 789 5999
Fax: 1 415 789 5888

COLORADO - BEAVER CREEK

The Inn at Beaver Creek
10 Elk Track Lane, Beaver Creek Resort, Colorado, 81620
Tel: 1 970 845 5990
Fax: 1 970 845 6204

MINI LISTINGS NORTH AMERICA

Condé Nast Johansens are delighted to recommend over 190 properties across North America, Mexico, Bermuda, The Caribbean, The Pacific.
Call 0800 269 397 or see the order forms on page 351 to order guides.

COLORADO - DENVER
Castle Marne
1572 Race Street, Denver, Colorado 80206
Tel: 1 303 331 0621
Fax: 1 303 331 0623

COLORADO - ESTES PARK
The Stanley Hotel
333 Wonderview Avenue, PO Box 1767, Estes Park, Colorado. 80517
Tel: 1 970 586 3371
Fax: 1 970 586 4964

COLORADO - MANITOU SPRINGS
The Cliff House at Pikes Peak
306 Cañon Avenue, Manitou Springs, Colorado 80829
Tel: 1 719 685 3000
Fax: 1 719 685 3913

COLORADO - STEAMBOAT SPRINGS
Vista Verde Guest Ranch
PO Box 770465, Steamboat Springs, Colorado 80477
Tel: 1 970 879 3858
Fax: 1 970 879 1413

COLORADO - VAIL
Sonnenalp Resort of Vail
20 Vail Road, Vail, Colorado 81657
Tel: 1 970 476 5656
Fax: 1 970 476 1639

DELAWARE - REHOBOTH BEACH
Boardwalk Plaza Hotel
Olive Avenue & The Boardwalk, Rehoboth Beach, Delaware 19971
Tel: 1 302 227 0441
Fax: 1 302 227 0561

FLORIDA - DELRAY BEACH
The Sundy House Resort
106 South Swinton Avenue, Delray Beach, Florida 33444
Tel: 1 561 272 5678
Fax: 1 561 272 1115

FLORIDA - KEY WEST
Simonton Court Historic Inn & Cottages
320 Simonton Street, Key West, Florida 33040
Tel: 1 305 294 6386
Fax: 1 305 293 8446

FLORIDA - MIAMI BEACH
Fisher Island
1 Fisher Island Drive, Miami Beach, Florida 33109
Tel: 1 305 535 6020
Fax: 1 305 535 6003

FLORIDA - NAPLES
Hotel Escalante
290 Fifth Avenue South, Naples, Florida 34102
Tel: 1 941 659 3466
Fax: 1 941 262 8748

GEORGIA - PERRY
Henderson Village
125 South Langston Circle, Perry, Georgia 31069
Tel: 1 478 988 8696
Fax: 1 478 988 9009

GEORGIA - SAVANNAH
The Eliza Thompson House
5 West Jones Street, Savannah, Georgia 31401
Tel: 1 912 236 3620
Fax: 1 912 238 1920

GEORGIA - SAVANNAH
Granite Steps
126 East Gaston Street, Savannah, Georgia 31401
Tel: 1 912 233 5380
Fax: 1 912 236 3116

GEORGIA - SAVANNAH
The President's Quarters
225 East President Street, Savannah, Georgia 31401
Tel: 1 912 233 1600
Fax: 1 912 238 0849

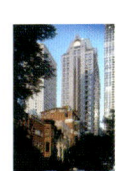

ILLINOIS - CHICAGO
The Sutton Place Hotel
21 East Bellevue Place, Chicago, Illinois 60611
Tel: 1 312 266 2100
Fax: 1 312 266 2103

LOUISIANA - NAPOLEANVILLE
Madewood Plantation House
4250 Highway 308, Napoleanville, Louisiana 70390
Tel: 1 985 369 7151
Fax: 1 985 369 9848

LOUISIANA - NEW ORLEANS
Hotel Maison De Ville
727 Rue Toulouse, New Orleans, Louisiana 70130
Tel: 1 504 561 5858
Fax: 1 504 528 9939

MARYLAND - ANNAPOLIS
The Annapolis Inn
144 Prince George Street, Annapolis, Maryland 21401-1723
Tel: 1 410 295 5200
Fax: 1 410 295 5201

MARYLAND - TANEYTOWN
Antrim 1844
30 Trevanion Rd, Taneytown, Maryland 21787
Tel: 1 410 756 6812
Fax: 1 410 756 2744

MARYLAND - WASINGTON D.C.
The George Washington University Inn
824 New Hampshire Avenue, N.W. Washington D.C., District of Columbia 20037
Tel: 1 202 337 6620
Fax: 1 202 298 7499

Mini Listings North America

Condé Nast Johansens are delighted to recommend over 190 properties across North America, Mexico, Bermuda, The Caribbean, The Pacific. Call 0800 269 397 or see the order forms on page 351 to order guides.

MISSISSIPPI - BILOXI

Green Oaks
580 Beach Boulevard, Biloxi, Mississippi 39530
Tel: 1 228 436 6257
Fax: 1 228 436 6225

MISSISSIPPI - JACKSON

Fairview Inn
734 Fairview Street, Jackson, Mississippi 39202
Tel: 1 601 948 3429
Fax: 1 601 948 1203

MISSISSIPPI - NATCHEZ

Dunleith Plantation
84 Homochitto Street, Natchez, Mississippi, 39120
Tel: 1 601 446 8500
Fax: 1 601 446 8554

MISSISSIPPI - NATCHEZ

Monmouth Plantation
36 Melrose Avenue AT, John A Quitman Parkway, Natches, Mississippi 39120
Tel: 1 601 442 5852
Fax: 1 601 446 7762

MISSISSIPPI - VICKSBURG

Anchuca Historic Mansion & Inn
1010 First East Street, Vicksburg, Mississippi 39183
Tel: 1 601 661 0111
Fax: 1 601 661 0111

MISSISSIPPI - VICKSBURG

The Duff Green Mansion
1114 First East Street, Vicksburg, Mississippi 39180
Tel: 1 601 636 6968
Fax: 1 601 661 0079

MISSOURI - ST LOUIS

Chase Park Plaza Hotel
212 North Kingshighway Boulevard, St Louis, Missouri 63108
Tel: 1 314 633 3000
Fax: 1 314 633 1133

NEW ENGLAND / CONNECTICUT - IVORYTON

Copper Beech Inn
46 Main Street, Ivoryton, Connecticut 06442
Tel: 1 860 767 0330

NEW ENGLAND / CONNECTICUT - MYSTIC

The Inn at Mystic
US1 & State 27, PO Box 216, Mystic, Connecticut 06355
Tel: 1 860 536 9604
Fax: 1 860 572 1635

NEW ENGLAND / CONNECTICUT - MYSTIC

Stonecroft Country Inn
515 Pumpkin Hill Road, Ledyard, Connecticut 06339
Tel: 1 860 572 0771
Fax: 1 860 572 9161

NEW ENGLAND / CONNECTICUT - NEW PRESTON

The Boulders Inn
East Shore Road, Route 45, New Preston, Connecticut 06777
Tel: 1 860 868 0541
Fax: 1 860 868 1925

NEW ENGLAND / CONNECTICUT - OLD MYSTIC

The Old Mystic Inn
52 MAIN STREET, OLD MYSTIC, CONNECTICUT 06372-0733
Tel: 1 860 572 9422
Fax: 1 860 572 9954

NEW ENGLAND / CONNECTICUT - RIDGEFIELD

West Lane Inn & The Inn at Ridgefield
22 West Lane, Ridgefield, Connecticut 06877
Tel: 1 203 438 7323
Fax: 1 203 438 8282

NEW ENGLAND / MAINE - CAMDEN

Blackberry Inn
82 Elm Street, Camden, Maine 04843
Tel: 1 207 236 6060
Fax: 1 207 236 9032

NEW ENGLAND / MAINE - CAMDEN

Camden Maine Stay
22 High Street, Camden, Maine 04843
Tel: 1 207 236 9636
Fax: 1 207 236 0621

NEW ENGLAND / MAINE - CAMDEN

Hartstone Inn
41 Elm Street, Camden, Maine, 04843
Tel: 1 207 236 4259
Fax: 1 207 236 9575

NEW ENGLAND / MAINE - GREENVILLE

The Lodge At Moosehead Lake
Upon Lily Bay Road, Box 1167, Greenville, Maine 04441
Tel: 1 207 695 4400
Fax: 1 207 695 2281

NEW ENGLAND / MAINE - KENNEBUNKPORT

The Captain Lord Mansion
6 Pleasant Street, Kennebunkport, Maine 04046-0800
Tel: 1 207 967 3141

NEW ENGLAND / MAINE - MOOSEHEAD LAKE

Greenville Inn
PO Box 1194, Norris Street, Greenville, Maine 04441
Tel: 1 207 695 2206
Fax: 1 207 695 0335

NEW ENGLAND / MAINE - NEWCASTLE

The Newcastle Inn
60 River Road, Newcastle, Maine 04553
Tel: 1 207 563 5685
Fax: 1 207 563 6877

314

Mini Listings North America

Condé Nast Johansens are delighted to recommend over 190 properties across North America, Mexico, Bermuda, The Caribbean, The Pacific.
Call 0800 269 397 or see the order forms on page 351 to order guides.

NEW ENGLAND / MAINE - ROCKLAND
Captain Lindsey House
5 Lindsey Street, Rockland, Maine 04841
Tel: 1 207 596 7950
Fax: 1 207 596 2758

NEW ENGLAND / MASSACHUSETTS - BOSTON
A Cambridge House
2218 Massachusetts Avenue, Cambridge, Massachusetts 02140–1836
Tel: 1 617 491 6300
Fax: 1 617 868 2848

NEW ENGLAND / MASSACHUSETTS - BOSTON
The Charles Street Inn
94 Charles Street, Boston, Massachusetts 02114–4643
Tel: 1 617 314 8900
Fax: 1 617 371 0009

NEW ENGLAND / MASSACHUSETTS - BOSTON
The Lenox Hotel
710 Boylston Street, Boston, Massachusetts 02116-2699
Tel: 1 617 536 5300
Fax: 1 617 236 0351

NEW ENGLAND / MASSACHUSETTS - CAPE COD
The Captain's House Inn
369–377 Old Harbor Road, Chatham, Cape Cod, Massachusetts 02633
Tel: 1 508 945 0127
Fax: 1 508 945 0866

NEW ENGLAND / MASSACHUSETTS - CAPE COD
Wedgewood Inn
83 Main Street, Route 6A, Yarmouth Port, Massachusetts 02675
Tel: 1 508 362 5157
Fax: 1 508 362 5851

NEW ENGLAND / MASSACHUSETTS - CAPE COD
The Whalewalk Inn
220 Bridge Road, Eastham (Cape Cod), Massachusetts 02642
Tel: 1 508 255 0617
Fax: 1 508 240 0017

NEW ENGLAND / MASSACHUSETTS - DEERFIELD
Deerfield Inn
81 Old Main Street, Deerfield, Massachusetts 01342-0305
Tel: 1 413 774 5587
Fax: 1 413 775 7221

NEW ENGLAND / MASSACHUSETTS - LENOX
Wheatleigh
Hawthorne Road, Lenox, Massachusetts 01240
Tel: 1 413 637 0610
Fax: 1 413 637 4507

NEW ENGLAND / MASSACHUSETTS - MARBLEHEAD
The Harbor Light Inn
58 Washington Street, Marblehead, Massachusetts 01945
Tel: 1 781 631 2186
Fax: 1 781 631 2216

NEW ENGLAND / MASSACHUSETTS - MARTHA'S VINEYARD
Hob Knob Inn
128 Main Street, po box 239, Edgartown, Massachusetts 02539
Tel: 1 508 627 9510
Fax: 1 508 627 4560

NEW ENGLAND / MASSACHUSETTS - MARTHA'S VINEYARD
Thorncroft Inn
460 Main Street, PO Box 1022, Vineyard Haven, Massachusetts 02568
Tel: 1 508 693 3333
Fax: 1 508 693 5419

NEW ENGLAND / MASSACHUSETTS - MARTHA'S VINEYARD
The Victorian Inn
24 South Water Street, Edgartown, Massachusetts 02539
Tel: 1 508 627 4784

NEW ENGLAND / MASSACHUSETTS - NANTUCKET
The Pineapple Inn
10 Hussey Street, Nantucket, Massachusetts 02554
Tel: 1 508 228 9992
Fax: 1 508 325 6051

NEW ENGLAND / MASSACHUSETTS - NANTUCKET
Union Street Inn
7 Union Street, Nantucket, Massachusetts 02554
Tel: 1 508 228 9222
Fax: 1 508 325 0484

NEW ENGLAND / MASSACHUSETTS - ROCKPORT
Seacrest Manor
99 Marmion Way, Rockport, Massachusetts 01966
Tel: 1 978 546 2211

NEW ENGLAND / NEW HAMPSHIRE - CHESTERFIELD
Chesterfield Inn
Route 9, PO Box 155, Chesterfield, New Hampshire 03443-0155
Tel: 1 603 256 3211
Fax: 1 603 256 6131

NEW ENGLAND / NEW HAMPSHIRE - HOLDERNESS
The Manor on Golden Pond
Route 3, PO Box T, Holderness, New Hampshire 03245
Tel: 1 603 968 3348
Fax: 1 603 968 2116

NEW ENGLAND / NEW HAMPSHIRE - JACKSON
The Inn at Thorn Hill
Thorn Hill Road, Jackson Village, New Hampshire 03846
Tel: 1 603 383 4242

NEW ENGLAND / RHODE ISLAND - BLOCK ISLAND
The Atlantic Inn
PO Box 1788, Block Island, Rhode Island 02807
Tel: 1 401 466 5883
Fax: 1 401 466 5678

Mini Listings North America

Condé Nast Johansens are delighted to recommend over 190 properties across North America, Mexico, Bermuda, The Caribbean, The Pacific. Call 0800 269 397 or see the order forms on page 351 to order guides.

NEW ENGLAND / RHODE ISLAND - NEWPORT
Cliffside Inn
2 Seaview Avenue, Newport, Rhode Island 02840
Tel: 1 401 847 1811
Fax: 1 401 848 5850

NEW ENGLAND / RHODE ISLAND - NEWPORT
The Francis Malbone House
392 Thames Street, Newport, Rhode Island 02840
Tel: 1 401 846 0392
Fax: 1 401 848 5956

NEW ENGLAND / RHODE ISLAND - NEWPORT
The Inn At Shadow Lawn
120 Miantonomi Avenue, Newport, Rhode Island 02842
Tel: 1 401 847 0902
Fax: 401 848 6529

NEW ENGLAND / RHODE ISLAND - PROVIDENCE
Historic Jacob Hill Inn
PO Box 41326, Providence, Rhode Island 02940
Tel: 1 508 336 9165
Fax: 1 508 336 0951

NEW ENGLAND / VERMONT - CHITTENDEN
Fox Creek Inn
49 Dam Road, Chittenden, Vermont 05737
Tel: 1 802 483 6213
Fax: 1 802 483 2623

NEW ENGLAND / VERMONT - CHITTENDEN
Mountain Top Inn & Resort
195 Mountain Top Road, Chittenden, Vermont 05737
Tel: 1 802 483 2311
Fax: 1 802 483 6373

NEW ENGLAND / VERMONT - LOWER WATERFORD
Rabbit Hill Inn
48 Lower Waterford Road, Lower Waterford, Vermont 05848
Tel: 1 802 748 5168
Fax: 1 802 748 8342

NEW ENGLAND / VERMONT - MANCHESTER VILLAGE
1811 House
PO Box 39, Route 7A, Manchester Village, Vermont 05254
Tel: 1 802 362 1811
Fax: 1 802 362 2443

NEW ENGLAND / VERMONT - MANCHESTER VILLAGE
The Village Country Inn
Route 7A, po box 408, Manchester Village, Vermont 05254
Tel: 1 802 362 1792
Fax: 1 802 362 7238

NEW ENGLAND / VERMONT - NEWFANE
Four Columns Inn
PO Box 278, Newfane, Vermont 05345
Tel: 1 802 365 7713

NEW ENGLAND / VERMONT - STOWE
The Mountain Road Resort At Stowe
PO Box 8, 1007 Mountain Road, Stowe, Vermont 05672
Tel: 1 802 253 4566
Fax: 1 802 253 7397

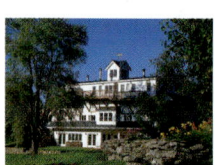

NEW ENGLAND / VERMONT - WEST TOWNSHEND
Windham Hill Inn
West Townshend, Vermont 05359
Tel: 1 802 874 4080
Fax: 1 802 874 4702

NEW ENGLAND / VERMONT - WESTON
The Inn At Weston
Scenic Route 100, Weston, Vermont 05161
Tel: 1 802 824 6789
Fax: 1 802 824 3073

NEW ENGLAND / VERMONT - WOODSTOCK
The Jackson House Inn
114-3 Senior Lane, Woodstock, Vermont 05091
Tel: 1 802 457 2065
Fax: 1 802 457 9290

NEW ENGLAND / VERMONT - WOODSTOCK
Woodstock Inn & Resort
Fourteen The Green, Woodstock, Vermont, 05091-1298
Tel: 1 802 457 1100
Fax: 1 802 457 6699

NEW MEXICO - SANTA FE
Hotel St Francis
210 Don Gaspar Avenue, Santa Fe, New Mexico 87501
Tel: 1 505 983 5700
Fax: 1 505 992 6340

NEW MEXICO - SANTA FE
Bishop's Lodge
PO Box 2367, Santa Fe, New Mexico, 87504
Tel: 1 505 983 6377
Fax: 1 505 989 8739

NEW MEXICO - TAOS
Casitas at El Monte
125 La Posta Road, PO Box 20, Taos, New Mexico 87671
Tel: 1 800 828 8267
Fax: 1 505 758 5089

NEW MEXICO - TAOS
The Inn on La Loma Plaza
315 Ranchitos Road, Taos, New Mexico 87571
Tel: 1 505 758 1717
Fax: 1 505 751 0155

NEW YORK - CAZENOVIA
The Brewster Inn
6 Ledyard Avenue, Cazenovia, New York 13035
Tel: 1 315 655 9232
Fax: 1 315 655 2130

Mini Listings North America

Condé Nast Johansens are delighted to recommend over 190 properties across North America, Mexico, Bermuda, The Caribbean, The Pacific.
Call 0800 269 397 or see the order forms on page 351 to order guides.

NEW YORK - EAST AURORA

Roycroft Inn
40 South Grove Street, East Aurora, New York 14052
Tel: 1 877 652 5552
Fax: 1 716 655 5345

NEW YORK - GENEVA

Geneva On The Lake
1001 Lochland Road (Route 14 South), Geneva, New York 14456
Tel: 1 315 789 7190
Fax: 1 315 789 0322

NEW YORK - ITHACA

William Henry Miller Inn
303 North Aurora Street, Ithaca, New York 14850
Tel: 1 607 256 4553
Fax: 607 256 0092

NEW YORK - NEW YORK CITY

Bryant Park Hotel
40 West 40th Street, New York, New York 10018
Tel: 1 212 869 0100
Fax: 1 212 869 4446

NEW YORK - NEW YORK CITY

The Kitano New York
66 Park Avenue New York, New York 10016
Tel: 1 212 885 7000
Fax: 1 212 885 7100

NEW YORK - NORTHERN CATSKILL MOUNTAINS

Albergo Allegria
#43 Route 296, Windham, New York 12496
Tel: 1 518 734 5560
Fax: 1 518 734 5570

NEW YORK - SARATOGA SPRINGS

Saratoga Arms
495–497 Broadway, Saratoga Springs, New York 12866
Tel: 1 518 584 1775
Fax: 1 518 581 4064

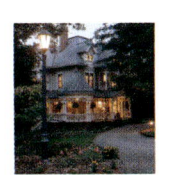

NORTH CAROLINA - ASHEVILLE

The Wright Inn & Carriage House
235 Pearson Drive, Asheville, North Carolina 28801
Tel: 1 828 251 0789
Fax: 1 828 251 0929

NORTH CAROLINA - BALD HEAD ISLAND

Theodosia's Bed & Breakfast
PO Box 3130, 2 Keelson Row, Bald Head Island, North Carolina 28461
Tel: 1 910 457 6563
Fax: 1 910 457 6055

NORTH CAROLINA - BALSAM

Balsam Mountain Inn
PO Box 40, Balsam, North Carolina 28707
Tel: 1 828 456 9498
Fax: 1 828 456 9298

NORTH CAROLINA - BEAUFORT

The Cedars Inn
305 Front Street, Beaufort, North Carolina 28516
Tel: 1 252 728 7036
Fax: 1 252 728 1685

NORTH CAROLINA - BLOWING ROCK

Chetola Resort
PO Box 17, North Main Street, Blowing Rock, North Carolina 28605
Tel: 1 828 295 5500
Fax: 1 828 295 5529

NORTH CAROLINA - BLOWING ROCK

Gideon Ridge
PO Box 1929, Blowing Rock, North Carolina 28605
Tel: 1 828 295 3644
Fax: 1 828 295 4586

NORTH CAROLINA - CASHIERS

Millstone Inn
119 Lodge Lane, Hwy 64 West, Cashiers, North Carolina 28717
Tel: 1 828 743 2737
Fax: 1 828 743 0208

NORTH CAROLINA - CHARLOTTE

Ballantyne Resort
10000 Ballantyne Commons Parkway, Charlotte, North Carolina 28277
Tel: 1 704 248 4000
Fax: 1 704 248 4005

NORTH CAROLINA - CHARLOTTE

The Park
2200 Rexford Road, Charlotte, North Carolina 28211
Tel: 1 704 364 8220
Fax: 1 704 365 4712

NORTH CAROLINA - DURHAM

Morehead Manor Bed & Breakfast
914 Vickers Avenue, Durham, North Carolina 27701
Tel: 1 919 687 4366
Fax: 1 919 687 4245

NORTH CAROLINA - EDENTON

The Lords Proprietors' Inn
300 North Broad Street, Edenton, North Carolina 27932
Tel: 1 252 482 3641
Fax: 1 252 482 2432

NORTH CAROLINA - GLENVILLE

Innisfree Victorian Inn and Garden House
PO Box 469, Glenville, North Carolina 28736
Tel: 1 828 743 2946

NORTH CAROLINA - HENDERSONVILLE

Claddagh Inn
755 North Main Street, Hendersonville, North Carolina, 28792
Tel: 1 828 697 7778

Mini Listings North America

Condé Nast Johansens are delighted to recommend over 190 properties across North America, Mexico, Bermuda, The Caribbean, The Pacific.
Call 0800 269 397 or see the order forms on page 351 to order guides.

NORTH CAROLINA - HIGHLANDS
Inn at Half - Mile Farm
PO Box 2769, 214 Half Mile Drive, Highlands, North Carolina 28741
Tel: 1 828 526 8170
Fax: 1 828 526 2625

NORTH CAROLINA - MANTEO
The White Doe Inn & Whispering Bay
PO Box 1029, 319 Sir Walter Raleigh Street, Manteo, North Carolina 27954
Tel: 1 252 473 9851
Fax: 1 252 473 4708

NORTH CAROLINA - RALEIGH - DURHAM
The Siena Hotel
1505 E. Franklin Street, Chapel Hill, North Carolina 27514
Tel: 1 919 929 4000
Fax: 1 919 968 8527

NORTH CAROLINA - ROBBINSVILLE
Snowbird Mountain Lodge
275 Santeetlah Road, Robbinsville, North Carolina 28771
Tel: 1 828 479 3433
Fax: 1 828 479 3473

NORTH CAROLINA - TRYON
Pine Crest Inn
85 Pine Crest Lane, Tryon, North Carolina 28782
Tel: 1 828 859 9135
Fax: 1 828 859 9135

NORTH CAROLINA - WAYNESVILLE
The Swag Country Inn
2300 Swag Road, Waynesville, North Carolina 28785
Tel: 1 828 926 0430
Fax: 1 828 926 2036

NORTH CAROLINA - WILMINGTON
The Verandas
202 NUN STREET, WILMINGTON, NORTH CAROLINA 28401-5020
Tel: 1 910 251 2212
Fax: 1 910 251 8932

NORTH CAROLINA - WINSTON SALEM
Augustus T Zevely Inn
803 South Main Street, Winston-Salem, North Carolina 27101
Tel: 1 336 748 9299
Fax: 1 336 721 2211

OREGON - GRANTS PASS
Weasku Inn
5560 Rogue River Highway, Grants Pass, Oregon 97527
Tel: 1 541 471 8000
Fax: 1 541 471 7038

PENNSYLVANIA - PHILADELPHIA
Rittenhouse Square European Boutique Hotel
1715 Rittenhouse Square, Philadelphia, Pennsylvania 19103
Tel: 1 215 546 6500
Fax: 1 215 546 8787

PENNSYLVANIA - PHILIDELPHIA
The Thomas Bond House
129 South 2nd Street, Philadelphia, Pennsylvania 19106
Tel: 1 215 923 8523
Fax: 1 215 923 8504

SOUTH CAROLINA - AIKEN
Rosemary & Lookaway Inn
804 Carolina Avenue, North Augusta, South Carolina 29841
Tel: 1 803 278 6222
Fax: 1 803 278 4877

SOUTH CAROLINA - CHARLESTON
Vendue Inn
19 VENDUE RANGE, CHARLESTON, SOUTH CAROLINA 29401
Tel: 1 843 577 7970
Fax: 1 843 577 2913

SOUTH CAROLINA - PAWLEYS ISLAND
Litchfield Plantation
Kings River Road, Box 290, Pawleys Island, South Carolina 29585
Tel: 1 843 237 9121
Fax: 1 843 237 1041

SOUTH CAROLINA - TRAVELERS REST
La Bastide
10 ROAD OF VINES, TRAVELERS REST, SOUTH CAROLINA 29690
Tel: 1 864 836 8463
Fax: 1 864 836 4820

TENNESSEE - KINGSTON
Whitestone Country Inn
1200 Paint Rock Road, Kingston, Tennessee 37763
Tel: 1 865 376 0113
Fax: 1 865 376 4454

TENNESSEE - WALLAND
Blackberry Farm
1471 West Millers Cove Road, Walland, Great Smoky Mountains, Tennessee 37886
Tel: 1 865 380 2260
Fax: 1 865 681 7753

TEXAS - BOERNE
Ye Kendall Inn
128 West Blanco, Boerne, Texas 78006
Tel: 1 830 249 2138
Fax: 1 830 249 7371

TEXAS - DALLAS
Hotel Adolphus
1321 Commerce Street, Dallas, Texas 75202
Tel: 1 214 742 8200
Fax: 1 214 651 3563

TEXAS - KYLE
The Inn Above Onion Creek
4444 Highway 150 West, Kyle, Texas 78640
Tel: 1 512 268 1617
Fax: 1 512 268 1090

MINI LISTINGS NORTH AMERICA

Condé Nast Johansens are delighted to recommend over 190 properties across North America, Mexico, Bermuda, The Caribbean, The Pacific.
Call 0800 269 397 or see the order forms on page 351 to order guides.

TEXAS - SAN ANTONIO

Havana River Walk Inn
1015 Navarro, San Antonio, Texas 78205
Tel: 1 210 222 2008
Fax: 1 210 222 2717

VIRGINIA - WILLIAMSBURG

Legacy of Williamsburg Inn
930 James Towmn Road, Williamsburg, Virginia 23185–3917
Tel: 1 757 220 0524
Fax: 1 757 220 2211

TEXAS - TYLER

Kiepersol Estates
21508 Merlot Lane, Tyler, Texas 75703
Tel: 1 903 894 3300
Fax: 1 903 894 4140

WYOMING - CHEYENNE

Nagle Warren Mansion
222 East 17Th Street, Cheyenne, Wyoming 82001
Tel: 1 307 637 3333
Fax: 1 307 638 6879

VIRGINIA - CHARLOTTESVILLE

200 South Street Inn
200 South Street, Charlottesville, Virginia, 22902
Tel: 1 434 964 7008
Fax: 1 434 979 4403

MEXICO - BAJA CALIFORNIA

Casa Natalia
Blvd Mijares 4, San Jose Del Cabo, Baja California Sur 23400
Tel: 52 624 14 251 00
Fax: 52 624 14251 10

VIRGINIA - CHARLOTTESVILLE

Clifton - The Country Inn & Estate
1296 Clifton Inn Drive, Charlottesville, Virginia 22911
Tel: 1 434 971 1800
Fax: 1 434 971 7098

MEXICO - CANCUN

Villas Tacul
Boulevard Kukulkan, KM 5.5, Cancun, Quintana Roo, 77500 Mexico
Tel: 52 998 883 00 00
Fax: 52 998 849 70 70

VIRGINIA - CHARLOTTESVILLE

Prospect Hill Plantation Inn
po box 6909, charlottesville, VIRGINIA 22906
Tel: 1 540 967 0844
Fax: 1 540 967 0102

MEXICO - ISLA MUJERES

La Casa De Los Sueños
Carretera Garrafon, S/N Isla Mujeres, Quintana Roo, Mexico 77400
Tel: 52 99887 70651
Fax: 52 99887 70708

VIRGINIA - CULPEPER

Prince Michel Restaurant & Suites
Prince Michel de Virginia, HCR 4, Box 77, Leon, Virginia 22725
Tel: 1 540 547 9720
Fax: 1 540 547 3088

MEXICO - RIVIERA MAYA

Maroma
highway 307 km 51, riviera maya, Quintana Roo, 77710 Mexico
Tel: 52 998 872 8200
Fax: 52 998 872 8220

VIRGINIA - MIDDLEBURG

The Goodstone Inn & Estate
36205 Snake Hill Road, Middleburg, Virginia 20117
Tel: 1 540 687 4645
Fax: 1 540 687 6115

MEXICO - ZIHUATANEJO

Hotel Villa Del Sol
Playa La Ropa S/N, PO Box 84, Zihuatanejo 40880, Mexico
Tel: 52 755 4 2239/3239
Fax: 52 7554 2758/4066

VIRGINIA - ORANGE

Willow Grove Inn
14079 Plantation Way, Orange, Virginia 22960
Tel: 1 540 672 5982
Fax: 1 540 672 3674

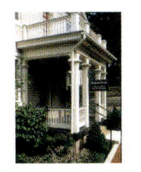

BERMUDA - DEVONSHIRE

Ariel Sands
34 South Shore Road, Devonshire, Bermuda
Tel: 1 441 236 1010
Fax: 1 441 236 0087

VIRGINIA - STAUNTON

Frederick House
28 North New street, Staunton, Virginia 24401
Tel: 1 540 885 4220
Fax: 1 540 885 5180

BERMUDA - HAMILTON

Rosedon Hotel
PO Box Hm 290, Hamilton Hmax, Bermuda
Tel: 1 441 295 1640
Fax: 1 441 295 5904

VIRGINIA - WHITE POST

L'Auberge Provençale
PO Box 190, White Post, Virginia 22663
Tel: 1 540 837 1375
Fax: 1 540 837 2004

BERMUDA - PAGET

Fourways Inn
PO Box Pg 294, Paget Pg Bx, Bermuda
Tel: 1 441 236 6517
Fax: 1 441 236 5528

Mini Listings North America

Condé Nast Johansens are delighted to recommend over 190 properties across North America, Mexico, Bermuda, The Caribbean, The Pacific.
Call 0800 269 397 or see the order forms on page 351 to order guides.

BERMUDA - PAGET
Newstead Hotel
27 Harbour Road, Paget Pg02, Bermuda
Tel: 1 441 236 6060
Fax: 1 441 236 7454

BERMUDA - SOMERSET
Cambridge Beaches
Kings Point, Somerset, MA02 Bermuda
Tel: 1 441 234 0331
Fax: 1 441 234 3352

BERMUDA - SOUTHAMPTON
The Reefs
56 South Shore Road, Southampton, SN02 Bermuda
Tel: 1 441 238 0222
Fax: 1 441 238 8372

BERMUDA - WARWICK
Surf Side Beach Club
90 South Shore Road, Warwick, Bermuda
Tel: 1 441 236 7100
Fax: 1 441 236 9765

CARIBBEAN - ANGUILLA
Frangipani Beach Club
PO Box 1378, Meads Bay, Anguilla, West Indies
Tel: 1 264 497 6442/6444
Fax: 1 264 497 6440

CARIBBEAN - ANTIGUA
Blue Waters
PO Box 256, St Johns, Antigua, West Indies
Tel: 1 268 462 0290
Fax: 1 268 462 0293

CARIBBEAN - ANTIGUA
Curtain Bluff
PO Box 288, Antigua, West Indies
Tel: 1 268 462 8400
Fax: 1 268 462 8409

CARIBBEAN - ANTIGUA
Galley Bay
Five Islands, PO Box 305, St John's, Antigua, West Indies
Tel: 1 268 462 0302
Fax: 1 268 462 4551

CARIBBEAN - ANTIGUA
The inn at English Harbour
PO Box 187, ST Johns, Antigua, West Indies
Tel: 1 268 460 1014
Fax: 1 268 460 1603

CARIBBEAN - BARBADOS
Coral Reef Club
St James, Barbados, West Indies
Tel: 1 246 422 2372
Fax: 1 246 422 1776

CARIBBEAN - BARBADOS
The Sandpiper
Holetown, St James, Barbados, West Indies
Tel: 1 246 422 2251
Fax: 1 246 422 0900

CARIBBEAN - CURAÇAO
Avila Beach Hotel
Penstraat 130, Willemstad, Curaçao, Netherlands Antilles, West Indies
Tel: 599 9 461 4377
Fax: 599 9 461 1493

CARIBBEAN - GRENADA
Spice Island Beach Resort
Grand Anse Beach, Box 6, St. George's, Grenada, West Indies
Tel: 1 473 444 4423
Fax: 1 473 444 4807

CARIBBEAN - JAMAICA
Blue Lagoon Villas
Fairy Hill, Port Antonio, Jamaica, West Indies
Tel: 1 876 993 7701
Fax: 1 876 993 8492

CARIBBEAN - JAMAICA
Grand Lido Sans Souci
PO Box 103, Ocho Rios, St Ann, Jamaica, West Indies
Tel: 1 876 994 1206
Fax: 1 876 994 1544

CARIBBEAN - JAMAICA
Half Moon Golf, Tennis & Beach Club
Montego Bay, Jamaica, West Indies
Tel: 1 876 953 2211
Fax: 1 876 953 2731

CARIBBEAN - JAMAICA
Mocking Bird Hill
PO Box 254, Port Antonio, Jamaica
Tel: 1 876 993 7134
Fax: 1 876 993 7133

CARIBBEAN - NEVIS
The Hermitage
Nevis, West Indies
Tel: 1 869 469 3477
Fax: 1 869 469 2481

CARIBBEAN - NEVIS
Montpelier Plantation Inn
Montpelier Estate, PO Box 474, Nevis, West Indies
Tel: 1 869 469 3462
Fax: 1 869 469 2932

CARIBBEAN - NEVIS
Nisbet Plantation Beach Club
St James Parish, Nevis, West Indies
Tel: +1 869 469 9325
Fax: +1 869 469 9864

MINI LISTINGS NORTH AMERICA

Condé Nast Johansens are delighted to recommend over 190 properties across North America, Mexico, Bermuda, The Caribbean, The Pacific.
Call 0800 269 397 or see the order forms on page 351 to order guides.

CARIBBEAN - ST KITTS
The Golden Lemon
DIEPPE BAY, ST KITTS, WEST INDIES
Tel: 1 869 465 7260
Fax: 1 869 465 4019

CARIBBEAN - ST KITTS
Ottley's Plantation Inn
PO BOX 345, BASSETERRE, ST KITTS, WEST INDIES
Tel: 1 869 465 7234
Fax: 1 869 465 4760

CARIBBEAN - ST KITTS
Rawlins Plantation Inn
PO Box 340, St Kitts, West Indies
Tel: 1 869 465 6221
Fax: 1 869 465 4954

CARIBBEAN - ST LUCIA
Anse Chastanet
PO Box 7000, Soufriere, St Lucia, West Indies
Tel: 1 758 459 7000
Fax: 1 758 459 7700

CARIBBEAN - ST LUCIA
Mago Estate Hotel
PO Box 247, Soufrière, St Lucia, West Indies
Tel: 1 758 459 5880
Fax: 1 758 459 7352

CARIBBEAN - ST. VINCENT
Camelot Inn - A Boutique Hotel
PO Box 787, Kingstown, The Grenadines, St Vincent, West Indies
Tel: 1 784 456 2100
Fax: 1 784 456 2233

CARIBBEAN - ST. VINCENT
Grand View Beach Hotel
Villa Point, Box 173, St Vincent, West Indies
Tel: 1 784 458 4811
Fax: 1 784 457 4174

CARIBBEAN - ST VINCENT & THE GRENADINES
Palm Island
ST VINCENT & THE GRENADINES, WEST INDIES
Tel: 1 800 345 0271
Fax: 1 954 481 1661

CARIBBEAN - TURKS & CAICOS ISLANDS
Point Grace
PO Box 700, Providenciales, Turks and Caicos Islands, British west indies
Tel: 1 649 946 5096
Fax: 1 649 946 5097

CARIBBEAN - TURKS & CAICOS
The Sands at Grace Bay
PO BOX 681, PROVIDENCIALES, TURKS & CAICOS islands, british WEST INDIES
Tel: 1 649 946 5199
Fax: 1 649 946 5198

FIJI ISLANDS - LABASA
Nukubati Island
PO Box 1928, Labasa, Fiji Islands
Tel: 61 2 93888 196
Fax: 61 2 93888 204

FIJI ISLANDS - LAUTOKA
Blue Lagoon Cruises
183 Vitogo Parade, Lautoka, Fiji Islands
Tel: 679 6661 622
Fax: 679 6664 098

FIJI ISLANDS - SAVU SAVU
Namale
Savu Savu, Fili Islands
Tel: 1 858 535 6380
Fax: 1 858 535 6385

FIJI ISLANDS - SUVA
The Wakaya Club
Wakaya Island, Fiji Islands
Tel: 1 970 927 2044
Fax: 1 970 927 2048

FIJI ISLANDS - TOBERUA ISLAND
Toberua Island Resort
PO Box 567, Suva, Fiji Islands
Tel: 679 347 2777
Fax: 679 347 2888

FIJI ISLANDS - VOMO ISLANDS
Vomo Island
PO BOX 5650, LAUTOKA, FIJI ISLANDS
Tel: 679 6668 122
Fax: 679 6668 500

FIJI ISLANDS - YASAWA ISLANDS
Turtle Island
YASAWA ISLANDS, PO BOX 9317, NADI AIRPORT, NADI, FIJI ISLANDS
Tel: 61 3 9823 8300
Fax: 61 3 9618 1199

FIJI ISLANDS - YASAWA ISLAND
Yasawa Island Resort
PO Box 10128, Nadi Airport, Nadi, Fiji Islands
Tel: 679 772 2266
Fax: 679 772 4456

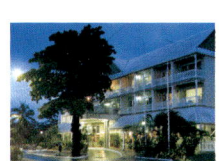

SAMOA - APIA
Aggie Grey's Hotel
PO Box 67, Apia, Samoa
Tel: 685 228 80
Fax: 685 232 03

Mini Listings Europe

Condé Nast Johansens are delighted to recommend over 320 properties across Europe and The Mediterranean. Call 0800 269 397 or see the order forms on page 351 to order guides.

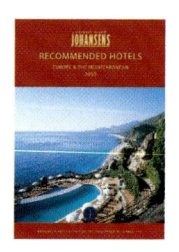

Andorra

PAS DE LA CASA
Font d'Argent Hotel Ski & Resort - C/ Bearn 20, 22, 24, Pas de La Casa, Andorra. Tel: +376 739 739

Austria

KÄRNTEN (PATERGASSEN)
Almdorf "Seinerzeit" - Fellacheralm, 9564 Patergassen, Austria. Tel: +43 4275 7201

KÄRNTEN (KLAGENFURT)
Hotel Palais Porcia - Neuer Platz 13, 9020 Klagenfurt, Austria. Tel: +43 463 51 15 90

KÄRNTEN (VELDEN)
Seeschlössl Velden - Klagenfurter Strasse 34, 9220 Velden, Austria. Tel: +43 4274 2824

NIEDERÖSTERREICH (DÜRNSTEIN)
Hotel Schloss Dürnstein - 3601 Dürnstein, Austria. Tel: +43 2711 212

SALZBURG (BAD GASTEIN)
Hotel & Spa Haus Hirt - An Der Kaiserpromenade 14, 5640 Bad Gastein, Austria. Tel: +43 64 34 27 97

SALZBURG (BAD HOFGASTEIN)
Das Moser - Kaiser-Franz-Platz 2, 5630 Bad Hofgastein, Austria. Tel: + 43 6432 6209

SALZBURG (BAD HOFGASTEIN)
Grand Park Hotel Bad Hofgastein - Kurgartenstrasse 26, 5630 Bad Hofgastein, Austria. Tel: +43 6432 63560

▼
TIROL (IGLS)
Schlosshotel Igls - Viller Steig 2, 6080 Igls, Tirol, Austria. Tel: +43 512 37 72 17

TIROL (IGLS)
Sporthotel Igls - Hilberstrasse 17, 6080 Igls, Tirol, Austria. Tel: +43 512 37 72 41

VORARLBERG (LECH)
Sporthotel Kristiania - Omesberg 331, 6764 Lech Am Arlberg, Austria. Tel: +43 5583 25 610

VORARLBERG (ZÜRS)
Thurnhers Alpenhof - 6763 Zürs – Arlberg, Austria. Tel: +43 5583 2191

WIEN (VIENNA)
Grand Hotel Wien - Kärntner Ring 9, 1010 Vienna, Austria. Tel: +43 1 515 80 0

Belgium

ANTWERP
Firean Hotel - Karel Oomsstraat 6, 2018 Antwerp, Belgium. Tel: +32 3 237 02 60

BRUGES
Hotel Acacia - Korte Zilverstraat 3A, 8000 Bruges, Belgium. Tel: +32 50 34 44 11

BRUGES
Hotel De Tuilerieën - Dyver 7, 8000 Bruges, Belgium. Tel: +32 50 34 36 91

BRUGES
Hotel Montanus - Nieuwe Gentweg 78, 8000 Bruges, Belgium. Tel: +32 50 33 11 76

BRUGES
Hotel Prinsenhof - Ontvangersstraat 9, 8000 Bruges, Belgium. Tel: +32 50 34 26 90

DE HAAN
Romantik Manoir Carpe Diem - Prins Karellaan 12, 8420 de Haan, Belgium. Tel: +32 59 23 32 20

FLORENVILLE
Hostellerie Le Prieuré de Conques - Rue de Conques 2, 6820 Florenville, Belgium. Tel: +32 61 41 14 17

KNOKKE~HEIST
Romantik Hotel Manoir du Dragon - Albertlaan 73, 8300 Knokke~Heist, Belgium. Tel: +32 50 63 05 80

KORTRIJK
Hotel Damier - Grote Markt 41, 8500 Kortrijk, Belgium. Tel: +32 56 22 15 47

MALMÉDY
Hostellerie Trôs Marets - Route des Trôs Marets, 4960 Malmédy, Belgium. Tel: +32 80 33 79 17

MARCHE~EN~FAMENNE
Château d'Hassonville - Route d'Hassonville 105, 6900 Marche~en~Famenne, Belgium. Tel: +32 84 31 10 25

Cyprus

LIMASSOL
Le Meridien Limassol Spa & Resort - Po Box 56560, 3308 Limassol, Cyprus. Tel: +357 25 862 000

Czech Republic

PRAGUE
Hotel Hoffmeister - Pod Bruskou 7, Klárov, 11800 Prague 1, Czech Republic. Tel: +420 2 51017 111

PRAGUE
Romantik Hotel U Raka - Cerninska 10/93, 11800 Prague 1, Czech Republic.. Tel: +420 2205 111 00

PRAGUE
Sieber Hotel & Apartments - Slezská 55, 130 00 Prague 3, Czech Republic. Tel: +420 2 24 25 00 25

Denmark

NYBORG
Hotel Hesselet - Christianslundsvej 119, 5800 Nyborg, Denmark. Tel: +45 65 31 30 29

Estonia

▼
PÄRNU
Villa Ammende - Mere Pst. 7, 80012 Pärnu, Estonia. Tel: +372 44 73888

France

ALSACE~LORRAINE (COLMAR)
Hostellerie Le Maréchal - 4 Place Six Montagnes Noires, Petite Venise, 68000 Colmar, France. Tel: +33 3 89 41 60 32

ALSACE~LORRAINE (COLMAR)
Hôtel Les Têtes - 19 Rue de Têtes, 68000 Colmar, France. Tel: +33 3 89 24 43 43

ALSACE~LORRAINE (COLMAR - ROUFFACH)
Château d'Isenbourg - 68250 Rouffach, France. Tel: +33 3 89 78 58 50

ALSACE~LORRAINE (GÉRARDMER – VOSGES)
Hostellerie Les Bas Rupts - 88400 Gérardmer, Vosges, France. Tel: +33 3 29 63 09 25

ALSACE~LORRAINE (MURBACH – BUHL)
Hostellerie St Barnabé - 68530 Murbach – Buhl, France. Tel: +33 3 89 62 14 14

ALSACE~LORRAINE (OBERNAI - OTTROTT)
A L'Ami Fritz - 8 Rue des Châteaux, 67530 Ottrott, France. Tel: +33 3 88 95 80 81

ALSACE~LORRAINE (STRASBOURG – OSTWALD)
Château de L'Ile - 4 Quai Heydt, 67540 Ostwald, France. Tel: +33 3 88 66 85 00

ALSACE~LORRAINE (THIONVILLE)
L'Horizon - 50 Route du Crève~Cœur, 57100 Thionville, France. Tel: +33 3 82 88 53 65

AUVERGNE - LIMOUSIN (SAINT~FLOUR)
Hostellerie Château de Varillettes - 15100 Saint~Georges par Saint~Flour, France. Tel: +33 4 71 60 45 05

Mini Listings Europe

Condé Nast Johansens are delighted to recommend over 320 properties across Europe and The Mediterranean.
Call 0800 269 397 or see the order forms on page 351 to order guides.

BRITTANY (BILLIERS)
Domaine de Rochevilaine - Pointe de Pen Lan, 56190 Billiers, France. Tel: +33 2 97 41 61 61

BRITTANY (LA GOUESNIÈRE – SAINT~MALO)
Château de Bonaban - 35350 La Gouesnière, France. Tel: +33 2 99 58 24 50

BRITTANY (AMBOISE)
Le Manoir Les Minimes - 34 Quai Charles Guinot, 37400 Amboise, France. Tel: +33 2 47 30 40 40

▼
BRITTANY (MOËLAN~SUR~MER)
Manoir de Kertalg - Route de Riec-Sur-Belon, 29350 Moelan~sur~Mer, France. Tel: +33 2 98 39 77 77

BRITTANY (PLOERDÜT)
Château du Launay - 56160 Ploerdüt, France. Tel: +33 2 97 39 46 32

BRITTANY (RENNES)
LeCoq~Gadby - 156 Rue d'Antrain, 35700 Rennes, France. Tel: +33 2 99 38 05 55

BRITTANY (SAINT MALO – PLEVEN)
Manoir du Vaumadeuc - 22130 Pleven, France. Tel: +33 2 96 84 46 17

BRITTANY (SAINT MALO – SAINT BRIEUC)
Manoir de la Hazaie - 22400 Planguenoual, France. Tel: +33 2 9632 7371

BRITTANY (TREBEURDEN)
Ti Al Lannec - 14 Allée de Mézo~Guen, BP 3, 22560 Trebeurden, France. Tel: +33 296 15 01 01

BURGUNDY - FRANCHE~COMTÉ (AVALLON)
Château de Vault de Lugny - 11 Rue du Château, 89200 Avallon, France. Tel: +33 3 86 34 07 86

BURGUNDY - FRANCHE~COMTÉ (AVALLON)
Hostellerie de la Poste - 13 Place Vauban, 89200 Avallon, France. Tel: +33 3 86 34 16 16

BURGUNDY - FRANCHE~COMTÉ (BEAUNE)
Ermitage de Corton - R.N. 74, 21200 Chorey~les~Beaune, France. Tel: +33 3 80 22 05 28

BURGUNDY - FRANCHE~COMTÉ (POLIGNY – JURA)
Hostellerie des Monts de Vaux - Les Monts de Vaux, 39800 Poligny, France. Tel: +33 3 84 37 12 50

BURGUNDY - FRANCHE~COMTÉ (VILLEFARGEAU – AUXERRE)
Le Petit Manoir des Bruyères - 5 Allée de Charbuy~les~Bruyères, 89240 Villefargeau, France. Tel: +33 3 86 41 32 82

BURGUNDY - FRANCHE~COMTÉ (VOUGEOT)
Château de Gilly - Gilly~lès~Cîteaux, 21640 Vougeot, France. Tel: +33 3 80 62 89 98

CHAMPAGNE - ARDENNES (ÉPERNAY)
Hostellerie La Briqueterie - 4 Route de Sézanne, 51530 Vinay – Épernay, France. Tel: +33 3 26 59 99 99

CHAMPAGNE - ARDENNES (TINQUEUX – REIMS)
L'Assiette Champenoise - 40 Avenue Paul Vaillant Couturier, 51430 Tinqueux, France. Tel: +33 3 26 84 64 64

CÔTE D'AZUR (CAGNES~SUR~MER)
Domaine Cocagne - Colline de La Route de Vence, 30, Chemin du Pain de Sucre, 08600 Cagnes~sur~Mer, France. Tel: +33 4 92 13 57 77

CÔTE D'AZUR (CANNES)
Le Cavendish - 11 Boulevard Carnot, 06400 Cannes, France. Tel: +33 4 97 06 26 00

CÔTE D'AZUR (ÈZE VILLAGE)
Château Eza - Rue de La Pise, 06360 Èze Village, France. Tel: +33 4 93 41 12 24

CÔTE D'AZUR (LE ROYAL – CANADEL~SUR~MER)
Le Bailli de Suffren - Avenue des Américains – Goffe de Saint~Tropez, 83820 Le Rayol – Canadel~sur~Mer, France. Tel: +33 4 98 04 47 00

CÔTE D'AZUR (MANDELIEU – CANNES)
Ermitage du Riou - Avenue Henri Clews, 06210 Mandelieu~La~Napoule, France. Tel: + 33 4 93 49 95 56

CÔTE D'AZUR (MOUGINS)
Le Mas Candille - Boulevard Clément Rebuffel, 06250 Mougins, France. Tel: +33 4 92 28 43 43

CÔTE D'AZUR (NICE)
Hôtel La Pérouse - 11, Quai Rauba~Capeu, 06300 Nice, France. Tel: +33 4 93 62 34 63

CÔTE D'AZUR (SAINT~TROPEZ - RAMATUELLE)
La Ferme d'Augustin - Plage de Tahiti, 83350 Ramatuelle, Nr Saint-Tropez, France. Tel: +33 4 94 55 97 00

CÔTE D'AZUR (SAINT~PAUL~DE~VENCE)
Le Mas d'Artigny - Route de la Colle, 06570 Saint~Paul~de~Vence, France. Tel: +33 4 93 32 84 54

CÔTE D'AZUR (SERRE~CHEVALIER)
L'Auberge du Choucas - 05220 Monetier~Les~Bains, Serre~Chevalier, Hautes~Alpes, France. Tel: +33 4 92 24 42 73

CÔTE D'AZUR (VENCE)
Relais Cantemerle - 258 Chemin Cantemerle, 06140 Vence, France. Tel: +33 4 93 58 08 18

LOIRE VALLEY (AMBOISE)
Château de Pray - Route de Chargé, 37400 Amboise, France. Tel: +33 2 47 57 23 67

LOIRE VALLEY (AMBOISE)
Le Choiseul - 36 Quai Charles Guinot, 37400 Amboise, France. Tel: +33 2 47 30 45 45

LOIRE VALLEY (CHINON)
Château de Danzay - RD 749, 37420 Chinon, France. Tel: +33 2 47 58 46 86

LOIRE VALLEY (CHISSAY~EN~TOURRAINE)
Hostellerie Château de Chissay - 41400 Chissay~en~Touraine, France. Tel: +33 2 54 32 32 01

LOIRE VALLEY (LANGEAIS)
Château de Rochecotte - Saint~Patrice, 37130 Langeais, France. Tel: +33 2 47 96 16 16

LOIRE VALLEY (MISSILLAC)
Domaine de La Bretesche - 44780 Missillac, France. Tel: +33 2 51 76 86 96

LOIRE VALLEY (SAUMUR-CHÊNEHUTTE~LES~TUFFEAUX)
Le Prieuré - 49350 Chênehutte~Les~Tuffeaux, France. Tel: +33 2 41 67 90 14

LOIRE VALLEY (TOURS - LUYNES)
Domaine de Beauvois - Le Pont Clouet, Route de Clere~les~Pins, 37230 Luynes, France. Tel: +33 2 47 55 50 11

LOIRE VALLEY (TOURS - MONTBAZON)
Château d'Artigny - 37250 Montbazon, France. Tel: +33 2 47 34 30 30

LOIRE VALLEY (TOURS - MONTBAZON)
Domaine de La Tortinière - Route de Ballan~Miré, 37250 Montbazon, France. Tel: +33 2 47 34 35 00

MIDI~PYRÉNÉES (CORDES~SUR~CIEL)
Le Grand Ecuyer - Haute de la Cité, 81170 Cordes~Sur~Ciel, France. Tel: +33 5 63 53 79 50

NORMANDY (BAGNOLES DE L'ORNE)
Bois Joli - 12, Avenue Philippe du Rozier, 61140 Bagnoles de L'Orne, France. Tel: +33 2 33 37 92 77

NORMANDY (BREUIL~EN~BESSIN)
Château de Goville - 14330 Breuil~en~Bessin, France. Tel: +33 2 31 22 19 28

NORMANDY (ETRETAT)
Le Donjon - Chemin de Saint Clair, 76790 Etretat, France. Tel: +33 2 35 27 08 23

NORMANDY (HONFLEUR – CRICQUEBOEUF)
Manoir de la Poterie - Chemin Paul Ruel, 14113 Cricqueboeuf, France. Tel: +33 2 31 88 10 40

NORMANDY (PACY~SUR~EURE)
Hostellerie Château de Brécourt - Douains, 27120 Pacy~sur~Eure, France. Tel: +33 2 32 52 40 50

NORTH - PICARDY (ABBEVILLE – ST. RIQUIER)
Abbatis Villa Hôtel Jean De Bruges - 18, Place de L'Eglise, 80135 St. Riquier, France. Tel: +33 3 22 28 30 30

NORTH - PICARDY (BETHUNE - GOSNAY)
La Chartreuse Du Val St Esprit - 62199 Gosnay, France. Tel: +33 3 21 62 80 00

NORTH - PICARDY (CALAIS - RECQUES~SUR~HEM)
Château de Cocove - 62890 Recques~sur~Hem, France. Tel: +33 3 21 82 68 29

▼
NORTH - PICARDY (ELINCOURT~SAINTE~MARGUERITE)
Château de Bellinglise - 60157 Elincourt~Sainte~Marguerite, France. Tel: +33 3 44 96 00 33

NORTH - PICARDY (ERMENONVILLE)
Hostellerie Château d'Ermenonville - 60950 Ermenonville, France. Tel: +33 3 44 54 00 26

NORTH - PICARDY (FÈRE~EN~TARDENOIS)
Château de Fère - 02130 Fère~en~Tardenois, France. Tel: + 33 3 23 82 21 13

NORTH - PICARDY (LILLE)
Carlton Hotel - Rue de Paris, 59000 Lille, France. Tel: +33 3 20 13 33 13

323

Mini Listings Europe

Condé Nast Johansens are delighted to recommend over 320 properties across Europe and The Mediterranean.
Call 0800 269 397 or see the order forms on page 351 to order guides.

NORTH - PICARDY (VERVINS)
La Tour du Roy - 02140 Vervins, France.
Tel: +33 3 23 98 00 11

PARIS (CHAMPS~ELYSÉES)
La Trémoille - 14 Rue de La Trémoille, 75008 Paris, France. Tel: +33 1 56 52 14 00

PARIS (CHAMPS~ELYSÉES)
Hôtel Plaza Athénée - 25 Avenue Montaigne, 75008 Paris, France. Tel: +33 1 53 67 66 65

PARIS (CHAMPS~ELYSÉES)
Hôtel San Regis - 12 Rue Jean Goujon, 75008 Paris, France. Tel: +33 1 44 95 16 16

PARIS (CHAMPS~ELYSÉES)
Résidence Alma Marceau**** - 5 Rue Jean Giraudoux, 75016 Paris, France. Tel: +33 1 53 57 67 89

PARIS (ÉTOILE – PORTE MAILLOT)
L'Hôtel Pergolèse - 3 Rue Pergolèse, 75116 Paris, France. Tel: +33 1 53 64 04 04

PARIS (ÉTOILE – PORTE MAILLOT)
La Villa Maillot - 143 Avenue de Malakoff, 75116 Paris, France. Tel: +33 1 53 64 52 52

PARIS (INVALIDES)
Hôtel Le Tourville - 16 Avenue de Tourville, 75007 Paris, France. Tel: +33 1 47 05 62 62

PARIS (JARDIN DU LUXEMBOURG)
Le Sainte~Beuve - 9 Rue Sainte~Beuve, 75006 Paris, France. Tel: +33 1 45 48 20 07

PARIS (MADELEINE)
Hôtel de L'Arcade - 9 Rue de L'Arcade, 75008 Paris, France. Tel: +33 1 53 30 60 00

PARIS (MADELEINE)
Hôtel Le Lavoisier - 21 Rue Lavoisier, 75008 Paris, France. Tel: +33 1 53 30 06 06

PARIS (OPÉRA – MONTMATRE)
Hôtel Lamartine - 39 Rue Lamartine, 75009 Paris, France. Tel: +33 1 48 78 78 58

PARIS (PANTHÉON)
Hôtel des Grands Hommes - 17 Place du Panthéon, 75005 Paris, France. Tel: +33 1 46 34 19 60

PARIS (PANTHÉON)
Hôtel du Panthéon - 19 Place du Panthéon, 75005 Paris, France. Tel: +33 1 43 54 32 95

PARIS (SAINT~GERMAIN)
ArtusHotel - 34 Rue de Buci, 75006 Paris, France. Tel: +33 1 43 29 07 20

PARIS (SAINT~GERMAIN)
Hôtel Le Saint~Grégoire - 43 Rue de L'Abbé Grégoire, 75006 Paris, France. Tel: 33 1 45 48 23 23

PARIS (SAINT~GERMAIN)
Hôtel Pont Royal - 7 Rue de Montalembert, 75007 Paris, France. Tel: +33 1 42 84 70 00

PARIS (SAINT~GERMAIN)
L' Hôtel - 13, Rue des Beaux Arts, 75006 Paris, France. Tel: +33 1 44 41 99 00

PARIS REGION (CERNAY~LA~VILLE)
Hostellerie Abbaye des Vaux de Cernay - 78720 Cernay~La~Ville, France. Tel: +33 1 34 85 23 00

PARIS REGION (ST. SYMPHORIEN~LE~CHÂTEAU)
Château d'Esclimont - 28700 St. Symphorien~Le~Château, France. Tel: +33 2 37 31 15 15

PARIS REGION (GRESSY~EN~FRANCE – CHANTILLY)
Le Manoir de Gressy - 77410 Gressy~en~France, Roissy Cdg, Nr Paris, France. Tel: +33 1 60 26 68 00

PARIS REGION (VILLE D'AVRAY)
Les Étangs de Corot - 53 Rue de Versailles, 92410 Ville d'Avray, France. Tel: +33 1 41 15 37 00

PARIS REGION (YERRES – ORLY)
Hostellerie Château du Maréchal de Saxe - Domaine de La Grange, 91330 Yerres, France. Tel: +33 1 69 48 78 53

POITOU~CHARENTES (COGNAC – CHÂTEAUBERNARD)
Château de L'Yeuse - 65 Rue de Bellevue, Quartier de echassier, 16100 Châteaubernard, France.
Tel: +33 5 45 36 82 60

POITOU~CHARENTES (POITIERS – MIGNALOUX)
Manoir de Beauvoir Golf & Hôtel - 635 Route de Beauvoir, 86550 Mignaloux – Beauvoir, France.
Tel: +33 5 49 55 47 47

POITOU~CHARENTES (POITIERS – SAINT~MAIXENT~L'ECOLE)
Logis St. Martin - Chemin de Pissot, 79400 Saint~Maixent~L'Ecole, France. Tel: +33 549 0558 68

PROVENCE (AIX~EN~PROVENCE)
Le Pigonnet - 5 Avenue du Pigonnet, 13090 Aix~en~Provence, France. Tel: +33 4 42 59 02 90

PROVENCE (GRIGNAN)
Le Clair de la Plume - Place du Mail, 26230 Grignan, France. Tel: +33 4 75 91 81 30

PROVENCE (GRIGNAN)
Manoir de la Roseraie - Route de Valréas, 26230 Grignan, France. Tel: +33 4 75 46 58 15

PROVENCE (LES~BAUX~DE~PROVENCE)
Mas de l'Oulivie - 13520 Les~Baux~de~Provence, France. Tel: +33 4 90 54 35 78

PROVENCE (LES SAINTES~MARIES~DE~LA~MER)
Mas de La Fouque - Route du Petit Rhône, 13460 Les Saintes~Maries~de~La~Mer, France.
Tel: +33 4 90 97 81 02

PROVENCE (SAINT~RÉMY~DE~PROVENCE)
Château des Alpilles - Route Départementale 31, Ancienne Route du Grès, 13210 Saint~Rémy~de~Provence, France.
Tel: +33 4 90 92 03 33

PROVENCE (UZÈS)
Château d'Arpaillargues - Hôtel Marie d'Agoult, 30700 Uzès, France. Tel: +33 4 66 22 14 48

RHÔNE~ALPES (CHAMBERY – COISE~SAINT~JEAN)
Château de La Tour du Puits - 73800 Coise~Saint~Jean, France. Tel: +33 4 79 28 88 00

RHÔNE~ALPES (COURCHEVEL 1850)
Hôtel Annapurna - 73120 Courchevel (1850), France. Tel: +33 4 79 08 04 60

RHÔNE~ALPES (COURCHEVEL 1850)
Le Kilimandjaro - Route de L'Altiport, 73121 Courchevel 1850 Cedex, France. Tel: +33 4 79 01 18 74

RHÔNE~ALPES (DIVONNE~LES~BAINS)
Château de Divonne - 01220 Divonne~les~Bains, France. Tel: +33 4 50 20 00 32

RHÔNE~ALPES (DIVONNE~LES~BAINS)
Le Domaine de Divonne Casino, Golf & Spa Resort - Avenue des Thermes, 01220 Divonne-les-Bains, France.
Tel: +33 4 50 40 34 34

RHÔNE~ALPES (LES GÊTS)
Chalet Hôtel La Marmotte - 61 Rue du Chéne, 74260 Les Gêts, France. Tel: + 33 4 50 75 80 33

RHÔNE~ALPES (LYON)
La Tour Rose - 22 Rue du Boeuf, 69005 Lyon, France. Tel: +33 4 78 92 69 10

RHÔNE~ALPES (SCIEZ~SUR~LÉMAN)
Château de Coudrée - Domaine de Coudrée, Bonnatrait, 74140 Sciez~sur~Léman, France. Tel: +33 4 50 72 62 33

SOUTH WEST (BIARRITZ)
Hôtel du Palais - Avenue de L'Impératrice, 64200 Biarritz, France. Tel: +33 5 59 41 64 00

SOUTH WEST (LE BUISSON~DE~CADOUIN)
Le Manoir de Bellerive - Route de Siorac, 24480 Le-Buisson~de~Cadouin, France. Tel: +33 5 53 22 16 16

SOUTH WEST (SAINT~JEAN~DE~LUZ)
Hotel Lehen Tokia - Chemin Achotarreta, 64500 Ciboure, Saint~Jean~De~Luz, France. Tel: +33 5 59 47 18 16

SOUTH WEST (SAINTE~RADEGONDE – SAINT~EMILION)
Château de Sanse - 33350 Sainte~Radegonde, France. Tel: +33 5 57 56 41 10

WESTERN LOIRE (CHAMPIGNÉ)
Château des Briottières - 49330 Champigné, France.
Tel: +33 2 41 42 00 02

WESTERN LOIRE (NANTES – LES SORINIÈRES)
Hostellerie Abbaye de Villeneuve - 44480 Nantes – Les Sorinières, France. Tel: +33 2 40 04 40 25

WESTERN LOIRE (NOIRMOUTIER)
Hostellerie du Général d'Elbée - Place du Château, 85330 Noirmoutier~en~L'Isle, France. Tel: +33 2 51 39 10 29

Germany

DÜSSELDORF – WASSENBERG
Hotel Burg Wassenberg **** - Auf Dem Burgberg 17, 41849 Wassenberg, Germany. Tel: +49 2432 9490

OBERWESEL – RHEIN
Burghotel auf Schönburg - 55430 Oberwesel – Rhein, Germany. Tel: +49 67 44 93 930

ROTHENBURG OB DER TAUBER
Hotel Eisenhut - Herrngasse 3-7, 91541 Rothenburg Ob Der Tauber, Germany. Tel: +49 9861 7050

Mini Listings Europe

Condé Nast Johansens are delighted to recommend over 320 properties across Europe and The Mediterranean.
Call 0800 269 397 or see the order forms on page 351 to order guides.

Great Britain & Ireland

ENGLAND (AMBERLEY)
Amberley Castle - Amberley, Nr Arundel, West Sussex BN18 9ND, England. Tel: +44 1798 831 992

ENGLAND (BAMBURGH)
Waren House Hotel - Waren Mill, Bamburgh, Northumberland NE70 7EE, England. Tel: +44 1668 214581

ENGLAND (DERBY - NOTTINGHAM)
Risley Hall Country House Hotel - Derby Road, Risley, Derbyshire DE72 3SS, England. Tel: +44 115 939 9000

ENGLAND (LONDON)
Beaufort House - 45 Beaufort Gardens, Knightsbridge, London SW3 1PN, England. Tel: +44 20 7584 2600

ENGLAND (LONDON)
Draycott House Apartments - 10 Draycott Avenue, Chelsea, London SW3 3AA, England. Tel: +44 20 7584 4659

ENGLAND (LONDON)
Kensington House Hotel - 15-16 Prince Of Wales Terrace, Kensington, London W8 5PQ, England. Tel: +44 20 7937 2345

ENGLAND (LONDON)
Number Eleven Cadogan Gardens - 11 Cadogan Gardens, Sloane Square, Knightsbridge, London SW3 2RJ. Tel: +44 20 7730 7000

ENGLAND (LONDON)
Number Sixteen - 16 Sumner Place, London SW7 3EG, England. Tel: +44 20 7589 5232

ENGLAND (LONDON)
Pembridge Court Hotel - 34 Pembridge Gardens, London W2 4DX, England. Tel: +44 20 7229 9977

ENGLAND (LONDON)
The Academy, The Bloomsbury Town House - 21 Gower Street, London WC1E 6HG, England. Tel: +44 20 7631 4115

ENGLAND (LONDON)
The Beaufort - 33 Beaufort Gardens, Knightsbridge, London SW3 1PP, England. Tel: +44 20 7584 5252

ENGLAND (LONDON)
The Colonnade, The Little Venice Town House - 2 Warrington Crescent, London W9 1ER, England. Tel: +44 20 7286 1052

ENGLAND (LONDON)
The Cranley - 10-12 Bina Gardens, South Kensington, London SW5 0LA, England. Tel: +44 20 7373 0123

ENGLAND (LONDON)
The Dorchester - Park Lane, Mayfair, London W1A 2HJ, England. Tel: +44 20 7629 8888

ENGLAND (LONDON)
The Halkin - 5 Halkin Street, Belgravia, London SW1X 7DJ, England. Tel: +44 20 7333 1000

ENGLAND (LONDON)
The Leonard - 15 Seymour Street, London W1H 7JW, England. Tel: +44 20 7935 2010

ENGLAND (LONDON)
The Milestone Hotel and Apartments - 1 Kensington Court, London, W8 5DL, England. Tel: +44 20 7917 1000

ENGLAND (LONDON)
Twenty Nevern Square - 20 Nevern Square, London SW5 9PD, England. Tel: +44 20 7565 9555

ENGLAND (LYNTON)
Hewitt's - Villa Spaldi - North Walk, Lynton, Devon EX35 6HJ, England. Tel: +44 1598 752 293

ENGLAND (MELTON MOWBRAY)
Stapleford Park Hotel, Spa, Golf & Sporting Estate - Nr Melton Mowbray, Leicestershire LE14 2EF, England. Tel: +44 1572 787 522

Greece

ATHENS
Hotel Pentelikon - 66 Diligianni Street, 14562 Athens, Greece. Tel: +30 10 62 30 650-6

CRETE
St Nicolas Bay Hotel - 72100 Agios Nikolaos, Crete, Greece. Tel: +30 2841 025041/2/3

CRETE
The Peninsula at Porto Elounda de luxe Resort - 72053 Elounda, Crete, Greece. Tel: +30 84 10 41 903

PAROS
Astir of Paros - Kolymbithres, Naoussa, 84401 Paro, Greece. Tel: +30 284 51976

Italy

CAMPANIA (POSITANO)
Hotel Villa Franca - Viale Pasitea 318, 84017 Positano (SA), Italy. Tel: +39 089 875655

CAMPANIA (POSITANO)
Hotel Poseidon - Via Pasitea 148, 84017 Positano (Salerno), Italy. Tel: +39 089 811111

CAMPANIA (RAVELLO)
Hotel Villa Maria - Via S.Chiara 2, 84010 Ravello (SA), Italy. Tel: +39 089 857255

CAMPANIA (SAN. AGATA SUI DUE GOLFI)
Oasi Olimpia Relais - Via Deserto 26, San Agata sui due Golfi, 80064 Hassa Lubrense (NA), Italy. Tel: +39 081 8080560

CAMPANIA (SORRENTO)
Grand Hotel Cocumella - Via Cocumella 7, 80065 Sant'Agnello, Sorrento, Italy. Tel: +39 081 878 2933

CAMPANIA (SORRENTO)
Grand Hotel Excelsior Vittoria - Piazza Tasso 34, 80067 Sorrento (Naples), Italy. Tel: +39 081 807 1044

EMILIA ROMAGNA (BAGNO DI ROMAGNA TERME)
Hotel Tosco Romagnolo - Piazza Dante Alighieri 2, 47021 Bagno di Romagna Terme, Italy. Tel: +39 0543 911260

EMILIA ROMAGNA (BOLOGNA)
Grand Hotel Baglioni - Via Indipendenza 8, 40121 Bologna, Italy. Tel: +39 051 225445

EMILIA ROMAGNA (BRISIGHELLA)
Relais Torre Pratesi - Via Cavina 11, 48013 Brisighella, Italy. Tel: +39 0546 84545

EMILIA ROMAGNA (FERRARA)
Ripagrande Hotel - Via Ripagrande 21, 44100 Ferrara, Italy. Tel: +39 0532 765250

EMILIA ROMAGNA (RICCIONE)
Hotel des Nations - Lungomare Costituzione 2, 47838 Riccione (Rn), Italy. Tel: +39 0541 647878

LAZIO (PALO LAZIALE – ROME)
La Posta Vecchia - Loc. Palo Laziale, 00055 Ladispoli, Rome, Italy. Tel: +39 0699 49501

LAZIO (ROME)
Hotel Aventino - Via San. Domenico 10, 00153 Rome, Italy. Tel: +39 06 5745 174

LAZIO (ROME)
Hotel Farnese - Via Alessandro Farnese 30 (Angolo Viale Giulio Cesare), 00192 Rome, Italy. Tel: +39 06 321 25 53/4

LAZIO (ROME)
Hotel Giulio Cesare - Via degli Scipioni 287, 00192 Rome, Italy. Tel: +39 06 321 0751

LIGURIA (FINALE LIGURE)
Hotel Punta Est - Via Aurelia 1, 17024 Finale Ligure, Italy. Tel: +39 019 600611

LIGURIA (SESTRI - LEVANTE)
Hotel Vis à Vis - Via della Chiusa 28, 16039 Sestri Levante, (GE), Italy. Tel: +39 0185 42661/480801

LOMBARDY (ERBUSCO - FRANCIACORTA)
L'Albereta - Via Vittorio Emanuele 11, 25030 Erbusco (Bs), Italy. Tel: +39 030 7760 550

LOMBARDY (MANTOVA)
Albergo San Lorenzo - Piazza Concordia 14, 46100 Mantova, Italy. Tel: +39 0376 220500

PIEMONTE (CUNEO)
Lovera Palace Hotel - Via Roma, 37, 12100 Cuneo, Italy. Tel: +39 0171 690 420

PIEMONTE (STRESA – LAKE MAGGIORE)
Hotel Villa Aminta - Via Sempione Nord 123, 28838 Stresa (VB), Italy. Tel: +39 0323 933 818

Mini Listings Europe

Condé Nast Johansens are delighted to recommend over 320 properties across Europe and The Mediterranean.
Call 0800 269 397 or see the order forms on page 351 to order guides.

PIEMONTE (TORINO)
Hotel Victoria - Via Nino Costa 4, 10123 Torino, Italy.
Tel: +39 011 56 11909

PUGLIA (SAVELLETRI DI FASANO)
Masseria San Domenico - Litoranea 379, 72010 Savelletri di Fasano (Brindisi) Italy. Tel: +39 080 482 7990

SICILY (ETNA)
Hotel Villa Paradiso dell'Etna - Via Per Viagrande 37, 95037 San Giovanni La Punta, Italy. Tel: +39 095 7512409

SICILY (GIARDINI NAXOS)
Hellenia Yachting Hotel - Via Jannuzzo 41, 98035 Giardini Naxos (ME), Italy. Tel: +39 (0)942 51737

SICILY (TAORMINA RIVIERA – MARINA D'AGRO)
Hotel Baia Taormina - Statale Dello Ionio 39, 98030 Marina D'Agro (ME), Italy. Tel: +39 0942 756292

▼
TRENTINO - ALTO ADIGE (MADONNA DI CAMPIGLIO)
Hotel Lorenzetti - Via Dolomiti Di Brenta 119, 38084 Madonna Di Campiglio (Tn) Italy. Tel: +39 0465 44 14 04

TRENTINO - ALTO ADIGE (MARLING – MERAN)
Romantik Hotel Oberwirt - St Felixweg 2, 39020 Marling – Meran, Italy. Tel: +39 0473 44 71 11

TRENTINO - ALTO ADIGE (MERAN)
Park Hotel Mignon - Via Grabmayr 5, 39012 Meran, Italy. Tel: +39 0473 230353

TRENTINO – ALTO ADIGE (NOVA LEVANTE)
Posthotel Weisses Rössl - Via Carezza 30, 39056 Nova Levante (Bz), Dolomites, Italy. Tel: +39 0471 613113

TRENTINO – ALTO ADIGE (SAN CASSIANO)
Hotel & Spa Rosa Alpina - Strada Micura de Rue 20, 39030 San Cassiano (BZ) Italy.. Tel: +39 0471 849500

TUSCANY (ASCIANO - SIENA)
CasaBianca - Loc. Casabianca , 53041 Asciano (SI), Italy. Tel: +39 0577 704362

TUSCANY (CASTIGLION FIORENTINO)
Relais San Pietro in Polvano - Località Polvano, 52043 Castiglion Fiorentino (AR), Italy. Tel: +39 0575 650100

TUSCANY (COLLE VAL D'ELSA - SIENA)
Relais della Rovere - Via Piemonte 10, Loc. Badia, 53034 Colle Val D'Elsa (SI), Italy. Tel: +39 0577 924696

TUSCANY (ELBA ISLAND - CAPOLIVERI)
Grand Hotel Elba International - Baia della Fontanella, Isola D'Elba, 57031 Capoliveri (LI), Italy. Tel: +39 0565 946111

TUSCANY (FLORENCE)
Hotel J and J - Via di Mezzo 20, 50121 Florence, Italy. Tel: +39 055 263121

TUSCANY (FLORENCE)
Villa Montartino - Via Gherardo Silvani 151, 50125 Florence, Italy. Tel: +39 055 223520

TUSCANY (LIDO DI CAMAIORE)
Hotel Villa Ariston - Viale C. Colombo 355, 55043 Lido Di Camaiore – Lucca, Italy. Tel: +39 0584 610633

TUSCANY (MONTERIGGIONI – SIENA)
Hotel Monteriggioni - Via 1 Maggio 4, 53035 Monteriggioni, Italy. Tel: +39 0577 305009

TUSCANY (MONTERIGGIONI – STROVE)
Castel Pietraio - Strada Di Strove 33, 53035 Monteriggioni, Italy. Tel: +39 0577 300020

TUSCANY (PIEVESCOLA)
Hotel Relais La Suvera - 53030 Pievescola – Siena, Italy. Tel: +39 0577 960300

TUSCANY (PORTO ERCOLE)
Il Pellicano - 58018 Porto Ercole (Gr), Tuscany, Italy. Tel: +39 0564 858111

TUSCANY (PORTO SANTO STEFANO – ARGENTARIO)
Hotel Torre di Cala Piccola - Porto Santo Stefano, 58019 Argentario, Italy. Tel: +39 0564 825111

TUSCANY (PUNTA ALA)
Hotel Cala del Porto - Via Del Pozzo, 58040 Punta Ana, Italy. Tel: +39 0564 922455

TUSCANY (RADDA IN CHIANTI)
Palazzo Leopoldo - Via Roma 33, 53017 Radda In Chianti, Italy. Tel: +39 0577 735605

TUSCANY (SIENA)
Hotel Certosa di Maggiano - Strada Di Certosa 82, 53100 Siena, Italy. Tel: +39 0577 288180

UMBRIA (ASSISI)
Romantik Hotel Le Silve di Armenzano - 06081 Loc. Armenzano, Assisi (PG), Italy. Tel: +39 075 801 9000

UMBRIA (COLLE SAN PAOLO - PERUGIA)
Romantik Hotel Villa di Monte Solare - Via Montali 7, 06070 Colle San Paolo - Panicale (PG), Italy. Tel: +39 075 832376

UMBRIA (GUBBIO)
Castello di Petroia - Località Petroia, 06020 Gubbio (Pg), Italy. Tel: +39 075 92 02 87 / 92 01 09

UMBRIA (OSCANO - PERUGIA)
Castello dell'Oscano Historical Residence - 06134 Perugia, Localita Cenerente, Italy. Tel: +39 075 584371

UMBRIA (PIAZZANO - CORTONA)
Villa di Piazzano - Località Piazzano, 06069 Tuoro Sul Trasimeno (PG), Italy. Tel: +39 075 826226

UMBRIA (SPOLETO)
Villa Milani - Residenza d'Epoca - Loc. Colle Attivoli 4, 06049 Spoleto, Italy. Tel: +39 0743 225056

UMBRIA (TODI)
Hotel Bramante - Via Orvietana 48, 06059 Todi (PG), Italy. Tel: +39 075 8348381/2/3

VENETIA (BASSANO DEL GRAPPA)
Hotel Ca' Sette - Via Cunizza Da Romano 4, 36061 Bassano del Grappa, Italy. Tel: +39 0424 383350

VENETIA (LIDO DI JESELO)
Park Hotel Brasilia - Via Levantina, 30017 Lido Di Jesolo, Italy. Tel: +39 0421 380851

VENETIA (MOGLIANO VENETO)
Hotel Villa Condulmer - Via Preganziol 1, 31020 Mogliano Veneto, Italy. Tel: +39 041 5972 700

VENETIA (NEGRAR – VERONA)
Relais La Magioca - Via Moron 3, 37024 Negrar (Verona), Italy. Tel: +39 045 600 0167

VENETIA (SARCEDO - VICENZA)
Casa Belmonte Relais - Via Belmonte 2, 36030 Sarcedo, Italy. Tel: +39 0445 884833

VENETIA (VENICE)
Hotel Giorgione - SS. Apostoli 4587, 30131 Venice, Italy. Tel: +39 041 522 5810

VENETIA (VENICE – LIDO)
Albergo Quattro Fontane - 30126 Lido Di Venezia, Venice, Italy. Tel: +39 041 526 0227

Luxembourg

REMICH
Hotel Saint~Nicolas - 31 Esplanade, 5533 Remich, Luxembourg. Tel: +352 2666 3

Monaco

MONTE~CARLO
Monte~Carlo Beach Hotel - Avenue Princesse Grace, 06190 Roquebrune – Cap~Martin, France. Tel: +377 92 16 25 25

The Netherlands

AMSTERDAM
Ambassade Hotel - Herengracht 341, 1016 Az Amsterdam, The Netherlands. Tel: +31 20 5550222

AMSTERDAM
Blakes - Keizersgracht 384, 1016 GB Amsterdam, The Netherlands. Tel: +31 20 530 20 10

AMSTERDAM
Seven One Seven - Prinsengracht 717, 1017 Jw Amsterdam, The Netherlands. Tel: +31 20 42 70 717

LATTROP
Hotel de Holtweijde - Spiekweg 7, 7635 Lattrop, The Netherlands. Tel: +31 541 229 234

▼
MAASTRICHT
Château St Gerlach - Joseph Corneli Allée 1, 6301 KK Valkenburg A/D Geul, Maastricht, The Netherlands. Tel: +31 43 608 88 88

OOTMARSUM
Hotel de Wiemsel - Winhofflaan 2, 7631 Hx Ootmarsum, The Netherlands. Tel: +31 541 292 155

Mini Listings Europe

Condé Nast Johansens are delighted to recommend over 320 properties across Europe and The Mediterranean.
Call 0800 269 397 or see the order forms on page 351 to order guides.

Norway

OPPDAL – DOVREFJELL
Kongsvold Fjeldstue - Dovrefjell, 7340 Oppdal, Norway.
Tel: +47 72 40 43 40

OSLO
Hotel Bastion - Skippergaten 7, 0152 Oslo, Norway.
Tel: +47 22 47 77 00

SOLVORN
Walaker Hotell - 6879 Solvorn, Sogn, Norway.
Tel: +47 576 82080

VOSS
Fleischers Hotel - 5700 Voss, Norway.
Tel: +47 56 52 05 00

Portugal

ALENTEJO (REDONDO)
Convento de São Paulo - Aldeia Da Serra, 7170 –120 Redondo, Portugal. Tel: +351 266 989160

ALGARVE (LAGOS)
Romantik Hotel Vivenda Miranda - Porto de Mós, 8600 Lagos, Portugal. Tel: +351 282 763222

LISBON & TAGUS VALLEY (LISBON)
Solar Do Castelo - Rua das Cozinhas 2, 1100–181 Lisbon, Portugal. Tel: +351 218 870 909

LISBON & TAGUS VALLEY (SINTRA)
Tivoli Hotel Palácio de Seteais - Rua Barbosa de Bocage, 10, Seteais, 2710 Sintra, Portugal. Tel: +351 219 233 200

▼
MADEIRA (FUNCHAL)
Quinta da Bela Vista - Caminho do Avista Navios 4, 9000 Funchal, Madeira, Portugal. Tel: +351 291 706400

MADEIRA (FUNCHAL)
Quinta das Vistas Palacio Gardens - Caminho de Santa Antonio 52-A, 9000-187 Funchal, Madeira, Portugal. Tel: +351 291 750 007

MADEIRA (FUNCHAL)
Quinta do Estreito - Rua José Joaquim da Costa, Estreito de Câmara De Lobos, 9325–034 Madeira, Portugal. Tel: +351 291 910530

MADEIRA (FUNCHAL)
Quinta do Monte - Caminho do Monte 192, 9050-288 Funchal, Madeira, Portugal. Tel: +351 291 780 100

MADEIRA (FUNCHAL)
Quinta Perestrello - Rua do Dr. Pita 3, 9000-089 Funchal, Madeira, Portugal. Tel: +351 291 706700

OPORTO & NORTHERN PORTUGAL (PINHÃO)
Vintage House Hotel - Lugar da Ponte, 5085-034 Pinhão, Portugal. Tel: +351 22 371 999 / 375 4633

Spain

ANDALUCÍA (ANTEQUERA)
Hotel Antequera Golf - Sta Catalina S/N, 29200 Antequera, Spain. Tel: +34 95 27 04 531

ANDALUCÍA (ARCOS DE LA FRONTERA)
Hacienda El Santiscal - Avda. El Santiscal 129 (Lago De Arcos), 11630 Arcos de La Frontera, Spain.
Tel: +34 956 70 83 13

ANDALUCÍA (BENAHAVIS – MARBELLA)
Amanhavis Hotel - Calle del Pilar 3, 29679 Benahavis, Málaga, Spain. Tel: +34 952 85 60 26

ANDALUCÍA (DOÑANA NATIONAL PARK)
El Cortijo de Los Mimbrales - Ctra del Rocio - Matalascañas, Km 30, 21750 Almonte (Huelva), Spain.
Tel: +34 959 44 22 37

ANDALUCÍA (GRANADA)
Hotel La Bobadilla - Finca La Bobadilla, Apto. 144, 18300 Loja, Granada, Spain. Tel: +34 958 32 18 61

ANDALUCÍA (JEREZ DE LA FRONTERA)
Hotel Villa Jerez - Avda. de La Cruz Roja 7, 11407 Jerez de La Frontera, Spain. Tel: +34 956 15 31 00

ANDALUCÍA (MÁLAGA)
Hotel La Casona de la Ciudad **** - C/Marqués de Salvatierra 5, 29400 Ronda, Málaga, Spain.
Tel: +34 952 87 95 95/96

ANDALUCÍA (MÁLAGA)
Hotel La Fuente de La Higuera - Partido de Los Frontones, 29400 Ronda, Málaga, Spain.
Tel: +34 95 2 11 43 55

ANDALUCÍA (MÁLAGA)
La Posada del Torcal - 29230 Villanueva de La Concepción, Málaga, Spain. Tel: +34 952 03 11 77

ANDALUCÍA (MÁLAGA)
El Molino de Santillán - Ctra. de Macharaviaya, Km 3, 29730 Rincón de La Victoria, Málaga, Spain.
Tel: +34 952 40 09 49

ANDALUCÍA (MARBELLA – ESTEPONA)
Las Dunas Beach Hotel & Spa - La Boladilla Baja, Crta. de Cádiz Km 163.5, 29689 Marbella – Estepona (Málaga), Spain. Tel: +34 952 79 43 45

ANDALUCÍA (MIJAS~COSTA)
Hotel Byblos Andaluz - Mijas Golf, 29650 Mijas~Costa, Málaga, Spain. Tel: +34 952 47 30 50

ANDALUCÍA (SEVILLA)
Cortijo El Esparragal - Ctra. de Merida, KM 795, 41860 Gerena (Sevilla), Spain. Tel: +34 955 78 27 02

ANDALUCÍA (SEVILLA)
Hacienda Benazuza El Bulli Hotel - 41800 Sanlúcar La Mayor, Seville, Spain. Tel: +34 955 70 33 44

ANDALUCÍA (SEVILLA)
Hotel Cortijo Águila Real - Ctra. Guillena–Burguillos Km 4, 41210 Guillena, Sevilla, Spain. Tel: +34 955 78 50 06

ANDALUCÍA (SEVILLA)
Hotel Hacienda La Boticaria - Ctra. Alcalá - Utrera Km.2, 41500 Alcalá de Guadaira, Sevilla, Spain.
Tel: +34 955 69 88 20

ANDALUCÍA (SEVILLA)
Palacio Marqués de la Gomera - C/ San Pedro 20, 41640 Osuna, Sevilla, Spain. Tel: +34 95 4 81 22 23

ANDALUCÍA (SEVILLA)
Palacio de San Benito - c/San Benito S/N, 41370 Cazalla de La Sierra, Sevilla, Spain. Tel: +34 954 88 33 36

ANDALUCÍA (SOTOGRANDE)
Almenara Golf Hotel & Spa - Avenida Almenara, 11310 Sotogrande, Spain. Tel: + 34 956 58 20 00

ARAGÓN (TERUEL)
La Parada del Compte - Antigua Estación de Ferrocarril, 44597 Torre del Compte, Teruel, Spain.
Tel: +34 978 76 90 72

ASTURIAS (VILLAMAYOR)
Palacio de Cutre - La Goleta S/N Villamayor, 33583 Infiesto, Asturias, Spain. Tel: +34 985 70 80 72

BALEARIC ISLANDS (IBIZA)
Cas Gasi - Apdo. Correos 117, 07814 Santa Gertrudis, Ibiza, Balearic Islands. Tel: +34 971 19 71 73

▼
BALEARIC ISLANDS (MALLORCA)
Ca's Xorc - Carretera de Deía, Km 56,1 07100 Sóller, Mallorca, Balearic Islands. Tel: +34 971 63 82 80

BALEARIC ISLANDS (MALLORCA)
Can Furiós Petit Hotel - Cami Vell Binibona 11, Binibona, 07314 Caimari, Mallorca, Balearic Islands.
Tel: +34 971 51 57 51

BALEARIC ISLANDS (MALLORCA)
Hotel Monnaber Nou - Possessió Monnaber Nou, 07310 Campanet, Mallorca, Balearic Islands.
Tel: +34 971 87 71 76

BALEARIC ISLANDS (MALLORCA)
Hotel Vistamar de Valldemossa - Ctra Valldemossa, Andratx Km. 2, 07170 Valldemossa, Mallorca, Balearic Islands. Tel: +34 971 61 23 00

BALEARIC ISLANDS (MALLORCA)
Read's - Ca'N Moragues, 07320 Santa María, Mallorca, Balearic Islands. Tel: +34 971 14 02 62

BALEARIC ISLANDS (MALLORCA)
Sa Posada d'Aumallia - Camino Son Prohens 1027, 07200 Felanitx, Mallorca, Balearic Islands. Tel: +34 971 58 26 57

BALEARIC ISLANDS (MALLORCA)
Scott's - Plaza de La Iglesia 12, 07350 Binissalem, Mallorca, Balearic Islands. Tel: +34 971 87 01 00

CANARY ISLANDS (FUERTEVENTURA)
Elba Palace Golf Hotel - Urb. Fuerteventura Golf Club, 35610 Antigua, Fuerteventura. Tel: +34 928 16 39 22

CANARY ISLANDS (GRAN CANARIA)
Gran Hotel Costa Meloneras **** - C/Mar Mediterráneo 1, 35100 maspalomas, Gran Canaria, Canary Islands.
Tel: +34 928 12 81 00

Mini Listings Europe

Condé Nast Johansens are delighted to recommend over 320 properties across Europe and The Mediterranean.
Call 0800 269 397 or see the order forms on page 351 to order guides.

CANARY ISLANDS (LANZAROTE)
Finca de Las Salinas - C/ La Cuesta 17, 35570 Yaiza, Lanzarote, Canary Islands. Tel: +34 928 83 03 25

CANARY ISLANDS (LANZAROTE)
Gran Meliá Volcán - Urb. Castillo del Aguila, Playa Blanco, Lanzarote, Canary Islands. Tel: +34 928 51 91 85

CANARY ISLANDS (TENERIFE)
Gran Hotel Bahía del Duque Resort - 38660 Adeje, Costa Adeje, Tenerife South, Canary Islands. Tel: +34 922 74 69 33/34

CANARY ISLANDS (TENERIFE)
Hotel Botánico *****GL - Avda. Richard J. Yeoward, Urb. Botánico, 38400 Puerto de La Cruz, Tenerife, Canary Islands. Tel: +34 922 38 14 00

CANARY ISLANDS (TENERIFE)
Hotel Jardín Tropical - Calle Gran Bretaña, 38670 Costa Adeje, Tenerife, Canary Islands. Tel: +34 922 74 60 00

CANTABRIA (VILLACARRIEDO)
Palacio de Soñanes - Bomo Quintanal 1, Villacarriedo, Cantabria, Spain. Tel: +34 942 59 06 00

CASTILLA~LA MANCHA (ALMAGRO)
La Casa del Rector - c/Pedro Oviedo 8, 13270 Almagro, Ciudad Real, Spain. Tel: +34 926 26 12 59

CASTILLA Y LEÓN (ÁVILA)
El Milano Real - C/ Toleo S/N, Hoyos del Espino, 05634 Ávila, Spain. Tel: +34 920 349 108

CASTILLA Y LEÓN (SALAMANCA)
Hotel Rector - Rector Esperabé 10–Apartado 399, 37008 Salamanca, Spain. Tel: +34 923 21 84 82

CASTILLA Y LEÓN (SEGOVIA)
Caserío de Lobones - Valverde del Majano, 40140 Segovia, Spain. Tel: +34 921 12 84 08

CATALUÑA (BARCELONA)
Hotel Claris - Pau Claris 150, 08009 Barcelona, Spain. Tel: +34 934 87 62 62

CATALUÑA (BARCELONA)
Hotel Colón - Avenida de La Catedral 7, 08002 Barcelona, Spain. Tel: +34 933 01 14 04

CATALUÑA (BARCELONA)
The Gallery - Rossellón 249, 08008 Barcelona, Spain. Tel: +34 934 15 99 11

CATALUÑA (COSTA BRAVA)
Hotel Rigat Park - Playa de Fenals, 17310 Lloret de Mar, Costa Brava, Spain. Tel: +34 972 36 52 00

CATALUÑA (GERONA)
Hotel Golf Peralada - C/ Rocaberti S/N, 17491 peralada, Gerona, Spain. Tel: +34 972 53 88 30

CATALUÑA (GERONA)
Mas Falgarona - Avinyonet de Puigventos, 17742 Gerona, Spain. Tel: +34 972 54 66 28

CATALUÑA (SITGES)
Hotel Estela Barcelona - Avda. Port d'Aiguadolç S/N, 08870 Sitges (Barcelona), Spain. Tel: +34 938 11 45 45

CATALUÑA (TARRAGONA)
Hotel Termes Montbrió Resort, Spa & Park - Carrer Nou 38, 43340 Montbrió del Camp (Tarragona), Spain. Tel: +34 977 81 40 00

CATALUÑA (VILADRAU - GERONA)
Xalet La Coromina - Carretera de Vic S/N, 17406 Viladrau, Spain. Tel: +34 938 84 92 64

MADRID (MADRID)
Antiguo Convento - C/ de Las Monjas, S/N Boadilla del Monte, 28660 Madrid, Spain.. Tel: + 34 91 632 22 20

MADRID (MADRID)
Hotel Villa Real - Plaza de Las Cortes 10, 28014 Madrid, Spain. Tel: +34 914 20 37 67

MURCIA (CARTAGENA - LA MANGA)
Hyatt Regency La Manga - Los Belones, 30385 Cartagena, Murcia, Spain. Tel: +34 968 33 12 34

VALENCIA (DÉNIA)
Hotel Buena Vista - Partida Tossalet 82, La Xara, 03709 Dénia, Spain. Tel: +34 965 78 79 95

VALENCIA (XÀTIVA)
Hotel Mont Sant - Subida Al Castillo, s/n Xàtiva, 46800 Valencia, Spain. Tel: +34 962 27 50 81

Sweden

BORGHOLM
Halltorps Gästgiveri - 38792 Borgholm, Sweden. Tel: +46 485 85000

HESTRA – SMÅLAND
Hestravikens Wärdshus - vik, 33027, hestra, Småland, Sweden. Tel: +46 370 33 68 00

LAGAN
Romantik Hotel Toftaholm Herrgård - Toftaholm Pa, 34014 Lagan, Sweden. Tel: +46 370 440 55

MALMO - GENARP
Häckeberga Manor - 24013 Genarp, Sweden. Tel: +46 40 48 04 40

TÄLLBERG
Romantik Hotel Åkerblads - 79370 Tällberg, Sweden. Tel: +46 247 50800

Switzerland

CHÂTEAU D'OEX
Hostellerie Bon Accueil - 1837 Château d'Oex, Switzerland. Tel: +41 26 924 6320

GSTAAD
Le Grand Chalet - Neueretstrasse, 3780 Gstaad, Switzerland. Tel: +41 33 748 7676

KANDERSTEG
Royal Park ***** Hotel - 3718 Kandersteg, Bernese Oberland, Switzerland. Tel: +41 33 675 88 88

Turkey

ANTALYA
Marina Residence & Restaurant - Mermerli Sokak No. 15, Kaleici, 07100 Antalya, Turkey. Tel: +90 242 247 5490

ANTALYA
Outdoor Centre Resort - Gift Gesmeier Mevkii, Beldibi, Antalya, Turkey. Tel: +90 242 824 9666

ANTALYA
Renaissance Antalya Resort - PO Box 654, 07004 Beldibi - Kemer, Antalya, Turkey. Tel: +90 242 824 84 31

ANTALYA
Talya Hotel - Fevzi Çakmak Caddesi No. 30, 07100 Antalya, Turkey. Tel: +90 242 248 6800

ANTALYA
Tekeli Konaklari - Dizdar Hasan Sokak, Kaleici, Antalya, Turkey. Tel: +90 242 244 54 65

ANTALYA
Tuvana Residence - Tuzcular Mahallesi, Karanlik Sokak 7, 07100 Kaleiçi - Antalya,Turkey. Tel: +90 242 247 60 15

BODRUM
Divan Palmira Hotel - Kelesharim Cad 6, 48483 Türkbükü – Bodrum, Turkey. Tel: +90 252 377 5601

BODRUM
L'Ambience Hotel - Bodrum - Eski ÇeSme Meukii, Gümbet Kavsagi, 48400 Bodrum - Mugla, Turkey. Tel: +90 252 313 83 30

GÖREME – CAPPADOCIA
CCS - Cappadocia Cave Suites - Gafelli Mahallesi, unlü Sokak, 05180 Göreme – Nevsehir, Turkey. Tel: +90 384 271 2800

KALKAN
Hotel Villa Mahal - P.K. 4 Kalkan, 07960 Antalya, Turkey. Tel: +90 242 844 32 68

UGHISAR - CAPPADOCIA
Museum Hotel - Tekelli Mahallesi 1, Urghisar - Nevsehir, Turkey. Tel: +90 384 219 22 20

ÜRGÜP - CAPPADOCIA
Ürgüp Evi - Esbelli Mahallesi 54, 5400 Ürgüp-Nevsehir, Turkey. Tel: +90 384 341 3173

NORTHERN CYPRUS (GIRNE - KYRENIA)
Hotel Bellapais Gardens - Crusader Road, Bellapais, Girne, Northern Cyprus. Tel: +90 392 815 60 66

NORTHERN CYPRUS (GIRNE)
The Hideaway Club - Karaman Road, Edremit, Girne, Northen Cyprus. Tel: +90 392 822 2620

THE WHITE COMPANY
LONDON

Elegant Toiletries and Guest Amenities available exclusively from Pacific Direct

Email: sales@pacificdirect.co.uk   www.pacificdirect.co.uk   Worldwide Sales Telephone (+44) 1234 347 140   USA Toll Free 1-877-363-4732

exceed your guests' expectations – luxury toiletries and amenities from **pacific direct**

Pacific Direct

www.pacificdirect.co.uk

international telephone:
(+44) 1234 347 140

e-mail sales@pacificdirect.co.uk

USA office:
call toll free 1-8777-363-4732

e-mail pdirectusa@aol.com

Index by Property

A

The Abbot's Fireside Hotel	Elham	119
Abbots Oak	Coalville	125
Aberdeen Lodge	Dublin	243
Acorn Inn	Evershot	85
Andrew's On The Weir	Porlock Weir	178
Apsley House	Bath	12
Ardeonaig	Killin	271
Ashwick Country House Hotel	Dulverton	175
The Austwick Country House Hotel	Austwick	220

B

Bae Abermaw	Barmouth	290
Balgonie Country House	Ballater	255
Ballachulish House	Ballachulish	257
Barcaldine House	Oban	259
Barnsdale Lodge	Rutland Water	128
Bath Lodge Hotel	Bath	17
The Beeches Hotel And Victorian Gardens	Norwich	147
Beechwood Hotel	North Walsham	145
The Bell At Skenfrith	Monmouth	294
Bella Luce Hotel & Restaurant	Guernsey	235
The Beresford	Birkenhead	133
Beryl	Wells	183
Bibury Court	Bibury	93
Biggin Hall	Biggin-By-Hartington	58
The Blue Bell Hotel	Belford	156
The Blue Lion	East Witton	223
Boar's Head Hotel	Burton Upon Trent	59
The Boar's Head Hotel	Harrogate	225
Bontddu Hall	Barmouth	291
Boscundle Manor	St. Austell	35
Bowfield Hotel & Country Club	Glasgow Airport	276
Broadoaks Country House	Windermere	55
Brook Meadow Hotel	Chester	25
Broom Hall Country Hotel	Thetford	152
Brovey Lair	Ovington	151
Browns Hotel, Wine Bar & Brasserie	Tavistock	80
Broxton Hall Country House Hotel	Chester	24
Bryn Tegid Country House	Bala	289
Buckingham's Hotel & Restaurant With One Table	Chesterfield	60
Burpham Country House Hotel	Arundel	204

C

Caldecott Hall	Great Yarmouth	137
Caragh Lodge	Caragh Lake	245
The Carpenters Arms	Stanton Wick	18
Cashel Palace Hotel	Cashel	250
Castle Hotel	Conwy	284
Castleton House Hotel	Forfar	256
Charlton Kings Hotel	Cheltenham	95
Chase Lodge	Hampton Court	197
The Chequers At Slaugham	Handcross	209
The Chequers Inn	Froggatt Edge	62
Chestnut House	Woolavington	187
Clarendon House	Kenilworth	199
Clarice House	Bury St. Edmunds	190
Cockliffe Country House Hotel	Nottingham	158
Combe House Hotel & Restaurant	Exeter	72
Compton House	Axbridge	173
Congham Hall	Kings Lynn	143
Conrah Country House Hotel	Aberystwyth	282
Coopershill House	Riverstown	249
Cormorant On The River, Hotel & Riverside Restaurant	Fowey	29
Corriegour Lodge Hotel	Fort Willam	265
The Cottage Country House Hotel	Nottingham	159
Coulsworthy House	Combe Martin	70
The Countryman At Trink Hotel	St Ives	36
The County Hotel	Bath	13
The Cricketers	Clavering	91

▼

Crosby Lodge Country House	Carlisle	43
Crouchers Country Hotel & Restaurant	Chichester	207
The Crown Hotel	Exford	176
The Crown Hotel	Stamford	131
The Crown House	Great Chesterford	92
Crown Lodge Hotel	Wisbech	22
Culduthel Lodge	Inverness	266
Culzean Castle – The Eisenhower Apartment	Ayr	277

D

Dale Head Hall Lakeside Hotel	Keswick	49
Dannah Farm Country House	Belper	57
Dunsley Hall	Whitby	228

E

The Eastbury Hotel	Sherborne	86
The Edgemoor	Bovey Tracey	68
Egerton Grey	Cardiff	300
Elderton Lodge Hotel & Langtry Restaurant	North Walsham	146
Emlagh House	Dingle	246
Eulah Country House	Jersey	238

F

The Falcon Hotel	Castle Ashby	154
Fallowfields	Oxford	163
Farthings Hotel & Restaurant	Taunton	180
Fayrer Garden House Hotel	Windermere	53
The Feathers Hotel	Ledbury	111
Felbrigg Lodge	Holt	141
Fernhill Hotel	Portpatrick	264
Forge Hotel	Chichester	208
The Four Seasons Hotel	Loch Earn	272
The Frog At Port Dunstaffnage	Oban	260
Frogg Manor Hotel & Restaurant	Chester	23

G

The George	Cavendish	193
The George Hotel	Dorchester-On-Thames	161
The George Hotel	Cranbrook	117
The George Inn	Warminster	216
Glangrwyney Court	Crickhowell	298
Glebe Farm House	Stratford-Upon-Avon	200
Glencot House	Wells	184
Glewstone Court	Ross-On-Wye	113
Gordleton Mill Inn	Lymington	106
Gorman's Clifftop House & Restaurant	Dingle Peninsula	247
The Granville	Brighton	201
The Great Escape Holiday Company	North Norfolk Coast	144
The Great House	Laleston	280
The Green Dragon Inn	Cheltenham	94
Grey Friar Lodge	Ambleside	40
Grove House	Hamsterley Forest	88

H

The Half Moon Inn	Petworth	210
Hell Bay	Isles Of Scilly	30
Hewitt's - Villa Spaldi	Lynton	76
Higher Faugan Country House	Newlyn	33
Hinton Grange	Bath	214
Hipping Hall	Kirkby Lonsdale	51
Hob Green Hotel And Restaurant	Harrogate	224
Holcombe Hotel	Oxford	162
Home Farm Hotel	Honiton	73
Hooke Hall	Uckfield	203
The Hope Anchor Hotel	Rye	202
Horsley Hall	Stanhope	89
Horton Grange Country House	Newcastle Upon Tyne	198
Hotel Eilean Iarmain	Isle Of Skye	267
Howfield Manor	Canterbury	116
The Hundred House Hotel	Telford	171
Hyland's Burren Hotel	Ballyvaughan	242

I

Ilsington Country House Hotel	Ilsington	74
Inn At The Elm Tree	St Brides Wentlooge	281
The Inn At Whitewell	Whitewell	124
The Inn on the Green	Maidenhead	20

J

J.D. Young	Harleston	138
The Jersey Arms	Oxford	164
Jubilee Inn	Pelynt	34

K

Kemps Country Hotel & Restaurant	Wareham	87
Killarney Royal Hotel	Killarney	248
Kilmokea Country Manor & Gardens	Kilmokea	251
The Kings Head Inn & Restaurant	Stow-On-The-Wold	168
Kingston House	Staverton	79
Kirkton House	Cardross	258
Kitley House Hotel & Restaurant	Plymouth	77
Knockendarroch House	Pitlochry	274

L

La Favorita Hotel	Guernsey	234
La Sablonnerie	Sark	239
The Lake Hotel	Port Of Menteith	275
The Lamb Inn	Burford	160

330

Index by Property

The Lamb Inn	Shipton-Under-Wychwood	167
Langley House	Taunton	182
Langrish House	Petersfield	109
The Lea Gate Inn	Coningsby	129
The Leatherne Bottel Riverside Inn	Goring-On-Thames	19
The Leathes Head	Keswick	48
Les Douvres Hotel & Restaurant	Guernsey	236
Les Rocquettes Hotel	Guernsey	240
Linthwaite House Hotel	Windermere	54
Littleover Lodge Hotel	Derby	61
Loch Melfort Hotel & Restaurant	Oban	261
The Lodge On The Loch	Onich	268
The Lord Haldon Country Hotel	Exeter	71

M

The Malt House	Chipping Campden	97
The Manor Hotel	Bridport	83
The Manor House	Great Snoring	136
Maryculter House Hotel	Aberdeen	254
The Maynard Arms	Grindleford	64
Melbourn Bury	Cambridge	21
The Mill at Harvington	Evesham	217
The Mill House Hotel	Ashington	205
The Mill & Old Swan	Oxford	165
The Mount Pleasant Hotel	Great Malvern	218
Mount Somerset Country House	Taunton	181

N

Nanny Brow Country House Hotel & Restaurant	Ambleside	41
The New Inn	Coleford	69
The New Inn At Coln	Cirencester	99
New Mill Restaurant	Basingstoke	102
New Park Manor	Brockenhurst	103
The Norfolk Mead Hotel	Norwich	148
Norton House Hotel And Restaurant	Mumbles	299
The Nurse's Cottage	Lymington	108

O

Oak Lodge Hotel	Enfield	132
Oak Tree Farm	Hopwas / Lichfield	189
The Old Manor Hotel	Loughborough	126
The Old Manor Hotel	Bath	212
The Old Quay House Hotel	Fowey	28
The Old Rectory	Norwich	150
The Old Rectory	Ilminster	177
The Old Rectory Country House	Llansanffraid Glan Conwy	286
The Old Tollgate Restaurant And Hotel	Brighton	206
Oldfields	Bath	14
The Otterburn Tower	Otterburn	157

P

Parklands Hotel & Acanthus Restaurant	Perth	273
Parva Farmhouse And Restaurant	Tintern	295
The Peacock Inn	Bakewell	56
Pen-Y-Dyffryn Hall Hotel	Oswestry	170
The Pend	Dunkeld	270
Percy's Country Hotel & Restaurant	Virginstow	82
Petersfield House Hotel	Horning	142

Peterstone Court	Brecon	297
Plas Dolmelynllyn	Dolgellau	292
The Plough Inn	Hathersage	65
The Plough Inn	Clare	194
Porlock Vale House	Porlock Weir	179
The Port William	Tintagel	37
Porth Tocyn Country House Hotel	Abersoch	288
Portland Arms Hotel	Wick	269
Preston House & Little's Restaurant	Saunton	78
The Pump House Apartment	Billericay-Great Burstead	90

Q

The Queen's Head Hotel	Hawkshead	46

R

The Red Lion	Burnsall	222
Redcoats Farmhouse Hotel And Restaurant	Stevenage	114
Ringlestone Inn and Farmhouse	Maidstone	120
The Rising Sun	Lynmouth	75
The Rock Inn Hotel	Halifax/Huddersfield	230
The Roman Camp Inn	Holt	140
Romney Bay House	New Romney	121
Rookhurst Country House Hotel	Hawes	226
Ross Lake House Hotel	Connemara	244
Royal Hotel	Tighnabruaich	262
The Royal Oak Inn	Winsford	186
Rudloe Hall	Bath	211
Rylstone Manor	Isle Of Wight	115

S

Santo's Higham Farm	Higham	66
Sawrey House Country Hotel & Restaurant	Hawkshead	47
The Sea Trout Inn	Totnes	81
The Shaven Crown Hotel	Shipton Under Wychwood	166
The Shibden Mill Inn	Halifax	229
Soulton Hall	Wem	172
Stanhill Court Hotel	Gatwick	196
Stanton Manor	Chippenham	215
The Steppes	Hereford	110
Stone Hall Hotel & Restaurant	Fishguard	296
Stow House Hotel	Aysgarth	221
The Stower Grange	Norwich	149
Stretton Hall	Church Stretton	169
The Suffolk Golf & Country Club	Bury St Edmunds	191
Sutton Bonington Hall	Nottingham	127
Swinside Lodge Hotel	Keswick	50
Sychnant Pass House	Conwy	285

T

Tan-Y-Foel	Betws-Y-Coed	283
The Tarn End House Hotel	Carlisle	44
Tasburgh House Hotel	Bath	15
Temple Sowerby House Hotel	Penrith	52
Thatched Cottage Hotel & Restaurant	Brockenhurst	104
Thornham Hall & Restaurant	Thornham Magna	195
Three Choirs Vineyards Estate	Newent	100
Tredethy House	Wadebridge	38
Tree Tops Country House Restaurant & Hotel	Southport	123

Trehaven Manor Hotel	Looe	31
Trehellas House Hotel & Restaurant	Wadebridge	39
Trelawne Hotel – The Hutches Restaurant	Falmouth	27
Trevalsa Court Hotel	Mevagissey	32

U

Underwood	Broughton-In-Furness	42

V

Vere Lodge	Fakenham	135
The Victoria At Holkham	Holkham	139
Villa Magdala	Bath	16

W

Wallett's Court	Dover	118
Waren House Hotel	Bamburgh	155
Washingborough Hall	Lincoln	130
The Weavers Shed Restaurant With Rooms	Huddersfield	231
The West Arms Hotel	Llanarmon Dyffryn Ceiriog	287
Western Isles Hotel	Tobermory	263
Westover Hall	Lymington	107
The White Hart Inn	Cheltenham	96
The White Hart Inn	Saddleworth	101
The White Horse	Brancaster Staithe	134
The White Horse Inn	Cambridge	192
The White House	Herm Island	237
The White Lion Hotel	Upton-Upon-Severn	219
White Moss House	Grasmere	45
The White Swan	Pickering	227
Whitley Ridge Country House	Brockenhurst	105
Widbrook Grange	Bath	213
The Wild Duck Inn	Cirencester	98
Willington Hall Hotel	Chester	26
Wilton Court Hotel	Ross-On-Wye	112
The Wind In The Willows	Glossop	63
The Windmill At Badby	Badby	153
The Woodborough Inn	Winscombe	185
Woolverton House	Bath	174

Y

Yalbury Cottage Hotel	Dorchester	84
Ye Horn's Inn	Preston	122
Ye Olde Bull's Head	Beaumaris	293
Ye Olde Dog & Partridge	Burton Upon Trent	188
Yeoldon House Hotel	Bideford	67

Index by Location

England

Location	Hotel	Page
Ambleside	Grey Friar Lodge	40
Ambleside	Nanny Brow Country House Hotel & Restaurant	41
Apuldram	Crouchers Country Hotel & Restaurant	207
Arundel	Burpham Country House Hotel	204
Ashington	The Mill House Hotel	205
Austwick	The Austwick Country House Hotel & Restaurant	220
Axbridge	Compton House	173
Aylmerton	The Roman Camp Inn	140
Aysgarth	Stow House Hotel	221
Badby	The Windmill At Badby	153
Bakewell	The Peacock Inn	56
Bamburgh	Waren House Hotel	155
Banbury	Holcombe Hotel	162
Basingstoke	New Mill Restaurant	102
Bath	Apsley House	12
Bath	Bath Lodge Hotel	17
Bath	Hinton Grange	214
Bath	The Old Manor Hotel	212
Bath	Oldfields	14
Bath	Rudloe Hall	211
Bath	Tasburgh House Hotel	15
Bath	Villa Magdala	16
Bath	Widbrook Grange	213
Bath	Woolverton House	174
Bath	The County Hotel	13
Belford	The Blue Bell Hotel	156
Belper	Dannah Farm Country House	57
Bibury	Bibury Court	93
Bideford	Yeoldon House Hotel	67
Biggin-By-Hartington	Biggin Hall	58
Billericay-Great Burstead	The Pump House Apartment	90
Birkenhead	The Beresford	133
Bledington	The Kings Head Inn & Restaurant	168
Borrowdale	The Leathes Head	48
Bovey Tracey	The Edgemoor	68
Bowness	Fayrer Garden House Hotel	53
Bowness	Linthwaite House Hotel	54
Box	Rudloe Hall	211
Bradford-On-Avon	The Old Manor Hotel	212
Bradford-On-Avon	Widbrook Grange	213
Bramber	The Old Tollgate Restaurant And Hotel	206
Brancaster Staithe	The White Horse	134
Bridport	The Manor Hotel	83
Brighton	The Granville	201
Brighton	The Old Tollgate Restaurant And Hotel	206
Broad Campden	The Malt House	97
Brockenhurst	New Park Manor	103
Brockenhurst	Thatched Cottage Hotel & Restaurant	104
Brockenhurst	Whitley Ridge Country House Hotel	105
Broughton-In-Furness	Underwood	42
Broxton	Broxton Hall Country House Hotel	24
Bryher	Hell Bay	30
Burford	The Lamb Inn	160
Burnsall	The Red Lion	222
Burpham	Burpham Country House Hotel	204
Burton Upon Trent	Boar's Head Hotel	59
Burton Upon Trent	Ye Olde Dog & Partridge	188
Bury St Edmunds	The Suffolk Golf & Country Club	191
Bury St. Edmunds	Clarice House	190
Cambridge	The Crown House	92
Cambridge	The White Horse Inn	192
Cambridge	Melbourn Bury	21
Canterbury	Howfield Manor	116
Carlisle	Crosby Lodge Country House Hotel	43
Carlisle	The Tarn End House Hotel	44
Castle Ashby	The Falcon Hotel	154
Cavendish	The George	193
Charlton Kings	Charlton Kings Hotel	95
Charlwood	Stanhill Court Hotel	196
Chartham Hatch	Howfield Manor	116
Cheltenham	Charlton Kings Hotel	95
Cheltenham	The Green Dragon Inn	94
Cheltenham	The White Hart Inn	96
Chester	Brook Meadow Hotel	25
Chester	Frogg Manor Hotel & Restaurant	23
Chester	Willington Hall Hotel	26
Chester	Broxton Hall Country House Hotel	24
Chesterfield	Buckingham's Hotel & Restaurant With One Table	60
Chichester	Crouchers Country Hotel & Restaurant	207
Chichester	Forge Hotel	208
Childer Thornton	Brook Meadow Hotel	25
Chilgrove	Forge Hotel	208
Chippenham	Stanton Manor	215
Chipping Campden	The Malt House	97
Church Stretton	Stretton Hall	169
Cirencester	The New Inn At Coln	99
Cirencester	The Wild Duck Inn	98
Clappersgate	Nanny Brow Country House Hotel & Restaurant	41
Clare	The Plough Inn	194
Clavering	The Cricketers	91
Coalville	Abbots Oak	125
Coleford	The New Inn	69
Coln St-Aldwyns	The New Inn At Coln	99
Coltishall	The Norfolk Mead Hotel	148
Combe Martin	Coulsworthy House	70
Coningsby	The Lea Gate Inn	129
Cookham Dean	The Inn on the Green	20
Copt Oak	Abbots Oak	125
Cranbrook	The George Hotel	117
Cricket Malherbie	The Old Rectory	177
Dartmoor	Ilsington Country House Hotel	74
Derby	Littleover Lodge Hotel	61
Dorchester	Yalbury Cottage Hotel	84
Dorchester-On-Thames	The George Hotel	161
Dover	Wallett's Court	118
Drayton	The Stower Grange	149
Dulverton	Ashwick Country House Hotel	175
Dunchideock	The Lord Haldon Country Hotel	71
East Stoke	Kemps Country Hotel & Restaurant	87
East Witton	The Blue Lion	223
Elham	The Abbot's Fireside Hotel	119
Enfield	Oak Lodge Hotel	132
Evershot	Acorn Inn	85
Eversley	New Mill Restaurant	102
Evesham	The Mill at Harvington	217
Exeter	Combe House Hotel & Restaurant	72
Exeter	The Lord Haldon Country Hotel	71
Exford	The Crown Hotel	176
Exmoor National Park	The Royal Oak Inn	186
Fakenham	Vere Lodge	135
Falmouth	Trelawne Hotel – The Hutches Restaurant	27
Felbrigg	Felbrigg Lodge	141
Formby	Tree Tops Country House Restaurant & Hotel	123
Fornham St Genevieve	The Suffolk Golf & Country Club	191
Fowey	Cormorant On The River, Hotel & Riverside Restaurant	29
Fowey	The Old Quay House Hotel	28
Fritton	Caldecott Hall	137
Froggatt Edge	The Chequers Inn	62
Gatwick	Stanhill Court Hotel	196
Glewstone	Glewstone Court	113
Glossop	The Wind In The Willows	63
Golant	Cormorant On The River, Hotel & Riverside Restaurant	29
Golcar	The Weavers Shed Restaurant With Rooms	231
Goosnargh	Ye Horn's Inn	122
Goring-On-Thames	The Leatherne Bottel Riverside Inn & Restaurant	19
Grasmere	White Moss House	45
Great Chesterford	The Crown House	92
Great Malvern	The Mount Pleasant Hotel	218
Great Snoring	The Manor House	136
Great Yarmouth	Caldecott Hall	137
Grimston	**Congham Hall**	**143**
Grindleford	The Maynard Arms	64
Halifax	The Shibden Mill Inn	229
Halifax/Huddersfield	The Rock Inn Hotel	230
Hampton Court	Chase Lodge	197

332

Index by Location

Hamsterley Forest	Grove House	88
Handcross	The Chequers At Slaugham	209
Harleston	J.D. Young	138
Harrogate	The Boar's Head Hotel	225
Harrogate	Hob Green Hotel And Restaurant	224
Harvington	The Mill at Harvington	217
Hatch Beauchamp	Farthings Hotel & Restaurant	180
Hathersage	The Plough Inn	65
Hawes	Rookhurst Country House Hotel	226
Hawkshead	The Queen's Head Hotel	46
Hawkshead	Sawrey House Country Hotel & Restaurant	47
Helland Bridge	Tredethy House	38
Henlade	Mount Somerset Country House Hotel	181
Hereford	The Steppes	110
High Crosby	Crosby Lodge Country House Hotel	43
Higham	Santo's Higham Farm	66
Hinton	Hinton Grange	214
Hitchin	Redcoats Farmhouse Hotel And Restaurant	114
Holkham	The Victoria At Holkham	139
Holt	Felbrigg Lodge	141
Holt	The Roman Camp Inn	140
Honiton	Combe House Hotel & Restaurant	72
Honiton	Home Farm Hotel	73
Hopwas / Lichfield	Oak Tree Farm	189
Hordle	Gordleton Mill Inn	106
Horning	Petersfield House Hotel	142
Huddersfield	The Weavers Shed Restaurant With Rooms	231
Hundon	The Plough Inn	194
Ilminster	The Old Rectory	177
Ilsington	Ilsington Country House Hotel	74
Isle Of Wight	Rylstone Manor	115
Isles Of Scilly	Hell Bay	30
Kenilworth	Clarendon House	199
Keswick	Dale Head Hall Lakeside Hotel	49
Keswick	Swinside Lodge Hotel	50
Keswick	The Leathes Head	48
Kings Lynn	Congham Hall	143
Kingston Bagpuize	Fallowfields	163
Kirdford	The Half Moon Inn	210
Kirkby Lonsdale	Hipping Hall	51
Lake Thirlmere	Dale Head Hall Lakeside Hotel	49
Langrish	Langrish House	109
Ledbury	The Feathers Hotel	111
Lincoln	Washingborough Hall	130
Littleover	Littleover Lodge Hotel	61
Littlestone	Romney Bay House	121
Longbridge Deverill	The George Inn	216
Looe	Trehaven Manor Hotel	31
Loughborough	The Old Manor Hotel	126
Lower Bockhampton	Yalbury Cottage Hotel	84
Loxley	Glebe Farm House	200
Lymington	Gordleton Mill Inn	106
Lymington	The Nurse's Cottage	108
Lymington	Westover Hall	107
Lynmouth	The Rising Sun	75
Lynton	Hewitt's - Villa Spaldi	76
Maidenhead	The Inn on the Green	20
Maidstone	Ringlestone Inn and Farmhouse Hotel	120
Markington	Hob Green Hotel And Restaurant	224
Mawnan Smith	Trelawne Hotel – The Hutches Restaurant	27
Melbourn	Melbourn Bury	21
Mevagissey	Trevalsa Court Hotel	32
Middleton Stoney	The Jersey Arms	164
Milford-On-Sea	Westover Hall	107
Millom	Underwood	42
Minster Lovell	The Mill & Old Swan	165
Near Sawrey	Sawrey House Country Hotel & Restaurant	47
New Romney	Romney Bay House	121
Newcastle Upon Tyne	Horton Grange Country House Hotel	198
Newent	Three Choirs Vineyards Estate	100
Newlands	Swinside Lodge Hotel	50
Newlyn	Higher Faugan Country House Hotel	33
Norfolk Broads	Petersfield House Hotel	142
North Norfolk	The Manor House	136
North Norfolk Coast	The Great Escape Holiday Company	144
North Walsham	Elderton Lodge Hotel & Langtry Restaurant	146
North Walsham	Beechwood Hotel	145
Northam	Yeoldon House Hotel	67
Norton	The Hundred House Hotel	171
Norton St Philip	Bath Lodge Hotel	17
Norwich	The Old Rectory	150
Norwich	The Stower Grange	149
Norwich	The Beeches Hotel And Victorian Gardens	147
Norwich	The Norfolk Mead Hotel	148
Nottingham	The Cottage Country House Hotel	159
Nottingham	Sutton Bonington Hall	127
Nottingham	Cockliffe Country House Hotel	158
Nr Bath	The Carpenters Arms	18
Nr Bridgwater	Chestnut House	187
Nr Canterbury	The Abbot's Fireside Hotel	119
Nr Daventry	The Windmill At Badby	153
Nr Durham	Grove House	88
Nr Looe	Jubilee Inn	34
Nr Malvern	The White Lion Hotel	219
Nr Okehampton	Percy's Country Hotel & Restaurant	82
Nr Totnes	Kingston House	79
Oswestry	Pen-Y-Dyffryn Hall Hotel	170
Otterburn	The Otterburn Tower	157
Outwell	Crown Lodge Hotel	22
Ovington	Brovey Lair	151
Oxford	Fallowfields	163
Oxford	Holcombe Hotel	162
Oxford	The Jersey Arms	164
Oxford	The Mill & Old Swan	165
Oxton	The Beresford	133
Pelynt	Jubilee Inn	34
Penrith	Temple Sowerby House Hotel	52
Petersfield	Langrish House	109
Petworth	The Half Moon Inn	210
Pickering	The White Swan	227
Plymouth	Kitley House Hotel & Restaurant	77
Ponteland	Horton Grange Country House Hotel	198
Porlock Weir	Porlock Vale House	179
Porlock Weir	Andrew's On The Weir	178
Preston	Ye Horn's Inn	122
Ringlestone	Ringlestone Inn and Farmhouse Hotel	120
Ripley Castle	The Boar's Head Hotel	225
Ross-On-Wye	Glewstone Court	113
Ross-On-Wye	Wilton Court Hotel	112
Rowsley	The Peacock Inn	56
Ruddington	The Cottage Country House Hotel	159
Rutland Water	Barnsdale Lodge	128
Rydal Water	White Moss House	45
Rye	The Hope Anchor Hotel	202
Saddleworth	The White Hart Inn	101
Saham Toney	Broom Hall Country Hotel	152
Saunton	Preston House & Little's Restaurant	78
Shanklin	Rylstone Manor	115
Sherborne	The Eastbury Hotel	86
Shibden	The Shibden Mill Inn	229
Shipton Under Wychwood	The Shaven Crown Hotel	166
Shipton-Under-Wychwood	The Lamb Inn	167
Skipton	The Red Lion	222
Slaugham	The Chequers At Slaugham	209
Southport	Tree Tops Country House Restaurant & Hotel	123
St Ives	The Countryman At Trink Hotel	36
St. Austell	Boscundle Manor	35
Stamford	The Crown Hotel	131
Stanhope	Horsley Hall	89
Stansted Airport	The Cricketers	91
Stanton Wick	The Carpenters Arms	18
Staverton	The Sea Trout Inn	81
Staverton	Kingston House	79
Stevenage	Redcoats Farmhouse Hotel And Restaurant	114
Stow-On-The-Wold	The Kings Head Inn & Restaurant	168
Stratford-Upon-Avon	Glebe Farm House	200
Sudbury	Boar's Head Hotel	59
Sutton Bonington	Sutton Bonington Hall	127
Swaffham	Brovey Lair	151
Sway	The Nurse's Cottage	108

Index by Location

Talkin Tarn	The Tarn End House Hotel	44
Tarporley	Willington Hall Hotel	26
Taunton	Langley House	182
Taunton	Mount Somerset Country House Hotel	181
Taunton	Farthings Hotel & Restaurant	180
Tavistock	Browns Hotel, Wine Bar & Brasserie	80
Telford	The Hundred House Hotel	171
Temple Sowerby	Temple Sowerby House Hotel	52
Thetford	Broom Hall Country Hotel	152
Thornham Magna	Thornham Hall & Restaurant	195
Thorpe Market	Elderton Lodge Hotel & Langtry Restaurant	146
Thorpe St Andrew	The Old Rectory	150
Tintagel	The Port William	37
Totnes	The Sea Trout Inn	81
Trebarwith Strand	The Port William	37
Tregrehan	Boscundle Manor	35
Trink	The Countryman At Trink Hotel	36
Troutbeck	Broadoaks Country House	55
Uckfield	Hooke Hall	203
Ullingswick	The Steppes	110
Upton-Upon-Severn	The White Lion Hotel	219
Virginstow	Percy's Country Hotel & Restaurant	82
Wadebridge	Tredethy House	38
Wadebridge	Trehellas House Hotel & Restaurant	39
Wareham	Kemps Country Hotel & Restaurant	87
Warminster	The George Inn	216
Washaway	Trehellas House Hotel & Restaurant	39
Washingborough	Washingborough Hall	130
Weardale	Horsley Hall	89
Weekly Lets	The Great Escape Holiday Company	144
Weekly Lets	The Pump House Apartment	90
Wells	Beryl	183
Wells	Glencot House	184
Wem	Soulton Hall	172
Wensleydale	The Blue Lion	223
Wensleydale	Rookhurst Country House Hotel	226
Wensleydale	Stow House Hotel	221
West Bexington	The Manor Hotel	83
West Cliffe	Wallett's Court	118
Whitby	Dunsley Hall	228
Whitewell	The Inn At Whitewell	124
Wilmington	Home Farm Hotel	73
Winchcombe	The White Hart Inn	96
Windermere	Broadoaks Country House	55
Windermere	Fayrer Garden House Hotel	53
Windermere	Linthwaite House Hotel	54
Winscombe	The Woodborough Inn	185
Winsford	The Royal Oak Inn	186
Wisbech	Crown Lodge Hotel	22
Withersfield	The White Horse Inn	192
Wiveliscombe	Langley House	182
Woolavington	Chestnut House	187
Woolverton	Woolverton House	174
Yealmpton	Kitley House Hotel & Restaurant	77
Yorkshire Dales	The Austwick Country House Hotel & Restaurant	220

Channel Islands

Fermain Bay	La Favorita Hotel	234
Herm Island	The White House	237
Sark	La Sablonnerie	239
St Helier	Eulah Country House	238
St Martins	Bella Luce Hotel & Restaurant	235
St Martins	Les Douvres Hotel & Restaurant	236
St Peter Port	Les Rocquettes Hotel	240

Ireland

Ballyvaughan	Hyland's Burren Hotel	242
Caragh Lake	Caragh Lodge	245
Cashel	Cashel Palace Hotel	250
Connemara	Ross Lake House Hotel	244
Dingle	Emlagh House	246
Dingle Peninsula	Gorman's Clifftop House & Restaurant	247
Dublin	Aberdeen Lodge	243
Killarney	Killarney Royal Hotel	248
Kilmokea	Kilmokea Country Manor & Gardens	251
Riverstown	Coopershill House	249

Scotland

Aberdeen	Maryculter House Hotel	254
Ayr	Culzean Castle – The Eisenhower Apartment	277
Ballachulish	Ballachulish House	257
Ballater	Balgonie Country House	255
By Glamis	Castleton House Hotel	256
Cardross	Kirkton House	258
Connel	The Frog At Port Dunstaffnage	260
Dunkeld	The Pend	270
Eilean Iarmain	Hotel Eilean Iarmain	267
Forfar	Castleton House Hotel	256
Fort William	Corriegour Lodge Hotel	265
Fort William	Ballachulish House	257
Glasgow Airport	Bowfield Hotel & Country Club	276
Highlands	Royal Hotel	262
Howwood	Bowfield Hotel & Country Club	276
Inverness	Culduthel Lodge	266
Isle Of Mull	Western Isles Hotel	263
Isle Of Skye	Hotel Eilean Iarmain	267
Killin	Ardeonaig	271
Loch Earn	The Four Seasons Hotel	272
Lybster	Portland Arms Hotel	269
Nr Loch Lomond	Kirkton House	258
Oban	Barcaldine House	259
Oban	The Frog At Port Dunstaffnage	260
Oban	Loch Melfort Hotel & Restaurant	261
Onich	The Lodge On The Loch	268
Perth	Parklands Hotel & Acanthus Restaurant	273
Perthshire	The Four Seasons Hotel	272
Pitlochry	Knockendarroch House	274
Port Of Menteith	The Lake Hotel	275
Portpatrick	Fernhill Hotel	264
Royal Deeside	Balgonie Country House	255
Tighnabruaich	Royal Hotel	262
Tobermory	Western Isles Hotel	263
Wick	Portland Arms Hotel	269

Wales

Abergavenny	Glangrwyney Court	298
Abersoch	Porth Tocyn Country House Hotel	288
Aberystwyth	Conrah Country House Hotel	282
Bala	Bryn Tegid Country House	289
Barmouth	Bae Abermaw	290
Barmouth	Bontddu Hall	291
Beaumaris	Ye Olde Bull's Head	293
Betws-Y-Coed	Tan-Y-Foel	283
Bontddu	Bontddu Hall	291
Brecon	Peterstone Court	297
Cardiff	Egerton Grey	300
Conwy	Castle Hotel	284
Crickhowell	Glangrwyney Court	298
Dolgellau	Plas Dolmelynllyn	292
Fishguard	Stone Hall Hotel & Restaurant	296
Ganllwyd	Plas Dolmelynllyn	292
Laleston	The Great House	280
Llanarmon Dyffryn Ceiriog	The West Arms Hotel	287
Llanhamlach	Peterstone Court	297
Llansanffraid Glan Conwy	The Old Rectory Country House	286
Monmouth	The Bell At Skenfrith	294
Mumbles	Norton House Hotel And Restaurant	299
Porthkerry	Egerton Grey	300
Skenfrith	The Bell At Skenfrith	294
St Brides Wentlooge	Inn At The Elm Tree	281
Tintern	Parva Farmhouse And Restaurant	295
Welsh Hook	Stone Hall Hotel & Restaurant	296

Index by Activity

≋ Hotels with heated indoor swimming pool

England

Cormorant On The River,
  Hotel & Riverside Restaurant ....Cornwall 29
Trelawne Hotel –
  The Hutches Restaurant ....Cornwall 27
Fayrer Garden House Hotel ....Cumbria 53
Underwood ....Cumbria 42
Ilsington Country House Hotel ....Devon 74
The Feathers Hotel ....Herefordshire 111
Wallett's Court ....Kent 118
Broom Hall Country Hotel ....Norfolk 152
Felbrigg Lodge ....Norfolk 141
Vere Lodge ....Norfolk 135
Dunsley Hall ....North Yorkshire 228
Glencot House ....Somerset 184
Oak Tree Farm ....Staffordshire 189

Clarice House ....Suffolk 190
The Suffolk Golf & Country Club..Suffolk 191
Widbrook Grange ....Wiltshire 213

Channel Islands

La Favorita Hotel ....Guernsey 234
Les Rocquettes Hotel ....Guernsey 240

Scotland

Bowfield Hotel & Country Club....Renfrewshire 276

Wales

Conrah Country House Hotel ......Ceredigion 282

≋ Outdoor pool

England

Hell Bay ....Cornwall 30
Higher Faugan
  Country House Hotel ....cornwall 33
Tredethy House ....Cornwall 38
Trehellas House Hotel
  & Restaurant ....Cornwall 39

Preston House
  & Little's Restaurant ....Devon 78
The Pump House Apartment ....Essex 90
New Park Manor ....Hampshire 103
Tree Tops Country House
  Restaurant & Hotel ....Lancashire 123
Washingborough Hall ....Lincolnshire 130
Brovey Lair ....Norfolk 151
Congham Hall ....Norfolk 143
The Great Escape
  Holiday Company ....Norfolk 144
The Norfolk Mead Hotel ....Norfolk 148
The Old Rectory ....Norfolk 150
Beryl ....Somerset 183
The Mill at Harvington ....Worcestershire 217

Channel Islands

Bella Luce Hotel & Restaurant ......Guernsey 235
Eulah Country House ....Jersey 238
Les Douvres Hotel & Restaurant ..Guernsey 236
The White House ....Herm Islands 237

Wales

Porth Tocyn
  Country House Hotel ....Gwynedd 288
Peterstone Court ....Powys 297

⛳ Golf course on-site

England

Hell Bay ....Cornwall 30
Caldecott Hall ....Norfolk 137
The Suffolk Golf & Country Club..Suffolk 191

🎾 Tennis

England

Oldfields......................................Bath & NE Somerset 14
Frogg Manor Hotel
  & Restaurant ....Cheshire........................23
Higher Faugan
  Country House Hotel ....Cornwall 33
Underwood ....Cumbria 42
New Park Manor ....Hampshire 103
Whitley Ridge
  Country House Hotel ....Hampshire 105
Romney Bay House ....Kent 121
Wallett's Court ....Kent 118
Abbots Oak ....Leicestershire 125
Sutton Bonington Hall ....Leicestershire 127
Congham Hall ....Norfolk 143
The Great Escape
  Holiday Company ....Norfolk 144
Vere Lodge ....Norfolk 135
The Boar's Head Hotel..................North Yorkshire 225
Dunsley Hall ....North Yorkshire 228
Stow House Hotel ....North Yorkshire 221

Fallowfields ....Oxfordshire 163
The Mill & Old Swan ....Oxfordshire 165
The Woodborough Inn ....Somerset 185
Woolverton House ....Somerset 174
The Mill at Harvington ....Worcestershire 217

Channel Islands

The White House ....Herm Island 237

Ireland

Ross Lake House Hotel ....Galway 244
Coopershill House ....Sligo 249
Kilmokea Country Manor
  & Gardens ....Wexford 251

Scotland

Royal Hotel ....Argyll & Bute 262

Wales

Porth Tocyn
  Country House Hotel ....Gwynedd 288
Peterstone Court ....Powys 297
Egerton Grey ....Vale Of Glamorgan....300

SPA Spa/health/fitness facilities

England

Clarice House ....Suffolk 190

Scotland

Bowfield Hotel & Country Club....Renfrewshire 276

M⁴⁰ Conference facilities for 40 delegates or more

England

Melbourn Bury ....Cambridgeshire 21
Willington Hall Hotel ....Cheshire........................26
Linthwaite House Hotel ....Cumbria 54
The Maynard Arms ....Derbyshire 64
Santo's Higham Farm ....Derbyshire 66
Combe House
  Hotel & Restaurant ....Devon 72
Kingston House ....Devon 79
Kitley House Hotel & Restaurant Devon 77
The Lord Haldon Country Hotel ..Devon 71
Acorn Inn ....Dorset 85
The Eastbury Hotel ....Dorset 86
Kemps Country
  Hotel & Restaurant ....Dorset 87
Horsley Hall ....Durham 89

335

Index by Activity

The Green Dragon Inn	Gloucestershire	94
The White Hart Inn	Greater Manchester	101
Langrish House	Hampshire	109
New Mill Restaurant	Hampshire	102
New Park Manor	Hampshire	103
The Feathers Hotel	Herefordshire	111
The George Hotel	Kent	117
Howfield Manor	Kent	116
Ringlestone Inn and Farmhouse Hotel	Kent	120
The Inn At Whitewell	Lancashire	124
Tree Tops Country House Restaurant & Hotel	Lancashire	123
Barnsdale Lodge	Leicestershire	128
Sutton Bonington Hall	Leicestershire	127
The Crown Hotel	Lincolnshire	131
Washingborough Hall	Lincolnshire	130
The Beresford	Mersyside	133
Caldecott Hall	Norfolk	137
Congham Hall	Norfolk	143
J.D. Young	Norfolk	138
The Norfolk Mead Hotel	Norfolk	148
Petersfield House Hotel	Norfolk	142
The Stower Grange	Norfolk	149
The Blue Lion	North Yorkshire	223
The Boar's Head Hotel	North Yorkshire	225
Dunsley Hall	North Yorkshire	228
The Red Lion	North Yorkshire	222
The Blue Bell Hotel	Northumberland	156
The Otterburn Tower	Northumberland	157
Cockliffe Country House Hotel	Nottinghamshire	158
Fallowfields	Oxfordshire	163
The Mill & Old Swan	Oxfordshire	165
Stretton Hall	Shropshire	169
Mount Somerset Country House Hotel	Somerset	181
Woolverton House	Somerset	174
The Plough Inn	Suffolk	194
The Suffolk Golf & Country Club	Suffolk	191
Thornham Hall & Restaurant	Suffolk	195
Stanhill Court Hotel	Surrey	196
Horton Grange Country House Hotel	Tyne & Wear	198
Clarendon House	Warwickshire	199
The Old Tollgate Restaurant And Hotel	West Sussex	206
The Rock Inn Hotel	West Yorkshire	230
The Shibden Mill Inn	West Yorkshire	229
The George Inn	Wiltshire	216
Stanton Manor	Wiltshire	215
The Mount Pleasant Hotel	Worcestershire	218

Channel Islands

La Favorita Hotel	Guernsey	234
Les Rocquettes Hotel	Guernsey	240

Ireland

Killarney Royal Hotel	Kerry	248
Cashel Palace Hotel	Tipperary	250

Scotland

Maryculter House Hotel	Abderdeenshire	254
Castleton House Hotel	Angus	256
Western Isles Hotel	Argyll & Bute	263
Hotel Eilean Iarmain	Highland	267
Portland Arms Hotel	Highland	269
The Four Seasons Hotel	Perth & Kinross	272
Bowfield Hotel & Country Club	Renfrewshire	276

Wales

The Great House	Bridgend	280
Conrah Country House Hotel	Ceredigion	282
Castle Hotel	Conwy	284
Bae Abermaw	Gwynedd	290
Peterstone Court	Powys	297

🔔 Licensed for wedding ceremonies

England

Brook Meadow Hotel	Cheshire	25
Broxton Hall Country House Hotel	Cheshire	24
Frogg Manor Hotel & Restaurant	Cheshire	23
Willington Hall Hotel	Cheshire	26
Boscundle Manor	Cornwall	35
Broadoaks Country House	Cumbria	55
Fayrer Garden House Hotel	Cumbria	53
Linthwaite House Hotel	Cumbria	54
The Maynard Arms	Derbyshire	64
The Peacock Inn	Derbyshire	56
Santo's Higham Farm	Derbyshire	66

▼
Combe House Hotel & Restaurant ....Devon 72

Hewitt's - Villa Spaldi	Devon	76
Kingston House	Devon	79
Kitley House Hotel & Restaurant	Devon	77
The Eastbury Hotel	Dorset	86
The Manor Hotel	Dorset	83
Horsley Hall	Durham	89
The Crown House	Essex	92
Bibury Court	Gloucestershire	93
The White Hart Inn	Greater Manchester	101
Langrish House	Hampshire	109
New Mill Restaurant	Hampshire	102
New Park Manor	Hampshire	103
Westover Hall	Hampshire	107
The Feathers Hotel	Herefordshire	111
Redcoats Farmhouse Hotel And Restaurant	Hertfordshire	114
The Abbot's Fireside Hotel	Kent	119
Howfield Manor	Kent	116
The Inn At Whitewell	Lancashire	124
Tree Tops Country House Restaurant & Hotel	Lancashire	123
Barnsdale Lodge	Leicestershire	128
Sutton Bonington Hall	Leicestershire	127
Washingborough Hall	Lincolnshire	130
Oak Lodge Hotel	London	132
The Beresford	Mersyside	133
Broom Hall Country Hotel	Norfolk	152
Congham Hall	Norfolk	143
The Manor House	Norfolk	136
The Norfolk Mead Hotel	Norfolk	148
The Stower Grange	Norfolk	149
The Austwick Country House Hotel & Restaurant	North Yorkshire	220
The Boar's Head Hotel	North Yorkshire	225
Dunsley Hall	North Yorkshire	228
Hob Green Hotel & Restaurant	North Yorkshire	224
The Red Lion	North Yorkshire	222
The Falcon Hotel	Northamptonshire	154
The Otterburn Tower	Northumberland	157
Cockliffe Country House Hotel	Nottinghamshire	158
Fallowfields	Oxfordshire	163
Stretton Hall	Shropshire	169
Compton House	Somerset	173
Farthings Hotel & Restaurant	Somerset	180
The Suffolk Golf & Country Club	Suffolk	191
Thornham Hall & Restaurant	Suffolk	195
Stanhill Court Hotel	Surrey	196
Horton Grange Country House Hotel	Tyne & Wear	198
Clarendon House	Warwickshire	199
The Old Tollgate Restaurant And Hotel	West Sussex	206
The Rock Inn Hotel	West Yorkshire	230
The Shibden Mill Inn	West Yorkshire	229
Rudloe Hall	Wiltshire	211

Channel Islands

Eulah Country House	Jersey	238
La Sablonnerie	Sark	239

Scotland

Maryculter House Hotel	Abderdeenshire	254
Castleton House Hotel	Angus	256
Loch Melfort Hotel & Restaurant	Argyll & But	261
Ballachulish House	Argyll & Bute	257
Barcaldine House	Argyll & Bute	259
Western Isles Hotel	Argyll & Bute	263
Corriegour Lodge Hotel	Highland	265
Hotel Eilean Iarmain	Highland	267
The Lodge On The Loch	Highland	268
Portland Arms Hotel	Highland	269
The Lake Hotel	Perth & Kinross	275
Bowfield Hotel & Country Club	Renfrewshire	276
Culzean Castle – The Eisenhower Apartment	South Ayrshire	277

Wales

Conrah Country House Hotel	Ceredigion	282
Sychnant Pass House	Conwy	285
The West Arms Hotel	Denbighshire	287
Bae Abermaw	Gwynedd	290
Bontddu Hall	Gwynedd	291
Glangrwyney Court	Powys	298
Peterstone Court	Powys	297
Egerton Grey	Vale Of Glamorgan	300

PERFECT HOSPITALITY BEGINS

WITH PERFECT FORM.

Classic furniture from Selva is the calling card of exclusive establishments.
By creating uniquely stylish surroundings, Selva spoils
not only your guests, but you, as well: with custom solutions,
creative ideas, and the most modern logistics. We would be happy to make
an appointment for you to visit our hotel furnishings showroom in Bolzano.

SELVA
HOTEL STYLE
A brand of Selva Style International

In UK and Ireland: Lidija Braithwaite - LPB Agencies   16 Lenham Avenue, Saltdean   Brigton, East Sussex BN2 8AE
Tel./Fax 01273 385 255   Mobile: 0771 852 2 746   e-mail: lpbagencies@cwcom.net

Selva AG/SpA, I-39100 Bolzano (Italy), Via Luigi-Negrelli-Straße 4
Tel. 0471 240111   Fax 0471 240211   e-mail: selva@selva.com   www.selva.com

Aichner Ciodi GGK — photo: © Moreno Maggi

North West England

Hotel location shown in red with page number

North East England

Hotel location shown in red with page number

CENTRAL ENGLAND
Hotel location shown in red with page number

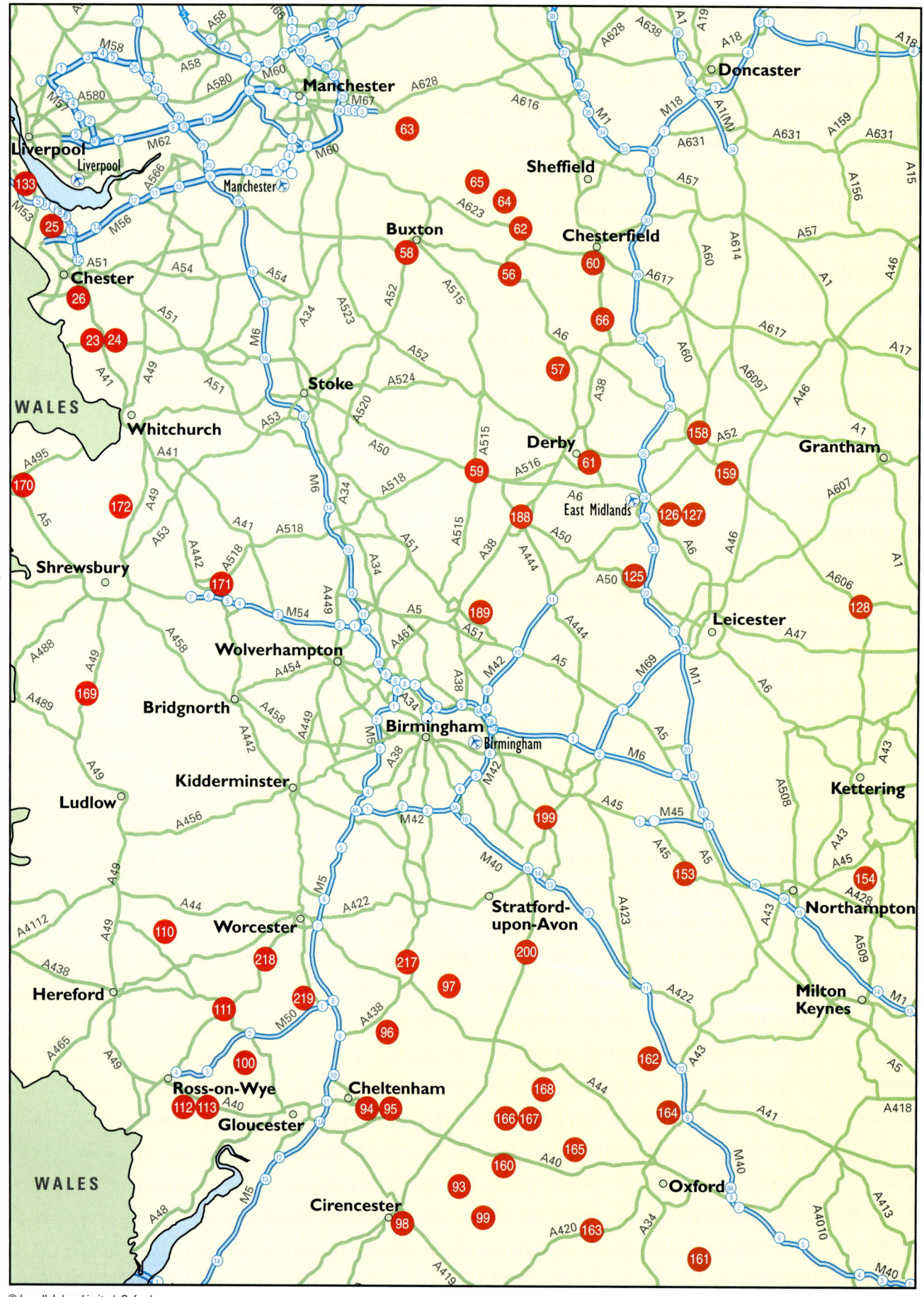

Eastern England

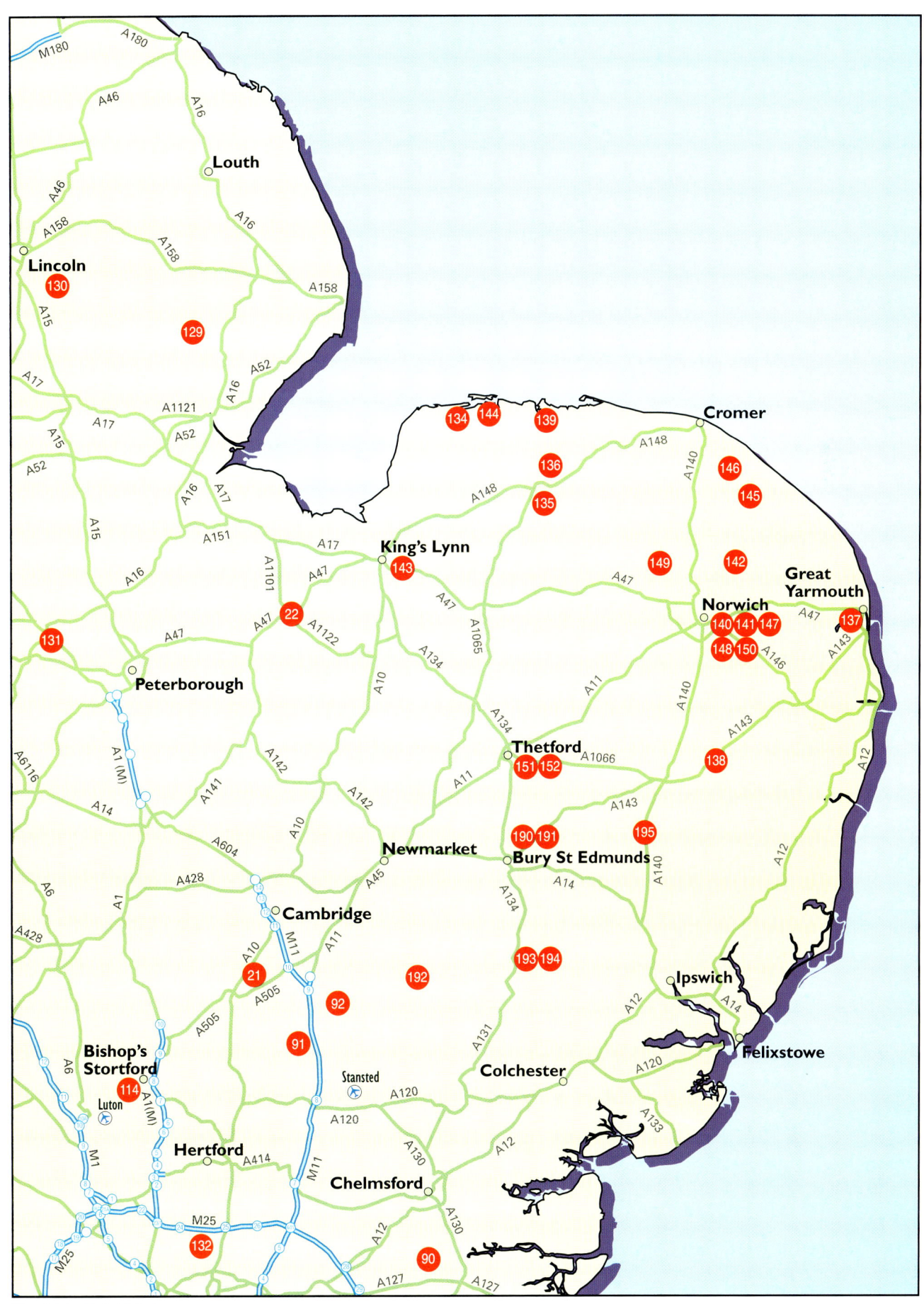

Hotel location shown in red with page number

CHANNEL ISLANDS & SOUTH WEST ENGLAND

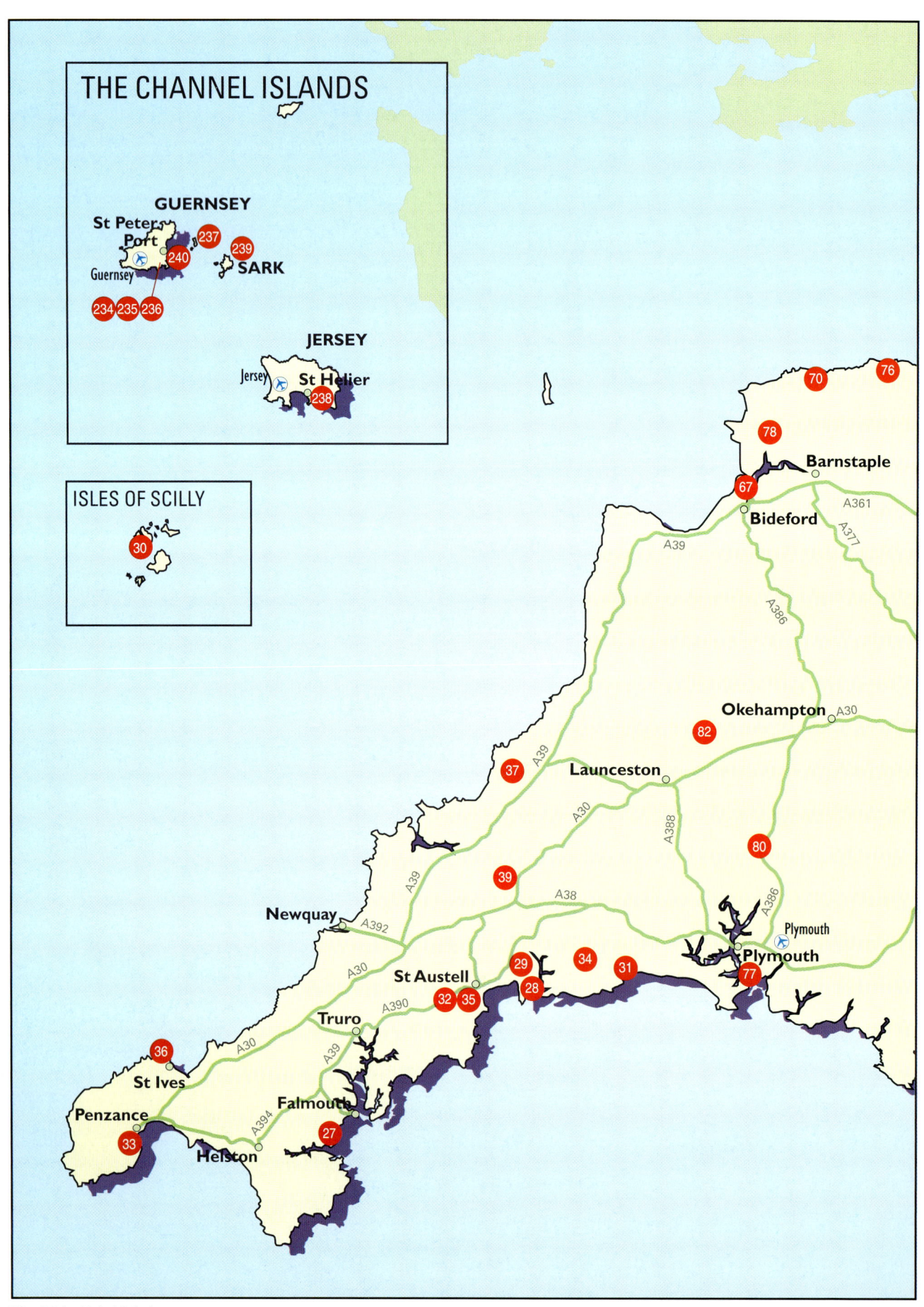

Hotel location shown in red with page number

SOUTH WEST ENGLAND

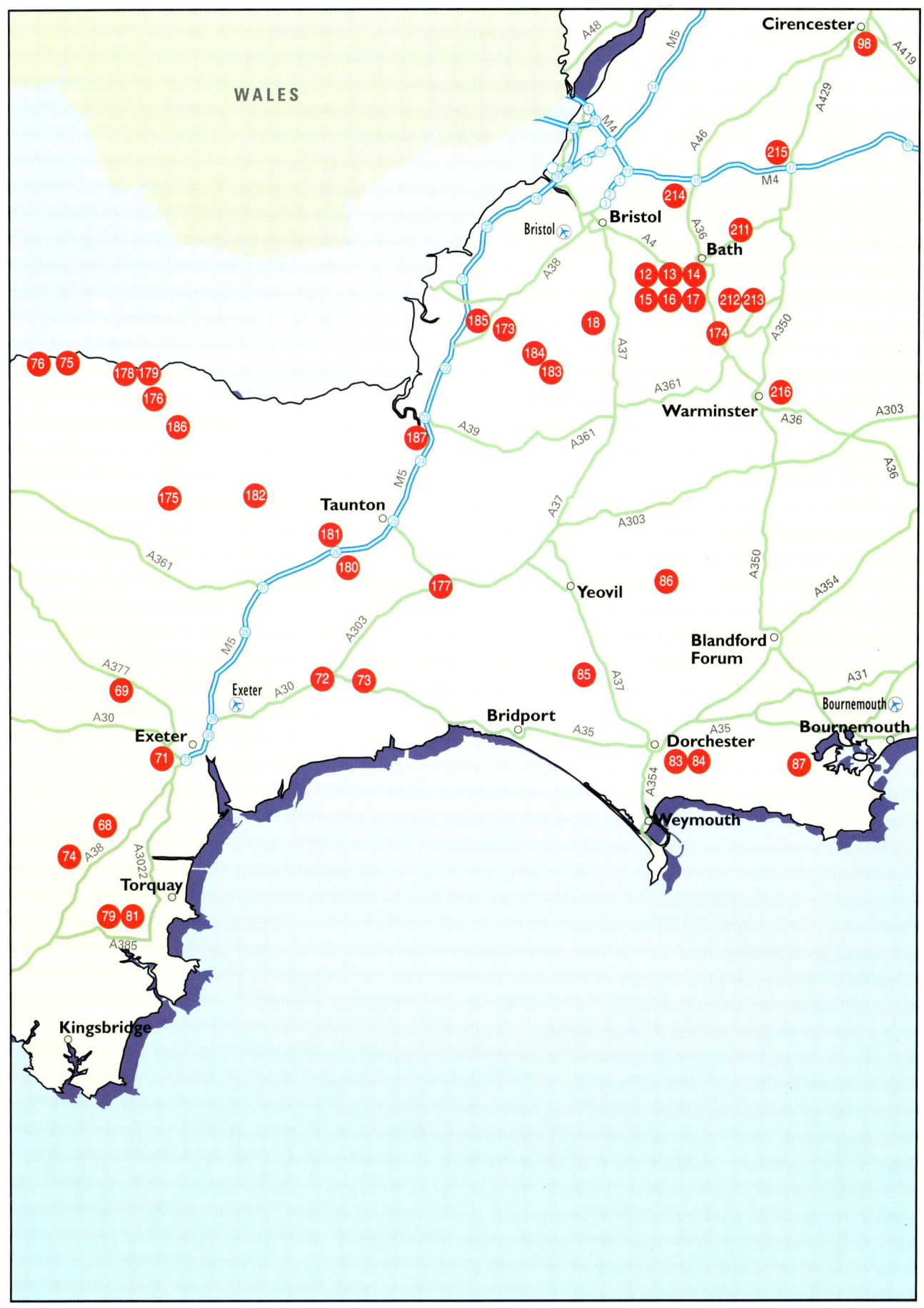

Hotel location shown in red with page number

343

Southern England

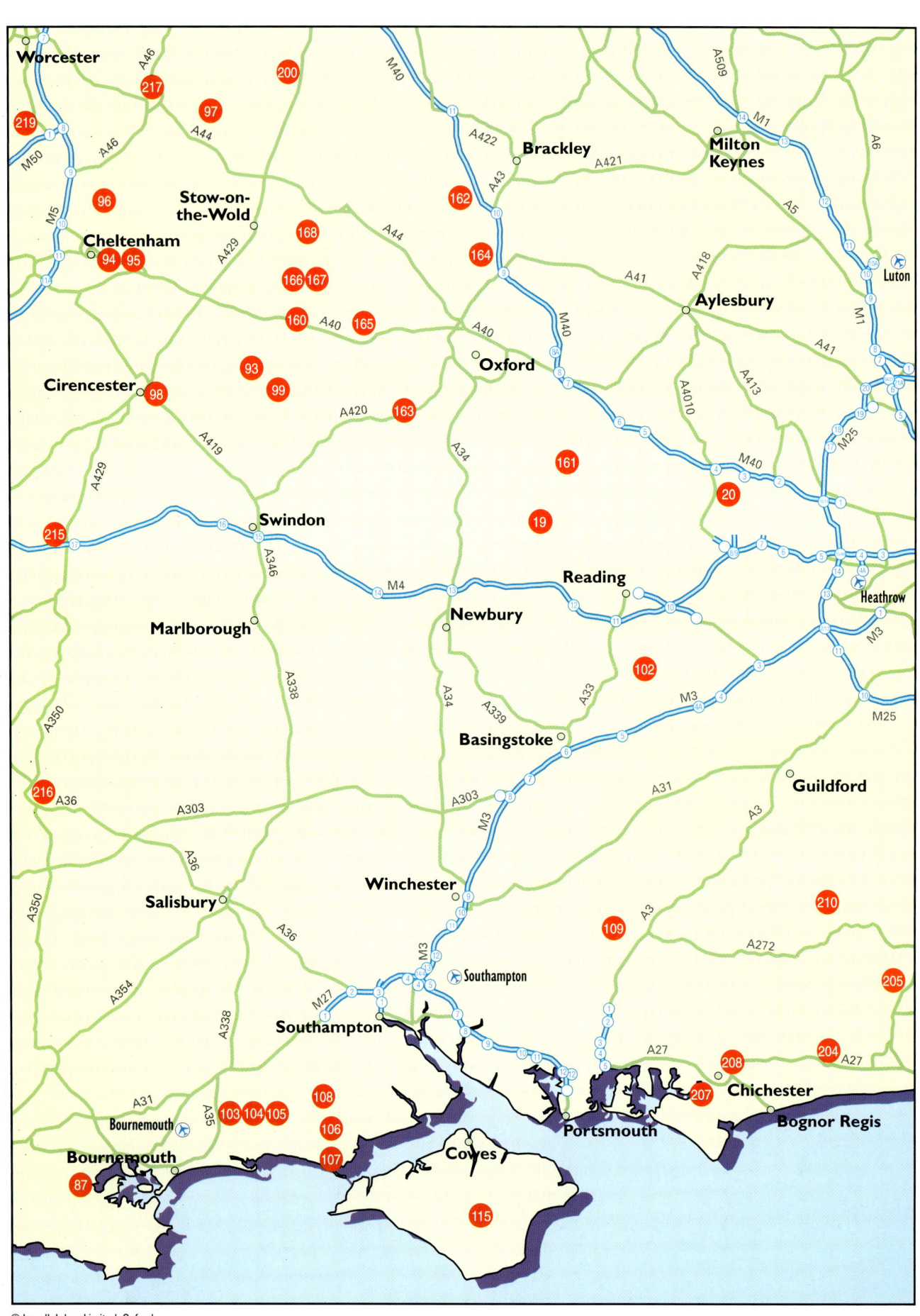

Hotel location shown in red with page number

South East England

Hotel location shown in red with page number

Ireland

Hotel location shown in red with page number

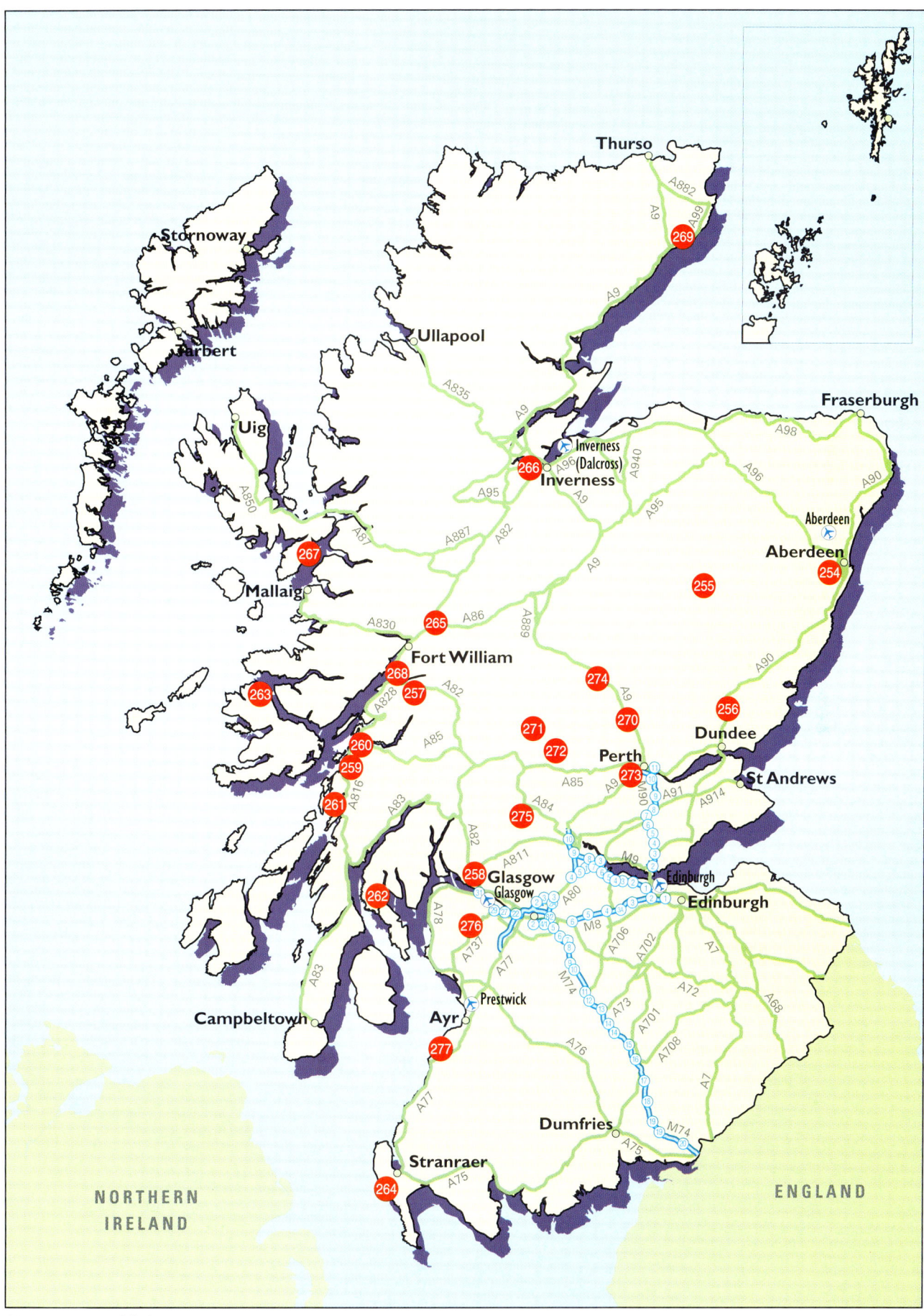

SCOTLAND
Hotel location shown in red with page number

WALES

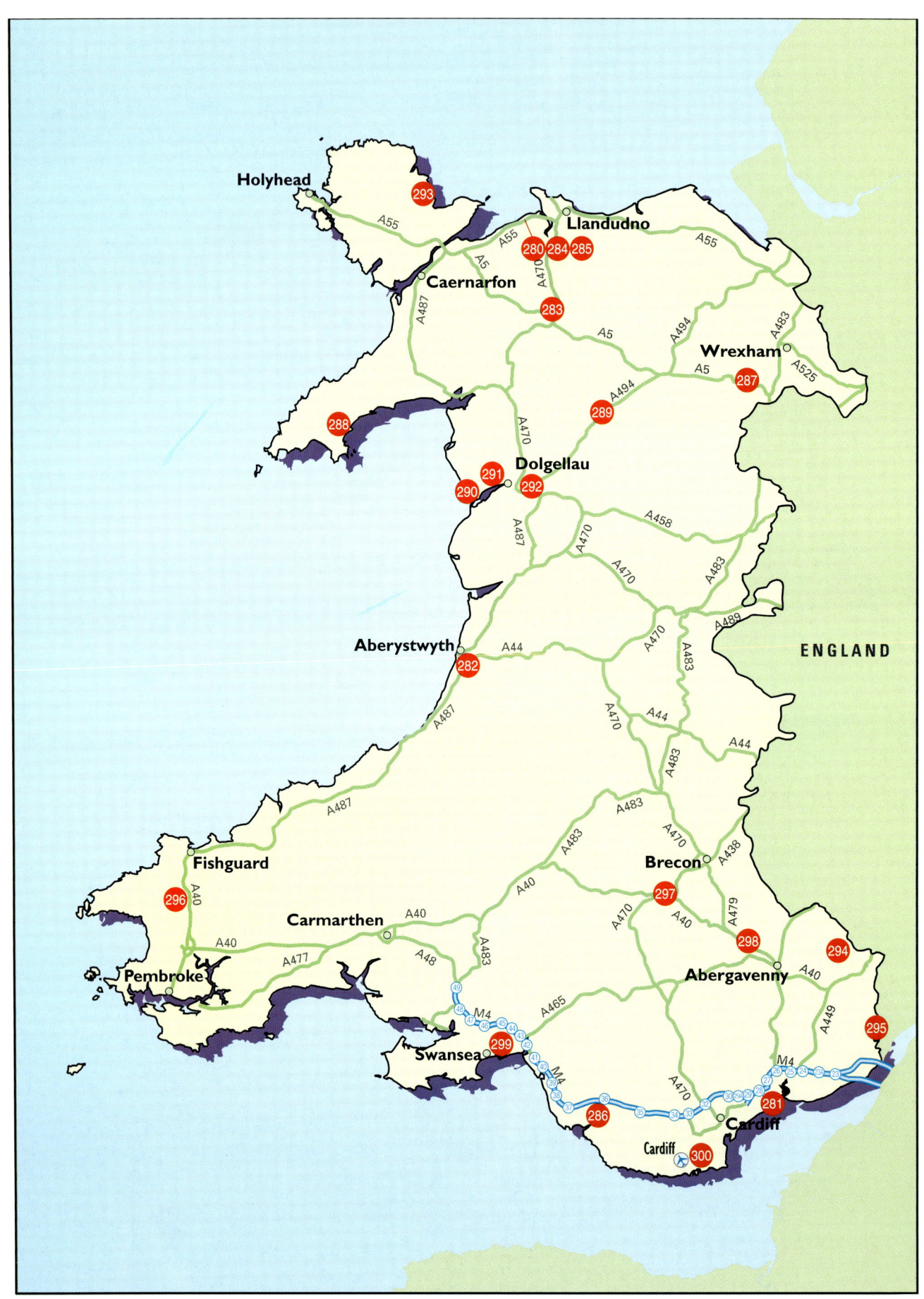

Hotel location shown in red with page number

Condé Nast Johansens Guides

Recommending only the finest hotels in the world

As well as this guide Condé Nast Johansens also publishes the following titles:

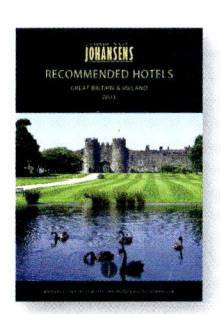

Recommended Hotels, Great Britain & Ireland

440 unique and luxurious hotels, town houses, castles and manor houses chosen for their superior standards and individual character

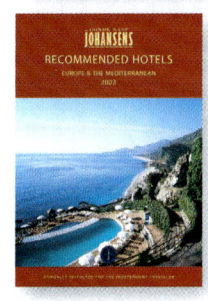

Recommended Hotels, Europe & the Mediterranean

320 continental gems featuring châteaux, resorts and charming countryside hotels

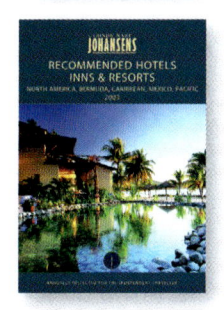

Recommended Hotels, Inns & Resorts, North America, Bermuda, Caribbean, Mexico, Pacific

200 hotels including many hidden properties from across the region

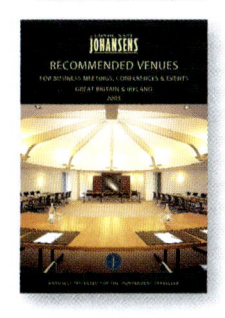

Recommended Venues for Business Meetings, Conferences and Events, Great Britain & Europe

230 venues that cater specifically for a business audience

Worldwide Listings Pocket Guide

Features all recommended hotels and serves as the perfect companion when travelling light

When you purchase two guides or more we will be pleased to offer you a reduction in the cost.

The complete set of Condé Nast Johansens guides may be purchased as 'The Chairman's Collection'.

**To order guides please complete the order form on page 351
or call FREEPHONE 0800 269 397**

Champagne for the Independently Minded

CHAMPAGNE
TAITTINGER
Reims

Condé Nast Johansens
preferred Champagne partner

HATCH MANSFIELD
Sole UK Agent for Champagne Taittinger
Tel 01344 871800 · Fax 01344 871871 · Email info@hatch.co.uk · www.hatchmansfield.com

ORDER FORM

CONDÉ NAST JOHANSENS

Choose from our wide range of titles below

Order **2** guides get **£5 off** • Order **3** guides get **£10 off** • Order **4** guides get **£20 off**

Order the Chairman's Collection worth £100 for just **£75**

Simply complete the form below, total the cost and then deduct the appropriate discount. State your preferred method of payment and mail to Condé Nast Johansens Ltd, FREEPOST (CB264), LONDON SE27 0BR (no stamp required). Fax orders welcome on 020 8655 7817

ALTERNATIVELY YOU CAN ORDER IMMEDIATELY ON FREEPHONE 0800 269 397, please quote ref: D008

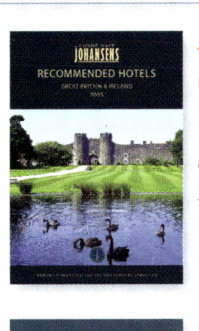

440 Recommendations
I wish to order
QUANTITY
copy/ies priced at £19.95 each.
Total cost
£

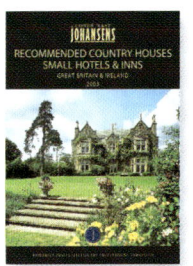

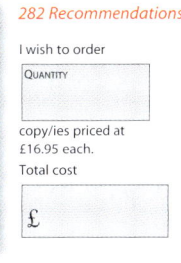

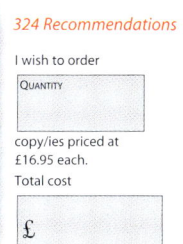

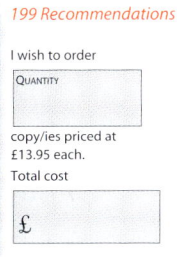

282 Recommendations
I wish to order
QUANTITY
copy/ies priced at £16.95 each.
Total cost
£

324 Recommendations
I wish to order
QUANTITY
copy/ies priced at £16.95 each.
Total cost
£

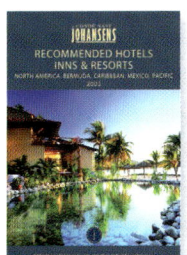

199 Recommendations
I wish to order
QUANTITY
copy/ies priced at £13.95 each.
Total cost
£

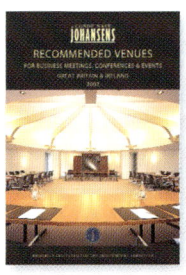

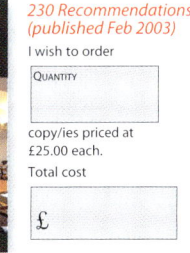

230 Recommendations (published Feb 2003)
I wish to order
QUANTITY
copy/ies priced at £25.00 each.
Total cost
£

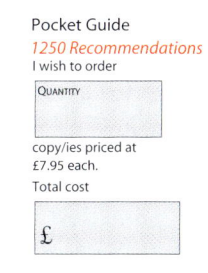

Pocket Guide
1250 Recommendations
I wish to order
QUANTITY
copy/ies priced at £7.95 each.
Total cost
£

Johansens Gold Blocked Slip Case priced at £5 each

Johansens Luxury Luggage Tag priced at £15 each

To order these items please fill in the appropriate section below

The Chairman's Collection
Order the complete collection of Condé Nast Johansens Recommended Guides for only **£75**
PLUS FREE Luxury Luggage Tag worth £15
PLUS FREE Slip Case worth £5

The Chairman's Collection contains all six titles pictured above. The Recommended Venues guide will be dispatched separately on publication in February 2003.

Now please complete your order and payment details

	tick	
I have ordered 2 titles - £5 off		−£5.00
I have ordered 3 titles - £10 off		−£10.00
I have ordered 4 titles - £20 off		−£15.00

Total cost of books ordered minus discount
(excluding the Chairman's Collection)
£

Luxury Luggage Tag at £15
Quantity and total cost: £

Johansens Gold Blocked SLIP CASE at £5
Quantity and total cost: £

I wish to order the
Chairman's Collection at £75
Quantity and total cost: £

Packing & delivery: (all UK orders) add £4.90
(Outside UK) add £6.00 per guide
or Chairman's Collection add £25.00
£

GRAND TOTAL £

I have chosen my Condé Nast Johansens Guides and (please tick)
I enclose a cheque payable to Condé Nast Johansens ☐
Please debit my credit/charge card account ☐
☐ MasterCard   ☐ Visa   ☐ Switch (Issue Number)

Card Holders Name (Mr/Mrs/Miss)

Address

Postcode

Telephone

E-mail

Card No.

Exp Date

Signature

NOW send to
Condé Nast Johansens Ltd, FREEPOST (CB264), LONDON SE27 0BR (no stamp required)
Fax orders welcome on 020 8655 7817

The details provided may be used to keep you informed of future products and special offers provided by Condé Nast Johansens and other carefully selected third parties. If you do not wish to recieve such information please tick this box ☐.
(Your phone number will only be used to ensure the fast and safe delivery of your order)

GUEST SURVEY REPORT

Evaluate your stay in a Condé Nast Johansens Recommendation

CONDÉ NAST JOHANSENS

Dear Guest,

Following your stay in a Condé Nast Johansens recommendation, please spare a moment to complete this Guest Survey Report. This is an important source of information for Johansens, to maintain the highest standards for our recommendations and to support the work of our team of inspectors.

It is also the prime source of nominations for Condé Nast Johansens Awards for Excellence, which are made annually to those properties worldwide that represent the finest standards and best value for money in luxury, independent travel.

Thank you for your time and I hope that when choosing future accommodation Condé Nast Johansens will be your guide.

Yours faithfully,

T. Sinclair

Tim Sinclair
Sales & Marketing Director, Condé Nast Johansens

p.s. Guest Survey Reports may also be completed online at www.johansens.com

1. Your details

Your name:

Your address:

Postcode:

Telephone:

E-mail:

2. Hotel details

Name of hotel:

Location:

Date of visit:

3. Your rating of the hotel

Please tick one box in each category below (as applicable)

	Excellent	Good	Disappointing	Poor
Bedrooms	○	○	○	○
Public Rooms	○	○	○	○
Food/Restaurant	○	○	○	○
Service	○	○	○	○
Welcome/Friendliness	○	○	○	○
Value For Money	○	○	○	○

4. Any other comments

If you wish to make additional comments, please write separately to the Publisher, Condé Nast Johansens Ltd, 6-8 Old Bond Street, London W1S 4PH

Please return completed form to **Condé Nast Johansens, FREEPOST (CB264), LONDON SE27 0BR** (no stamp required).
Alternatively send by fax to 020 8655 7817